THE MAN
WHO OWNED
A WONDER
OF THE WORLD

ALSO BY EVAN J. ALBRIGHT

*Cape Cod Confidential: True Tales of Murder, Crime,
and Scandal from the Pilgrims to the Present*

*Explore Chichén Itzá: A Complete Guide to the Ruins,
How to Get There, Where to Go, What to Do*
(as editor)

*Cape Cod Babylon: True Tales of Murder, Crime,
and Scandal among the Rich and Famous*

The Man Who Owned a Wonder of the World

The *Gringo* History of Mexico's Chichén Itzá

EVAN J. ALBRIGHT

The Man Who Owned a Wonder of the World
The Gringo History of Mexico's Chichén Itzá
Copyright © 2015 by Evan J. Albright.

All rights reserved. No part of this book may be reproduced in any form by any electronic or mechanical means including photocopying, recording, or information storage and retrieval without permission in writing from the author.

Book and Cover design by Ryan Sawyer
Cover Photography by Joseph Ivan Sabido Yver

Portions of this book were previously published in Mexico in a limited abridged edition.

ISBN: 978-1-939607-02-7

A Pickwick Book
An imprint of Bohlin Carr Inc.
www.bohlincarr.com
info@bohlincarr.com

DEDICATION

To those I had the honor to meet—

Fernando Barbachano Gomez Rul
Virginia (Thompson) Kuykendall
George Stuart
Ben Muse
Jean Jacques Rivard
(David) Warren Thompson
Edward Hamlin Thompson
Priscilla C. Thompson
"Cap'n Bill" Stout
Curtis Ray Harrison
David Legters

—and to those I wish I had,
this book is dedicated.

CONTENTS

Prologue: 1926 1
Prologue: Present Day 7

PART ONE

The Dead City of the Maya 13
A Brick-Maker's Son 21
Interviewing Edward thompson 27
An Offer He Could Refuse 31
A Sunset Revelation 35
Their Man in Yucatán 41
Fernando in the Flesh 51
Miguel Barbachano 61
Progreso 67
Thompson's Explorations 73
Chichén Itzá, Finally 81
Maudslay 87
Carlos (Thompson) Marrufo 93
Teobert Maler 97
The Ballad of Carlos Marrufo 101
The World's Fair 105
Doña Maria Luisa 109
Buying Chichén Itzá 115
Touring Chichén Itzá 123

The High Priests' Grave 127
Inside the Pyramid 133
American Ferment Company 139
Meeting the Marrufos 143
A Strange Place 145
Francisco Gomez Rul 155
Exploring the Cenote Sagrado 161
Meridá of Years Past 167
One Shovel at a Time 171
Goodbye to Yucatán 177
'The Find of the Century' 179
The Thompson Learn the Truth 183

PART TWO

Revel in the Glory 189
Other Expeditions to the Sacred Well 195
Willard and Morley 201
Sacred Well, Round Two 207
To the Depths 217
The Fate of the Treasure 225
Edward Thompson, Hacendado 229
Hurricane Wilma 235
The Return of Morley 239
Pyramid Death Dive 247
Flight in the Face of Revolution 253
99 Years of Memories 259
The Fires of Socialism 261
'We Go to Chichén Itzá!' 267
The Dream of Gomez Rul 273

PART THREE

Return to Yucatán 279
From Spy to Socialite 283

Trapped in Chiquila	287
Mrs. Alma Reed	291
Love at the End	297
Scoop	301
Family Matters	307
Red Tiger with Eyes of Jade	309
Family Matters	315
Rebuilding Chichén Itzá	317
Iguana Love	327
'The City of the Sacred Well'	331
INAH	339
The Big Find	343
Equinox	347
The Mayaland	353
More Barbachanos	365
The Women of Chichén Itzá	369
Fiesta!	379
Morley Falls, Mexico Rises	383
Back at Bibiano's	393
The End of Thompson	395
The Best Things in Life	401
Barbachano vs. the Government	405
The Thompsons Meet the Barbachanos	411
'So What?'	413
The Artifacts Today	421
Balankanche	429
A Dios Don Fernando	441
Chichén for Sale	447
Epilogue	461

ACKNOWLEDGEMENTS, AFTERWORD, AND BIBLIOGRAPHIC ESSAY

Toutes les Americanistes deviennent fous
(All the students of ancient America go mad)

Edward Herbert Thompson

PROLOGUE
1926

IT WAS THE BIGGEST TREASURE THEFT since Hernando Cortes and the Spanish Conquest. Or so the Mexican government believed.

On Sept. 6, 1926, Mexico charged Edward Herbert Thompson, a citizen of the United States, with "the crime of robbery of artifacts of archaeological objects of the property of the nation." Thompson had looted the ruined city of Chichén Itzá, one of the great capitals of what had been the ancient Maya civilization, the government charged. The stolen artifacts were considered "priceless" but that did not stop the prosecutor from placing a value on them: $1,036,500 in Mexican currency, slightly more than a half million U.S. dollars.

Thompson was part of a larger, more nefarious plot, the government's prosecutor believed. He accused two of the most prestigious institutions in the United States, the Peabody Museum at Harvard University and the Field Museum in Chicago, of conspiring with Thompson to smuggle the artifacts out of Mexico. Although the government leveled no formal charges, the prosecutor demanded that the museums' respective directors come to Mexico to be interrogated.

A week later in a courtroom in Mérida, the capital of Yucatán state, Judge Roberto Castillo Rivas opened a hearing into Thompson's alleged crime. The government's first witness, Juan Martínez Hernández, was one of the world's leading scholars of the ancient Maya. Martínez Hernández, nearly sixty, told the court that twenty-one years earlier he had been at

Chichén Itzá and seen Edward Thompson and several Maya men next to a large dredge perched over a giant, water-filled sinkhole known as the Cenote Sagrado or Sacred Well. The Mayanist said he saw the American examine a load of mud that he assumed had been brought up from the floor of the sinkhole.

Martínez Hernández claimed Thompson had been financed by Charles P. Bowditch, the main benefactor of the Peabody Museum at Harvard. Thompson had recovered innumerable artifacts that had been flung into the Cenote Sagrado by the ancient Maya. Many of the artifacts were gold, Martínez Hernández said, and at least one gold object had come into the possession of Thompson's foreman, Juan Olalde, who in turn had sold it to a friend who melted it down into a rosary. Another man, Carlos Marrufo, who resides at Chichén Itzá, owned several pieces of carved jade from the Cenote Sagrado that he kept in a biscuit tin, Martínez Hernández said.

A few days later, members of the court rode out to Chichén Itzá, more than 100 kilometers away, to interview more witnesses and view firsthand the suspected burglarious tool, the dredge. This part of the hearing was open to reporters. "The proceedings promise to be sensational," was the prediction of one of the local daily newspapers, *Diario de Yucatán*.

The setting was spectacular. The judge and entourage arrived in several motor vehicles that parked next to the giant pyramid known as *El Castillo*—"The Castle." Rising majestically more than twenty-five meters from ground level, the structure was in ruin, but a team from the Mexican government had been working on two of the four sides, reassembling the fallen stone.

To the east, in sharp contrast, was a giant temple that looked almost new. Half the height of El Castillo, the newly named "Temple of Warriors" was massive, three giant ascending terraces with a wide staircase in the center. To the north of the staircase, the temple façade was rough and unfinished, but the other side had been reconstructed. In the front of the temple were more than fifty pillars, many intricately carved with martial figures standing atop victims or slaves or beaten opponents. Next to the Temple of Warriors were several tantalizing mounds, still waiting to give up their secrets. To the west the Great Ball Court, two giant vertical walls with rings embedded in the upper center, where according to legend the ancient Maya played a game that ended in ritual execution.

The judge and others were led north to what appeared to be a wide path through the forest but was, in fact, an ancient road. It terminated at a giant sinkhole. The Sacred Well is more than fifty-five meters across and descending straight down some twenty-five meters where the bottom was filled with sickly green water. The dredge Thompson had employed was no longer there, but Martínez Hernández pointed out several tree trunks near a ruined temple at the lip of the sinkhole where two decades before it had been anchored. He showed the prosecutor and judge a nondescript mound, which he said were the dredge's tailings. Some of the men began to poke around the mound, and they unearthed fragments of jade, potsherds, and a single human tooth, which everyone agreed was the remains of a long-ago Maya sacrifice.

The judge, the prosecutor, and the coterie walked back to El Castillo, where in the pyramid's shadow the federal Inspector of Ruins maintained quarters. There they interviewed the man who reportedly had served as Thompson's foreman, Juan Olalde, fifty-five. Olalde testified he had gone to work for Edward Thompson in 1897 at his plantation. Thompson had begun dredging the Cenote Sagrado in November 1904 and continued for eight months, then resumed in April 1906 for almost four months, stopping only because money from his sponsors had dried up. The dredge had pulled up gold and copper objects, as well as pottery and a Maya form of incense, copal, he testified. Olalde had been told that Thompson shipped the artifacts to museums in Mexico City. He later found out the objects had been shipped out of the country, although he did not know to whom. He flatly denied he had ever sold gold from the cenote, nor did he own anything taken from there.

The court found the infamous dredge on Olalde's property not far from the ruins. They located the dredge's winch in a storeroom near Thompson's plantation house a few hundred feet from Olalde's hut. A photographer took shots of the dredge and winch from several angles, and one of the representatives of the court dutifully recorded the serial numbers. The judge ordered the dredge seized, but because it weighed several hundred pounds, it could not be taken to Mérida. Instead, it was placed into the custody of the federal Inspector of Ruins, to be moved to his headquarters at Chichén Itzá.

The court returned to the inspector's encampment where the prosecutor continued the examination of witnesses, among them several local Maya who admitted through an interpreter to operating the dredge for Thompson (although they claimed they were ignorant of what Thompson found or did with the artifacts). The most damning testimony came from several members of the Tun family. Bernardino Tun told the court that he had been at Thompson's plantation in 1921 shortly before socialist rebels had burned it down. In a warehouse next to the main building, he saw wooden boxes filled with human bones, incense, and small, metal bells, all of early Maya origin. After the fire, he witnessed Thompson pick through the burned building, gathering objects from the floor and putting them carefully into fresh boxes. Another Tun, named Pablo, told the court that he also had seen the dredge in operation, although he could not say what type of objects had been found. Faustino Tun said he had a cornfield near the cenote and had witnessed the dredge pulling up copal and human bones. When Thompson noticed he was being watched, he began concealing what he had found, Faustino testified. On one occasion, the witness said he had seen Thompson retrieve a large object that appeared to be made of gold. Faustino claimed that he had seen this object many times inside Thompson's home.

The main subjects of the inquiry—Thompson and the respective directors of the Field and Peabody museums—were no-shows, which surprised no one. The Field Museum, at least, had sent its regrets. As its attorney relayed to the Mexican consulate in Chicago, "They take the position they are not compelled by law to testify in this matter."

The Mexican court did not need Thompson, for it already had his confession: his biography, *The City of the Sacred Well*, written by T.A. Willard and published in the United States. In it, Thompson described in detail how he had imported a dredge, employed it to scoop the bottom of the Cenote Sagrado, and had found hundreds, if not thousands of artifacts from the ancient Maya civilization that once occupied Chichén Itzá. Thompson's description of all the objects he recovered ran more than twenty pages. "The golden objects brought up, if simply thrown into the goldsmith's melting pot, would net several hundreds of thousands of dollars in bullion," Willard quoted Thompson.

Even more helpful to the prosecution was an inventory at the end of the book of the best objects. The prosecutor had transcribed the list, attached an estimate in pesos of each find, and submitted it to the court as proof of damages: An ancient golden bowl, twelve inches in diameter, weighing about a pound, was worth $150; an ornate forehead band or tiara ("This magnificent object of gold is the best that has been found in the Maya region")—$1,000; figures of frogs, bats, and monkeys, cast from solid gold—$30 each; a mask of solid gold, seven inches wide, "with eyes closed representing a person sleeping or dead, and having on the right eyelid a crossed figure resembling an elephant's trunk"—$3,000. The inventory ran several pages and at the end was a total: $1,036,410.

To anyone who attended the hearings, there was little doubt of the outcome. Thompson would be prosecuted for stealing the patrimony of the nation of Mexico. On the train back from Chichén Itzá, prosecutor José Castillo Rivas told a reporter that he would begin the process of attaching Thompson's property, which would be forfeited to Mexico should he be found guilty.

That property was known as the "Hacienda Chichén," which according to the reporter was "a few meters from the ruins of the same name, which permitted Mr. Thompson during many years to operate freely." Thompson's hacienda included a large main house, several outbuildings, and adjoining fields, he wrote.

But the reporter got it wrong. Thompson owned the Hacienda Chichén, that was true; but he also owned Chichén Itzá. One of the greatest cities of the ancient Maya civilization belonged to a gringo—for now.

PROLOGUE
PRESENT DAY

WHAT MUST IT BE LIKE TO OWN CHICHÉN ITZÁ? Thompson is dead, but there is one man who knows. Fernando Barbachano Gomez Rul has owned Chichén Itzá since inheriting it from his father, Fernando Barbachano Peón, upon the latter's death in 1964. Now the patriarch of the Barbachano clan, "don" Fernando (although he says he does not like the title because it is usually associated with old men) defends Chichén Itzá from all the plethora of public and private interests seeking to strip him of it.

Owning Chichén Itzá is a never-ending battle, he explains from his mansion in Mérida, the capital of Yucatán state, about 100 kilometers from Chichén Itzá. Says he, "I have devoted a major part of my life to the study of the Maya civilization, while protecting the site of Chichén Itzá from vandals; corporations like Coca-Cola wanting to display obnoxious advertising on top of the temples; the majority of Mexican archaeologists who are, by their clear-cut communist ideologies, worse than vandals; and from some international, irreverent beings posing as scholars looking for fame by producing garbage..."

There is one group more despised than all the others combined, don Fernando says: the government. Ever since the Barbachanos purchased Chichén, the government has done everything in its power to undermine the family's legitimate and court-validated ownership, he says. "Our top government officials are corrupt, liars and thieves, from the governor down," he says. "I have said so not just in several radio and TV interviews, but also in published articles with my signature! Do they dare answer? Not a word. Do they dare take me to court for saying untruthful incriminations against them? No single action."

If don Fernando hopes to engage either the state or federal government in debate, he is wildly mistaken. As Edward Thompson learned seventy-five years earlier, the government does not participate in a dialog, it hits you where it hurts. And for don Fernando, it chooses to hit him in the pocketbook.

The Barbachano family operates two resorts next to Chichén Itzá, the Mayaland and the Hacienda Chichén, the former home of Edward Thompson. These resorts have their own entrance to Chichén Itzá. Guests of the Barbachano resorts enter the archaeological zone for free. Or they did, until the day don Fernando escorts a group of guests to his entrance to Chichén Itzá, only to be met by several dozen armed men from Yucatán's *Secretaría de Protección y Vialidad* (the Yucatán Department of Protection and Roads). Wielding automatic weapons, the state militiamen bar don Fernando and his party from entering the archaeological zone.

"I have never, ever, been so highly recognized," don Fernando says later, barely hiding his glee. "Do you know any other human being so honored? Not one, not two, not three, but fifty *paramilitars* with machine guns in hand to stop me from entering my own property under orders of the government."

Don Fernando goes to the newspapers to complain about the action taken against him and the government is not amused. In a familiar echo from the days of Edward Thompson, the state announces it will seize Chichén Itzá. "If they want my property, go ahead," Don Fernando says, but adds slyly that he expects a fair price.

The owner of Chichén Itzá sues the state government, demanding it not only recognize his rightful ownership of the ancient city, but also pay him 470 million pesos, which according to the lawsuit is the state's portion of ticket revenue collected over the past eight years. If the state of Yucatán wants to make don Fernando pay to enter his own land, then don Fernando will make the state give up all the ticket money it has earned from Chichén Itzá.

The battle lines drawn, the state of Yucatán and the owner of Chichén Itzá take their conflict to the courts. But what neither could predict was that this would be a fight that was going to spill into the streets and onto the ancient pathways of Chichén Itzá.

Fernando Barbachano Gomez Rul

Edward Thompson and Maya "guide,"
after a studio portrait, circa 1890

PART ONE

Some things need to be examined with a telescope; some with a microscope; Mexico, with a kaleidoscope.

—*Edward Herbert Thompson*

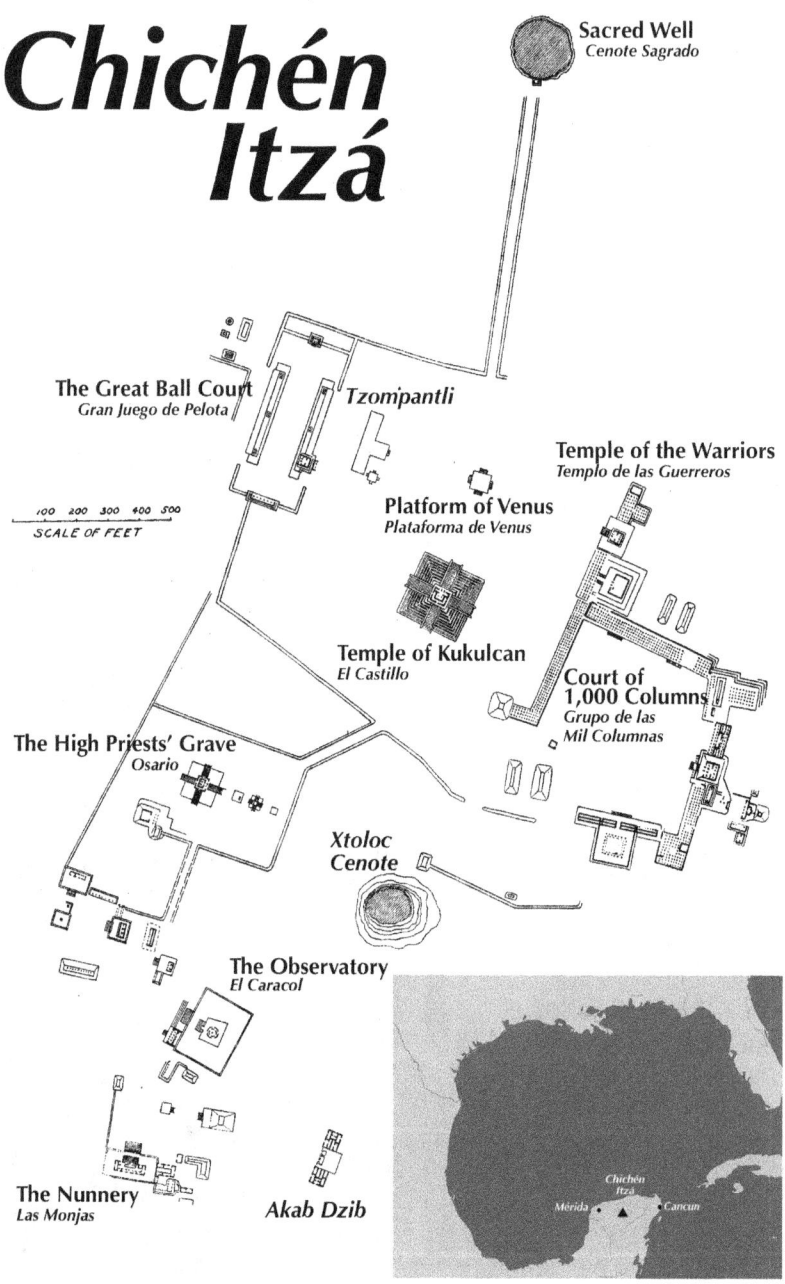

THE PRESENT

THE DEAD CITY OF THE MAYA

CHICHÉN ITZÁ MAY BE ONE of the most famous archaeological sites in the world but I don't recognize the name at all. When it comes to the ancient civilizations of the Americas, I can't tell you the difference between the Maya, the Inca, or the Aztecs.

But what I do know is a good story when I see one. In my hands is an old newspaper clipping from 1926. The headline, as headlines go, is pretty awful. Newspapermen (and women), of whom I count myself one, relish a juicy "hed." It's hard to beat the classic *New York Post* "Headless Body in Topless Bar;" that one you get the feeling pretty much wrote itself. This particular headline did not thrill so much as thud: "ACCUSED ARCHAEOLOGIST IN RESOLVE TO PROTECT OBJECTS." Beneath it is another headline: "Edward H. Thompson, Now at West Falmouth, Says Mexico's Charges Will Not Swerve Him From His Decision."

The article had appeared in the Nov. 6, 1926 edition of the *Yarmouth Register*, a small, weekly newspaper on Cape Cod where I had worked several years before. It was one of hundreds of articles that I had copied from the newspaper's "morgue" that had served as source material for a regular column on the history of local crime I called "Cape Cod Confidential."

The reporter had interviewed Thompson at his small beach cottage on the Cape. According to the article, the Mexican government had accused Thompson of stealing millions of dollars worth of valuable antiquities and had seized his hacienda in Mexico until the case could be resolved in the courts.

The quotes from Thompson were pure gold. He did not deny taking the artifacts. "I hold it to be self evident that these finds, taken from the Sacred Well, do not belong to any one Nation of this New World," Thompson told the reporter. "They are part of prehistory." In Thompson's mind, Mexico of 1926 could not be responsible for such treasures. "In doing what I have done, I feel that I have protected Mexico against herself," he said. "Until Mexico can give this guarantee of permanent safety I shall protest against the surrender of a single object that I have brought from Yucatan to the United States and placed in the museums of this country for safety and for the use of those who desire to study them."

The story failed to answer the most elementary questions: How could someone physically smuggle millions of dollars worth of gold and jade out of a country? What was the Sacred Well? The reporter described Chichén Itzá as the "great dead city of the Mayans in the Yucatán," but what exactly did that mean? This brief article hinted at a much bigger story. And it made me afraid.

There had been this other story, you see, about a rape trial on Cape Cod from 1921. Like this article, it was only a few paragraphs long but it hinted at a much, much larger story. I dug into it and found that rather than getting answers, I was uncovering more mysteries. It became an obsession. I spent ten years researching that one, consuming a good portion of my spare time. I found the answers I was seeking, but at what cost? Lori, my wife, still gets upset when she thinks about it. I had conducted my research completely on my dime, but in the end, I recovered those costs by selling the story to magazines. According to Lori, it was not the money that mattered, but the time this quest took me from her and our two children. "Even when you weren't working on it, you were thinking about it," she says.

Which is why I had put this article about Thompson and Chichén Itzá away in a folder shortly after finding it. It had many of the same qualities of that earlier tale. What is so compelling are not the parts of the story that are missing—any good reporter can find that out—but *why* those parts are missing. The "why" often is obscured and getting at the answers is like trying to grab smoke. The challenge beckoned to me like a dope dealer: "C'mon, just one little taste." But I resisted and filed away Edward Thompson and Chichén Itzá for another day.

That had been a decade ago. Earlier this year I published my first book, a collection of stories about Cape Cod crime, and it seems to be selling. I am already at work on a sequel, but I'm a few stories short. I pull out the folder that contains the Thompson clipping. I read it again. *With a little research, I can knock this out in a day or two*, I think. I am lying to myself. Despite my better judgment, I begin digging into the story of Edward Thompson and the Sacred Well of Chichén Itzá.

Step one, hit the internet. Chichén Itzá, I learn, is one of the major attractions in all of Mexico. Every year more than a million visitors tour the ancient city while on vacation to Cancún or Playa del Carmen, the resort playgrounds along the east coast of Mexico, a region called "the Mayan Riviera." Chichén Itzá is two hours away by air-conditioned bus, the preferred method to get there. Every day thousands arrive around the same time, swarming the archaeological zone like army ants for a ninety-minute feast of ancient culture. Despite the heat, the long lines, and the few bathrooms, most come away with a sense of awe.

The city had been constructed by what today is called the "ancient

Maya civilization," a group of peoples that flourished for a thousand years between what is today southern Mexico and El Salvador. The "ancient" tag is a little misleading, as the Maya civilization entered its "Classic" period at the same time Europe was in the Middle Ages. Perhaps they are called ancient because they come across *ancienty*: spears, human sacrifice, and their own version of gladiatorial combat, a soccer-like ball game where the stakes, supposedly, were life or death.

The Maya's magnificent cities were as big as those built by the Romans and Greeks and they did it without metal tools, the wheel, or beasts of burden. They favored grand pyramids, or to be more precise, ascending platforms topped by ornate temples. They created a calendar as accurate as the one we have today, except that it ran out in December 2012. Their civilization collapsed long before their calendar and all these big cities fell to ruin, overtaken by the forest until being rediscovered in the nineteenth century.

The most famous Maya city of all is Chichén Itzá, located in the middle of Mexico's Yucatán peninsula. While Chichén is far from the prettiest or the biggest, it is the most impressive. Immense structures rise majestically above broad, flat platforms.

For most of the world, Chichén Itzá is synonymous with the ancient Maya. Type "Maya pyramid" into an internet search engine and Chichén's great pyramid, El Castillo (also known as the Temple of Kukulcan) will come up four times out of five. Again, it isn't the largest or the most ornate, but everybody knows it. Mexico should trademark it because just looking at it says "ancient Maya."

Surrounding the pyramid are other dramatic structures. To the west is the Great Ball Court, the largest in the world, with lurid bas-relief carvings of two ball teams and a decapitated ball player. To the south, a massive, three-story structure called Las Monjas, and near that a round building named the Caracol that many believe served as an observatory. To the east rises another giant platform, the Temple of the Warriors, surrounded by square pillars, many of them carved with the images of Maya soldiers. And to the north, at the end of an ancient man-made road, is a giant sinkhole or cenote (say-noh-tay), alternately called the Cenote Sagrado (Sacred Cenote), the Well of Sacrifice, or the Sacred Well. It is for this impressive feature that Chichén Itzá got its name. *Chi* is Maya for "mouth;" *che'en* means "well;" and Itzá is the name of the one of the peoples who settled there. Put it all together and Chichén Itzá means "at the mouth of the well of the Itzá". Chichén was the Mecca of the ancient Maya world. A millennium ago pilgrims from all over southern Mexico traveled across some of the most inhospitable terrain on the planet to stand at the edge of the Cenote Sagrado and hurl tributes of gold, carved jade, and even people into the fetid green waters below.

Then, in the early 1900s, Edward Thompson comes along and digs it all up.

I forage local libraries for information about Chichén. The world of Maya studies turns out to be one of the most picked-over subjects in the world; there is a lot to wade through and a lot to absorb. A theme emerges and it ties the tale of Edward Thompson to anyone else who explored Chichén Itzá and the Maya: obsession. The ancient Maya are the archaeological equivalent of the *tabula rasa*; despite the grand monuments that litter the landscape, little is known about how they lived. The desire to learn anything about them gripped men (and women) with a fever, prompting them to abandon reason and trudge into the jungle and forest in search of answers.

That same narcotic influence reaches out to me, except the ancient Maya are of little interest. My fascination is with the obsessed, the walking dead: the explorers who hacked through jungles, excavated monuments, and dived in cenotes, to peel back the secrets of a civilization that had disappeared centuries before. From the outset, I vow to focus my research solely on Edward Thompson. I find a biography and his autobiography, and part of the mystery is explained. How was Thompson able to get access to Chichén Itzá and the Sacred Well? He bought it. Now I see what the big deal about Thompson is all about. Chichén Itzá is to Mexico what Stonehenge is to England, the Tower of Pisa to Italy, the Forbidden City to China. Thompson was not some looter who sneaked into the ruins. For fifty years a gringo owned Mexico's greatest archaeological treasure. Imagine the outrage if Great Britain owned Plymouth Rock, if Canada owned Niagara Falls, or if Mexico owned the Grand Canyon—actually, Plymouth had been a British colony, much of Niagara Falls is in Canada, and the Grand Canyon at one time was part of Mexico until the United States went to war and took it, which explains, in part, why Mexicans today are so sensitive about Chichén Itzá. When the Mexican government charged Thompson with theft of the artifacts, it did not seize Thompson's *plantation*; it seized *Chichén Itzá*.

This story has now grown too large for my book, so I pitch it to a magazine and, curse my luck, they accept. I have a few weeks to turn in a 2,000-word article. Just when I begin to feel confident that I have my arms around this story, it takes a crazy turn. In a conversation with an archaeologist who had written a book about one of the early explorers of Chichén Itzá, he asks if I had heard about the fellow who today claims to own the ancient city, just as Thompson had owned it in a century earlier. "I think his name is 'Barbachano,'" he tells me.

After we hang up, I search the internet for "Chichén Itzá" and "Barbachano." I find a page in Spanish that, if I understand correctly, describes how the Mexican government is fighting a gentleman named Fernando Barbachano G. Rul, who claims to be Chichén's owner. I find an e-mail address for a "Fernando Barbachano Gomez Rul." A few days after the beginning of the New Year I shoot a note into the ether:

Buenos Dias,

Pardon my English, por favor, as my Spanish is very bad.

I am a writer seeking information about Chichen Itza. I am researching the men who came to the Yucatan seeking their fame and/or fortune at Chichen, specifically E.H. Thompson.

It has come to my attention that a Fernando Barbachano G. Rul is pursuing a claim of ownership of Chichen. Would that be you? If so, would you be available for an interview?

Kind regards,

Evan J. Albright

Ten hours later I receive a response:

Helow, E.J.

Yes, it was I that owned the private land on which the ancient Maya buildings of Chichén Itzá sit. This particular tract of land was deeded by my father to me in 1964, so I actually owned it for 40 years.

As of mid December I deeded it to my grandson Hans T. Barbachano. Yes, we both would be open for an interview, and more.

If you are writing a book about the Maya and you give me credit for my research that brings these ancient people as the oldest civilization in the world, I would not mind your interview in this regard.

When are you planning to come to Yucatán, E.J.?

He signs the e-mail, "Fernando."

"When are you planning to come to Yucatán, E.J.?" What an odd question. I have no plans to visit Yucatán. I'm just writing an article, right?

THE PAST

A BRICK-MAKER'S SON

EDWARD HERBERT THOMPSON WAS BORN in Worcester, Massachusetts in 1857. Worcester today is the second largest city in Massachusetts, but during Thompson's childhood, it was reinventing itself, transforming from an agricultural center into a manufacturing powerhouse thanks to its strategic location as a transportation hub for goods passing between Boston, Providence, New York City and all points west. No fewer than five rail lines originated in Worcester, spreading in all directions like spider legs, not only to the large cities in the Northeast, but also to Canada, the Midwest, and West. As a boy Thompson watched Worcester's population double, then redouble, much of it by immigrants from Ireland, Poland, and Sweden who moved there seeking work in the rapidly expanding factories.

Thompson's father had arrived in Worcester with the immigrant wave, but he was born of old New England stock. The Thompsons had emigrated from England to the Massachusetts Bay Colony in the 1600s and were among the original settlers of the Massachusetts town of Woburn, today a suburb of Boston. Thompson's father, Josiah Augustus Thompson, had moved to Worcester as an adult, finding work in the lumber trade. He married Mary Thayer on Aug. 13, 1856 and a little more than a year later their first child, Edward Herbert Thompson, was born. Over the next seven years, the family added another son and two girls and moved into a house in downtown Worcester on a tiny side road that paralleled Main Street, optimistically named Eden Street.

When Thompson was fifteen, his father bought a half-acre along the seashore in Falmouth, Mass., a Cape Cod town some seventy-five miles away. A rail line recently had opened to Cape Cod and a summer colony of Worcester residents had sprung up along the Falmouth shoreline. During the family's visits, Josiah learned of clay deposits in a section of town known as West Falmouth. In colonial times there had been a community brick kiln, but that had been abandoned for decades. Josiah purchased the abandoned clay pit and rebuilt the kiln. He hired a carpenter from Worcester to build barracks and work buildings reportedly from lumber scavenged from Falmouth's last windmill. The clay, not surprisingly, contained a large percentage of Cape Cod sand, so while bricks fired from it lacked the tensile strength needed to support walls or chimneys, they were ideal for scouring. Homes used scouring bricks to polish metal, sharpen knives and clean hard surfaces; in construction, scouring bricks were employed to scrape and smooth hard surfaces, such as removing excess material from concrete forms. Josiah found buyers for his scouring bricks, so he moved full-time to Falmouth to manage the new business. Mary stayed behind in Worcester to raise the children and see to their schooling.

As a young man, Edward Thompson enrolled in the Worcester Free Institute of Industrial Science, a school whose purpose was to produce the future middle managers of Worcester's growing industries. Thompson studied engineering but dropped out after little more than a year. One possible reason for his failure to finish his studies might have been that his father needed his help in Falmouth. Another reason may have been that he spent more time dreaming of faraway places than buckling down to his books. "During my engineering course I studied Japanese with a view to going later to Japan and investigating the origin of the Ainus, that mysterious white race of the Flowery Kingdom," Thompson revealed in his biography.

He also began studying civilizations a little closer to home. The ancient Maya, a group of peoples that inhabited Central America and eastern Mexico, captured his interest. They had built giant cities of stone that rivaled those found in Greece or Egypt. Thompson had read a best-selling account by John Lloyd Stephens, a New Yorker who had visited the Maya ruins of Yucatán in the 1840s. The book contained breathtaking drawings by Englishman Frederick Catherwood, such as this one of El Castillo:

Thompson also didn't have to look too far from home to find another expert on Maya ruins. A few blocks away from his house was the office of Stephen Salisbury III, one of Worcester's elite citizens, who had toured the ruins of Yucatán in the 1860s and recently had financed an expedition to Chichén Itzá by the explorer Augustus Le Plongeon. Salisbury served on the board of directors of the American Antiquarian Society (his father was president), which published Le Plongeon's findings as well as scientific papers about the calendar and the pictographic writing of the Maya. Even though Thompson and Salisbury did not run in the same social circles they might have run into each other on the street. Whether Thompson knew Salisbury personally or by his writings and the writings of the Society, he had to have been influenced.

A bigger influence was the Abbé Charles-Étienne Brasseur de Bourbourg, a French writer, who theorized in the 1860s that the ancient Maya civilization of Yucatán and Central America were descendants of Atlantis. The Greek philosopher Plato had written that deep in mankind's past there had been an advanced civilization that lived on a continent somewhere in the Atlantic Ocean. According to legend, a cataclysm sank Atlantis and its civilization disappeared. Thompson took Brasseur de Bourbourg's theories even further and began composing the essay that would change his life: "Atlantis Not a Myth."

The Atlanteans, "having no further accession to their numbers, and being continually decimated by savages and disease, they slowly retreated before the ever-advancing hordes," Thompson wrote, adding that they "were forced back to their cities on this continent, that had been spared them from the universal destruction of their country, where the dense and almost impenetrable forests afforded them their last refuge." Their descendants built the Maya pyramids and were the origins of all the civilizations found in North America.

It took Thompson more than a year to find a publisher for his theory, but when it finally reached print, it made a splash. The editors of *Popular Science Monthly* apparently liked it so much that they made it a featured article in the October 1879 issue. "Atlantis Not a Myth" received wide notice and was reprinted in the prestigious *Journal of Science* in London. Thompson may have been a wee bit ahead of his time. Four years later Ignatius Donnelly published his book-length treatise on the subject, *Atlantis: The Antediluvian World*, which became a wide bestseller.

On his father's property in West Falmouth, Thompson built a small cabin where he could get away from the kiln to write. He failed to match the success of "Atlantis Not a Myth," for his subsequent articles only found a home in local newspapers. As his literary career failed to gain traction, Thompson settled down to his life's labors in the brick and abrasives trade. Between the family business on Cape Cod and his job in Worcester, his career path appeared assured. It was now time to get married and raise a family. For this next phase of life, he looked no further than his own neighborhood. Down the road from the brick kiln, in a big, rambling captain's house, lived the Hamblin family. John Hamblin, a whaling captain, had died in 1875 and left behind his wife Mary and seven children, with one more on the way. The oldest was a daughter Thompson's age named Henrietta after her maternal grandmother. "Etta," as her family called her, had helped raise her siblings after her father died. She was a no-nonsense woman, exactly the opposite in temperament and outlook from Edward Thompson. Despite these differences, Etta and Edward married in 1883. Perhaps Thompson realized that he needed a partner in life who would be able to rein in his wilder impulses. Or maybe, just maybe, Thompson was attracted to her because she had lived the life of adventure that he so desired. When Etta's father took to the sea in search of whale, he brought his wife and family with him. A month before Etta turned one, she went to sea and sailed around the world for almost four years, spending much of her early childhood in the Indian Ocean, with stops in Australia and the Polynesian Islands. The voyage was so long that Etta left the United States an only child and came back with two siblings and a third on the way.

The birth of Etta and Edward's first child was in a far less romantic setting than on a ship in the Indian Ocean. Alice Louise Thompson was born at home in West Falmouth in the middle of winter. With her arrival, Edward Thompson must have had a crystal clear vision for his life, at least for the next several years: continue to grow the business with his father and brother, buy or trade for more land, have more children with Etta. It promised to be a good life, a very normal life. Which must be why only a few days after Alice was born, Edward Thompson decided to throw all of it away, risking his life and that of his family, to explore the wilds of Yucatán.

THE PRESENT

INTERVIEWING EDWARD THOMPSON

MY NEW BEST FRIEND Fernando Barbachano Gomez Rul and I begin a daily exchange of e-mail. When I learn something new from a book or article, I ask Fernando about it. Our online conversations are a delight. No subject is off limits and we trade thoughts about everything, including politics and religion. While I greatly enjoy these exchanges, I begin to feel as if I'm losing Edward Thompson in the process. I've exhausted the resources of the internet and local libraries. I now own and have read a half-dozen times Edward Thompson's autobiography, *People of the Serpent*, and a third-person account of Thompson's explorations in Yucatán, *The City of the Sacred Well*, by T.A. Willard, which reportedly had been the reason Thompson had been kicked out of Mexico. The book contains an appendix that lists "the more important gold and jade objects found in the Sacred Well." If accurate, it is easy to see why the Mexican government had gotten so upset. According to Willard, there were bowls of "fine gold," including one that weighed about a pound; dozens of gold disks, embossed with figures and archaic designs; molded or shaped animal figures of "massive gold and finely worked"; the list went on and on, describing hundreds of figures, amulets, bells, and other objects of gold and carved jade. Willard concludes the list with a big, fat et cetera: "A thousand other articles of great value to archaeology."

I have learned as much as I can from my armchair and from Fernando. I need to humanize Edward Thompson. More importantly, I want—no need—to talk to real people, not just by e-mail or telephone. Thompson had died in 1935. I am certain that there are people alive today who knew him. Probably not children, but certainly grandchildren.

Where to start the search? Although Thompson was from Worcester, he called Cape Cod home for most of his adult life. If he was a true Cape Codder, I shouldn't have to go very far. As someone once observed, "the Cape Cod man, let him go to whatever part of the world he may, is sure to come back. His local tastes never die out; and where'er he roams, at every step away, he drags a lengthening cable." I open the telephone book. There he is. "Edward Thompson," and an East Falmouth address. My Edward Thompson was from West Falmouth, some two miles as the crow flies, so it is conceivable they are related. I pick up the phone and punch in the number. An elderly woman answers, a good sign. I ask to speak to Edward Thompson. "Ed!" she shouts, an indication he either is in another part of the house or deaf.

"Hello," says a man in a voice so hoarse he has to be at least eighty. I introduce myself and explain I am looking for ancestors of Edward Herbert Thompson, who had owned Chichén Itzá. "He was my grandfather," Ed says. Bingo!

Ed tells he would be amenable to an interview. He invites me to his house, because, he explains, it is hard for him to get out. We agree to meet the next day.

The Thompson home is a modest Cape, indistinguishable from the others in the neighborhood. I knock and Ed's wife, Priscilla, answers. She drags a small cart behind her that contains a canister of oxygen; a thin plastic tube runs to her nostrils. Ed is in the bathroom, she explains. Soon I hear a flush and he comes out to meet me, dragging his own can of air.

Ed and Priscilla are old, no doubt about it. But I can't tell how old, so I ask. "Ninety," Ed answers. Plenty old enough to have known his grandfather, I calculate.

I'm directed to a small parlor. After we make ourselves comfortable, Ed tells me that his grandfather moved to West Falmouth because his father Josiah had purchased a clay pit on Brick Kiln Road. Edward Thompson "came down to the Cape and started his acquisition of land, about a hundred, a hundred ten years ago," Ed says. In my head, I figure it was closer to 125 years ago, but don't say anything. I want Ed to tell the story.

Later the family moved to Yucatán, where Ed's father, Edward Josiah Thompson, was born and raised. Having grown up in Mexico, Ed's father had a heavy Yucatecan accent, and when he moved to the United States the only position he could find was as a Spanish teacher in New Jersey. "He couldn't get any other kind of job, but he could speak Spanish," Ed says. "Put two and two together..."

Being a teacher had its benefits. It meant summers off and the family returned every year to spend a few weeks on Cape Cod at his grandfather's property in West Falmouth. That house, no longer in the family, recently burned down, Ed adds. The only property owned by the senior Edward Thompson that is still in the family is a small cabin on West Falmouth's Black Beach overlooking Buzzards Bay.

I knew from Edward Herbert Thompson's autobiography that he first had gone to Yucatán with his wife, Henrietta, and oldest daughter who was a baby. How many children did they have? "Six," Ed says. Were they all born in Yucatán except for the oldest? "I believe so, yes," Ed replies.

"I know that much later, when Ed's mother was expecting him, she came back to have him born here," Priscilla says.

That meant Ed had been conceived in Yucatán. "So you've got some Mexican in you?" I ask.

"Yeah, get up and do a Mexican dance," Priscilla says, and we laugh. Ed's dancing days are long over.

I ask if they get many requests for interviews. "All the time," Priscilla laughs. She remembered a documentary by a British company that had flown to Cape Cod to interview Ed and other members of the family. When the Thompsons saw the program, "we really didn't appreciate it too much," Priscilla says. The filmmakers never came out and said it, but they hinted that Thompson had gotten rich from his explorations at Chichén Itzá. And that, according to Priscilla, was flat out wrong. The Thompsons never had any money, she says.

THE PAST

AN OFFER HE COULD NOT REFUSE

A FEW DAYS AFTER THE BIRTH of Alice Thompson on Feb. 1, 1885, Stephen Salisbury III requested the pleasure of Edward Thompson's company for dinner. The invitation must have come as a bit of a surprise even though they probably knew each other. The two men were separated by a generation (Thompson was twenty-seven, Salisbury forty-nine), by wealth (with the recent passing of his father, Salisbury was one of the richest men in the United States), and by class. The Thompsons had been in Worcester since the 1850s; the Salisburys arrived in 1767 and owned much of the city. Edward Thompson had attended Worcester Free Institute of Industrial Science; the Salisbury family had founded the school, but none of the family had gone there (Stephen, of course, had attended Harvard). Thompson had joined the Worcester Society of Antiquity, whose members were amateur historians and wrote about local history; Salisbury now was president of the prestigious American Antiquarian Society, which had its own headquarters and funded explorers and their excavations across North America.

In the middle of winter, Thompson made his way to the stone mansion known by everyone in Worcester. Though only two stories tall, the

Salisbury House was one of the largest homes in the city. It had been built in the Greek revival style that was more Sparta than Athens. In typical New England Yankee fashion, its façade, though prepossessing, eschewed opulence for utility. Six unadorned Doric columns supported the porch, framing a door that was sturdy but not elaborate. The sole significant decorative elements were five tiny circular windows under the roofline that were trimmed with moldings in the form of carved Greek-style wreaths.

The interior, however, was a different matter. Thompson could not help but be impressed by the bright white doorways and trim, and the light marble, so different from the dark wood paneling that was in fashion at the time. The square, straight lines of the exterior hid the most sublime feature of the home: a magnificent rotunda that rose through the center of the house, capped by a mini-dome.

The dinner was equally impressive, not so much for the food as for the company. Salisbury had asked a couple of friends to join them. George Frisbie Hoar, the "moon-faced junior senator from Massachusetts," like Thompson and Salisbury, was a resident of Worcester. His visage was instantly recognizable, framed by his famous mutton chop whiskers, bookish eyeglasses, and cleft chin. Also present was Hoar's former pastor, the noted author and minister Edward Everett Hale. Hale was an American icon, thanks to his novella, "The Man Without a Country," which had been published during the Civil War. His eyes were set deep over melancholy saddlebags and the rest of his face hidden behind a bushy gray beard that projected from his jaw like a ledge, Hale looked like the literary vagabond he was. These men were some of the most influential in New England, carved from the Puritan mold, born to a manner that believed in public service and who had the money to pursue such a lifestyle. Thompson, at twenty-seven and beginning a career as a manufacturer of scouring brick, must have wondered why he had been invited among such august company.

The answer was not long in coming. Salisbury wished to offer him a job: "After dinner my host, in the simple, direct style habitual to him, informed me that the American Antiquarian Society and the Peabody Museum of [Harvard] desired to have certain ruined groups on the peninsula of Yucatán scientifically investigated, and that they had chosen me to be the investigator," Thompson recalled years later. Senator Hoar had persuaded President Chester A. Arthur to appoint Thompson consul to Yucatán and Campeche, so he would have a salary to support these investigations.

Salisbury's interest in the Maya ruins had been sparked by a Harvard classmate, David Casares of Mérida, Yucatán. During the American Civil War, Casares invited Salisbury to visit him and, as wealthy young men could buy their way out of the military, the young millionaire skipped the battle of Shiloh and spent several weeks in Mexico, during which he toured many of the ruins. This began a lifelong interest in the ancient civilization that once controlled the region and Salisbury employed his fortune to ferret out its secrets. During the latter half of the nineteenth century, no one would invest more to study of the Maya civilization of Yucatán. He wanted as his agent Edward Thompson.

Why Thompson? The future archaeologist thought it had been because Salisbury had read "Atlantis Not a Myth" six years before and had always kept Thompson in mind.

What Thompson may not have known was that Salisbury and company desperately needed someone and needed him soon. The offer to Thompson came with a condition: He had to accept on the spot. If he didn't, there was a good chance the consul appointment would go to someone else, someone neither Salisbury nor Senator Hoar could influence. Grover Cleveland would soon be inaugurated as president, the first Democrat in a quarter century. The Republican Party had been putting their own people in federal office since Reconstruction, but now it was the Democrats' turn and there was a long list of favors to be repaid.

"Mr. Salisbury then asked me if I would accept the appointment," recalled Thompson, who no doubt weighed his options. He could continue to work for his father on Cape Cod, digging clay, pressing it into bricks, firing it in the kiln and then hoping someone would buy it, or he could pack up his family and move to Mexico, where adventure and a guaranteed income awaited. "It was an unnecessary question."

The Senate confirmed Thompson on Feb. 14, a little more than two weeks before Cleveland took office. A month later Thompson, Henrietta, and baby Alice departed their Cape Cod home and boarded a steamship in New York for Yucatán where Thompson could begin his life's work.

THE PRESENT

A SUNSET REVELATION

I'M FOLLOWING EDWARD, Henrietta, and Alice to Yucatán, because of what their descendants tell me today. It begins with something Priscilla reveals near the end of our time together. She turns out to be a fount of information about the Thompson family, even though she married into it. Ed doesn't know much about the history of the family. As he sees it, no one in the family is much interested in either Edward Thompson's adventures or in Mexico. None of Edward Thompson's six children ever expressed any interest in archaeology, Priscilla says. I find that difficult to comprehend. These children had grown up among the ruins of Chichén Itzá. "I don't think anybody talked about it," Ed says. He certainly didn't, even though his grandparents eventually came to live with them. Ed was a teenager at the time "and I wasn't interested. But if there was any talk, I didn't hear it. I don't think there was. It was just life to them."

"And if they did talk about it, it wasn't a pleasant subject to discuss either," Priscilla says, and then starts to explain, but I am already asking my next question. In my eagerness, I violate the cardinal rule of interviewing: Keep the subject talking and they will tell you something juicy. And as I discover later, the reason the Thompsons of an earlier generation didn't talk about Chichén Itzá is the exact reason why I have to go.

According to Priscilla, the member of the Thompson family who knows the most about Edward Thompson the explorer is Ed's sister, Virginia. "She's younger and she's interested in the family, like me," she says. "Ginny," as she is called, owns that little piece of Cape Cod from Edward Thompson's day, the small cabin on Black Beach. She lives in Upton, a town between Boston and Worcester, but she frequently comes down to the Cape. "She might even be there now," Priscilla says. She gives me the number for the beach house.

I call Ginny's Black Beach house when I get back home. A woman answers who sounds much, much younger than Ed or Priscilla, so this can't be Ginny, who was born four years after her brother. It turns out to be Ginny's daughter, Heleni. Her mother is at home off-Cape, she tells me, but will be down in a few weeks. I explain why I am calling and then, out of the blue, Heleni asks if I would like to visit her at Black Beach. I really want to see this property. Black Beach is one of the jewels of Cape Cod, with expensive beach houses. If there is a Thompson fortune, this has to be it. We arrange a date to meet.

But first I have to talk to her mother, Ginny. I catch up with her by phone at home in Upton.

I like her immediately. At eighty-six her mind is keen. She keeps atop the news, about which she is very opinionated (a family trait, I am to learn). Everything she says is punctuated with her wry sense of humor. Her voice is husky, which comes from a lifetime of smoking.

Ginny calls her grandfather, "Pappagrande." She adored him. "He was the kind of person everybody loved," she says. "He was interested in people. He loved to tell these stories."

Edward and Henrietta in their dotage came to live with Ginny's father and mother. She got to know her grandfather very well during that period and came to learn something about his business affairs as well. "When I was in high school...they sold the hacienda to someone named Barbachano for ten thousand dollars," she says. I stop her. The Mexican government had seized the property, I say. How could the Thompsons sell it if did not belong to them? "I know that they sold the property," Ginny insists. I make a note to ask don Fernando to explain how this was possible.

The previous summer there had been a big Thompson family reunion. "My son had wanted to see some of Pappagrande's things at the Peabody [Museum at Harvard]," she says. "We had forty or fifty family members who went to see the museum and there wasn't a lot there. What they had was interesting, but it wasn't nearly as much as I assumed they might have." I tell her that according to my research, the Peabody Museum gave back many objects to Mexico, although I had yet to confirm that. I was happy to learn that there were at least some of the artifacts still there and mentally made another note to visit the Peabody to see them.

Like Priscilla, Ginny has abhorred how the media has portrayed her grandfather. She also did not care for the British documentary. The family had been invited to watch it and she had wanted to walk out because she had been so disgusted with the veiled accusations that her grandfather had taken treasure for himself. But what really set her off was a magazine article that had appeared in the 1940s that not only accused her grandfather of running off with the treasure of the ancient Maya, but also of killing someone to protect the secret. "I lived with him," she says. "I know he would not be the type of person to kill somebody."

Before I hang up I promise to visit Ginny next time she's on Cape Cod. I tell her that daughter Heleni has invited me to see the beach house and to watch a sunset.

Days later I drive to the beaches along West Falmouth Harbor. This is one of the few sections of beach on Cape Cod that face west. Across

Buzzards Bay, you can make out the opposite shoreline, not far from New Bedford where Henrietta Thompson's family sailed from 150 years ago to hunt whales. The sun hangs low over the horizon, but I still have plenty of time. I find the dirt road turnoff protected by the obligatory sign telling me that I am on private property. I pay it no attention. If I am stopped, I will say I am on my way to meet Miss Heleni Thayre, daughter of Ginny (Thompson) Kuykendall. If whoever stops me is really interested, I'll tell them about Edward Herbert Thompson, Chichén Itzá, and the Sacred Well of the Maya.

I drive past one expensive beach house after another. I wonder how I'm going to identify Ginny's because house numbers are difficult to pick out, as if the residents of this road like their privacy. It doesn't turn out to be too hard. Ginny's family refers to the house as a "camp." Compared to the other houses, Ginny's is downright primitive, where you would expect to find Henry David Thoreau or Henry Beston spending a solitary year.

Ginny's shack sits on a short dune. She owns three acres, but only one is habitable; the rest consists of protected dunes and salt marsh. For tax purposes, her camp is valued at almost a half million dollars. Of that, $30,000 is for the building, about the same as the cost of my car. It was once again evidence that if Edward Thompson had made a fortune on Maya relics, this branch of the family has never seen it.

The camp is a box, twenty-five feet square. I knock on the door and a voice inside tells me to walk around to the back. There I find a large deck with a spectacular view of Buzzards Bay. Heleni emerges through a screen door, bearing wine, cheese, and crackers. Although she is in her early sixties, she moves and acts like a woman much younger. She is a ball of energy and more than a little ADD. She flits from subject to subject like a bee sampling blossoms. She has an opinion on everything and, like her mother, is not reluctant to share it. I just sit back and watch the show.

As the sun dips below the horizon and rewards us with a rose-colored finish, I ask her about Edward Thompson. "Your great-grandfather and Henrietta had a bunch of kids—"

"—And he had an affair," Heleni interrupts. "Did mother tell you about that? He had some Mexican children down there."

I fumble for something to say. "That I didn't know," I admit.

"There was a terrible scandal, so bad, that nobody wanted to deal with it," she says. Throughout the interview we keep returning to the subject of her grandfather's secret life. But it is a secret that didn't bother Heleni in the least. She admires her great-grandfather. "He was physically quite courageous," she says. A few years ago she visited Chichén Itzá. "I would be walking in broad daylight and I would be thinking, are there any jaguars here? He was there all by himself, no tourists at all, climbing into caves, going into ruins where there would be snakes and spiders and all he had was his courage. He went down in the Sacred Well with the Mayans saying, 'Don't go down there, Kukulcan will get you!'"

Today Chichén Itzá is one of Mexico's biggest tourist attractions and according to Heleni, various grandchildren and great-grandchildren of Edward Thompson have gone to Mexico to see the ruins and old hacienda. But to her knowledge, none of Edward Thompson's children ever went back after the last left Yucatán around the time of the Mexican Revolution.

"Sometimes the reason they don't go back is because it gets *interesting*," I suggest

"Or *too interesting*," Heleni adds.

Sitting on the deck, where almost a century before Edward Thompson had once enjoyed the very same breezes off the bay, I know what I have to do. I had spent the past few weeks chasing down descendants of Edward Thompson in the United States. But that was only half the story. I have to go to Mexico and find the children and children's children he left behind.

Montejo House, downtown Merida, late 1800s

THE PAST

THEIR MAN IN YUCATAN

EDWARD THOMPSON ARRIVED in Yucatán before his credentials. Considering how quickly his appointment had been made, it was more than possible no one knew he was coming. He paid a courtesy visit to Yucatán's governor, but because he had no official papers the meeting was perfunctory.

Four days later his credentials arrived and Thompson took up the duties of American Consul in Yucatán. The office was, at least according to Thompson, a mess. There were financial irregularities, including the disappearance of several hundred dollars the office had been holding, part of the estate of a U.S. seaman who had died in Yucatán. The State Department ordered Thompson to investigate his predecessor, Louis Henri Aymé.

Thompson tracked down Aymé in Oaxaca, a Mexican state to the southwest of Yucatán. The former consul was conducting archaeological explorations on behalf of the Smithsonian to collect ethnographic and archaeological objects for the National Museum in Washington, D.C.

Aymé told Thompson that to his knowledge the records of the funds were in the consulate office. Thompson could not find them, possibly because Aymé's former clerk mysteriously disappeared a few weeks into

Thompson's tenure. The scandal of the missing money haunted Aymé for months and he had to repay the funds from his own pocket. It was an embarrassing end to what had been a promising career in the Foreign Service.

It was also an end to his archaeological career. Possibly Thompson's investigation and the smear on his professional record soured him, for Aymé, like Thompson, was a dual career man. Thompson may not have known it, but he was not the first explorer sent by Messrs. Salisbury and Hoar to explore the Yucatán.

Aymé was born in New York in 1855, the son of a surgeon with political ties. He grew to be a strapping man of almost six feet, with jet-black hair and a prominent black beard. He applied for West Point but ended up attending Columbia College. He eventually followed in his father's footsteps and studied medicine, but never became a practicing medical doctor.

Like Thompson, he came to the attention of Salisbury and Hoar, who in 1880 offered him the American Consul post in Yucatán in exchange for his services as an archaeological explorer. Unlike Thompson, Aymé at least had some professional experience with science, with government and with overseas travel. In 1874 he had voyaged to Queenstown, New Zealand, as part of an official government expedition to observe the "transit of Venus." Twice every 105 to 121 years the orbit of Venus crosses between the sun and the planet Earth, creating a mini-solar eclipse. The purpose of Aymé's expedition was, in part, to generate a series of measurements that would allow scientists to accurately estimate the distance of the Earth from the sun. His job was listed as "photographic assistant," a crucial position as the plan was to take dozens of plates of negatives during the several-hour Venus transit. While in Queenstown, Aymé also collected specimens of birds, shellfish, and reptiles that he later donated to the American Museum of Natural History in New York.

Aymé became nationally famous, unintentionally, in 1879 for a failed attempt to reach Patagonia from New York City by horseback. He joined an expedition headed by a man with the ultimate Anglophile name of "Henry St. Patrick Tudor." Tudor's expedition became the butt of jokes in newspapers around the country ("Champion Idiot on Horseback" was the headline in the *Cincinnati Enquirer*; "It is also rumored that he carries a bottle in his saddlebags," warned the *Atlanta Constitution*). Aymé had joined the trip to collect scientific samples along the way, but the expedition apparently never made it out of the United States. Instead it petered out somewhere in the American South, reportedly after Tudor almost lost a foot to an alligator.

The connection to Tudor did not soil Aymé's reputation. Although he was not trained in archaeology (not many people in the world at that time were), Salisbury and Hoar must have been happy to obtain the services of such an educated and articulate gentleman. Others also were impressed by the enthusiasm and energy that Aymé employed toward his duties as consul and his side occupation as explorer of ancient ruins. Of the latter, he received special attention. When the writer Frederick Ober visited Yucatán in 1881, Aymé and his wife joined him on a trip to Kabah, a Maya ruin south of Mérida. Ober called Aymé "a gentleman every way fitted for the position" and he "possessed rare accomplishments as an educated gentleman and devotee of science." According to Ober, "Aymé is an enthusiastic explorer, who is indefatigable in his search after objects of interest to the antiquarians of America."

Aymé was on track to become one of the beacons of Maya archaeology. But his undoing began long before he was accused of stealing money from the U.S. Consulate. If one were to pick a moment where it all went wrong, it was when Aymé chose to cross swords with another explorer, Augustus

Le Plongeon.

Le Plongeon was more force of nature than scientist and he was a natural rival to Aymé. Both had French roots yet were United States citizens; Aymé had a full beard, as did Le Plongeon; Aymé courted all archaeologists and scientists, presumably to further his career, but Le Plongeon courted no one as he preferred to work solely with his wife, Alice.

Relations between Aymé and Le Plongeon began cordially and the two men treated each other as respectful colleagues. Alice described Aymé as "our amiable American Consul" when writing about his involvement in Mérida's Carnaval in the winter of 1881. In June, Aymé visited the Le Plongeons at Uxmal, a ruin that rivals Chichén Itzá in its grandeur. Augustus shared his method for taking moulds of the carved stones. Aymé, in turn, praised some of the finds Le Plongeon had made there.

But a few months later Aymé's archaeological affections soon turned to another, the French explorer Désiré Charnay. When Aymé met Charnay in the late fall of 1881, he could only be described as smitten. Charnay returned the warm feeling. Charnay began taking his meals at Aymé's home and the two became close. Aymé is "an energetic archaeologist, well acquainted with the ruins," wrote Charnay. The explorer mentored Aymé in his methods of making paper moulds of Maya monuments and sent him to Uxmal unsupervised to oversee the making of several moulds there.

At the end of the year, Aymé and Charnay headed an expedition of 150-200 men (kindly supplied by the governor of Yucatán) to explore Chichén Itzá. The explorers camped atop El Castillo and deployed the men to alternately stand watch for hostile Maya insurgents, known as sublevados, or swing machetes to clear the brush from the ruins so they could be photographed.

While clearing the Great Ball Court, Aymé noticed that a vine was obscuring the view of one of the giant stone rings that projected from the wall, some twelve meters above the ground. "I asked why this was not cut away and an Indian replied that it was impossible—too dangerous," Aymé recalled years later. "I had always told the natives that nothing was impossible to a white man." The Maya, with a smile, handed Aymé his machete and said that if nothing was impossible, "you cut it!" A few minutes later, Aymé found himself leaning over the top of the wall swinging uselessly at the vine just out of reach a meter below. Aymé then noticed a piece of limestone that projected from the wall near the top and figured he could throw one leg over the side, rest a foot on that stone, and then have the leverage to reach and cut the vine. Once he had moved into position, he swung the machete at the vine and the stone under his foot broke loose. Aymé began to topple off the wall. "I heard a scream of terror from below," Aymé wrote. "Instinctively I threw up my right hand and felt it grasp something. It was the stem of a pliant plant growing near the brink, in some way spared by the Indians who had been clearing there." The vine held and Aymé narrowly escaped splattering on the stones below. The event still was a tragedy, for none of the images of the ball court ring was usable.

Had Aymé been smart, he would have kept his opinions regarding Charnay and Le Plongeon to himself, but instead he began comparing the two men. After Charnay taught Aymé his method for making moulds, Aymé wrote Stephen Salisbury in Worcester, who was one of Le Plongeon's patrons. "Mr. Charnay's process is far superior to that used by Dr. Le Plongeon. He has given me, under conditions of secrecy, the whole process and kindly furnished me with sufficient material for two years work."

Le Plongeon might have dismissed Aymé's fickleness, except that he and Charnay were in competition for the same limited source of funds available to explore the Yucatán, and by the early 1880s, Charnay was getting the lion's share. He had convinced another of Le Plongeon's longtime patrons, tobacco millionaire Pierre Lorillard, to finance a major expedition to Mexico and Central America (Charnay, however, says that Lorillard approached him). In addition, Charnay had credentials from the French government, which helped smooth getting permissions from Mexican officials to conduct explorations.

Le Plongeon, on the other hand, was doing his expeditions on the cheap. He could only afford to bring along his photographic equipment and his wife, Alice. He was jealous of Charnay even before his expedition began, writing Salisbury with the prediction that his fellow Frenchman's work would be revealed to be "a great HOAX."

Charnay frequently claimed he held no ill will toward Le Plongeon, but he also never hesitated to make a special point when his discoveries contradicted Le Plongeon's theories. Le Plongeon believed the Maya civilization to be 10,000 years old; Charnay posited that it was much newer, that the great cities of the Maya had been inhabited when the Spanish arrived in the late fifteenth century. Neither man was correct, at least according to archaeologists today.

Le Plongeon's gripes about Charnay fell on deaf ears, so he directed his full fury at Aymé. Augustus and Alice returned to Yucatán in the spring of 1882 and two months later mounted a full-out assault on the reputation of the consul. When Aymé was inducted into the Stephen Salisbury-run American Antiquarian Society, Le Plongeon fired off a poisonous letter to Salisbury, announcing he could no longer be affiliated with an organization that admitted a fraud such as Aymé. Le Plongeon sarcastically described the consul as "That excellent photographer—who cannot yet turn out a picture. That most learned of Mayan scholars who cannot even say 'good morning' in Maya."

Le Plongeon sent letters to Senator Hoar and to the State Department with specific charges against Aymé. Le Plongeon claimed that in addition to joining scientific societies on false pretenses, Aymé cheated on his debts, stole money from friends, spread false gossip about the Le Plongeons that put their lives in danger, and that he was a coward, a liar, and a man without honor. Many of the accusations were more of a reflection of Le Plongeon's character, than Aymé. For example, he was outraged that when a Mexican general insulted Aymé the consul "accepted said insult rather than fight a duel to the death."

Despite the ridiculousness of some of the charges, Aymé responded to each one, even though, as he wrote to his superiors in Washington, "they are, after all, simply charges, no proofs are advanced." For twelve pages he described the events that spawned them and provided a reasonable explanation for all of them. For example, when Le Plongeon claimed that Aymé wore a ribbon on his coat that indicated he was a recipient of the French Legion d'Honneur, Aymé explained it was just a ribbon.

There was one accusation leveled by Le Plongeon that Aymé believed required the strongest possible denial. The explorer reported that the consul had used "the seal of the Consulate to cover exportations of antiquities from Yucatán." Aymé called the charge "an 'absolute, whole cloth, damnable' falsehood." Le Plongeon, Aymé wrote, "has most falsely and vilely twisted an innocent use of the seal into an apparent misdemeanor." According to the consul, on three prior occasions he certified a package contained nothing subject to export or import duties: one contained chocolates, another a chocolate pot used by the natives and the third was a parcel belonging to Le Plongeon that the consul never opened but now believed contained antiquities.

Aymé's superiors in the State Department apparently were satisfied with his responses for no action was taken. But Le Plongeon did not give up. During an 1883 visit to Chichén Itzá, the Le Plongeons discovered that one of the ancient murals in a temple overlooking the Great Ball Court had been damaged and learned from a witness that Aymé was the culprit when he attempted to scrape off dirt with a knife or machete when he had been there with Charnay two years before. Alice reported this alleged vandalism in a *Scientific American* article.

Aymé around this time began behaving in ways that from outward appearance seemed erratic and extreme. In January 1882 he had reported to his superiors that he was the object of a conspiracy by prominent businessmen in Yucatán, presumably because the consul had refused to go along with their schemes. "At first they tried intimidation, then bribery, and now are endeavoring, both these having failed to procure my dismissal," Aymé wrote his superiors. The businessmen wanted to replace Aymé with another American, William Tappan, who ran a counting house that supposedly served their interests in the city of Progreso. But then Aymé reversed his position at the end of 1883 and submitted Tappan's name to serve as his assistant. A few days after that, he wrote Salisbury to report he had sold everything he owned, sent his wife to New York, and now planned to strike out south and photograph ruins.

In May 1884 Mexican customs officials in Progreso confiscated three boxes Aymé attempted to ship out of the country. The boxes contained what the Mexican officials characterized as Maya artifacts. Aymé reported to his superiors that the boxes contained "fragments," which the consul claimed were not subject to the Mexican prohibition against shipping antiquities.

Aymé was in the United States on a leave of absence when the controversy erupted. He delayed his return to work in Yucatán, possibly because he knew what was waiting for him. He wrote Salisbury that he planned to resign as consul and had applied to the State Department for a transfer to Peru. Word of Aymé's difficulties reached Le Plongeon, who was back in the United States at his residence in Brooklyn, and he fired off an "I told you so" letter to Salisbury, reporting that Aymé was thinking of resigning because, "I expect the place is too hot for him."

When Aymé returned to Yucatán in September, he received a telegram from his superiors and immediately resigned. He accepted the commission from the Smithsonian to explore Oaxaca, but it was to be his last-ever archaeological expedition. His consul career had ended in scandal. Not long after his return to the United States, his wife sued him for divorce. At thirty-one, he was washed up.

Augustus LePlongeon

Désiré Charnay

Louis Aymé

Chichén Itzá, 1880s

THE PRESENT

FERNANDO IN THE FLESH

THE FLIGHT TO MERIDA, YUCATÁN, is uneventful except for a pen that bursts on the first leg of the trip to Houston, leaving my writing hand appropriately jaguar spotted. My seatmates are two men heading home to Texas. One introduces himself as "Doy," which he has to spell for me, and the other has a five-dollar name that is so long, I don't bother to have him spell it; Doy calls him "A-to-Z" or "Alphabet." They are excited about heading home because awaiting them is a party where some 300 pounds of crawfish would be served.

They had been in Boston to attend a conference on hammering. "You mean learning how to pound nails with a hammer?" I ask.

For some of those boys, it sure seemed that way," Doy says, and we laugh.

Across the aisle sits my family. I can't quite remember who had suggested that all of us go, but it probably was me. Several months ago, shortly before I rediscovered the story of Edward Thompson and the Sacred Well, Lori and I had been discussing future vacation spots. While we couldn't reach agreement on where to go, both of us were certain about where we didn't want to go: Mexico.

I have to say that Lori took it well when I announced a few weeks later that I just had to see Chichén Itzá and visit my new best friend, Fernando Barbachano Gomez Rul. At some point the idea originated that my quest to see Yucatán should be a family adventure, so here we are. Lori sits quietly across the aisle with my fifteen-year-old son, Sam, and nineteen-year-old daughter, Sarah.

We change planes in Houston to catch one of the two flights a week to Mérida. Once we're in the air, I take a few moments to look around the cabin. Everyone seems to be reading. One fellow studies a Spanish phrase book. A woman flips through The Maya by Michael Coe, which I haven't read but is said to be one of the best books about the ancient Maya civilization. A few rows up a man studies a big green binder with individual pages in plastic sleeves. I can see pictures of Maya monuments and maps, so I assume he is a tour guide. In front of him are two women dressed in what I would call "gypsy chic" pass crystals back and forth. Everyone looks like gringos. Where are the Mexicans?

I find them when I get up to use the washroom to scrub more ink off my hands. While the front twenty rows of the aircraft are filled with light-skinned people, the back rows are filled with darker-skinned people. Can that be a coincidence?

The descent into Mérida is steep and the landing hard and fast. As we get off the airplane, we are met with a blast of sharp heat. This was to expected as April is one of the hottest months in Yucatán, far warmer than summer.

The Mérida airport is small and compact. As we get off the plane we are met by a blast furnace of heat, even though the sun went down some time ago. This is April, one of the hottest months of the year, even hotter than summer.

We retrieve our bags and clear immigration and customs. As we head out of the terminal, we look for don Fernando in the lobby and even though I have never met him, I know who he is immediately. Apparently I am not what he expects because he looks past me down the corridor as I approach and introduce myself.

Fernando sits in a wheelchair, the result of complications related to diabetes and non-functioning kidneys. He rises and shakes my hand vigorously. "EJ," he calls me. "Sam," he says as he shakes my son's hand. He calls Lori and Sarah by name and each receive kisses. Fernando is nearly eighty, his shoulders hunched but his eyes bright and energetic. He wears a white traditional shirt, the guayabera, with its distinctive dual pleats running top to bottom in parallel with the buttons. His hair is white and thin, and cut like Julius Caesar; his face framed by a white beard and sideburns but no mustache, like an old Amish man.

He introduces the man standing next to him. "This is my, uh, son, Hans," says Fernando. From our e-mails, I know their relationship is much more complicated than that, hence the hesitation. Hans had been married to Fernando's eldest daughter, Maruja, but even after the divorce, the two men remained close and now Hans serves as Fernando's primary care provider. Hans is slightly shorter than me, with similar northern European features, no surprise as he was born in Germany.

Outside Fernando has two Mercedes sedans waiting; He directs Lori and the kids into one with a driver who appears to be Maya; I join Fernando and Hans in the other. There is an awkward moment while I stand at the door waiting for Fernando to get into the car. It turns out he is waiting for me. Manners and protocol appear very important and I am clueless about them.

Our arrival has come after sunset and soon we are whisked through downtown Mérida. My first look at the capital of Yucatán state is underwhelming. Streets are unattractively illuminated by jaundice yellow sodium vapor streetlights and sterile blue, low-energy fluorescents.

Buildings loom prisonlike and in the low light I can see no decoration on them, only flat, featureless stucco. Everywhere is peeling paint and all the windows are barred. It reminds me of the time we accidentally got off the New Jersey Turnpike in East Orange and drove for several blocks past burned out buildings protected by security bars.

Along the way we chat about my quest. I tell Fernando that I intend to find Thompson's descendants in Yucatán. According to Fernando, Thompson had taken as a mistress his cook, a woman named Victoria. "I believe she had one son by Thompson," Fernando says. "I became very close friends with Thompson's son, whose name was Carlos." According to Fernando, "Doña Victoria had a little place at Chichén, two huts, one to live in and one to dispense food for the workers of Thompson." As Fernando remembers it, after his father bought Chichén Itzá, Victoria claimed that she owned the land under her huts. Her husband, who Fernando said was named "Marrufo," wanted to build a small hotel on the property. Fernando's father would not allow that and had them evicted. According to Fernando, Marrufo also was the name of Thompson's son—"Carlos Marrufo." He was quite a bit older than Fernando, maybe by twenty years, so if he is still alive he'd be almost 100.

Fernando takes us to our hotel, which proves slightly difficult to find. I have the address, but not the number. I only know it is on "Calle 55 x 64 y 66," which means it is on Fifty-fifth Street between Sixty-fourth and Sixty-sixth streets. Street signs are painted on buildings, very hard to make out in the murky light. All the structures have the same general appearance, continuous broad walls with slits of narrow doors and windows, making it impossible with the naked eye to discern a hotel from a car repair shop from a pharmacy from a private residence, all of which could share the same block. When we get to the address, I have to get out of the car and creep down the street to find the hotel entrance. But find it I do. Fernando and I make plans to meet the next day and with that, he and Hans bid us goodnight.

The next morning, sunlight transforms the city. The scary, fortress-like buildings of the night before are now bright, multi-colored homes and businesses with a myriad of individual architectural features. The facades, which had appeared to be institutional concrete, now welcome us with colorful stucco. The result makes me feel as if our fortunes are much brighter. I have an appointment to interview don Fernando in the late morning at his home, so we decide to kill a few hours a few blocks away in the Museo de Antropologia.

The museum presents an appropriate introduction to Maya history and culture. We walk through on our own, but most of the explanatory plaques are in Spanish, which I can't read. A small man approaches me, dressed in a light blue shirt, dark vest, and dark slacks, with a lanyard around his neck threaded through a laminated card that proclaims him to be an official guide. He asks if I would like a tour. "I only want to see artifacts from Chichén Itzá," I tell him. "No problem," he says and away we go. Lori and the children, however, have had enough of the museum and tell me they will wait outside.

My guide introduces himself as Antonio Patrón Orozco. I ask if he is related to Yucatán's governor, Patricio Patrón Laviada and he says he is, confirming what Fernando already has warned me, that everyone in Yucatán is related. Antonio walks me along the display cases and as he promised, points out all the objects from Chichén. He shows me several artifacts that had come from the Cenote Sagrado—skulls, a small gold frog, tools, and a wooden stool. I tell him that my understanding was that all the objects from the Sacred Well were either at the Peabody Museum in Harvard or in Mexico City; he explains that no, they have numerous artifacts in their collection.

He points out a ceramic platter, beautifully painted with Maya figures and glyphs on it. In the center a small hole has been punched out. "The Maya believe there is life in everything," he explains, including inanimate objects. Before it could be sacrificed to the Cenote Sagrado, the plate had to be "killed."

We walk around a corner and there, before me, is a version of the most famous statue in Mexico—the "chac-mool." The form is instantly recognizable: A life-sized carving of a man sitting in an awkward and uncomfortable position, his knees drawn up and his upper torso propped up by his elbows. The sculpture was made famous by Augustus Le Plongeon, who excavated the "first" one at Chichén Itzá in 1875. He called the statue "Chaacmol," which derived from two Maya words: chaac, which was the name of the Maya rain god but also could mean "thunder" or "tempest," and mol, which is the "paw of a carnivorous animal." Together as chaacmol it meant "the paw swift as thunder." Le Plongeon's sponsor, Stephen Salisbury III, changed the spelling to "chac-mool" and that is the name that stuck.

Because the statue was too large and heavy to move far, Le Plongeon had to leave it in the woods not far from Chichén Itzá. He then returned to Mérida to announce the find and his intention to send the statue to the U.S. Centennial Exposition to be held in Philadelphia in 1876. Le Plongeon's announcement generated tremendous interest, but not what the explorer expected. Instead the state of Yucatán sent an expedition to find the statue and bring it back. It took more than 150 Maya to drag the chac-mool to Izamal, the largest city between Chichén and Mérida, where the sculpture was feted like a conquering hero. Speeches were made, poems were read, all in tribute to what was described as the greatest archaeological find ever made in Yucatán.

From there the statue was brought to Mérida where it was installed in the state museum. The director of the museum, Juan Peón Contreras, gave Le Plongeon all the credit for the find, referring to him as "a genius." But he made it clear that regardless of what Le Plongeon believed, the statue was not his. "Ignorant of the laws of the country, this American traveller thought that he might at once call himself the proprietor of the statue," wrote Peón Contreras. "The indefatigable traveller came to Mérida, where, in the meantime the Government of the State asserted that the statue was the general property of the nation and not that of the discoverer."

Peón Contreras was wrong. It was legal to own ancient artifacts in Mexico, but as Le Plongeon learned, the law is only as good as the people or governments that enforce them. In the case of the chac-mool, the government had no intention of ever giving it back to him.

In tribute to Le Plongeon, Peón Contreras planned to put the chac-mool behind a wooden fence with a placard that contained the following legend (but in Spanish, of course):

The discovery of the wise archaeologist. Mr. Le Plongeon,
in the ruins of Chichén-Itzá.

General Protasio Guerra being Governor of the State of Yucatán.
It was brought to the Museo Yucateco on the 1st of March, 1877,
by Juan Peón Contreras, Director of the Museum.

There is no sign or fence around the chac-mool in front of me. It is not even the chac-mool that Le Plongeon excavated. It is one of a dozen or so other versions of the sculpture that have been found to date within a few hundred feet of where Le Plongeon excavated the first at Chichén. It turns out the form is relatively common, although primarily among other Mexican peoples, not the Maya. Different versions of the statue have been found in central Mexico, indicating a link of some kind between the civilization that preceded the Aztecs and the Maya of Chichén Itzá.

As for the chac-mool that Le Plongeon discovered, it is no longer in Merida. In 1877 Mexico's new president, Porfirio Diaz, decided that the statue was indeed a national treasure, so he confiscated it from the state of Yucatán and had it shipped to the national museum in Mexico City, where it rests today.

After the tour I rejoin my family outside. Even though April is one of the hottest months in Yucatán, the morning is comfortable. The museum is on Paseo de Montejo, which has been called the Champs Elysee of Mérida. The wide, tree-lined boulevard, named after Yucatán's conqueror, runs from the center of the city to the north. It is lined with majestic mansions from the turn of the previous century; the museo is in one, a "palace" formerly owned by one of Yucatán's governors, Felipe Cantón Rosado.

At the appointed time I lead Lori and the kids down the boulevard to don Fernando's home. We stop in front of a wrought-iron gate, behind which are two large mansions, almost identical, each one about half the size of a city block. Lori laughs. "You met this man on the internet?" she says.

I'm have been told that houses that come in pairs are not unusual in Yucatán and there is even a word for them—gemelas, the Spanish word for twins. These two had to be among the biggest gemelas on the peninsula. Don Fernando's mansion is on the left. Lori's driver from last night, whose name we learn is Chaco, sees us and opens the gate. His wife, Juanita, who is the maid and cook, directs us to the front entrance, which opens into a ballroom-sized foyer with a large, sweeping marble staircase and a ceiling that extends to the roof. The interior is dark and it is difficult to make out much detail in the gloom. Hans appears at a railing on the floor above and announces that Fernando is up and soon will be joining us. A few minutes later we hear Fernando's voice, followed by the whirr of what sounds like a heavier version of a child's remote-control toy car. Fernando rides his wheelchair down the stairs aboard a small tractor. He tilts back like an astronaut while Hans guides the machine down the staircase.

At the bottom of the stairs, he insists again upon getting out of his chair to greet us. He offers to take us on a tour of the first floor and shuffles ahead a large room off to our left. It is somewhat bare, obviously not used, and Fernando points out the reason. The ceiling, seven meters over our heads, has been patched. Hurricane Isidore, a category three storm, lifted one corner of the roof, he explains, and water poured in, damaging the entire south side of the mansion and some of the French furniture that had been in the house since it was built in the early 1900s.

Fernando slowly guides us back into the foyer and to a room he tells us is his office. He points out that everything in the house is original, including the light switches and the internal telephone system. There were no telephones in Mérida when the mansion was constructed, says Fernando, but the owner of the house had his own service put in (this turns out not to be correct; Mérida had a telephone exchange by the turn of the century). The office, with an old desk and chair, appears to be rarely used and later I would learn that Fernando has another, bigger office in the basement. Fernando gingerly walks to a portrait of a man with a mustache and soul-patch beard dressed in nineteenth century garb. He explains that this is one of his great uncles, Miguel Barbachano y Tarrazo, the former governor of Yucatán and signer of the Mexican constitution. I already know who he is—the central figure at the very heart of the *Guerra de Castas*—"War of the Castes," the bloody civil war between Maya and Mexican that tore Yucatán in half for more than sixty years.

Miguel Barbachano

THE PAST

MIGUEL BARBACHANO

TENSIONS THAT HAD BEEN BUILDING in Mexico for centuries would shatter the nation into pieces, like shards of ancient pottery that littered Chichén Itzá.

Not long after Mexico threw off the yoke of Spain in 1821, pressures from within and pressures from without began lopping off large chunks of Mexican territory. While the most famous example, at least to gringos, is the independence of Texas (which brought on the Mexican-American War and cost Mexico what is today the American Southwest), there was a similar independence movement in Yucatán and at the center was a second-generation Mexican, Miguel Barbachano.

His rise emerged from the rivalry between the two great cities on the Yucatán Peninsula. For centuries Mérida, the capital of Yucatán, and Campeche, the second largest city in the state to the south, had quarreled. While there was little the two cities could agree upon, they had one thing in common: distrust of the Mexican government. In 1840 Yucatán broke from Mexico and the new independent government split power between Campeche and Mérida: Santiago Méndez, a conservative, methodical man, ran Campeche; Barbarchano, a young, brash, and colorful politician, ran Mérida. The new government unanimously selected Méndez, the former vice governor and the elder of the two, governor. Barbachano, the younger, was made vice governor in a compromise vote. Despite their combined declaration of independence, the uneasy truce between the two cities was tenuous. Soon the rivalry and the battle for dominance over the newly independent peninsula would, as one contemporary writer put it, cast a shadow of discord, hatred, favoritism, and black passions "that soon had to sink to Yucatan into an abyss of blood and ruins." In their respective drives to get the upper hand, these two cities would inadvertently break the social contract with the indigenous Maya and unleash a class war that would plunge the peninsula into a sixty-year conflict that still resonates today.

Barbachano, like Méndez, had been born in Campeche, but when Campechanos sided with Mexico against Spain in 1824, the city expelled its Spanish-born citizens, which included Barbachano's parents. The family moved backed to Spain, where Babachano received his education. When he returned to Yucatan around 1837, he moved to Mérida, where he joined his brothers, Manuel and Francisco. The siblings became involved in Yucatecan politics, but it was Miguel who demonstrated a passion and flair for elected office. "Still young, learned, well educated, with a charming manner, a voice that was sweet and ingratiating, and quickly ready to speak, he soon acquired a great influence on the Mérida youth, and when he embraced warmly the cause of freedom, they recognized him as their natural leader," wrote one contemporary. When Yucatán flew its new flag atop the *Palacio Municipal*, the 34-year-old vice-governor "was the most enthusiastic about this symbolic act, imagining for himself the title of vice president or better."

When Mexico eventually got around to sending an army in the summer of 1842 to force the defiant Yucatán back into the fold, Méndez resigned the governorship to defend Campeche and Barbachano assumed command of the state. Yucatán raised an army of 6,000. The Maya were recruited heavily, and Barbachano promised any indigenous man who volunteered an exemption from civil and religious taxes.

The Mexican army massed close enough to Mérida to see the towers, according to one historian, but the city was saved by divine providence. By mistake a messenger delivered a letter to Barbachano that had been intended for a Yucatecan who was the leading Mexican sympathizer inside the city. The Mexican general outside the city sought an estimate of Yucatán's troop strength. Barbachano, the story goes, pretended to be the traitor and replied that 4,000 troops protected the city and that 11,000 armed Maya were on the march to join them. In addition France agreed to send a battalion to succor the Yucatecans. Mexico withdrew its forces and opened negotiations with Barbachano. Yucatán agreed to return to Mexico as a quasi-independent state.

The truce was shortlived. Mexico's president reneged on the deal, but then the new president, Antonio López de Santa Anna, reneged on the reneging and restored Yucatán's independence. In early 1846 the barbachanistas won control of the state congress and in August, war loomed with the U.S., so Barbachano agreed to rejoin Santa Anna's Mexico. Barbachano was once again named governor and in September the barbachanistas imposed a new constitution that failed to win support from the Campechano representatives. The Yucatán congress ordered them to sign it and when they refused, they were deposed. With that, Méndez's party revolted and Yucatán plunged into civil war.

The two sides were evenly matched. The party of Méndez controlled all of Campeche. The barbachinistas ran Mérida, which was larger, but their hold was not complete; there were members among the clergy and the *Casta Divina*—the ruling families of Yucatán descended from the initial Spanish settlers. When it came to Barbachano, the "divine caste" *odiaban de corazon* ("despised the heart," that is, "hated his guts"). Barbachano was not a member of the Yucatecan elite because his parents had come from Spain 250 years too late. He married into the Camaras, who were Casta Divina, but while his wife forever would be a member of that distinguished class, he always would be considered an outsider.

So Méndez controlled Campeche and Barbachano control most of Mérida. Outside of those two cities, Méndez supporters appeared to hold an edge; his party had political control of most of the other towns, all of which were relatively small. The one exception was Yucatán's third largest city, the frontier town of Valladolid.

Valladolid had long been a city where political ambitions exploded into violence. The city had been sacked and pillaged more times than Jerusalem. After a series of failed negotiations between the two parties, hostilities broke out in December 1846. In armed conflicts in the towns of Ticul and Tekax the Méndez loyalists routed the barbachanistas. In Peto, a combined force of 2,000 comprised of Méndez party loyalists and Maya took Peto, then in January moved on to Valladolid. In the minds of many, this was where the Guerra de Castas began. The invaders not only drove out the Barbachano forces, but then went on a six-day rampage that included murder, rape, dismemberment, and torture. "They committed such acts of revenge and barbarism...that impartial men could not help but be horrified and see in these events a prelude to the Caste War, which, blown by poisoned parties, leveled the Yucatán," according to an 1861 account of the war.

Barbachano resigned as governor and spent a few weeks in Havana until the violence had cooled. Yucatán had crossed a threshold; the fight was no longer with Mexico or Campeche, but from the Indians. As historian Terry Rugeley put it, "Maya peasants...were now armed, angry, and–to a degree never true before–organized."

Over the next several months rebels rose up against their former masters. By the spring of 1848, the situation in Yucatán was dire. Méndez was once again governor and appealed to the United States for arms and assistance, even if the price were becoming a U.S. territory. Just as Congress was about to vote on the matter, the Yucatán government reached an accord with the rebel Maya. Barbachano had returned to Mexico and had inserted himself into the peace negotiations, which were less negotiation than capitulation. The government agreed to all the Maya demands, which included:

Various taxes and contributions demanded of the Maya were to be abolished, and fees reduced.

Maya lands were now free to be used "without threat of rent or seizure."

Abolition of all debts of indentured workers.

Arms confiscated during the war were to be returned to the Maya.

Jacinto Pat, one of the leaders of the Maya resistance, was named governor of the Maya. And Miguel Barbachano was named "governor for life" of Yucatán.

THE PRESENT

PROGRESO

'WHY WAS BARBACHANO** named to be governor by the Mayas?" Don Fernando asks rhetorically. "They recognized Barbachano as one who was in favor of the Maya people. When they [reliquished] their arms, Barbachano decorated two of the generals. Ever since, the Barbachanos and the Maya have had a good relationship."

I tell don Fernando of a letter I had found written at the time of the treaty from Santiago Méndez to Commodore Matthew C. Perry of the U.S. Navy. Without U.S. assistance, Méndez wrote, "it will leave us to perish; and take pleasure in the spectacle of the prolonged agony, and the destruction of a civilized and friendly people, who, perhaps, on account of their being friendly, are now involved in this terrible calamity."

Méndez turned over the governorship to Barbachano, he wrote, to facilitate the treaty. "Mr. Barbachano had to ratify it with closed eyes." The agreement "covered us with shame," of which Barbachano got the worst because the provision making him governor for life made it appear that "the insurrection was to place him in the governorship, which is absolutely false." The purpose of the treaty was to buy time; by making peace with the forces controlled by Jacinto Pat, the meager Yucatán military could focus upon the remainder of the rebel Maya. But it didn't work. "The convention has been disregarded by [the Maya], and they have invaded other towns, slaughtering a multitude of victims," Méndez wrote. The rebel Maya were twelve leagues from Campeche and the people expected a siege.

Not only did the treaty fail to buy the needed time, it also was a major factor in the U.S. Congress's decision to table action on sending military aid to Yucatán. All looked grim as Maya soldiers convened outside Campeche and Mérida, but the invasion never materialized. Edward Thompson, years later, spoke with veterans on both sides of the conflict and one explanation was that cities had been saved by flying ants. As Thompson had heard it, when ant drones and queens take to the air, the Maya know that the rainy season is near, which means they must return home and plant their corn or face starvation.

Fernando tells me that the tide of war turned not long after that. Many Maya were captured, he says. What to do with the prisoners? "Miguel Barbachano…could not feed them, he could not kill them," Fernando tells me. "Killing them would have had to be done by shooting and there wasn't enough ammunition. So he made a deal with Cuba where he sent these human beings as slaves in exchange for arms and food."

Fernando finances a lot of charitable work to help rural Maya, so I ask him if he does it because he feels guilt for his great-great-great uncle's action. Fernando snorts at the very idea. "I cannot be held responsible for something that happened one hundred fifty years ago," he says.

One of the servants comes in to tell Fernando that his wife, Maruja, will be joining us. A few minutes later Hans guides the mini-tractor down the stairs. If the astronaut position is awkward for Fernando, it is worse for doña Maruja, who must contend with a skirt. I have to give her credit: she pulled it off with aplomb. We meet her at the bottom of the stairs where introductions are made and she greets us warmly. We plan the afternoon. We need to pick up a rental car, so Hans drives Fernando, Lori and me to the agency; our children stay with doña Maruja, who will meet us at a restaurant for lunch.

Hiring the car is uneventful. Soon I'm behind the wheel of a small sedan. Lori takes the back seat and Fernando rides shotgun. He could have ridden in safety and comfort with Hans in the Mercedes.

Within a couple of minutes of leaving the car rental agency, I am grateful Fernando is in the car. Not only do I have no idea where I'm going, but I'm flummoxed by the driving practices of Yucatecans. I had read before coming down how dangerous the roads could be, but nothing could have prepared me for the simultaneous skill and carelessness of drivers. "Lanes," or any other lines on the road, are but a guideline, like the diamonds on a bowling alley. They suggest where one is to drive, but as with all suggestions, they can either be accepted or rejected. Cars move into my lane unmindful whether I am there or not. The streets are narrow and as the buildings come right up to the sidewalk, one makes turns at their own risk for you can't sneak out far enough to see oncoming traffic. The road system makes no sense, with one-way streets and dead ends the norm. Fernando guides me out of the core of downtown—*Centro*, as it is called—and onto the broad Paseo de Montejo. From our earlier walk I know we are about to reach a traffic circle (*glorieta* in Spanish), so I ask Fernando what the rules are. Cars within the traffic circle have the right-of-way over those entering, he tells me. "Just like New England," I say, and when I reach my first one, there is a break in the traffic so I jump my car into the circle. What I didn't count on was the average Yucatecan driver's insistence upon driving in a straight line. At the center of the circle is a giant carved monument, so I steer to avoid it. The car to my right, however, has other plans and cuts straight across the circle and nearly sideswipes me. I brake and swerve and swear. But now I know the rules. At the next glorieta Fernando directs me to exit to the left. I enter and as I curve to the left,

I look quickly and, seeing a car on my right moving to cut me off, I give it a little gas, pull ahead, and drive three-quarters around. As I am about to exit don Fernando shouts "Stop!" and I do, narrowly avoiding getting creamed by a truck. "I thought I had the right-of-way?" I ask.

He shakes his head. "Not here," he says quietly.

I curse myself for driving in the first place. I come to understand that drivers in Yucatán are like fish. If you've ever watched a school in a pond, they seem to move as one, turning sharply as a group yet never bumping into each other. Piloting a car in Yucatán is like that. To survive I had to dart all over the road with my brother and sister fishes. It was exhausting.

We leave the city and head north on an open highway to a restaurant, the Hacienda Xcanatun, a former plantation. A century ago it grew henequen, Fernando tells us, a giant spiny member of the agave family. But rather than produce tequila like its cousin, fibers from the leaves of the henequen plant can be spun into durable rope and twine, he says. In the late 1800s and early 1900s Mérida had more millionaires per capita than any other city in the world, thanks to the demand for henequen rope in the United States. One of the henequen millionaires had built his mansion, he says. While there is still a market for henequen today, it is no longer the excuse to print money that it once had been. Many of the old haciendas are like this one, being converted into resorts or restaurants.

The lunch is delicious. We say our thank yous and bid goodbye to Fernando, Maruja, and Hans. We are on to Progreso, the coastal city north of Mérida. During my research I had read many letters by Thompson, acting as American consul, written from his office in Progreso. I hope to find some trace of him or of the Progreso of the turn of the century. Also, I figure a day at the beach will put my family in a good mood, a reward, if you will, for the heat of Merida; Chichén Itzá will be hotter.

We arrive in the late afternoon. We have reservations to stay at Casa

Quixote owned by an expatriate Curtis Harrison. I can't find the address of the hotel, but I figure I can drive along the shore and find it. Progreso, however, turns out to not be some small fishing village, but a sprawling vacation community. We drive up and down the shoreline and neighboring streets, but no Casa Quixote. I look again through my travel bag and this time I find the address, "Calle 23 x 48 y 50," which means Twenty-Third Street between Forty-Eighth and Fiftieth. Except there turns out to be no street numbered twenty-three at that address. There is a Twenty-First and Twenty-Fifth, but nothing in between. The sun is starting to get low on the horizon and I have this horrible vision of driving around Progreso well after dark. Then, while driving on Calle 21, there's the hotel! For some mysterious reason Calle 21 has become Calle 23, but only for a couple of blocks or so.

We are late and the hotel appears abandoned. There is no one in the reception area. I walk from one end to the other and don't find a soul—no guests, no staff, no one. As I'm running contingencies through my mind, a gringo saunters up from down the street. It can only be Curtis. He says had been expecting us several hours earlier and tells us matter-of-factly we were lucky to catch him, for his was on his way to a friend's birthday party. He shows us to our rooms: The kids and Lori get a large room on the second floor and I have a small room on the first.

Curtis ambles off to his party and we head to the ocean, a block away, to catch the sunset. The beach is filthy, with bottles and wrappers everywhere. The evening breeze blows hot. After sunset we eat in a restaurant that had been recommended by Curtis. It is nearly empty. My fish isn't what I ordered and worse, it's so greasy I can only eat half of it. We head back to the hotel and I crash in my room. I sleep apart from the rest of my family because I snore like a Harley. Sitting alone in my room, I begin to despair. I feel out of place in Mexico, where nothing makes sense and not just the language. I wonder what the hell I'm doing here.

By the next morning, I've had it with Mexico. I join my family for breakfast in the hotel restaurant. Curtis is there, enjoying a cup of coffee. In his native Texas drawl he asks about our stay. Though he isn't expecting it, I unload on him, everything from the crazy drivers to the bizarre road numbering system and everything in between. Curtis listens patiently. When I finish, he asks if I want a piece of advice. "Sure," I tell him.

"If it doesn't make any sense, check your passport," he says.

I don't understand, I say. "Exactly," he says. "*You* don't have to understand. All you need to know is that *they* understand it." Yucatecans are not confused by the roads, by the customs, by what I perceive to be cultural idiosyncrasies. Just because something doesn't make any more sense to me than poop on fine china doesn't mean that it's chaos or anarchy.

Curtis's words are magical. Maybe I am worrying about my family or maybe my expectations for this trip are so high, but I am letting Yucatán get to me instead of my usual practice of going with the flow. I find great comfort in Curtis's advice. Who am I to argue with a culture that is more than 500 years old? I vow to relax and take Yucatán as it comes. Energized, I am ready to see Chichén Itzá.

THE PAST

THOMPSON'S EXPLORATIONS

EDWARD THOMPSON DID NOT GO to Chichén Itzá, at least not right away. He'd been in Yucatán almost four years by the spring of 1889 when he boarded a narrow-gauge train in Mérida for Izamal, roughly halfway. At Izamal he hired a wagon unique to Yucatán called a *volan coché*. Pulled by three mules, the volan consisted of a mattress suspended by leather straps over an axle supporting two large wagon wheels. The highway from Izamal extended to Valladolid and was one of the better country roads on the peninsula, but it was far from level. Yucatán is well known for being flat, especially near Mérida, but past Izamal the terrain begins to undulate like the back of an oyster shell, scored with sharp ridges of limestone. As one traveler observed, "these ripples are moving from north to south, recalling the waves of the sea, they are increasing in height as you approach Valladolid, reaching an average height of fifteen to twenty feet." The volan's trio of mules provided the horsepower to get up the ridges and the stability to prevent you from traveling going too fast or too recklessly on the way down. The wide wheelbase and high clearance enabled the volan to go over almost any terrain, but the ride was far from comfortable for the passenger on the mattress, who was bounced around and frequently suffered bumps and bruises from encounters with the wagon frame. At times luggage came free and the passengers could find themselves trampolining with a heavy steamer trunk.

At the town of Dzitas, Thompson hired a horse and pack-mule. The path to Chichén Itzá was no better than it had been in Le Plongeon's time. Thompson picked his way through the acacia forest and after traveling for several hours was rewarded with the magnificent view of the giant pyramid El Castillo. "Pen cannot describe or brush portray the strange feelings produced by the beating of the tropic sun against the ash-colored walls of those venerable structures," Thompson recalled more than forty years later. "Old and cold, furrowed by time, and haggard, imposing, and impassive, they rear their rugged masses above the surrounding level and are beyond description."

His recollection must have been colored by nostalgia, for his correspondence at the time of the trip reveals a completely different assessment. Chichén Itzá was not worth exploring, he wrote, for the same reason the adventurous don't visit the site today—too many tourists.

"The walls…are simply covered with tourists' names, poems of more or less demerit and the like," Thompson complained to a patron in Boston. The principal structures had suffered from being used for cattle and horses when the site was a working plantation, and the floors of the monuments "are paved with fragments of beer bottles and sardine cans."

The ancient city was within the range of marauding bands of rebel Maya, but that threat had failed to discourage other explorers. According to Thompson, "a dozen different people have been to Chichén Itzá and Uxmal and taken moulds and made plans." Thompson had come to Chichén to visit one of those explorers, Alfred Maudslay, who was planning to stay several months studying the site. "Of one thing I am certain, that Maudslay's work will not in any way approach in value our work done and to be done in the future," Thompson wrote. If Chichén Itzá did not deserve study, what did? According to Thompson, it was the city of Labná.

If Thompson had died before buying Chichén Itzá, he probably would be known today for his work at Labná, where he made several expeditions and spent several months. Labná is Maya for "old, ruined buildings," an interesting name as it had some of the prettiest and well preserved structures in the region. Thompson selected Labná to focus his efforts because it was a virgin site: ignored by the Spanish, who had plundered other ruins for stone to build their haciendas; ignored by the post-contact Maya, for it had no source of fresh water; and ignored by time, as many of the ruins were in excellent condition.

The challenge to explore ruins in Yucatán for men such as Thompson—that is, someone with a career, wife, and young children—was that you needed to hire men for labor and for protection. Thompson was not wealthy and therefore, like Blanche Dubois, "depended on the kindness of strangers." Thompson found one such stranger in Carlos Peón Machado, a member of Yucatán's elite Casta Divina, and one of the richest men in Yucatán, the owner of more than a dozen haciendas. Peón Machado was an intellectual of the highest order. He was an active patron of the arts and apparently didn't mind redirecting some of his fortune toward the archaeological explorations of Edward Thompson. "This family and the name of Peón is all over Yucatán a synonym for sturdy, uncompromising loyalty, is noted for its broad, progressive ideas and generous hospitality," Thompson wrote. "Long may their numbers increase and furnish guides for Yucatan's true prosperity."

Don Carlos, unfortunately, did not own any of the haciendas that contained the most famous Maya cities, such as the Hacienda Uxmal (which belonged to another member of the Peón family) or the Hacienda Chichén (which reportedly was abandoned, a casualty of the never-ending War of the Castes). But one of his estates, the Hacienda Tabi, was considered one of the finest properties in all of Yucatán and its boundaries encompassed some of the most beautiful and fascinating ancient Maya ruins that had been little explored.

A few months after arriving in Yucatán, Thompson had made his first trip to Labná. After a long horse ride from Mérida in which he leapfrogged from pueblo to hacienda to pueblo, Thompson rode into a range of low hills and then dropped into a shallow valley with rich, dark soil, unlike the hardscrabble, flat landscape around Mérida. His horse cut through fields dedicated to the cultivation of sugarcane, bisected by small stone channels, a simple irrigation system to provided water to the parched land. He wound his way along a trail that could almost be called a road to arrive at the Hacienda Tabi.

The main casa of the hacienda was one of the most magnificent in all Yucatán, two stories tall and extending the length of a football field. It anchored a broad courtyard, also framed by a sugarcane factory, stables, and a church. In Thompson's time, everything would have looked either new or well repaired, save the fallen-down church (Don Carlos was a rabid anti-Catholic). The air would have been filled with the clang of machinery and the cloying smell of cooking sugarcane. Some 300 laborers worked the plantation and Thompson was pleased to learn that many had been put to his disposal for his expedition to Labná.

Peón Machado probably wasn't at the hacienda when Thompson arrived— few *hacendados*, the owners of haciendas, lived on their plantations. While don Carlos may have provided the permission, it fell to his superintendent Antonio Tejardo to organize the expedition resources. He put the Maya laborers of the hacienda to work on Thompson's projects, not only clearing ruins, but also cutting roads to them from the hacienda.

On that first trip, Thompson and the Maya from Tabi reached Labná as the late afternoon sun glinted off the sole monument visible, a small temple atop a steep mound that rose ten meters above the forest. When John Lloyd Stephens visited Labná more than forty years before, he had been captivated by the compact but distinctive monument, which he called "the most curious and extraordinary structure we had seen in the country." On top was an elaborate roof comb, more than twice the height of the one-story temple. At one time it had been richly decorated with carved figures in relief, but by the time Stephens and Thompson saw it, only pieces of legs and arms remained.

The forest had overtaken Labná and one could pass within fifty meters of any temple "and still remain unaware of their existence," according to Thompson. Thanks to Stephens, Thompson knew what to look for, but the search for ruins would have to wait until morning. As nightfall approached, members of his party had either seen or heard *"un tigre."* The original plan had been to make camp in one of the structures, but Thompson decided they should stay close to the horses to prevent them from being carried away by the jaguar.

The arch at Labná

Over the next several days Thompson had the men clear the monuments. Under the trees and vines they found several palace-like buildings in excellent preservation. One structure in particular captivated Thompson, as it has later visitors to the site: a richly ornamented portal, known today as the Labná Arch. It divided two courtyards and had survived the centuries intact while the structures around it fell to ruin.

Thompson had limited time during that initial visit to explore Labná, but he made the most of it. He and his team discovered secret rooms, skeletons buried beneath floors, numerous remains of huts of the common people and, arguably his most important find, the Mayan innovation that enabled the civilization to construct cities in areas without a water supply—the *chultun*. Chichén Itzá has cenotes; at Uxmal the Maya had built reservoirs. But as Thompson discovered, at Labná the Maya had constructed a series of underground cisterns, dug out of the limestone bedrock by hand and coated with fine stucco that made them impermeable.

After that initial visit, Thompson knew he had found the focus of his archaeological investigations in Yucatán. "I have chosen this city of Labná as my special field of study, not only because it is a rich field for archaeological research, but also because it has thus far escaped the hands of modern vandals," he wrote in a report to the American Antiquarian Society. "Too near the haunts of the dreaded sublevados to suit the taste of curiosity seekers, it has escaped their visitations, while no hacienda exists in its neighborhood to covet the worked stones that it contains. It thus realizes my ideal object of archaeological study—an undisturbed ruined city."

Thompson proposed a fuller expedition to Labná. Stephen Salisbury was interested, but unwilling to commit to the full expense. Thompson needed another deep pocket. To help prime the financial pump, Thompson sent to the American Antiquarian Society a sample of the type of work he planned to do, a mould of an intricate doorway above which was a mask with the large, hooked nose of the Maya rain god Cha'ac. Earlier explorers had suggested it was representative of an elephant and thereby proof that the people of the Americas originated from Asia or, as Thompson himself had suggested only a decade before, the lost continent of Atlantis. After having seen the ruins in person, he recanted, writing, "I believe the civilization of the Mayas to have been a distinct and an original one," he wrote. "And while at some period it may have had contact with that of the East, this contact was too slight to impress itself decidedly upon it."

Thompson's mould of the Labná doorway was installed in the foyer of the society, looming two stories high. As impressive as it may have been, it failed to attract funding for another expedition to Labná. Thompson would have to look elsewhere. The challenge, of course, was that he was in Yucatán and those with disposable incomes who might be predisposed to investing in archaeology were in the United States. But then Thompson had a stroke of luck, the very kind he would have over and over again in his career, in the form of a Bostonian named Charles Pickering Bowditch.

Like many of his generation, Bowditch must have thought that nothing in his life could match his experience during the U.S. Civil War. He was a Boston Brahmin, the New England equivalent of Yucatán's Casta Divina. His great-grandfather had been George Washington's secretary of state, his grandfather a famous mathematician, his father a successful businessman, and his brother a world-famous doctor. Like many young men his age, he felt the lure of battle and left Harvard to accept a lieutenant's commission among the Massachusetts volunteers. Rather than join one of the existing regiments, Bowditch agreed to help lead the Massachusetts 55th—the second African American volunteer company behind the 54th, today known as a "Glory" regiment. In June 1864 he transferred to be with his brother Henry to command the first African American cavalry regiment, the 5th Massachusetts. He had only been with the regiment a week when he had his first taste of action joining in the assault on Petersburg, Va. When the regiment failed to distinguish itself in the eyes of the military brass, it was ordered off the front lines to guard a prisoner-of-war camp, and soon after that Bowditch resigned his commission and went into business, beginning with oil exploration in Pennsylvania, and later back in Massachusetts where he managed his fortune and those of his other Brahmins.

In the early 1880s he became vice president of the American Bell Telephone Company and in 1885 was named a director of the new national company, the American Telegraph & Telephone Company (AT&T). His wealth assured, his children grown, Bowditch cast about for something new to devote his energies. He and a friend decided to visit Mexico and in February 1888 found himself in the company of American Consul Edward H. Thompson, who took him on a tour of Labná and a giant cavern, called Loltun.

The Maya ruins bewitched Bowditch. From that first visit to Yucatán to his death more than thirty years later he would place his fortune at the disposal of those who sought the secrets of the ancient Maya civilization. Edward Thompson has found his sugar daddy.

THE PRESENT

CHICHÉN ITZÁ, FINALLY

IT HAD TAKEN Edward Thompson three days to get to Chichén Itzá from Mérida; we make it in less than two hours. Actually it takes an hour longer, because we have to drive back to Progreso to pick up my glasses which I had forgotten back at the Casa Quixote because I was excited and in a hurry to get to Chichén. Rushing is not the Mexican way. Taking one's sweet time is not only good for the nerves, it is necessary to survive. The faster you go, the slower you go; there is always *mañana*. However, as Curtis, the owner of the hotel, had warned me, "'Mañana' does not mean 'tomorrow;' 'mañana' just means 'not today.'"

The trip from Progreso to Chichén Itzá is over excellent highways. The condition of the cars that drive upon it—not so much. We see a man driving two motorcycles welded together to make a car. We pass entire families—father, mother, child—riding a motorcycle all at once. Most drivers do not drive defensively or with what I would consider the minimum of safety. Yesterday I found that upsetting, but this is the new me. I feel as if I belong. Driving in Yucatan reminds me of my childhood. I grew up in a rural community and it was not unusual to see a group of workers perched precariously in the back of a pickup on their way to some job. A few miles outside of Mérida, one of those pickups drives next to me on the highway. The driver (with the requisite worker or two hanging on for dear life in the bed) waves frantically, pointing at my car's rear. I pull over and find that my trunk lid is open. The only thing that has saved our belongings from being strewn all over the highway is that our car is so small I had to wedge all the gear in to get it to fit. I will forever be grateful to that gentleman who took the trouble to let us know of the danger. It turned out to be but one of several kindnesses that Yucatecans showed us as we bumbled through their country.

We will be staying at the Hacienda Chichén, which I have been told is next to the archaeological zone if not actually in it. This was the hacienda that Edward Thompson owned and operated. He rebuilt it beginning in 1894 and lived there on and off until 1925. Don Fernando's father converted the hacienda into a hotel in the 1950s and it has been receiving guests ever since. The hacienda is owned by don Fernando's sister, Carmen and is managed by Fernando's daughter, Belisa.

To get there we have to drive through Pisté and my first take is that it is a small town of filthy streets, cheap hotels, and a tourist bus-filled highway. I'm not particularly bothered by its appearance because it reminds me, for some odd reason, of that little desert town where I grew up. But if the Hacienda Chichén turns out to be as "quaint" as Pisté, I know I will be in for some of Lori's rolling of eyes. To our collective relief, the Hacienda Chichén has been transformed into a first-class resort. The landscaping is lush and birds fill the trees. The cottages, which at one time had been the temporary homes of some of the world's greatest Maya archaeologists, have been upgraded with air conditioning, ceiling fans, and new bathrooms. Each cottage has its own décor.

As we check into the resort, a short, thick man of Maya heritage wearing a guayabera, the same style of shirt that don Fernando favors, introduces himself as Antonio Bustillos Castillo. He is to be our guide to Chichén

Itzá, he explains. The reception desk is in the main casa, most of which has been converted into a restaurant, but food is far from my mind. Even though it is well past lunchtime and we haven't eaten since breakfast, I'm too excited to wait. I beg my family to explore the archaeological zone. "There'll be a snack bar or a restaurant in there somewhere," I tell them.

I've brought along recording gear, so I ask my son to run the microphone while I carry the recorder and listen with headphones. I want to make sure I catch Antonio's every word. As we walk toward the entrance to the Chichén Itzá archaeological zone, he tells us that he began working for the Barbachanos thirty years ago, eventually managing their resort at Uxmal. "In 1998 I retired from the hotel and became a freelancer and since then been working as a tour guide," he says.

The Hacienda Chichén is next to the Mayaland, the original Barbachano hotel, which according to Antonio was built in 1930. We walk by its

Hacienda Chichén

entrance, which looks out upon the Maya observatory known as the *Caracol* (Spanish for "snail," to describe the circular staircase that winds inside of the temple). This unusual building is round, not square like other Maya structures. The upper part is in ruins, but still visible are little windows. "There were eight of them for people to watch the celestial bodies," Antonio says. He turns around and indicates the Mayaland, which is owned by don Fernando's eldest son, Fernando Barbachano Herrero. There are plans to add another restaurant to the hotel, he says. *Enough about restaurants*, I think. My family looks longingly inside. The resort is beautiful, I tell Antonio. "When Fernando does things, he likes to do them most impressive," Antonio says.

He leads us to the entrance to Chichén Itzá, where I purchase tickets at a long counter manned by two people. One person takes my pesos, another stamps some tickets and gives them to me along with paper wrist bands. Once we are inside the gate, Antonio offers his translation of the name Chichén Itzá: "'Chi' means 'mouth'; 'chen' means 'well'; 'itz' means 'magic'; and 'ha' means 'water'…Chi-chén Itz-ha, which means 'the land of the well where the water comes out as magic.'"

He points out what I take to be a low wall running next to the path. "This is what we call a 'white road,'" Antonio says, or in Maya, sacbé. These raised pathways run throughout Chichén Itzá, he says. Ahead to the left is a large arch, looking almost out of place standing by itself off the main path. Antonio says it was built six months ago, a restored ruin. The archaeologists supposedly found most of the original stones and were able to reconstruct the arch from the rubble.

As we walk along the well-trod path, the sun beats down on us. A light breeze kicks up and brings the sweet scent of blossoms. I ask Antonio what I'm smelling and he tells me it is a flower the Maya call *its its chek*. I don't see any flowers, however, just the gray pathway, the gray woods, gray dust in the air; the bland surroundings only increase awareness of the heat. This is the heart of the dry season. I worry briefly about my family, but only briefly.

Antonio explains that what we will soon be seeing is the Toltec portion of Chichén Itzá. The Toltecs were from Central Mexico, he explains, and were the ones who brought human sacrifice when they conquered the Maya of Chichén Itzá sometime in the tenth century. Before that the Maya did not believe in human sacrifice, he says.

He walks us past a few ruins in various stages of reconstruction: Some are mounds of rubble, some have been cleared but not rebuilt, and others appear to be finished, although Antonio explains that when the Maya ruled Chichén Itzá, the walls would have been covered with stucco and brightly painted.

We've been in the archaeological zone for almost an hour when Antonio guides us to what must be the money shot. We walk into a clearing and before us is the pyramid El Castillo—"Casteeya" is how Antonio pronounces it. Across a wide, flat open space is the Temple of Warriors and behind us, the exterior of the Great Ball Court. Over the last few months I've seen hundreds of photographs, many taken from this very spot, but nothing prepares me for the majesty of these structures, or how massive and imposing they are in real life. Antonio is telling us something about what we're seeing, but I don't hear him. I'm enthralled that I'm finally here.

"I have to sit down," comes a weak voice from behind me. It's Sam. His face is ashen and his eyes are glassy, almost rolling back into his head. He looks like he is about to drop the microphone. I know instantly what's wrong: He has not eaten since eight that morning, nor taken a sip of water since we left the hacienda.

I don't need to look at Lori to know what expression is on her face. I can feel the heat and it's not the Yucatán sun. It's Lori, and she's furious.

Alfred Mauldslay

THE PAST

MAUDSLAY

IT TOOK A LOT to make Alfred Maudslay angry, if, indeed, he ever angered at all. But Yucatán certainly tried his patience.

Maudslay, a tall, thin Englishman, disembarked at Progreso on Christmas Eve of 1888. Unlike his predecessors Le Plongeon or Charnay, Maudslay was a "real" archaeologist, at least as much of one as existed in the 19th century. "His aim was perfection, and his published scientific works show that his ideal was accomplished," wrote his good friend T.A. Joyce. "As a scholar, he refused to be satisfied with hazy generalizations, and sought the truth. Mr. Maudslay's work can never be equaled."

Over the past seven years he had hiked throughout Central America and Mexico, studying the ancient Maya cities of Copan, Tikal, Quirigua, Menche, and Yaxchilan. His careful reports of these cities had been feted by the great scientific societies of Europe. But at Chichén Itzá, he must have wondered if he had met his match.

He arrived in Mérida before his baggage. He had been promised letters of introduction by Mexican authorities, yet no letters awaited him. He was anxious to get started on his study of Chichén Itzá, but instead he wasted weeks in Mérida. "Here I passed a month in much discomfort," he wrote. He found Mérida without charm and worse, very, very expensive.

The so-called "White City" had gone green. The hacendados were making a fortune growing the "green gold" of henequen and their wealth was driving up prices throughout the city. Mérida, like any other boomtown, had runaway inflation. Maudslay found the cost of food and shelter much higher than elsewhere in Mexico and every able man in the peninsula had been recruited to plant and tend and harvest henequen. For Maudslay this spelled potential disaster, because he needed workers to clear the ancient monuments so he could photograph and measure them.

While he waited for his credentials, he managed to get out of Mérida twice, to Uxmal and a "flying visit" to Labná, where Edward Thompson was working. Thompson's new patron, Charles Bowditch, had hired him to map, photograph, and make moulds of the ruins for the Peabody Museum at Bowditch's alma mater Harvard. Thompson, who was coming to the end of his third year in Yucatán, finally had received the financial backing to conduct what would be his first major expedition.

With Bowditch's support, Thompson had brought to Yucatán two Harvard men, Clifton H. Paige, an engineer, and Henry N. Sweet, a photographer. They set up camp in front of the large structure known as the Palace and from there mapped the center of the city. "During this survey not only were topographical notes carefully made, but those in other lines were copiously recorded: the humus and forest depositions on edifice top, terrace level, and forest bottom were studied and carefully noted, as were also the insect and bird life, and the growth of the plants on special sites and places, including a beautiful and fragrant lilac-tinted orchid found growing on a bay tree on the side of the temple pyramid," Thompson wrote.

Maudslay left Thompson to return to Mérida where he resumed organizing his own expedition. In all it took two months, but in February 1889 he rode into Pisté. The small town was still in the midst of its slow crawl back from the ravages of the Caste War, but there had been progress. Maudslay found it almost a functioning town again. It even had a government administrator, called a *commisario*, who invited Maudslay to stay with him until he could get established at Chichén Itzá. Commisario Estéban Martín (to Maudslay he was "Stephen") was a *thanks*, meaning he was part Maya and part something else, usually Spanish. In the cultural pecking order that was Yucatán, those of Spanish descent were the upper classes, the Maya were the laborers, and the mestizo a class all its own, which filled the middle management ranks. Foremen on plantations, for example, were often mestizo. Martín, Maudslay said, "was a capital specimen of a half-caste yeoman," although the explorer disapproved of what he perceived as a weakness for liquor.

Martín had a four-year-old son who instantly took to Maudslay and Maudslay to him. Maudslay found him "a child who would have attracted attention in any part of the world for his robust beauty and his charming and genial manners and fearless ways." The entire village "adored the boy," Maudslay wrote, adding, "I don't think I ever met a child who attracted me so much."

Maudslay had little success at hiring workers in Mérida or in Valladolid, where he had passed some time before arriving at Chichén. Pisté, unlike other parts of Yucatán, was outside the so-called henequen zone. Maudslay found locals willing to clear the brush from the monuments.

Martín's son proved to be a welcome distraction amidst the hard labor. "He never showed any shyness of me and we became fast friends," Maudslay wrote. "He used to prattle away to me in Maya about all that was going on, although I could not understand a word of his language." He added, "It was hard to believe that he was related to the people around him, for he seemed to belong to some superior race."

Maudslay must have appreciated the company of the young boy, for

Chichén Itzá was lonely work, especially at night when the laborers would return to their huts in Pisté and leave Maudslay by himself. The explorer lived in the ruins, first in the Casa Colorada and later in the top story of the majestic Las Monjas. There were occasional visitors who would arrive without warning. In early March Thompson and his photographer, Henry Sweet paid a visit, the same trip where Thompson had determined Chichén was not worth studying.

Sweet had finished his commitment to Thompson and was seeing the sights before heading back to Boston. Maudslay suggested that he extend his stay and come to Chichén to help him. The offer irritated Thompson. "It is not very pleasant to think that the expedition [at Labná] has furnished a man to work for a rival Society of a rival nation," Thompson wrote to his sponsors at the Peabody Museum, "but Mr. Maudslay is rich and generous, and has no thought of the money he spends."

Sweet promised to consider the offer and returned with Thompson to Mérida. Shortly after they left, Maudslay's foreman approached him. His mother was dying, he said, and asked for two weeks off to return to Mérida to be with her. Maudslay gave the fellow a token payment toward his wages and instructions on how to get the remainder from his agent in Mérida. As if things couldn't get worse, Commisario Martín arrived "in a state of great distress" for his son had been seriously ill for three or four days and the father was certain death was near. Maudslay stopped in Pisté on his way to Izamal to find additional workers and visited the boy, who was in the grips of fever and delirium. There was little Maudslay could do, but he had supplies brought from his camp at Chichén that he hoped would keep up the lad's strength and break the fever.

Maudslay continued on to Izamal and while he was recruiting more help, by happenstance he learned that his foreman had been there the night before "apparently quite forgetful of his dying mother." The man apparently had boasted "that he well understood how to manage" the gringo Maudslay and that he was on his way to Mérida to have fun at Carnaval. Maudslay sent a telegram to his agent in Mérida advising him to withhold wages from the now *ex*-foreman. Maudslay never heard from him again.

His effort to attract additional workers failed, so he returned to Chichén. As he rode through Pisté, he stopped to ask how Martín's son was faring and learned the boy had been buried that morning. Martín appeared, "looking haggard and wretched," and as Maudslay found out later, he was in the middle of a two-week bender. The explorer went to pay his respects to the boy's mother and found the house prepared for a service. The table where Maudslay had done his writing when he lived there had been converted into a makeshift altar with a white cloth. They had no pictures of saints, so the family had cut out two advertisements from a magazine, one of a German woman touting beer and the other of a Spanish-looking woman enjoying white wine. They had no vase, so someone had gathered some beer bottles into which they put funereal bouquets. The heartbreaking scene soon became macabre when two of the village elders approached Maudslay with a proposal. They wanted to unearth the boy's body and have Maudslay take a photograph, as no image of the child existed. Despite their insistence, Maudslay managed to beg out of the gruesome request.

Work resumed at Chichén. Maudslay does not say how deeply he was affected by the death, but it may be significant that nowhere in his published books and articles about his experience at Chichén does the name of the boy appear. The experience changed Maudslay, for he began to see the Maya as people. Their distress over the passing of the young boy "was touching and utterly unlike the usual callousness of the American native," he wrote. "But, as I have said, the child was possessed of exceptional beauty and charm of manner, and he had won his way to all their hearts."

Maudslay, with typical British stoicism, pressed on with the task at hand. That was why he was delighted when Henry Sweet came riding into his camp. "I secured a charming companion for the remainder of my stay at the ruins," Maudslay wrote, "and without his timely help my expedition must have proved almost a failure."

THE PRESENT

CARLOS (THOMPSON) MARRUFO

IT'S A HUSBAND'S LOT to be forever wrong. In my single-minded quest, I had endangered the family, Lori tells me. Poor Antonio suddenly finds himself without a tour. As we hustle out of the archaeological zone, he tries to stop and explain some feature to us, but Lori just stares straight ahead and keeps walking for the exit. Once we're out, he and I make a date to resume the tour the next day—if I survive that long.

Sam recovers quickly once he has some water and something to eat. Lori's temper takes a little longer. We head to our bungalows. We are in two adjoining rooms in "Thompson's Cottage," which originally thrilled me until I learn it was named after the archaeologist J. Eric Thompson. In fact, there is little, if any of the legacy of Edward H. Thompson that I can see, even though he owned the hacienda for fifty years. True, Edward Thompson is a controversial name in Mexico, but the Barbachanos would not own the hacienda if it had not been for him.

The air conditioning in our room helps cool Lori's temper. She stretches out on the bed, enjoys a cervesa from the mini-bar, and begins to relax. There is a softening with regard to the Sam calamity, but I know this event has been entered into that ever-growing list that will be brought up for the rest of our collective lives as an example of what a dunderhead I can be.

Marriage is but a string of debacles occasionally broken by apologies and make-up sex.

With Lori collapsed in the room, I check on the kids. They're on the *pórtico*, sitting in hammocks and reading Harry Potter books, no doubt for the tenth time. I tell Lori I'm going for a walk. In truth, I'm once again on my single-minded, self-centered quest to find Edward Thompson.

The bungalows are spread throughout the hacienda property, connected by narrow concrete walkways that are raised four or five inches above ground level. They remind me of the ancient Maya walkway, the sacbé, that Antonio had pointed out. I figure this area must get flooding or heavy rains to warrant such an ankle-breaking height to the sidewalks.

The landscaping is spectacular, a tropical mélange of palms and other trees, obviously native, that I don't recognize. I am particularly struck by a thick-trunked tree, almost white like a birch, with giant thorns and branches that span outward at sharp right angles. This is the ceiba, a tree sacred to the Maya. Beneath the trees are flowers of every description and in some delicate orchids grow. The trees are filled with birds that chirp and screech constantly. The air smells rich and alive, and feels thicker than it does back home.

I walk to the *casa principal*, or main building, which, like the bungalows, has been painted a cheerful yellow that glows in the late afternoon light. I have seen a handful of photographs of it from Thompson's day. From what I can tell, the core structure is much the same. Five large arches, borne by thin, almost delicate, columns, run along the front. These support a roof that projects over a veranda that runs two-thirds the length of the building. The rear of the hacienda house has a similar design, although there are only three arches in the center, and the terraza is correspondingly shorter. Again, this is identical to Thompson's time. The former living quarters in the center of the building has been replaced with a reception area and a restaurant, yet while the functions have changed, the casa is the same as when Thompson lived here a century ago. In Thompson's day, the front was the back and the back was the front.

The casa had been built from limestone blocks taken from Chichén Itzá. Several of the stones in the façade had been carved in ancient times, including one of a tiny man with hands held above the head, a pose called *atlante* or *carydid*. The ceiling is fifteen to twenty feet high, supported by rough-hewn beams of some unrecognizable wood. The doorways at the center of the building are open to the elements, both front and back, and there doesn't appear to be anyway to close them. At one end of the building is a closed-in dining room; at the other is some kind of library or office.

Just off the front of the building is a small, uncovered terraza with several tables dressed in white tablecloths with a colorful sash of purple and blue, colors from the Guatemala highlands. There's a small building, a bodega I think they call it, with a bar. I decide to sit for a spell and have a cocktail. A man in a crisp white shirt and dark slacks approaches and takes my margarita order. I notice everyone here looks Maya. Now that I think about it, I don't see anyone working who isn't descended from the Maya.

I gaze out toward the front of the property. When Thompson was here it served as a corral for the cattle. Today there is a bushy tree, the size of a small building, surrounded by a hedge. I can't tell what kind of tree it is, but it doesn't look native. Beyond that is a large, free-standing arch. Just looking at it gives me a chill as I remember something I read in Thompson's autobiography. During the Caste War, the rebel Maya would bring the men and women they had captured on their raids to the arch. There they divided their spoils of war. The human booty was divided as well, the men as slaves and the women as wives of the soldiers. It did not matter if the captive was white or Indian, according to Thompson's source. In my research I had come across a brief newspaper item written in the early days of the Caste War. It told the same story, but with one major difference: the men who were not fit to be slaves were hung from the arch. Thompson called it "The Gateway of Sadness." Today the Barbachanos use the arch as part of the hacienda logo.

My reverie is broken by the arrival of my margarita, which comes in what can only be described as a goblet. It's enough drink for two or three people. The man who brings it starts to walk away, but I call him back. "Excuse me," I say. "But do you know of a man who once lived around here named Carlos Marrufo?"

Without hesitation the man nods. "But he is dead," he tells me. As he would be around 100, that comes as no surprise, but then the man says, "His wife, doña Maria Luisa, lives in Pisté. You should speak to her."

THE PAST

TEOBERT MALER

RIVALRIES BETWEEN ARCHAEOLOGISTS are nothing new. Explorers outnumber potential patrons, making competition for the funding of excavations fierce. Most of the struggles between archaeologists are of the Edward Thompson/Alfred Maudslay variety, resulting in the occasional pique or hurt feeling. Some blow up into full-blown feuds, such as Augustus Le Plongeon and Thompson's predecessor Louis Aymé. But none matched Thompson's thirty-year war with Teobert Maler.

Maler, the son of a diplomat from the German Confederation's Duchy of Baden, was born in 1842 during one of his father's missions to Rome. His mother died when he was a year old, which left care of the infant to his father, who Maler later described as "a gloomy, distrustful, and miserly man, whose mean attributes even grew into a certain degree of insanity." The acorn did not fall far from the oak, for those very words could have been applied to Maler, who spent his dotage in Mérida saloons swilling cerveza and issuing screeds against his favorite target, don Eduardo Thompson. But that came much, much later.

At twenty-one Maler moved to Vienna and became an Austrian citizen. He went to work for a prestigious architect, but abandoned that career and joined a military unit recruited by Austrian Archduke Maximilian to aid the French in Mexico. Napoleon III had assumed control of the nation for non-payment of debts and installed Maximilian to be the new Mexican emperor. In early 1865 Maler landed in Mexico and fought for Maximilian to suppress revolts by insurrectionists in Veracruz and Puebla.

The French occupied Mexico over the objections of the United States, but as that country was preoccupied with civil war, it could take no action. By the middle of 1865 the American Civil War was over and the U.S. turned its attention to Mexico. Because France had been an ally to the Union, the U.S. chose not to go in with guns blazing but instead encouraged the end of support for Maximilian. France's money dried up, Maximilian was overthrown, and in typical Mexican fashion, put before a firing squad and shot. Maler went into hiding, but unlike most of his comrades, did not return to Europe. He liked Mexico and decided to stay.

For the next decade he wandered throughout the country, studying its people and the remains of the great civilizations that once thrived there. The turning point for him was in 1877 when he visited the ancient Maya city of Palenque in Chiapas. After a week of sketching and photographing ruins, he decided that he would devote his life to exploring the remains of the ancient Maya. Unfortunately, he was out of money. His father had died in 1875 and the new government had confiscated his estate in Germany. Maler returned home for the first time in twelve years to press his claim. It took him six years, but he won a settlement and with that money returned to Mexico in 1885, the same year Thompson arrived. Maler was forty-three.

He explored Chichén Itzá in late 1891. Like Maudslay two years before, he hired locals to clear the monuments, lived in Las Monjas, photographed and mapped the ruins. His work was identical to Maudslay's, but not as detailed or extensive. His report on Chichén was not published until long after his death in 1917 and by then was of interest to few archaeologists.

While the report lacked new information about Chichén Itzá, it provided keen insight into the mental state of Maler, for in it he revealed the disdain he felt for all of his contemporaries. Maler hated other archaeologists and found them his inferior. He considered Charnay soft, "not the man for such expeditions who sees the discomforts and risks inseparable from such a distant trip." He accused Le Plongeon of *"profanaciones,"* of desecrating Chichén during his excavations and said that he was an "exploiter" versus an "explorer" because of his "frequent and gross abuses of our famous monuments of antiquity." Maudslay was much too well respected to attack directly, so Maler instead attacked those who assisted him.

One explorer became a lifelong enemy: Edward Thompson. In his Chichén Itzá report, Maler went on a two-page tirade about Thompson's excavations, claiming he had damaged the substructure of one of the monuments at Labná. With his pen engaged in full hyperbolic mode, Maler compared the site after Thompson was done to "the catastrophe that blew up the island of Krakatoa." According to Maler, Thompson had deceived the government by describing himself as an "artista," seeking permission to paint pictures of the site, when in fact he had hired forty men "with crowbars and pickaxes" to tear the city apart. At no time, Maler wrote, did the government ever send a representative to see "what kind of 'watercolors' those 'artistas' were using."

Maler must have believed there had to be a special ring of hell reserved for "artistas" such as Thompson. What Thompson did not know was that Maler would devote the remainder of his days to making Thompson's life on earth a living hell.

Teobert Maler

Previously unpublished Maler photos from Chichén Itzá, 1891-2

THE PRESENT

THE BALLAD OF CARLOS MARRUFO

AFTER HAVING STARVED my family earlier in the day, I treat them to a lavish dinner at the Hacienda Chichén. We sit on the terraza where I had had my drink. Now that the sun is down, cool breezes sweep through the palms and trees. The stars emerge from the murky blackness of the sky.

Lori and I order margaritas and the tension between us earlier in the day melts away in a haze of alcohol. Sarah, who is nineteen, decides that now is the time to have her first drink, a piña colada. I don't offer any protest because Lori thinks it's a capital idea and I don't want to rock the boat if I can help it.

We talk about the schedule tomorrow. Lori tells me that she is not interested in participating in any more tours. She suggests that I go with Antonio, and she and the children will explore on their own. She knows I'll agree with anything.

I tell her and the children about my brief exchange with the waiter earlier the day. At some point I have to go into Pisté and find Carlos Marrufo's widow, I tell them. Suddenly the air swells with guitars and singing. A trio of musicians moves through the restaurant, singing ballads to tables of patrons. "It's called la trova," I tell Lori. The style of three musicians playing guitars singing melancholy songs had its roots in Cuba, but was popularized in Yucatán a century ago. Three men in white guayaberas carrying guitars wander from the main part of the restaurant and approach our table. Two of the men are Maya and look to be around the same age as me; both are short and stocky. The third is a young man, probably a little older than Sarah, slightly taller and thinner than the older men, and looks mestizo. I ask if they would mind if I record a couple of songs. They are thrilled at the idea.

Author's wife with trova musicians

I pull out the recorder and set it up. I think for an instant of giving the microphone to Sam, but then decide I don't want to go down that road again. "What are we going to hear first?" I ask.

"We're going to sing special for you a Mayan song," says one of the older men. He appears to be the leader. "We're going to dedicate this song for you and then for everybody. From Chichén Itzá to the United States and all over the world, a Mayan song."

He strums his guitar and the other two join in on cue. They sing a folk melody, but with lyrics in the Maya language. The only words I pick out are the names of Maya cities: "Chichén Itzá," "Mayapan," "Uxmal," "Izamal."

When they finish, I ask what the song was about. "This is a special song dedicated to Kukulcan," the leader tells us. Kukulcan is name the Maya give the "principal man," he says, although in the rest of Mexico he is known as "Quetzalcoatl." "All those names belong to just one people," he tells us

The trio performs another, this time about Chichén Itzá. It is in Spanish and again I don't understand it, but I recognize some of the words: "El Castillo," "Caracol," "chac-mool," "cenote."

We applaud enthusiastically after each song. At the end, I say, "You have to tell me your names."

The leader of the trio leans into my microphone. "Bibiano. Uh. Tun.," he says. He seems to spit out each of his names

"Justo Tek Mex," says the man with the glassy eye.

"Joel Geobani Uh Marrufo," says the young man.

We talk for a few minutes, until I register what's been said. "Did you say 'Marrufo?'" I ask. "Do you know Carlos Marrufo? Or his widow, Maria Luisa?"

"Si," Joel says. "She is..." he struggles to find the word.

"She is his grandmother," Bibiano says. "That is my wife's mother. Carlos Marrufo was her father."

Serendipity.

I start blurting out about Edward Thompson and how I came to Yucatán in search of his descendants. I can't believe it. Standing next to me is Thompson's great grandson. I search his face for some resemblance, but I don't see it. I don't not see it either. I ask to meet his grandmother, to learn the story of Carlos Marrufo.

"I will take you to her," Bibiano offers. He explains that doña Maria Luisa does not speak English, but he will translate for me. He asks me to meet him in front of the church in Pisté tomorrow morning and he will introduce me to the widow of Carlos Marrufo.

Bibiano Uh Tun (Pereira photo)

THE PAST

THE WORLD'S FAIR

IN THE YEAR 1892, anthropology came into its own.

To recognize the 400th anniversary of Columbus's discovery of America, a group of Chicago businessmen proposed building a world's fair. The World Columbian Exposition would be the biggest in history. The organizers had their eye on the Paris exposition of 1889, which had brought the world the Eiffel Tower. The Chicago fair, to be built on almost 700 acres in Chicago's South side, would be four times bigger and while there would be exhibits from around the world, it would emphasize the Americas.

One of the first things the organizers did after getting permission from Congress in 1890 to hold the fair was hire Frederic W. Putnam from Harvard's Peabody Museum to put together an entire building devoted to anthropology. They gave him a $100,000 budget to collect artifacts from around the world to fill it.

Putnam not only sought objects to be displayed inside the Anthropology Building, but outside as well, and for that he turned to Edward Thompson. "He wrote me at once to make direct moulds, full-sized, an absolutely accurate, in papier-mache...of certain typical facades in the ruined groups of Yucatán, the finest existing remains of the once great Maya civilization," Thompson wrote. These giant moulds would serve as casts to erect copies of the monuments in the courtyard in front of the anthropology building.

Thompson additionally pledged to bring a Maya family to Chicago where they would stay in a replica of a na, a Maya thatch-covered house. One member of the family would be a potter who would demonstrate his craft.

Thompson was granted "an unlimited leave of absence" from his consul post, which he believed was the first time such a privilege ever had been granted.

Putnam sent Thompson a list of structures he wanted to be reconstructed: the great arch at Labná, a decorated arch from the House of the Governor in Uxmal, one of the temples from Chichén Itzá, and the post-conquest façade of the conquistador Montejo's casa in Mérida. "I confess I was somewhat startled," Thompson said of the ambitious list. Putnam trimmed the demand to five large moulds from structures at Uxmal and the magnificent arch at Labná. In all, Thompson was to cast 10,000 square feet of ruins, ship the moulds to Chicago, and then cast and reconstruct them on the grounds of the exposition.

Uxmal, like Chichén Itzá, is one of the largest Maya ruins on the Yucatán peninsula. But unlike Chichén, "the whole region is a pest-hole, a breeding place of malignant fevers, the home of dancing clouds of virulent mosquitoes." When the Maya built the city, they designed an ingenious system of reservoirs, because there were no cenotes or lakes for water. After the city fell to ruin, the water system became "mud-filled and stagnant," and a breeding ground for malaria-carrying insects. When John Lloyd Stephens and Frederick Catherwood stayed there a half century earlier, both men came down with fevers; Catherwood became so ill he had to return to the United States to recover and Stephens would suffer relapses for the remainder of his life.

Thompson led a team of forty Maya to Labná and then to Uxmal. As expected, workers began dropping from fever until half the crew were confined to their hammocks, including Thompson. According to one of his assistants, Thompson's face was "as pale as yellow wax," and the whites of his eyes "were as red raw meat." His voice was weak and trembled, his feet were constantly cold, and he suffered from cramps. His men, at least those still standing, feared he was near death.

Thompson revived sufficiently to supervise the remaining work at Uxmal, but several of his men died. He collapsed again, he said, once the last crate of moulds was packed aboard a steamer for New York. He was so weak when he arrived in the United States that he could not even hold a pen. By October, he was well enough to travel to Chicago to assist in casting the moulds and assembling the giant replica structures on the grounds of the exposition.

The fair opened in the spring of 1893 and during its five-month run, hosted more than 26 million visitors from around the world who came to see some 65,000 exhibits in more than 200 buildings. For the first time, the world could see reasonably accurate depictions of the monuments of the ancient Maya at a one-to-one scale.

After the fair closed on Hallowe'en 1893, the life-sized casts from Uxmal and Labná were destroyed. What the ancient Maya built had lasted more than 500 years; Thompson's monuments didn't even stand for 500 days.

Reproductions of Labná (above) and Uxmal (below) at the Columbian Exposition in Chicago

THE PRESENT

DOÑA MARIA LUISA

I AM UP WITH THE SUN. Bibiano and I had agreed to meet early because I have to hook up with Antonio at Chichén to resume our tour. I load my recorder, camera, and other equipment in the car and drive into Pisté.

The road from Chichén goes directly into the center of Pisté village. There are several taxis parked in front of the church, so I pull past them and stop in front of the entrance. The church is closed, apparently for good, according to the sign out front. It looks to be in better shape than when the big four of Charnay, Le Plongeon, Maudslay, and Maler were here in the 1880s and 1890s. Pisté is today a thriving community. Behind me, across the highway, is a small outdoor restaurant—a *cocina economica*. A little further down the street is a butcher and someone is already at work, cutting up meat for the day. There must be a school nearby, because there are a lot of children wearing uniforms. At the intersection next to the church there is a police officer, blowing a whistle and directing traffic. The scene is so normal and so natural I can't help but smile.

The sun already feels hot. I try not to look conspicuous, but a six-foot three-inch gringo sticks out. No one pays attention to me, so in a place like Pisté that gets hundreds of tourists each day, I'm not that unusual.

Bibiano comes wheeling up on a small child's bicycle. He waves for me to follow him up the street. I get back into the car and drive behind him. He can only go about five miles an hour because the pedals are too small for him to work up much speed. I notice we are on the road that leads to the Cuota, or toll road, that we had taken yesterday to come to Chichén Itzá.

He leads me past small stores (*tiendas*), a pharmacy (*farmacias*), Maya nas, and cement houses to a low, but relatively modern-looking home set back from the road with a front yard—unusual for a place that usually has houses built next to the sidewalk. The front door is open and there are children running around. Bibiano and I are met by a short, slight woman, possibly in her sixties, wearing a shapeless white shift with colorful embroidery around the neck and bottom hem. This is a *huipil*, the traditional Yucatecan shift. Her black hair has little gray and is pulled back from her face. She greets me with a warm smile. I cannot keep from grinning. This is doña Maria Luisa Nah Rodriguez, wife of Carlos Marrufo.

She waves me into her parlor and indicates I am to sit down. She speaks to me in Spanish, but I don't understand a word. Bibiano explains she wants to know if I would like anything. I say no thank you. There is a little dog running in and out of the house yapping constantly. In the next room a television blares out in Spanish and two or three young children are watching. They don't seem too curious to see me.

We are joined by Victoria, Bibiano's wife and daughter of Maria Luisa. She looks like her mother and, like her son, I don't see any resemblance to Edward Thompson.

I explain why I have come and Bibiano translates what I say into Spanish. He appears to be up to the task, although I have no idea what he is telling his mother-in-law.

I say I have heard that Carlos Marrufo was the son of Edward Thompson and she says that it was true. Carlos also had two brothers, Hector and Alfredo, and a sister, Ofelia. "Were they also by Thompson?" I ask, and the answer seems to be yes. I say "seems to be," because the translations were coming fast and furious. One of the brothers married an American woman and moved to the United States. A few years ago some of their children visited Chichén Itzá and were staying at one of the hotels next to Chichén Itzá where doña Maria Luisa worked. Today, however, the family has no contact with them.

I say that I have heard that Carlos Marrufo was a mechanic. Bibiano translates and everyone laughs. He was not just a mechanic, he was "*muy mechanico*," they tell me. "He repairs everything," Bibiano explains.

Carlos Marrufo Manjarrez, early 1970s

Carlos and Maria Luisa had eight children and seven survived into adulthood. Victoria was the oldest, followed by seven boys: Carlos, Ariel, Reynaldo, Javier, Guillermo, and Miguel are the ones still alive. The boys built Maria Luisa this house after Carlos died, she says.

"I have some sensitive questions to ask," I say. I have been in contact with Edward Thompson's family in the United States and they are concerned that what I might learn is that when Thompson left Mexico, he left doña Victoria with nothing. Is that true? I ask. What did he leave her?

Bibiano translates my question and the answer is long, but his reply is one word. "Nothing," he says. "After Edward Thompson left, Victoria tried to live in the hacienda because she believed it was for her. When the Barbachanos come, they say she needs to leave that place." She moved in with Carlos, Bibiano says, near what today is the Pisté bus station. "She got sick, it was not a very good hut, so she went to Mérida where she died," he says.

It was as I feared, but it was pretty much what I had expected. "When I go back, I'd like to share this information with the children in the United States," I tell them and Bibiano translates. This provokes a lot of conversation in Spanish, to which Bibiano then asks, "They want to know, how many children does he have?"

I explain that Edward Thompson had five children who survived into adulthood. They are all dead, I say. "I have met two of his grandchildren and I have met two of his great-grandchildren. His granddaughter who cared for him when he was old and sick and when he died, is the one who asked me, if I find the children of Thompson and doña Victoria, to let her know." Bibiano draws a sharp breath and nods. I tell them how I had conveyed to her that she may not like what I discover. "I told her I might find out that Thompson left Yucatán and left doña Victoria nothing and she said, 'Yes, I still want to know.' I don't know if his granddaughter will find that shameful. I don't know."

I have to return to the Hacienda Chichén to meet Antonio. As I say my goodbyes, Bibiano takes me aside. "Where is your family?" he asks. I explain they are probably still sleeping. He nods in the direction of doña Maria Luisa. "They want to know your family," he says.

"You want to meet my family?" I ask somewhat stupidly. He nods.

I explain that we are headed for the archaeological zone and then we will leave Chichén to return to Mérida. Bibiano looks at me as serious as church and tells me I must bring my family. I start to explain how that might not be possible, but he insists. He won't let me depart until I agree.

"Well," I say, "we're leaving around noon and we have to drive down this road. Would you like us to stop by?" He smiles and nods. I get in my car, say a few more adioses, turn the car around, and head back to Chichén Itzá.

Apparently they had expected me to bring Lori and the kids on this interview. To me, I was there on business. But as I just learned, a lesson that would be repeated many times, the business of Yucatan is family.

Maria Luisa Nah (Pereira Photo)

Victoria Marrufo Nah (Pereira photo)

THE PAST

BUYING CHICHÉN ITZÁ

FAMILY WAS OF THE GREATEST IMPORTANCE to Edward Thompson. He and Henrietta had arrived in Yucatán in 1885 with one child; by 1894 Henrietta had given birth to five more. In September 1886 Edward Josiah Thompson was born; in May 1888 Ernest Hamblin Thompson; in January 1890 Mary Abbie Thompson, although she did not survive the year; in December 1891 Margarita Thompson; and sometime in the winter of 1893-94, Henrietta became pregnant again and would have a girl who would be named Abby May Thompson. About the time Henrietta would have suspected she was with child, her husband lost his job.

Thompson's patron in Congress, the Hon. George Frisbie Hoar, was no match for the Democratic wave that roared over the civil service when Grover Cleveland returned as president in 1893. Thompson had been appointed consul at Mérida just days before Cleveland took office the first time in 1885. He might have skated through Cleveland's second term, except for the bad luck and poor health of Marcellus L. Davis. Davis had been among the Democratic faithful in Arkansas and for his support, Cleveland appointed him Consul to the British colony of Trinidad off the coast of Venezuela. Unfortunately for Thompson, Davis took ill and needed an assignment closer to home. The president's people chose Mérida.

Ironically, Grover Cleveland and Edward Thompson were now neighbors. Cleveland had purchased a summer home only a few miles from Thompson's cottage on Cape Cod. Both men's houses looked out upon Buzzards Bay and both enjoyed dipping a line. Thompson had been home during much of the summer of 1892, so it's possible they might have crossed paths on the open seas. If they had, it apparently did not affect Cleveland's decision. Thompson was out as consul and Davis was in.

Thompson received official notice that he had been replaced on Jan. 10, 1894. If it came as a shock, Thompson was over it by April when he wrote Frederick Ward Putnam, "I miss the income of the Consulate but I have my own pretty little place in the suburbs of Mérida where I retired to after being relieved." Unlike most consuls who return to the United States upon completing their assignments, Thompson elected to stay in Yucatán. "I thus have to pay no rent and not only that but my garden under the supervision of an old American aided by the 'Chinese cheap labor' is commencing to yield me quite a little income without any personal efforts of my own, thus helping a great deal in allowing me to give the most of my time to my chosen work. Beside I have not lost all hope of again being Consul. *Quién sabe*? ["Who knows?"]"

Besides the revenue from his "garden," Thompson had found a new patron, Allison V. Armour of Chicago. "By the kindness of Mr Armour I am assured of ample funds for the continuance of my work here," he wrote.

Thompson congratulated Putnam on his excellent work at the Columbian Exposition, calling it "the archaeological event of the century." Thompson was writing, in part, to let him know that he had completed the last of the contracted work at Labná. The moulds were ready to be shipped and

Thompson reported he had already sent along a selection of skulls and a small idol his party had found. He also sent a "beam from Uxmal."

The moulds were still sitting in Mérida a month later. Furthermore, Thompson had not made any progress on documenting the expedition. "You and Mr. Bowditch must not feel annoyed at my delay in reporting on the Labná work," Thompson wrote Stephen Salisbury in May. He sent Salisbury several cylinder recordings he had made of Maya speakers reciting poems, the days of the week, numbers, and more. He had also recorded some music from a Maya ritual. "We have preserved and saved for posterity that which would otherwise would have inevitably become lost within the next generation." Thompson wrote. The ex-consul was keeping busy. "I am working hard and obtaining good results in various ways."

And then he bought Chichén Itzá.

According to Thompson's autobiography, "The idea of purchasing an abandoned plantation and, incidentally, a ruined city and the Sacred Well, came to me when I visited Chichén Itzá." As Thompson tells the story, he had been sitting atop the giant monument Las Monjas, looking out over the ancient city, when he noticed another batch of ruins that, to his trained eyes, did not look as if they were Maya structures.

"You are right, don Eduardo," his assistant told him. Everyone in Yucatán by this time called him "don Eduardo," except for Teobert Maler who, when not calling him epithets, referred to him derisively as "Papacito" ("daddy"). His assistant told him that the ruins were the former buildings of the hacienda, unoccupied for more than forty years since the outbreak of the Caste War. Thompson resolved right then and there to buy Chichén Itzá. "Upon my return to Mérida I sought out the heirs and offered to purchase the place for a reasonable sum," Thompson wrote. "They were young men who evidently had given up any idea of restoring the plantation," he wrote, and they were afraid of the sublevados. With the help of Allison Armour "who had frequently visited the ruins with me," Thompson bought the Hacienda Chichén which included the ancient city of Chichén Itzá.

That was one story. In another version, which Thompson related to T.A. Willard, he had dreamed of buying Chichén even before moving to Yucatán. Once he was in Mexico, he tried "for a long time" to attract investors, "but organizing a stock company to raise sunken galleons along the Spanish Main would be a simple task as compared with my difficulties in promoting what seemed a will-o'-the-wisp project."

Those were, as with all things Edward Thompson, stories with kernels of truth. Purchasing Maya ruins was an old idea, but not Thompson's. John Lloyd Stephens fifty years earlier had attempted to purchase Copan in Honduras. Stephens had told the supposed owner of the ruins that he "wished to return with spades, pickaxes, ladders, crowbars, and men, build a hut to live in, and make a thorough exploration." However, he could not risk such an expedition on the off chance the rightful owner would refuse him access. Stephens, "in plain English," asked,"What will you take for the ruins?" The owner "was not more surprised than if I had asked to buy his poor old wife," Stephens wrote.

The man wanted to sell but was afraid that because Stephens was a gringo that it would bring him trouble with the government. Stephens, who ostensibly was in Central America on a diplomatic mission, pulled out what he called his "diplomatic coat," made of fine material and decorated with large shiny buttons embossed with eagles. The owner had never seen such a fine coat, Stephens wrote, and the buttons sealed the deal.

"The reader is perhaps curious to know how old cities sell in Central America," Stephens explained. "Like other articles of trade, they are regulated by the quantity in market and the demand; but, not being staple articles, like cotton and indigo, they were held at fancy prices, and at that time were dull of sale. I paid fifty dollars for Copan. There was never any difficulty about price. I offered that sum, for which don Jose Maria thought me only a fool; if I had offered more, he would probably have considered me something worse."

When Stephens returned to the United States, he received a communication that the deal had fallen through. He related the story of the almost-sale in his best-selling book, *Incidents of Travel in Central America, Chiapas, and Yucatán*, which Thompson had surely read, so it is possible that he had been thinking about buying Chichén for some time. And it wasn't as if the ancient city wasn't for sale. It had been offered to Désiré Charnay during his first visit in the early 1860s for two thousand pesos, approximately $1,000 U.S. "It was a small amount, but, alas! I was too poor to buy it and live too far away to take advantage of so many precious things; abandoned to the ravages of time, exposed to the barbarity of some travelers, these magnificent ruins are deteriorating every day, and in even a few centuries not one stone will stand to remind people the existence of these extinct civilizations."

Who was the man who claimed to Charnay to be the owner of Chichén Itzá? The explorer never provides a name. In the years leading up to the beginning of the Caste War, the owner was Juan Sosa Arce. According to local legend, the owner had been killed in the opening salvos of the Caste War. But Sosa Arce was alive and fit as a fiddle in 1860, some years into the war. It is possible he offered to sell Chichén to Charnay.

When Thompson purchased the Hacienda Chichén in 1894, the Sosa family no longer owned it. The sellers were three men: Delio Moreno Cantón, Emilio García Fajardo, and Leopoldo Cantón Frexas. Thompson described them as young and naïve. They certainly were young, in their twenties. But naïve? Within four years all three had served or were serving in Yucatán's state legislature. They were members of the Casta Divina: Moreno Cantón was the nephew of the politically powerful Francisco Cantón Rosado, who would serve as governor of the state when the three men were in Yucatán's legislature; García Fajardo would later own Yucatán's leading newspaper; and Cantón Frexas, who was a cousin to Governor Cantón Rosado, became one of Yucatán's major hacendados who also promoted an interest in the ancient Maya. The very idea that Thompson could put one over on any of these three men is laughable. That they would be afraid of sublevados is almost insulting, especially to those related to Cantón Rosado, who had built his reputation as a soldier and officer in the Caste War.

The real story of how Thompson purchased Chichén Itzá appears much more complicated. Contrary to Thompson's claim that he had long planned to buy Chichén, the decision had come together quickly. Thompson, who was fond of boasting of his plans well in advance of doing them, makes no mention of the Chichén deal in any of his letters prior to the purchase. It is unlikely that he ever solicited American investors, for there is no mention of such a business opportunity in correspondence between his largest patrons, Stephen Salisbury and Charles Bowditch.

It is more probable that the idea to buy Chichén was not even Thompson's. The three men involved in the sale were not, as Thompson claimed, the heirs of the original owner. The three were middle children from wealthy families and although at least two were related, they were no closer than cousins several times removed. That these three seemingly random individuals were the rightful heirs to Chichén is just as believable as to say all three were next in line for the Spanish crown. These three men were from some of the most powerful families in Yucatán and it is more likely they were there to grease the wheels of the ponderous Mexican bureaucracy.

According to one Yucatecan writer, the man behind the plan to sell Chichén Itzá to Thompson was Yucatán's bishop, Crescencio Carrillo y Ancona, a great scholar on the ancient and contemporary Maya. When Thompson needed someone to speak Maya for his cylinder recordings, he had turned to the bishop, who spoke the language expertly. He recited the "Lord's Prayer" in Maya and pronounced names of Maya places. According to Thompson, the two men had known each other for years.

At around the same time Thompson recorded the bishop, the Mexican Congress passed a major revision to laws pertaining to abandoned lands: Anyone could make a legal claim to any property that did not have a clear title. It appears that Messrs. Moreno Cantón, García Fajardo, and Cantón Frexas claimed the 800 hectares of the Hacienda Chichén at Bishop Carrillo y Ancona's urging and then sold it to Thompson for a nominal sum, officially 300 pesos. Thompson easily could have afforded that figure (approximately $150 U.S.) and would not have required the financial assistance of Armour, so the actual cost of the property must have been much, much more. It is a common practice in Mexico, even today, to report one sale price to the government, upon which its valuation for taxation is established, yet sell the property for a much higher figure, with the bulk of the transaction kept off the books.

Thompson indicated that the new law was the reason he was able to purchase the hacienda. In writing Putnam two days after officially completing the sale, he claimed he was able to buy the property thanks to "the peculiarly favorable auspices that now exist." He added that now he can pursue his research "calmly and thoroughly knowing that no one except the federal government can interrupt me in my doings upon my own property." The federal government maintained a level of control over the hacienda because of a brief clause in the new law that stated that "areas of ruined monuments," regardless of whether they be abandoned or not, "will always remain the domain" of the Mexican federal government. This also included whatever land required "for the care and conservation of them."

Some scholars and later legal experts have suggested that the clause means archaeological sites such as Chichén Itzá cannot be sold (and some have gone so far as to say the sale to Thompson was illegal). If that were the case, sales of property throughout Mexico would be almost impossible as the nation has thousands of ruins. Today all but a handful of ancient ruins are on private lands, many of them scooped up in the land-office rush that resulted from the new abandoned property law. The Mexican courts would later uphold Thompson as the "undisputed owner" of Chichén Itzá.

If Thompson had not bought Chichén, someone would have. Around twenty percent of Yucatán's lands were acquired as a result of it. If it was Carrillo y Ancona who masterminded the sale, and it makes sense that he was, he made sure it went into the hands of someone who cared about the Maya ruins upon it and who had could attract the funds required to seek out its secrets.

THE PRESENT

TOURING CHICHÉN ITZÁ

ANTONIO WAITS FOR ME at the hacienda—Edward Thompson's hacienda, although I imagine it didn't look anything like this when he bought it in 1894. I run to check on my family, but find they have already left for the archaeological zone.

This time we decide to go in by the main entrance, which means I have to drive around the archaeological zone to get there. There is a gated lot where it costs ten pesos to park. We enter under the giant "A," a modern version of the Maya arch, a contemporary architect's homage to the ancient culture beyond. I buy a ticket and resume the tour where we left off the other day, in front of the giant pyramid El Castillo.

Antonio takes me to a large platform and shows me bas-relief carvings of eagles and jaguars, their claws and paws holding human hearts, their mouths poised to devour them. This was what Le Plongeon called the "Mausoleum of Chaacmol," today known as the Temple of the Eagles and the Jaguars. I walk over to the information sign to see if they mention either Le Plongeon or the chac-mool sculpture he found buried underneath it. Nothing, not a word, and I mention it to Antonio.

"He's the one who dynamited—" Antonio starts to say, and I begin to laugh.

"That's just a story," I tell him. "Everybody seems to think he blew up a monument. Not true." Le Plongeon railed against people who defaced the monuments. The dynamite story came from a notice Le Plongeon placed in a Mérida newspaper announcing that he had booby-trapped monuments in Uxmal with dynamite to prevent looting. It was a stupid bluff and it backfired, as evidenced by Antonio's belief today that Le Plongeon had dynamited monuments in search of treasure.

The platform has been restored. I can't even tell which side Le Plongeon tore down to pull out the chac-mool. I tell Antonio about Augustus and Alice and their strange notion that the Maya were progenitors of human civilization. They also were the first explorers to learn to speak Maya and talk with the natives. "I have a theory," I tell Antonio. "Chac-mool" in Maya can mean "red jaguar"; what if Le Plongeon had been told by a Maya elder that there was a sculpture known as the "red jaguar" at Chichén? When he finds a statue, he assumes that's what it is. "What if oral tradition had it that there was a chac-mool—a 'red jaguar' at Chichén Itzá?" I ask. I point up to El Castillo behind us. "Because inside that pyramid, archaeologists found such a statue, the red jaguar throne."

Antonio agrees it could have been possible. The oral tradition is strong among the Maya and there could have been someone near Chichén who knew the old legends. But it was, at best, a theory.

He continues his tour, describing an intricate carving inside a structure known as the Lower Temple of the Jaguars. Except that I can't see what he's referring to, because there is scaffolding inside the temple and a woman who appears to be doing some kind of work on the bas relief carving. Antonio explains that she must be with INAH, the federal agency that supervises the ruins. For the first time it occurs to me that there are archaeologists here who are still conducting research at Chichén Itzá. I thought these ruins had pretty much been studied to death.

We walk into the Great Ball Court. It is even bigger than it appears in photographs. Giant perpendicular walls, from where you could imagine hundreds if not thousands of people watching the game on the floor below. About six meters above the ground in the center of each wall is a ring, more than a meter in diameter with a hole slightly more than half a meter wide. According to Antonio, the idea of the game was to put a ball through the ring without using your hands. I am skeptical. I don't think I could throw a ball through there if you gave me all day.

There is a lot of speculation, Antonio says, whether it was the winners or the losers of the game who were sacrificed at the end of the ball game. Someone surely was killed, because there are carvings on panels in the ball court that show one of the ball players, decapitated, with blood pouring in streams from his neck. Those streams turn into plants and flowers. Antonio gave me his opinion. "Don't think of this as 'sacrifice,' think of it as 'offerings.' And you offer the gods the best. So it was the winner who was sacrificed."

We walked out of the ball court and down a slight rise. There is a large, open structure with a palm roof, a palapa, which contains a gift shop. There are also people along the paths selling handicrafts and trinkets, either on blankets on the ground or on makeshift tables. "So the locals, they get a permit to work in here?" I ask.

"They don't have permission," Antonio says sharply. "They just—that's the way they are protesting the concessions that don Fernando's family have in the palapas." Antonio says they don't bother him, but it is clear to me he is irritated. "Sometimes they get closer and start offering their products." He points out one young man holding some kind of wooden trinkets in his hand, approaching a group of tourists in front of us. I can't make out what he's telling them, but according to Antonio he's saying, "One dollar! One dollar! One dollar!"

"What will eventually happen, I think, is someone will go too far and it will blow up," I say.

Antonio seems doubtful. "The government does not want to have any–arguments—with them," he says. "There are—interests." He doesn't explain further.

We approach what appears to be a smaller version of the pyramid El Castillo. This is the Osario, Antonio tells me, also known as the "High Priest's Tomb." I knew a little something about it. "Edward Thompson excavated this," I say. It was his first at Chichén Itzá.

The High Priest's Grave or Osario today (Pereira Photo)

THE PAST

THE HIGH PRIEST'S GRAVE

MOST EARLY ANTIQUARIANS and archaeologists struggled to find a single patron, but Edward Thompson had an embarrassment of riches. In the months before his purchase of Chichén Itzá as well as the years that followed he spent a lot of energy keeping all his patrons on the hook, even though he wildly over-committed. Reading through his correspondence of the period, one can see his approach was to take money up front for work and then put off completion as long as he could, sometimes indefinitely. He owed a lot to the Peabody Museum, including his report on Labná and the cavern of Loltun. He took money from Allison Armour in Chicago for additional projects. And he negotiated with the Peabody Museum for more archaeological work.

He assured Frederick Ward Putnam at the Peabody that his involvement with Armour in Chicago was a good thing. "He [Armour] has generously arranged that the results of my work go with me to whatever institution I connect myself," Thompson wrote. "To the Chicago University if the arrangements planned are consummated; if not then elsewhere as I may elect." The implication of his letter was clear: "Continue to be nice to me and perhaps you will get some or all of the finds." The reason Thompson probably did not come out and say that was because it could not be true. Armour was on the board of Chicago's Field Museum; it is highly unlikely he would have permitted Thompson to conduct work for any other museum on his dime. Putnam warned him not to get too involved with the Field, which he felt was more interested in "drive and rush and sensational effects," but Thompson was never one to pass up a paycheck, especially as he no longer had the security of a consulate salary.

To further complicate matters, Thompson proposed to Armour and the Field Museum to conduct an investigation of the Maya city of X'Kichmook. That must have irritated his sponsors in Massachusetts as Thompson had discovered the city in 1886 while working for Stephen Salisbury and had done a lot of exploratory work while working for the Peabody Museum. In his report on X'Kichmook published by the Field Museum in 1898 there is no mention of his Massachusetts underwriters, only a thank you to "the kind liberality of Mr. Armour."

Armour further solidified their relationship by proposing an expedition of his own to Yucatán with Thompson as guide. On Dec. 30, 1894 he anchored his yacht *Ituna* off Progreso. Armour had brought along an all-star scientific team: William Henry Holmes and Charles F. Millspaugh, directors of anthropology and botany, respectively, at the Field Museum, as well as Princeton art historian Allan Marquand. For three months the men cris-crossed Mexico, visiting Palenque, Teotihuacan, Mont Alban, as well as sites on the Yucatán Peninsula such as Cozumel, Isla Mujeres, Uxmal, and, of course, Chichén Itzá. While visiting Thompson's new home, Yucatán's newest hacendado let slip to Holmes one of his brilliant ideas for exploring Chichén Itzá involving the Cenote Sagrado, which Holmes published in his journal of the trip. "There has been some talk of exploring the accumulations forming the bottom of this cenote with the expectation of securing works of art or other treasures," Holmes wrote, "but the task is a most formidable one and will require the erection of strong windlasses and efficient dredging apparatus. It is doubtful if promised results warrant the outlay necessary for carrying out the work in a thorough manner."

From far right, counter-clockwise: Edward Thompson, Henry Holmes, Allison Armour, Allan Marquand, Charles Millspaugh

As the Field Museum apparently was not interested in the challenge of exploring the Sacred Well, Thompson cast around for some project that would meet the museum's approval. Between the pyramid El Castillo and Las Monjas was a shapeless mound which, at the top, had large, intricately carved columns with giant feathered serpent heads, similar in style to El Castillo. In his second year as Chichén's new owner, Thompson cleared the debris at the top of the temple and found what appeared to be two large tablets embedded into the floor between the feathered serpent pillars. Thompson and his Maya crew pried them up and found beneath them "a well-like opening" that pierced the center of the temple.

From his experience excavating the chultunes of Labná. Thompson had mastered the techniques required to explore deep caves and wells. He never explained *how* he learned his procedures, but from the context one assumes it was by painful trial and error. The first thing was to determine if the air in the shaft was breathable. If the seal had been airtight, it was more than possible that all the oxygen in the hole had been exhausted over the centuries. Thompson lowered a lighted candle on a cord down into the hole. If the flame faded, he would know he would need to run bellows and pump fresh air in before proceeding.

After checking the air quality and finding it acceptable, Thompson descended into the shaft. He wore a high-crowned hat filled with rags in case, as he was being lowered into the hole, one of the workers should dislodge a stone onto his head. "I held between my teeth a heavy and very sharp hunting knife," he wrote, to slice off the head of poisonous snakes that might reside in the hole. "Then with one foot in the noose of a stout rope and one hand free, my men let me over the edge and down into space."

The shaft descended four meters to a pile of rubble. As the sides of the tunnel were perfectly formed, Thompson concluded the debris, which consisted of large, worked stones, had been thrown in intentionally. He ordered his men into the shaft to excavate and after they removed a little over a meter of loose stones they found a skeleton and two red pottery vessels, one smashed and one intact. Beneath that burial, they found another skeleton and more artifacts. In all, Thompson and his men uncovered seven burials, one on top of the other. Some contained more than one body and all yielded artifacts, including two large copper bells and many small ones, which to Thompson's knowledge was only the second time such artifacts had been discovered in Yucatán. There were also fine worked jade ornaments, amulets, and beads, and in one grave, a glob of material that turned out to be pom, or incense. Once excavated, the shaft including the graves turned out to be ten meters high, or roughly the height of the pyramid. It also had narrowed from almost two meters wide at the top to less than 120 centimeters at the bottom.

As he had excavated to ground level, Thompson thought he had found everything, but a worked stone embedded in the floor caught his eye. With little room to maneuver (Thompson was a few centimeters short of two meters tall), he managed to pry up the stone and exposed another hole approximately a meter square half-filled with a mixture of dirt, ashes, scorched stones, burned artifacts, and charred human bones. As Thompson removed the soil, he uncovered a narrow stairway. He also found artifacts that were whole and unburned, including a large, jade pendant. He came again to another stone that he knew capped another chamber or passage. "I gradually loosened the stone and as I lifted it away, I found beneath an opening as black as night, from which poured a rush of air as chill as the breath of death," Thompson recalled.

According to Thompson, his assistants became frightened. "It is the mouth of the underworld," they told him.

"If it is, we will soon have a chance to see what the underworld is like," Thompson said.

Thompson had exposed an opening to a cavern where the floor was ten meters below. The next day he brought a rope and tackle and had his men lower him to the cave floor. There he found amidst a deep pile of debris more human bones and artifacts, including in one corner what appeared to be an altar.

The excavation had been a tremendous success. Thompson dubbed the pyramid "The High Priest's Grave," for he believed that whoever had been buried there had been an important personage. The name today is the

Osario, Spanish for burial chamber. Later excavation and study revealed that the skeletons were not priests—unless priests happened to be children.

The 'High Priests Grave' before reconstruction, looking much as it did when Thompson excavated it

THE PRESENT

INSIDE THE PYRAMID

THE OSARIO TODAY is restored, but visitors are not allowed to climb to the top to see the hole Edward Thompson found. I had read somewhere that the chamber he found deep in the earth has a passageway that some believe goes due east and empties out into the cenote known as Xtoloc, which served as the main source of potable water for Chichén Itzá.

Antonio and I press on. A little further down the path we come to the *Casa Colorada*, Maudslay's first headquarters at Chichén. Beyond that the forest opens and in front of us is Las Monjas, "the Nunnery," a massive three-story building that makes up the southern boundary of the main archaeological zone of Chichén. It draws so much of my attention as we approach that I almost miss the large ruin to my left, the Caracol. It looks like an observatory, with a ruined dome on the top. "This is the only round building in Chichén Itzá," Antonio says. He explains that it got the name Caracol, Spanish for snail, from the winding staircase inside that took priests to the top.

The Caracol is roped off, so we can't get any closer than ground level. "It must have been great twenty years ago or so when you could climb all over these monuments," I say.

"When I started guiding, there was a ladder and you could climb all the way to the top," Antonio says. He understands why the government had blocked access to prevent vandalism, but things have gotten much better. "In the last decade, I notice that people have more respect," he says. They no longer scratch their names on walls or do other damage.

Leaning next to a tree is a man in a light blue shirt looking official. Antonio exchanges a few words with him in Spanish, and apparently the answer is yes. We walk down a path to a low and long single-story building I recognize immediately, *Akab Dzib*, where Le Plongeon conducted his first excavation. I don't tell Antonio, but this is my favorite ruin at Chichén and I can't wait to see the carving inside. Except the entryway is blocked by a giant screen.

"Don't worry, we're not doing anything illegal," he says as he pushes it back into the chamber, creating a space for me to slide through. Perhaps he mistook the expression on my face for worry rather than excitement. I am more than happy to end up in a Mexican prison to see the inside of the building whose name translates to "The House of Obscure Writing."

We step into a chamber, maybe three meters deep and in the opposite wall is a low passageway to another chamber. Once my eyes adjust to the gloom, I can see over the low door a lintel containing my first carved Maya glyphs. Le Plongeon thought it described a telegraph between Valladolid and Mérida. Antonio tells me that if you crawl through the passageway and look up, there is another carving of a sitting priest performing the Maya fire ceremony. I pull out my camera and shoot the glyphs, then lean in and photograph the carving of the sitting priest. I came prepared, for my camera has a night vision setting and it records the carving in the dark without a flash.

We walk back to Las Monjas and enter a courtyard at one end. There is the most intricately carved façade I have seen so far. I recognize it, for above a doorway is what some have suggested is a space man. Only it doesn't look much like an ancient astronaut of any kind when you see it in person and close up. What I had never noticed before was how many different things are represented besides the little man over the doorway. There are carvings of fish, turtles, lizards, jaguars, and plants, especially maize. The corners of the building are decorated with horrible masks of a figure with a long, hooked nose—the rain god Chaac.

Next to the courtyard is a two-story building called the *Iglesia* or "Church." I can't see how it got its name because it doesn't look very church-like to me. Antonio takes me inside a chamber. He has me look up and I can see the room is vaulted in the traditional Maya arch. This, he tells me, is one of the oldest examples of the arch at Chichén Itzá, and that if I compare it to the trusses that support the thatch roof of a Maya hut I'll find the design is identical. I don't tell him that it was Edward Thompson who first published on that, about how he supposedly sat atop Las Monjas just a few feet away and decided to buy Chichén Itzá. I think he finds it a little off-putting how much I know, or worse, think I know.

We exit the Iglesia, with Las Monjas looming to our left, the round Caracol to our right, and there, in the center under a tree, is Sam, ignoring these wonders of the ancient world for a handheld video game.

Lori and Sarah are not far behind, so I thank Antonio, who has to lead another tour. We have some time before we have to head back to Mérida, so we all go back to check out El Castillo, the pyramid. Once there, the kids decide to climb the ninety-one stairs to the top. I want to see the throne room inside the pyramid, so I stand in line next to a door cut into the base of the pyramid's northern staircase. El Castillo, the temple of Kukulcan, had been built atop a smaller, older pyramid. In the 1930s Mexican archaeologists discovered this and tunneled into the throne room that capped the old pyramid. Inside they found another chac-mool and a red jaguar throne, with spots of inlaid jade. If you wait in line long enough, they let you go up and look at the throne room.

I notice the fellow running the door is Antonio's friend, the one who let us see Akab Dzib. I introduce myself. "Antonio is an excellent guide," I tell him. "He must be the best guide at Chichén."

"Second-best guide," the man tells me. "I'm the best."

As we wait for the group in the throne room to come down, I notice a large bug land on the hand of the best guide at Chichén. I stare. It's a flying ant. I am reminded of Thompson's tale that Mérida was saved during the Caste War because the arrival of flying ants told the attacking rebels that it was time to return home to plant their milpa. *Le major guía* looks down and flicks the winged ant away. He does not seem inclined to leave his post to plant corn.

Instead, he waves me into the doorway. "Go ahead," he says. "No se flash, por favor. No flash, amigos." I follow a young couple through the door and into a tunnel, again with the Maya arch. After about four meters or so, we make a sharp right and walk for another four meters before coming to a staircase. Like most stairs on Maya monuments, the risers are very steep and the treads narrow, at least for my large feet. I had expected the tunnel to be cool, but it is quite the opposite, very hot and very humid. The air feels thin and I am quite winded once I get to the top where there is a small platform. Before us is what looks like a door to a jail cell. Behind the bars is fine mesh chicken wire. They really don't want you to go inside the throne room. Just past the door is a chac-mool, clumsy in execution, at least when compared to the one Le Plongeon found. Behind the chac-mool is another chamber and in the center is the red jaguar throne. It might have been red, but it is so gloomy I can't be sure of the color.

More people pile up the stairs behind me. The platform in front of the jail door is a meter or so deep and two meters wide. There isn't a lot of room for many people. I snap a couple of quick photos using once again the infrared setting on my camera, and then head back down.

I gulp the fresh air once I'm out into the open. Gazing up the pyramid I recognize two pairs of spindly legs projecting from the top step. My children are enjoying the view. I begin the long climb. The steps appear to be half to twice as high as your average staircase back home and the pads very narrow. I make it about two-thirds the way up before I have to stop, I'm so winded. Once I catch my breath I finish the climb and join Sarah and Sam at the top.

The temple atop El Castillo is bigger than it looks from the ground. The rooms inside are spacious. The platform outside the temple is wide, although it becomes dangerously narrow when you pass another tourist on it.

The view is spectacular. The pyramid is twice as tall as the surrounding forest that extends to the horizon. This view must have been reserved for the elites. I can't see that the laborers would have been allowed to come up here. But this would have been an ideal place to commune with one's gods. Sarah and Sam enjoy the vantage point, but with minimum communing..

Stretched out at the top of one of the staircases is a street dog, a female, with mangy fur and protruding ribs. I can't imagine how it got up here or how it intends to get back down. Then I wonder how I'm going to get back to ground level. Looking down the staircase makes it appear even more frighteningly steep. I begin my descent in a serpentine pattern so I can put most of my foot on the narrow step. Once I run out of staircase on one side, I have to steady myself with my hand on an upper step to turn the opposite direction. About two-thirds of the way down I congratulate myself for not being like the other tourists who are coming down on their butts, until I am passed by a man about half my age trotting straight down the stairs.

I meet Lori at the base of the pyramid. She didn't want to climb. The children soon join us. We still have a little time, so we head north to see the Cenote Sagrado.

You can tell that you are walking on what at one time was an ancient sacbé. In places the roadbed is three or four meters above the grade. The sacbe stretches several hundred yards before it drops over a slight rise to a tiny ruin perched next to the one of the most ominous holes in the ground I've ever seen. I get as close to the lip as I can and look thirty meters down to the rankest, most vile, most evil looking water one can imagine. From where we are perched, the Cenote Sagrado looks perfectly round and the walls drop straight down. It's so large, that I can't get it all in one photograph. That's fine because I've never seen a photograph that has done it justice. It is obvious why the Maya believed this was a special place, a straight shot to their version of the underworld.

Next to the Sacred Well is another large palapa, the second of don Fernando's gift shops. This seems to be a grisly location from which to sell t-shirts and snacks, but I buy Sam an ice cream. That people were once sacrificed here does not bother him one little bit.

THE PAST

AMERICAN FERMENT COMPANY

WHEN EDWARD THOMPSON PURCHASED the Hacienda Chichén, he had two main objectives: to conduct archaeology and to restore the hacienda into a working (and profitable) plantation. He lacked the capital to rebuild the hacienda, but as it had throughout his life, fortune smiled on him once again.

A few months after closing on Chichén Itzá, Thompson received a visit in Mérida from Fred Kilmer, who, according to Thompson, was "a well known expert chemist." Kilmer revealed that his purpose in Yucatán was not as a tourist, but business. He represented a concern called the American Ferment Company, which was scouting suitable locations for the cultivation of papaya. From papaya American Ferment produced a dietary supplement known as "papaina." The papain enzyme in papaya breaks down proteins, so the chemical was useful as a remedy to aid digestion of the typical Victorian diet of heavy meats and potatoes.

Kilmer said his company was seeking a new source of the papaya extract because the plantations in Jamaica had met with "disastrous and costly results." Kilmer was certain that Yucatán was the ideal environment to grow papaya on a large scale, as it was already cultivated in the region. The chemist believed Thompson was just the man to undertake such an enterprise and said he would pay $200 U.S. gold for every pound of extract produced. A single tree, according to Kilmer, could produce one to five pounds of crystal extract. In the first year Thompson found "that the average output per tree was decidedly less than ten ounces." This meant that to be profitable, Thompson had to cultivate more trees. He contacted Kilmer and received a loan of several thousand dollars to plant a sufficient number of papaya at the Hacienda Chichén to make the enterprise worthwhile.

In his third year as a papaya farmer, Thompson received the welcome news that Republican William McKinley had been elected the new president, replacing Democrat Grover Cleveland. With the change in administrations came the inevitable rush of federal offices, including the post of consul to Mérida. In June 1897 Edward Thompson returned to his consular duties and the steady annual salary.

Thompson could not be a full-time archaeologist, a full-time plantation owner, and a full-time U.S. consul at the same time. He had for years juggled two of those jobs, but three were too many. Something had to go. So he trained one of his men at the Hacienda Chichén how to care for the sprawling papaya operation and left him in charge.

Thompson's plan might have worked, except the Mexican government decided that the time had come, after more than half a century, to finish the Caste War once and for all. Federal troops launched a major offensive into the territory east of Chichén Itzá that was under control of the rebel Maya. In retaliation, the sublevados resumed hostilities against towns along the boundary of their perceived domain. In late 1899 and early 1900, they attacked and held the villages of Okap and Saban. When word of the raids reached the Hacienda Chichén, sixty-five kilometers away, all of Thompson's workers fled and refused to return. Within weeks the entire papaya crop had gone to rot.

Thompson owed thousands to the American Ferment Company, which turned over his debt to a collection agency. When it failed to get any money from Thompson, the bill collector contacted his employer, the U.S. State Department. Thompson's bosses demanded an explanation from their man in Yucatán, whose job it was to point out opportunities for American businesses, not go into business. For Thompson it was an embarrassment, but he explained to his superiors that the deal with the American Ferment Company had occurred before he had been reinstated as consul. In his mind, turning over the debt to a collection agency had been a grave injustice, but injustice or no, it was one he had to make right and find the money somewhere. Allison Armour, who had helped Thompson buy the Hacienda Chichén, had moved on to other scholarly pursuits, so Thompson sought and received a loan from his original patron, Stephen Salisbury.

Thompson's grand plan to become the papaya magnate of Yucatán, like his fields, had been choked to death. The American Ferment Company somehow managed to survive despite Thompson's failure. It grew into two companies: Johnson & Johnson, today one of the world's biggest corporations; and Mead Johnson, one of the world's leading manufacturers of nutritional products for babies. Dr. Kilmer went on to become head of the research division of Johnson & Johnson, where he also served as chief of publicity. His son, Joyce Kilmer, inherited his father's gift for words and became a world-famous poet by writing about, of all things, trees. "I think that I shall never see/A poem lovely as a tree," the younger Kilmer wrote. Edward Thompson's appreciation of poetry is unknown, but after the papaya tree debacle, the last thing he wanted to do was read a poem about it.

Mexican descendants of Edward. H. Thompson, the Marrufo and Uh Tun Marrufo clans

THE PRESENT

MEETING THE MARRUFOS

WE ARE DONE with Chichén Itzá, at least for now. It's time to check out of the Hacienda Chichén and get back to Mérida. Of course we have one stop to make before we split town.

Lori is less than thrilled with the idea of visiting a group of people she has never met. The whole thing strikes her as odd. "Me, too," I say, but explain how adamant Bibiano had been.

We pull up to the curb next to doña Maria Luisa's yellow casa. Everyone piles out of the car and with me in the lead, we open the gate and walk into the front yard. "Hola! Hola!" I shout. People come pouring out from everywhere: doña Maria Luisa, her grandchildren, one or two of her sons, Bibiano's wife Victoria. It was a blur of family. I look around. "Where's Bibiano?" I ask, and then say, *"Donde* Bibiano?" Victoria lets out a rush of Spanish and all I understand is *"trabajo"*—work—and "hacienda." I gather that he had to go to work at the hacienda.

"Se habla ingles?" I ask. She smiles and shakes her head. No one, I learn, speaks English. I look over to Lori, who is shaking hands and smiling. This is going to be a trainwreck, I think.

Except it isn't.

Sarah and Sam have picked up enough Spanish in school to be able to exchange a few sentences and if one of us can't speak enough English or Spanish to get a thought across, we move on to something else. Though we are divided by language, culture, and geography, we are members of the same club and have more in common than not. I learn zero information about Edward Thompson or doña Victoria, but I see what has emerged from that relationship and more importantly, at least to me, my wife and children see it, too. In turn, the Marrufos view me as a human being, not just a man there to ask questions.

Victoria has something important for me to see back at her house, which, if I understand correctly, is a short distance away. We say our goodbyes to doña Maria Luisa and her family, and follow Victoria down the street. She leads us to a house that sits about a meter below the grade of the road. There is a sitting porch and in one corner a religious shrine. We wait on the sidewalk while she goes inside and comes back with several photographs. I study one, a black and white photo of a man in his fifties, in front of a car from the late 1960s and one of the monuments from Chichén Itzá in the background. I know right away who it is. "Carlos Marrufo?" I ask.

"Si, Carlos Marrufo," Victoria says softly. "Papa."

She has several photographs of him. I ask if I can copy them, then photograph the photographs. I promise her that when I return, I will bring copies. I'm not certain she understands what I am saying, but I like to think she does, especially about the part where I will come back.

We walk back up the street to our car and say our final goodbyes. And then we are off, back to Mérida.

Much later, when we are getting ready to leave Mexico, I ask Sam what his favorite part of the trip had been. He doesn't even hesitate. "Meeting the Marrufos," he says.

Yeah, me too.

THE PAST

A STRANGE PLACE

BACK IN NEW ENGLAND, another patron of Thompson's archaeological research, Charles Bowditch, was at his wits' end. He was nearing sixty, too old and too busy to go to Mexico and Central America to seek the answers that he craved about the ancient Maya. He had to rely on intermediaries and to date every expedition he had financed had ended in some form of disappointment. It was not saying a lot that his best agent in the field had been Edward Thompson, who consistently over-promised and under-delivered, always with some excuse. Bowditch also feared Thompson was cheating him on his contracts.

If only he could find someone who was more malleable, someone who could follow instructions and see them through. In the 1880s and 1890s, after burning through several promising candidates on a series of expeditions, he gave up his search for that brilliant young archaeologist and, admittedly, he settled—for a young Harvard graduate who was "not over strong intellectually."

Alfred Marston Tozzer was twenty-four and had been scratching out a living as an anthropologist and linguist. After getting his degree, he performed fieldwork for Bowditch's Peabody Museum, first in California where he studied the languages of American Indian tribes, and then in the

Southwest conducting linguistic and anthropological research among the Navajos.

Bowditch was less than enthusiastic about Tozzer's abilities. "Whether he has got the stamina to hold his own with the uncivilized races and whether he is going to be one who will do honor to the work with which we propose to entrust him, I hardly like to venture an opinion," Bowditch wrote Frederick Ward Putnam. Perhaps it was Tozzer's physique, which was rail-thin, or his height, which was well under six feet. Whatever the reason, Bowditch concluded, "He does not impress me."

Impressed or not, Bowditch needed someone and needed them now. For years he had been trying to interest the Archaeological Institute of America to send an expedition to Mesoamerica, that region that included the ancient peoples of Mexico and Central America. He eventually had to fund it himself, but in 1901 the AIA agreed to create its first "traveling fellow" for the Americas, a four-year scholarship for a promising student. Tozzer won the award because there was no one else.

The position was not without strings. Tozzer would be dispatched to Yucatán, ostensibly to study and learn the language of the Maya and to seek out its purest form, which would, it was hoped, help to decipher the ancient hieroglyphs. But he also would be going as a spy, to keep Bowditch informed as to the activities of Edward Thompson and to make certain he was doing the archaeological work he was under contract to perform.

In the end, Tozzer surprised everyone, including himself. Bowditch, despite his initial reservations, had found a companion and colleague with whom he would share his interest in the Maya for the rest of his life. Thompson, who had no patience for writing laborious archaeological reports, was about to meet the man who would spend decades documenting and analyzing the discoveries for which he would become famous. When Tozzer stepped off the boat in Progreso in January 1902, no one could have predicted that he would become one of the most important Maya archaeologists in history or that within hours after arriving in Yucatán, his life would be inextricably bound with Edward Thompson's.

In Yucatán, Tozzer entered a world and culture unlike any he had experienced. Over the course of his young life he had travelled through much of the United States and Europe, yet Yucatán, he wrote his mother, is "a strange place, in fact the strangest place I was ever in, nothing American and still more nothing Spanish." The architecture he identified as Mexican, but the Yucatecans are a combination of "Mexican and Indian."

Tozzer checked into the "best hotel" in Mérida, an execrable place called the Hotel Moro-Muza, that in later years would become one of the city's havens for prostitutes. That first night, however, Thompson invited him to join his family at their home, "Quinta Acadia." "It is one of the most delightful places that can be imagined," Tozzer observed. "The house stands in the midst of a grove of cocoanut palms, orange, and banana trees." The house was Thompson's pride and joy, and sat on a small mound that had once been an ancient Maya ruin. He had purchased the property not long after moving to Mérida, designed the house and supervised its construction. Thanks to "the liberal use of dynamite," he had excavated the limestone scrubland and transformed it into a "luxuriant garden."

The house matched the garden's beauty, and like other similarly sized Yucatecan homes, the rooms were enormous, with ceilings more than twenty feet high, floors covered in tile, and windows barred but without glass. The house was large and had to be, for the Thompsons by this time had six children. All were bilingual except for the youngest, who at three years old could speak only Spanish.

Tozzer's first night in Yucatán coincidentally turned out to be one of the Thompson family's last nights in Quinta Acadia. Thompson had just sold the house, which was on the outskirts of Mérida, and was preparing to move the family into the city. Tozzer thought nothing of it, but this should have been his first clue that something was amiss with Thompson's finances. Tozzer naively believed Thompson to be wealthy. "He is a very sharp business man and has amassed a small fortune," Tozzer wrote his mother several days later. "He has invested nearly the whole in [the Hacienda Chichén] which he expects to yield large returns financially in order to pay his scientific work," he wrote. "He is now selling most of his land holdings in Mérida, they have arrived at the figure he has been waiting for these many years." Only much later would Tozzer learn the real reason don Eduardo was selling everything he owned.

The next morning Thompson helped Tozzer purchase what he would need to live in the bush—a hammock, mosquito netting, and a wide-brimmed straw hat. The elder man also took the young anthropologist on a tour of Mérida, but it turned out there would be no time for dilly-dallying as Tozzer learned that the train he had planned to take to Chichén Itzá the next day was now leaving that day at noon.

Somehow the young anthropologist got to the station on time. He arrived at Dzitas at dusk and the driver who would take him by volan to Chichén was nowhere to be found, no doubt because of Tozzer's early departure. Tozzer took it in stride. He found dinner in the home of one of the locals, and hung his hammock up in the train station where he spent the night.

The next day Tozzer's driver arrived and took him to Chichén. Tozzer had been warned about the condition of the road, but he assumed it could not be worse than some of the mountain passes he had ridden over in the mountains of California. "Now I see I was wrong to make any such exception," Tozzer noted. "The road here is without exception the very worst I ever saw. In any other vehicle than the one we had, the journey would have been impossible."

He arrived at the Hacienda Chichén after two and "my highest hopes of the place were fully realized." Tozzer was installed in the main casa. The big house recently had been renovated and had five large rooms: In addition to the room assigned to Tozzer, there was a guest room, a workroom, a long dining room, and the room Mr. Thompson shared with Mrs. Thompson.

In only a short time he was at work and productive. "Life here has quickly settled into a routine," he wrote his mother after only a few days. "How quickly one becomes accustomed to the newest and strangest places. I have been here since Saturday and yet I already feel very much at home even in so strange a place. And then when I think of you in perhaps a snow-bound north, it all seems like a dream that there was such a thing as snow anyway."

Every day Tozzer was up at seven for a small breakfast of tortillas left over from the day before and "coffee," a bluish-grey beverage made from Veracruz beans; Maya lessons and translation at eight with Felisiano Cordero, an older man assigned to work with him; break at eleven for a bath, as per custom of the Maya; supper at noon; back to work at two with the Maya language; exploring Maya ruins at four; a light dinner at seven, and then, after reviewing the day's work, bed in the hammock, "which I think of adopting instead of a bed when I return north."

Tozzer marveled over the day-to-day lives of the men and women who worked the hacienda. Everything seemed to fascinate him. Of the humble tortilla he wrote:

> Unlike some things, these are very palatable after they are seen being made. Tortillas are the main food of the people. First corn, after being soaked in water, is ground on a stone metate [the stone mortar upon which corn is ground] with another stone much resembling our rolling pin. Unlike the Navajos, the Yucatecan women stand when grinding. The

metate has four stone legs and rests in one end of a shallow cedar tray. When I saw the process last night, two women were grinding each with a metate at either end of the cedar tray, which in turn stood on legs. The corn is ground very, very fine and being mixed with a little water makes a sort of thick paste. The woman then takes a small hand full of this and moulds the tortilla with her fingers on a green banana leaf. When done, it is perfectly round about five inches in diameter and as thick as thin card board. This is then baked in an iron resting on three stones over an open fire. It is taken off when just beginning to turn brown and placed in the hot ashes below when the two sides separate from each other. She takes it out, slaps it against a stone to let out the air in the middle and you have the finished tortilla, a thin, flexible disk almost like thick cloth in texture, but very good to eat, especially when brought hot from the fire. You tear off a piece of it, and take up your meat, using it as you would a piece of paper so as not to soil your fingers. When you are through your meal, use another as a napkin and then finish finally by eating your napkin. So, if one stops to think, during the course of one meal, you eat a fork every time you take a mouthful, eat your plate as well, and finally your napkin, for food is often served on the "tortillas" themselves.

The idyll of hacienda life proved to be short. It wasn't long before the cracks in paradise started to show, beginning at the top with the superintendent, José Sierra, who Tozzer saw as lazy and corrupt. "We who live here all the time know how pigs have been sold, cows and oxen slaughtered, corn picked green all to enrich the pocket and line the nest of Don José. Mr. Thompson either sees or does not dare, or dares and does not see."

Tozzer's Maya instructor, Felisiano, somehow earned the ire of Don José, who one day abruptly announced to Tozzer that he would be working with another man. Tozzer was certain that Don José was taking a third of the wages he was paying Felisiano, all of seventy-five *centavos* per day; perhaps the bite had gotten too big and when the man complained, Don José replaced him. Tozzer solved the problem by paying the wages directly to the new man—minus Don José's twenty-five centavo commission, as he would "keep the extra quarter myself."

The new man, Benito, turned out to be a gem. Intelligent and enthusiastic, Tozzer found him a vast improvement over old Felisiano. Tozzer's relationship with the Maya man grew to a point that when Benito fell from a tree and injured his leg, the young linguist went to his house to continue their studies. "He seemed surprised that I was willing to come over there to work," Tozzer wrote. "The centuries of almost slavedom which the race has suffered shows everywhere. It is as instinctive as breathing for the hand to go up to the hat when they meet me or anyone other than a native Mayan…And so Benito regards it as strange that I, Señor don Alfredo, should so far condescend as to be willing to work in his common hut."

The switch of Benito for Felisiano did not disrupt Tozzer's routine, but that was not the case two weeks into his stay with the arrival of an Englishwoman, Adela Breton, who blew into Chichén like a norté storm. At first Tozzer did not know what to make of her:

> *Miss Breton is a character as I will try and show you. She is an English maiden lady of much means direct from England where she has been at her home on a vacation. Her appearance is typical of an independent, unmarried spinster of fully sixty, tall, thin, and with a long face, grey hair, a few scattered hairs on her chin, considerably more on her lip, extremely near sighted, but straight as an arrow. She wore a short skirt, a dark blue shirt-waist with standing collar attached, and a brimmed straw hat covered with flowers and planted perfectly flat upon her head,*

but the surprise comes when she starts to talk. She in En-glish, *you know,* En-glish *to the very bone and her speech is as exaggerated as any affected English you ever heard upon the state.*

She traveled with a Mexican servant, Pablo, who cooked and cleaned and made her life as comfortable as possible. This was her third season at Chichén Itzá. Breton was an artist and Alfred Maudslay had sent her to check and correct his drawings of the ruins for his forthcoming study of Chichén Itzá. Normally Breton lived with Pablo in the ruins, eschewing the hacienda, but on this trip she decided to stay in one of the huts on the hacienda property.

Tozzer quickly warmed to Breton. The two spent every available evening together. She had brought along her own food, which Pablo cooked for her, and she always shared with Tozzer. She had been coming to Mexico for almost ten years and she regaled him with stories of her travels. She also was free with her opinions. Over the course of her two previous seasons at Chichén, she had seen enough of Edward Thompson's work to come to the conclusion that he was a poor archaeologist. Tozzer also had begun to see Thompson in a new light, not only for his archaeological expertise, which he described as "half popular, half scientific," but also for certain practices at the hacienda that were more nefarious.

"Yucatan needs a Harriet Beecher Stowe and a Garrison as much as our country did before our war," Tozzer wrote. "A hacienda is nothing more than a second slave-holding plantation of the South." Workers receive the equivalent of what would be a United States quarter-dollar per day, which Tozzer could see was not enough to meet expenses, so the workers become indebted to the hacienda. "The owner never expects and does not, in fact, wish this debt to be paid off for as long as there is a debt, so long the hacienda has the power of life and death over the person." The

Hacienda Chichén was not exempt from the wage slave system, Tozzer found. Workers were bound for life to the hacienda and were not allowed to leave without permission. If a man refused to work, another seventy-five centavos for each day missed would be added to his debt.

"So in plain terms, our American consul is a slave owner," Tozzer wrote.

Tozzer learned of the cruelties of the system when the man who lived in the hut next reportedly was whipped. "It seems rather impossible to believe that a ranch owned and controlled by a consul of the American Republic which stands for freedom if for nothing else, should witness what is nothing more than a slave whipped at the post and this when the owner was present in the hacienda even if not an actual witness. Doubtless the man had done wrong, but it was no reason why all his self respect should be robbed from him in such a barbaric way." Tozzer had not been witness to the beating, but the man showed him the rope marks on his back. Still, he could not bring himself, even privately, to condemn completely his host at the Hacienda Chichén. "The fact is this, the Thompsons have lived so very long in Yucatán that even the tradition and principles of their native land have escaped them. They are more Yucatecans than Americans, and for this they can be excused."

Tozzer's new friend, Benito, was not exempt from wage slavery. When Tozzer had told Don José that he would be paying Benito directly, the superintendent of the hacienda ordered Benito work at another plantation that Thompson owned. Benito refused, saying his leg had not healed enough to allow manual labor. Don José told him he would be docked the seventy-five centavos for refusing an order to work, so Tozzer took his case to Edward Thompson. "I told Mr. Thompson I wanted Benito to try and pay off some of his debt and he said, 'We don't want him to, for then we would have no hold on him.'" Thompson told the young anthropologist that he could have Benito for as long as he needed him, but he had to uphold the hacienda way of doing things. Thompson told Benito he had "done wrong in flatly refusing to carry out the command" of Sierra, the *majordomo*, but that he could continue to work with Tozzer until Thompson's friend, a doctor, would arrive to examine him to determine if he was physically able to work.

Thompson then took Tozzer aside and told him that he expected the doctor in "a month or two"—or "perhaps never," which meant Benito would be available to assist him through the duration of his stay. And with that, Thompson showed Tozzer that even if you can't beat the system, you don't have to join it..

THE PRESENT

FRANCISCO GOMEZ RUL

BACK IN EDWARD THOMPSON'S ERA, haciendas relied on debt peonage, which made up seventy-five percent of the workforce. Debt peonage was abolished after the Mexican Revolution. Bibiano and his family work at the Hacienda Chichén as employees, with all the rights and privileges that entails under Mexican law. Much has changed from a century ago. The Barbachano family had known from the beginning that the way to make money with the Hacienda Chichén was not by growing crops or raising livestock. The value of Chichén Itzá was not the land, but the ancient monuments it contained and the desire of the world to see them.

Don Fernando's father, Fernando Barbachano Peón, had been the first to see this, which was why he built the Mayaland Hotel—at least as I had understood the story. But according to Fernando, the one who had the initial foresight in the family was his mother's father, don Francisco Gomez Rul. Although his father gets the credit for pioneering the tourism industry on the Yucatán Peninsula, he was carrying out the vision of his father-in-law, who saw the future of Chichén Itzá long before most—or so Fernando tells us.

We are back in Mérida, sitting in Fernando's study in the mansion on Paseo de Montejo. The windows are open and breezes sweep the room, which, with tall ceilings that trap the heat, keep us all comfortable. We are here to conduct a series of interviews for the book and it is a true family affair: I ask the questions, Sam records the audio, Sarah shoots video, and Lori relaxes in one of the padded leather chairs.

Family is very much on my mind after our experience in Pisté with the Uh Tuns and the Marrufos. After hearing about our adventures, don Fernando regales us with tales of his family, especially of the grandfather he never knew.

"Don Francisco was born in Malaga, Spain, in 1872 and died in Mérida in April 1926, one week before my birth," Fernando tells us. He had been a young fifty-four when he was struck and killed by a train.

Francisco had wanted to be a priest and had even graduated from a Jesuit seminary, "but he enjoyed the company of women rather than wear a skirt for life," says Fernando. According to Barbachano lore, don Francisco's family sent him to Mexico to check on its investments and properties in the vicinity of Mexico City. During his investigation, he was shot on two separate occasions. The second time he slipped out of the hospital, intending to beat a retreat back to Spain, except that he never made it. He found himself stranded in Mérida, awaiting funds and a ship to take him home. But like many a young man, he was waylaid by a beautiful *señorita*, a charming young lady of Castilian and English stock. Isabel Castillo Rivas was unique among Merida's young women. She was tall, slender, with blue eyes and hair of gold. Francisco was smitten and he remained in Mérida to be with her.

He cobbled together a living in the arts: as a writer, a photographer, a painter, a teacher. In 1906 he even shot and directed one of the first films in Yucatan, "*El Tobaco*." He was the founder of Yucatán's first school of fine arts (his daughter, Carmen, was one of the earliest graduates), where a bust of him rests to this day. He directed plays and even dance groups.

It was his work as a photographer that brought him to the attention of Edward Thompson. Gomez Rul became Thompson's regular photographer, Fernando tells us. "Thompson never photographed anything," snorts Fernando. This isn't true for I know of many photographs that could only have been taken by Thompson, but many from the latter part of his life were stylistically similar to those taken by Gomez Rul, who always liked to include people in his shots. Outside of his relationship with Thompson, Gomez Rul took dozens if not hundreds of photographs of Maya ruins.

His interest in the remnants of the ancient Maya went far beyond the scientific; Gomez Rul was a believer that the Maya civilization was linked with other ancient civilizations around the world. He became a Theosophist, with its beliefs in spiritual healing, lost continents of Atlantis and Lemuria, and spiritualism. "My grandfather was the head of the Yucatán American Theosophical Society," Fernando says. He also was a Mason, 33d Degree, and "started the first Masonry religious group in Yucatán."

More than two decades after his death the family learned that Francisco Gomez Rul had a secret life. In 1949 Fernando and the women in his life—his wife Maruja and the two Carmens, mother, and sister—took their first trip to Europe. They visited England and toured the continent, and ended their trip in Spain to visit family. Before leaving Mexico they had exchanged correspondence with Maruja's relatives, but had never received any response from the Gomez Rul side of the family. "Once in France, my mother sent another letter to her Aunt Carmen, elder sister of her father" to let them know they were coming. When they arrived at what they believed was the Gomez Rul home in Malaga, "no one was expecting us!" Fernando says. They told the maid at the door they were the Gomez Rul family from Mexico and that they were there to see the woman that

Fernando's mother had been named after, doña Carmen Gomez Rul.

"You must be at the wrong address as there is no such person in this house," the maid told them.

"My mother, who would not be stopped by anyone, much less a maid, said, 'Tell doña Carmen that her niece Carmen, daughter of her brother don Francisco, has just arrived from Mexico to visit her.'" The maid closed the door but quickly returned and led the Barbahanos into a parlor where a white-haired woman awaited. She instantly recognized Fernando's mother. "You are my brother's daughter from Mexico," she said, welcoming her with a kiss. "What is this Gomez Rul name you use?"

That was when the family learned that don Francisco had been living in Merida under an assumed name. His real name, according to Fernando, was Francisco Cebrián de la Tovilla y Pérez Gálvez. "He wanted to return to Spain with his family, but never had enough money," Fernando says. He was too embarrassed to ask his family for financial assistance.

Don Francisco corresponded with his family in Spain through a trusted friend, Fernando said, but had never told his Mexican family his true name, nor, apparently, told his family in Spain he was living under an assumed name. When he was tragically killed in an accident, he never had the chance to set the record straight. Even though his Mexican family knew where the ancestral home was in Malaga, their letters went unanswered; in turn don Francisco's family never learned of his fate.

Fernando confided one more secret about his grandfather's family. His great aunt was in line for the Marquesa of Orepesa, a title the Spanish court bestowed upon members of Incan royalty and, as his great aunt had no children, Fernando's mother could have inherited the title, if she had so desired. She didn't, he tells me.

But what Fernando never says (possibly he did not know) is that his grandfather had belonged to what had been one of the wealthiest families in Mexico. The Pérez Gálvez family owned more than a dozen giant haciendas and numerous productive mines at the time of the first Mexican Revolution. One hacienda alone, not far from Mexico City, had 150,000 goats and sheep, and of the former, 200 were slaughtered each day for their meat and tallow.

The Mexican side of the family had died out by the 1860s and apparently the property and wealth transferred to family back in Spain. Being absentee landlords, the family's holdings in Mexico by the latter half of the 19th century were threatened by competitors and by the government, so it was more than plausible that young Francisco had been sent to investigate their status. It is also more than possible that those who coveted the family's assets would stop at nothing, including eliminating descendants of the Pérez Gálvez family. It made sense that don Francisco would change his name, as his ancestors in Mexico included members from the wealthy Gomez and Rul families, that would explain where his alias originated.

I am skeptical about Fernando's claim that the family comes from Incan royalty. After we return to the United States, I do some research on the Orepesa title. As Fernando had said, the title descended from one of the last Incan kings, Atahualpa. Orepesa means "weight in gold." The name is somewhat of a misnomer, because King Atahualpa, after being captured by Spanish conquistadores, offered as ransom not his weight in gold, but a room full of the rare metal and two more rooms filled with silver. The Spanish killed him anyway. Atahualpa's nephew, Túpac Amaru, led a revolt forty years later and, like his uncle, was executed. Amaru's niece married a Spanish nobleman and it was their daughter who was bestowed the title "Marquesa de Orepesa."

By the 1940s the title had been vacant more than two centuries. It is more than possible don Fernando's great aunt had a right to the title. Then I stumble across a book, *Los Aborígenes de América*, written in 1894 by Rafael Delorme Salto. I had downloaded the book from the Internet because it contained some brief information about Chichén Itzá. While digitally flipping through it I come across a brief mention of the Incan Tupac Amaru. According to the author, there were three women in Malaga, Spain, who had rights to the Orepesa title. The son of one of those women was Francisco de Paula Cebrián de la Tovilla, better known to me as Francisco Gomez Rul.

I'll be damned.

But that discovery is in the future. Today, Don Fernando sits before me, gleefully retelling the tale of his family's Incan ancestry. But then he adds, "Please consider this confidential—and do not dare start calling me 'the duke!'"

Francisco Gomez Rul

THE PAST

EXPLORING THE CENOTE SAGRADO

THE NORTHERN LOWLANDS of the Yucatán Peninsula is a giant slab of limestone, formed when the entire region was underwater. For millions of years, dying fish and mollusks left their carcasses on the bottom of this ocean, a gently falling rain of bone and shell. When the seas withdrew between 20,000 and 30,000 years ago, left behind was a flat shelf of calcified earth. The geology resembles a baguette: a thin, hard crust over a soft, mushy center. The world above is arid, almost desert-like, but beneath the surface there is a network of underground rivers. Ground water seeps through the earth and when it finds a spongy section, natural acids dissolve the limestone, leaving behind a void in the bedrock. Sometimes the crusty limestone on the surface collapses and exposes the bubble to the air, creating what the Maya called a *dzonot*—today, "cenote."

Northern Yucatán is dotted with thousands of cenotes, but the most famous is at Chichén Itzá. "The [cenote at Chichén Itzá] was the largest and the wildest we had seen," explorer John Lloyd Stephens wrote in 1843. "In the midst of a thick forest, an immense circular hole, with cragged, perpendicular sides, trees growing out of them and overhanging the brink, and still as if the genius of silence reigned within."

From one side to the other, the cenote is sixty-five meters across at its widest point and twenty-five meters to water level. The steep walls comprise large, white bands of limestone, broken by thinner dark bands of sediment. Erosion has allowed some of the layers of white limestone to jut out to form a ledge, upon which persistent but scrawny bushes and trees perch. The wall is dotted with dozens of caves, some big enough for a man and filled with bats. The bottom is a pool that offers no cool invitation, but evokes putridity, glowing with a sickly green. "A mysterious influence seemed to pervade it," Stephens noted.

The central plaza of Chichén Itzá connects with the Sacred Well by way of a broad sacbé. A few hundred feet from the pyramid El Castillo the Maya built the ceremonial road which punctures the forest and terminates at a small, ruined shrine and platform at the lip of the Sacred Well. If the legends are true, this is where Mayan priests cast sacrifices. Surrounding the shrine are ascending tiers of limestone that form a small, natural amphitheater. Human sacrifices into the cenote would have provided great drama, but these must have been the cheap seats. The better view would have been on the opposite side of the cenote. Those who sat so close to the shrine would not have seen the crowd-satisfying splash as flailing bodies crashed into the water.

Edward Thompson loved to bring visitors to the Cenote Sagrado. As he stood next to the lip by the ruin, he would dramatically describe for visitors the ritual of sacrifice made by the Maya priests to appease Chaac, the god of rain. "In times of drought, pestilence, or disaster, solemn processions of priests, devotees with rich offerings, and victims for the sacrifice wound down the steep stairway of the Temple of Kukil Can [Kukulcan], the Sacred Serpent, and along the Sacred Way to the Well of Sacrifice," Thompson would intone. "There, amid the droning boom of the *tunkul*, the shrill pipings of the whistle and the plaintive notes of the flute, beautiful maidens and captive warriors of renown, as well as rich treasures, were thrown into the dark waters of the Sacred Well to propitiate the angry god who, it was believed, lived in the deeps of the pool."

Friar Diego De Landa, the future bishop of Yucatán, repeatedly mentioned the practice of human sacrifice in his *Relacion de la Cosas de Yucatan* of 1566. According to de Landa, the Maya believed that the victims would emerge from the depths on the third day "even though they never did see them reappear."

In 1579, the mayor of the nearby town of Valladolid confirmed de Landa's account in a letter to King Charles of Spain. The Maya lords of Chichén, after sixty days of "fasting and abstinence," at daybreak threw women over the cliff and into the water, he wrote. Those that survived until noon were hauled out. The priests encircled the survivors in smoky fires of Maya incense, called copal. They asked the women what they had seen. According to the mayor:

> *When they recovered their senses, they said that below there were many people of their nation, men and women, and that they had received them. When they tried to raise their heads to look at them, heavy blows were given them on the head, and when their heads were inclined downward beneath the water they seemed to see many deeps and hollows, and they, the people, responded to their queries concerning the good or the bad year that was in store for their masters.*

Maya from all over Yucatán reportedly had been throwing tributes into the Sacred Well for centuries. As Friar de Landa speculated, "If this country had possessed gold it would be this Well that would have the greater part of it."

Thompson was very familiar with de Landa's descriptions of the Sacred Well. "From the moment I read the musty old volume the thought of that grim old water pit and the wonderful objects that lay concealed within the depths became an obsession with me," he wrote in his autobiography. "For days and weeks after I purchased the plantation, I was a frequent worshiper at the little shrine on the brink of the Sacred Well. I pondered, mused, and calculated. I made measurements and numberless soundings, until, not satisfied but patiently expectant, I put my notebook aside and awaited the accepted time."

The "accepted time" turned out to be almost ten years after he purchased Chichén Itzá. If Thompson was so certain that de Landa and others were correct, why wait almost a decade to test the theory? Because he had no choice.

Thompson's finances were dire. For years he had been seeking a partner in the Hacienda Chichén who could spring him from debt. He sent his first "prospectus" to the man who first brought him to Yucatán, Stephen Salisbury. In a letter to the Worcester millionaire, Thompson described the current state of the hacienda with the enthusiasm of a time-share salesman. "The right person will see a large, well-made stone house, airy cool rooms, large arched corridors, stone-tiled, forty-five servants with families, four carts, thirty mules, three hundred handsome cattle, carpenter shop with tools, blacksmith shop, plantation store well stocked with goods, native carriages (volanes), horses, brood mares, studs, pure-blooded Holstein to raise the standard of the native-stock, a large field of sugar cane flourishing, to be ground next December, and lastly, over thirty-five square miles of rich land, timberland, cane, fruit and pasturage."

Thompson wanted Salisbury to be his partner, because, in a sense, they already were. The don of Chichén Itzá owed the don of Worcester more than $8,000 U.S. for debts that went back to Thompson's first days in Yucatán in 1885. Salisbury had kept a careful accounting of every dime he loaned Thompson and for good reason: Thompson made only three payments on the loans the entire time he was in Mexico.

Salisbury declined Thompson's offer of partnership, but Thompson did not give up trying to tap that well. In 1902 he sought $2,000 to construct a seventeen-kilometer railroad spur line between Dzitas and Chichén Itzá. The loan never came to fruition and from Salisbury's financial records one can deduce that Thompson had been cut off.

So Thompson, backed into a financial corner, proposed the only kind of enterprise that he knew would attract investors. He approached Salisbury and Bowditch to finance an exploration of the Cenote Sagrado. Salisbury agreed but with some very, very long strings attached. He would underwrite the expedition, but as a loan, for which he would receive the deed to Chichén Itzá as collateral. In view of Thompson's credit history, Salisbury would have been assured that Thompson would never be able to repay his debts and that the property would be his. Or so he thought. Once their deal was signed, Salisbury learned that Thompson had been borrowing from others. And not just anyone.

In November 1899 Thompson mortgaged Chichén for $15,000 Mexican at eight percent annual interest. The lender was don Juan Francisco Molina Solis, Merida's resident historian and younger brother of the most powerful man in Yucatán, the current governor, Olegario Molina Solis. Salisbury had been unaware of the loan, but must have been horrified to learn that Thompson had never made so much as a single payment on the note, which by 1904 had ballooned to more than $20,000 Mexican. Salisbury was holding a second mortgage.

The Worcester industrialist immediately contacted his friend and lawyer in Mérida, David Casares, to buy up the Solis mortgage for the equivalent of $9,000 U.S. gold. The transaction doubled Thompson's debt to Salisbury to more than $21,000 U.S. To prevent any future shenanigans, Salisbury took the deed to Chichén.

Above, the Hacienda Chichén, early 20th century.
Below, a Pisté street scene from the same period. Parked
is the infamous *volan*.

THE PRESENT

MÉRIDA OF YEARS PAST

WHY DID FRANCISCO MOLINA agree to sell his financial interest in Chichén Itzá to Stephen Salisbury? When Salisbury's agent came to pay Thompson's mortgage, why didn't Molina instead take the property, which would have been his right as Thompson had never made a payment on the note?

I ask don Fernando. Why did the Casta Divina, who had all the money world, did not seem to care about the mysterious ruins throughout their land. Or to be more precise, their actions indicated that they were happy to let others outside Mexico explore their lands.

The great families of Yucatán, Fernando explains, were indifferent to Chichén Itzá and to the mysteries it contained, especially during that period. As a people they were very self-absorbed and were interested only in their own lives and their status in society, for it was a time of great change, he says. Francisco Molina's brother Olegario, the governor, was turning Merida into a cosmopolitan city as advanced as any in the world. He compelled the hacendados to finance a series of public works projects, such as a modern hospital and prison. He ordered the paving of Merida's dirt streets and the construction of a showplace for the city, the wide boulevard Paseo de Montejo. The members of the Casta Divina all rushed in to build beautiful mansions along this street. And one of the grandest of all is the house where Fernando and I sit.

The man who built the mansion, Fernando says, was Ernesto Camara Zavala, eldest son of one of Yucatan's most prestigious families, and ambassador to France for Mexico President Porfirio Diaz. While in France, Camara Zavala came to admire the work of a German-born architect, Gustave Umbdenstock, who had designed two buildings for the Exposition Universelle (the Paris Exposition) in 1900. "He is said to have told the architect, 'Go to my hometown and build your dream house for me,'" Fernando tells me.

"Can you imagine an architect building a structure where there are no wives, no mothers, no sisters, all requesting absurd changes to the project?" he asks. "Umbdenstock must have had orgasm after orgasm as he completed the project to perfection, with all the required money and no questions asked!"

The Camara family reportedly sold three of their haciendas to complete the project, says Fernando. They brought to Yucatan specialists in the construction trades—iron workers, electricians, plumbers, stained glass window artists, stone workers, and masons, many of whom settled in Mérida after the house was finished. According to Fernando, the house sparked a trend for wrought iron work for window treatments, gates and fences, a motif that is common in Mérida today.

The house was state of the art for its time, with its own phone system. The furniture, he explains, was handmade in France for the Exposition, and much of it fills the house today. "You can still find the stamps on the back from Mexican customs," don Fernando says.

Ernesto was a bachelor when he built the house, but he did not spend his life alone. "The story goes further," don Fernando tells me, but it is one of which the Camara family will not speak. "One night, the ambassador arrived home in Paris to a special evening reception. As he entered he caught the eye of a very young lady who he invited to dance. They danced all night, love at first sight on both sides. Not a word was passed in accordance to the rituals of the time as they had not been officially introduced." Both were in for a surprise.

The young woman happened to be the ambassador's niece, born in Merida while he was in France. "They had never met; she was visiting France for the first time," Fernando says. The couple was too much in love to break it off. "They even went to the Pope for permission to marry: denied."

It did not matter. "It is said they lived as husband and wife," Fernando says. This unusual arrangement was accepted in Merida, because at the time high society consisted of individuals who were *libre pensadores*—free thinkers, and non-religious, says Fernando.

It was into this world that don Fernando's father was raised, he says. Fernando Barbachano Peón was born in Puebla, but both of his parents were from Merida and soon removed him to there. From the beginning, his life was caught up in scandal, Fernando says. His parents divorced, which at the time was a rare occurrence in Yucatán, especially among the wealthy class. Living with your niece apparently was accepted, but divorcing your wife was a no-no.

"My grandmother was fighting my grandfather," he says. During that period, one side of the family or the other would kidnap young Fernando. The couple would then reconcile and remarry, only to divorce again. "They divorced three times," says Fernando. "Unbelievable."

Fernando blames it on his grandmother's family, the Peóns, one of the founding families of Yucatán. "The Peón family have brilliant people and 'too brilliant' people—meaning cuckoo," he says. His grandmother was of the "too brilliant" variety. The public fights between his grandparents and the frequent kidnappings proved traumatic to young Fernando Barbachano Peón. He would endure the effects of that trauma for the rest of his life, Fernando says.

I change the subject to my recent visit with the Marrufos. I delicately tell him what doña Maria Luisa had said, that Fernando's father had bought Chichén and then evicted Victoria, Thompson's mistress. Fernando says that it was true. When his father purchased Chichén Itzá in 1944, Victoria was running a hotel on the property. "My father went to Victoria and told her that she could live for the rest of her life on the hacienda, but not if she ran a hotel," Fernando says. Her husband refused, so Fernando's father got the courts to evict them, he says.

"Her husband?" I ask. Doña Maria Luisa had said that Victoria had no husband.

"Yes, her husband," Fernando says. "Marrufo." I show him a picture doña Maria Luisa gave me. I point to the man in a mustache who doña Maria Luisa could not identify. Fernando thought he could be Marrufo, but could not remember. But it was Marrufo who insisted on running a hotel there, of that don Fernando was certain.

Now I was completely confused. Carlos Marrufo, Thompson's son, had a stepfather named Marrufo? How could that be?

THE PAST

ONE SHOVEL AT A TIME

ONCE THOMPSON COMMITTED to explore the Sacred Cenote and retrieve the artifacts he believed it contained, he considered three methods—draining, diving, or dredging—and each presented its own unique challenges. Draining the well would require a fleet of pumps and a commensurate number of windmills to drive them. Even if such a pumping system was possible, it was doubtful a cenote so large could be emptied before underground springs replenished it. Diving would be difficult, because of the limited visibility in the water. Dredging had been attempted before by explorer Désiré Charnay in 1882, but his small equipment could not pierce the centuries of fallen rock, trees, and other debris that covered the bottom.

"I concluded at last that it could be dredged, and with comparatively simple equipment consisting of a stiff-legged derrick with a hand windlass, a long boom which might be swung out over the well, and a steel orange-peel buck-scoop, or bucket," Thompson wrote.

He acquired the biggest dredge he could reasonably ship to Yucatán. The boom was ten meters long and constructed of sturdy New England oak, as was the derrick. The windlass had been cast from heavy iron, and together with the orange-peel bucket weighed more than a ton.

Thompson had little difficulty shipping the dredge from the United States to Yucatán, but transporting it from the port of Progreso to Chichén Itzá, 100 kilometers in the interior, proved an enormous undertaking. Once in Progreso, Thompson's agents put the dredge aboard a train to Mérida, then transferred it to another rail line for shipping to Dzitas. From there it was seventeen kilometers to Chichén Itzá "over the poorest excuse for a road," Thompson said. Maya workers carried the dredge overland on foot, because no wagon outside of the compact volan could make the rugged trip. "The equipment was moved piecemeal, until, after months and months of the hardest work I have ever done, it was all piled beside the Sacred Well," Thompson said.

He planned to begin dredging in 1903, but a yellow fever epidemic paralyzed Yucatán and shut down his project before it could begin. He had to wait until March 1904 before he could dip the bucket in the well.

A month into the project, the young Harvard anthropologist Alfred Tozzer returned to Yucatán. Before his departure the previous year, Thompson had told him something big was in the works. Privately Tozzer had scoffed believing it was just so much talk. But now he had to eat crow: Thompson was dredging the Sacred Well, which just by itself Tozzer had to admit was an astounding achievement.

Before heading to Chichén to begin his second season of work, Tozzer met with Leon J. Cole, a Ph.D. candidate from Harvard. Cole had ostensibly come to the Yucatán to help Thompson with the dredging, but, like Tozzer the year before, his job may have been to spy on Thompson on behalf of Charles Bowditch. Cole "shows surprisingly little interest in the archaeology and the ethnology of the country," Tozzer observed. That should not have been surprising because Cole was not an archaeology student, but working on a doctorate in zoology. The subject of his thesis was the vertebrates of Yucatán and he had come to the area on behalf of

Harvard's Museum of Comparative Zoology. Somehow he was loaned to the Peabody Museum and, instead of spending the majority of his time collecting animal specimens, he slogged through the tailings brought up by Thompson's dredge in search of Maya artifacts. Despite his newly directed priorities, Cole managed, between bucket loads, to identify 128 species of birds.

Cole's lack of interest in all things Maya made him the impartial observer to the early days of dredging the cenote. His field diary from Chichén proved once again that Thompson was not a man to let the facts get in the way of a good story. One of the great dramatic moments in Thompson's autobiography, written almost thirty years later, is the discovery of the first artifact. Thompson wrote:

> *The day was gray as my thoughts and the thick mist dropped from the leaves of the trees as quiet tears drop from half-closed eyes. I plodded through the dampness down to where the staccato clicks of the dredge brake called me and, crouching under the palm leaf lean-to, watched the monotonous motions of the brown-skinned natives as they worked at the winches. The bucket slowly emerged from the heaving water that boiled around it and, as I looked listlessly down into it, I saw two yellow-white, globular masses lying on the surface of the chocolate-colored muck that filled the basin. As the mass swung over the brink and up to the platform, I took from it the two objects and closely examined them.*
>
> *They seemed to be made of some resinous substance. I tasted one. It was resin. I put a piece into a mass of lighted embers and immediately a wonderful fragrance permeated the atmosphere. Like a ray of bright sunlight breaking through a dense fog came to me the words of the old H'Men, the Wise Man of Ebtun: "In ancient times our fathers burned*

*the sacred resin—*pom*—and by the fragrant smoke their prayers were wafted to their God whose home was in the Sun."*

These yellow balls of resin were masses of the sacred incense pom, and had been thrown in as part of the rich offerings mentioned in the traditions. That night for the first time in weeks I slept soundly and long.

Thompson's recollection, which he claimed he could remember "as if it were but yesterday," may have been just that—a memory he made up the day before he wrote his autobiography. Cole's field diary reveals four days into the dredging, Thompson left for Progreso to tend to his duties as consul. He wasn't at the cenote when the bucket brought up incense. Even if he had been, he would not have had to light the substance to know what it was, for he had found pom when he excavated the Osario. Also, Cole reported that the dredge began recovering human bones and pottery shards almost from the beginning, not after "days and days," as Thompson later described.

Cole saw through Thompson "as anyone can who is with the man more than a day," Tozzer noted, but still felt kindly toward him because of the hospitality he received at the hacienda. Cole even named a bird after his host, the *otus choliba thompsoni*, a Yucatecan species, appropriately enough, of screech owl.

Cole described for Tozzer the objects recovered so far. The most exciting was what appeared to be a wooden scepter with a carved face that had been gilded, the first gold ever recovered in Yucatán. "This is a most important find, and really quite a boom [sic], for Thompson needs all the pushing he can find," Tozzer wrote. The dredge also recovered numerous jade beads and copper bells.

A couple of days later Tozzer went to see the cenote operation for himself. "I came back covered in head to foot with mud," he wrote. "One simply can't resist getting into the very midst of the pile of soft mud as each load comes up." The importance of the finds could not be exaggerated, Tozzer thought. "Mr. Thompson expects at any moment to be stopped by the authorities as they will naturally resent such a success of a foreigner." One trunk of artifacts, he reported, had already been shipped out of Yucatán. Tozzer did not say how this happened, but he was soon to learn firsthand.

Thompson and the dredge

176   Evan J. Albright

Maya workers at the Hacienda Chichén guide the dredge while floating in the Cenote Sagrado.

THE PRESENT

GOODBYE TO YUCATÁN

I PROMISE DON FERNANDO that I will stop by the Casa Camara one more time to say goodbye before leaving Yucatán. My children and I raid the local gift shops to find some Yucatán treasure of our own before returning to the hotel for what will be our final night in Mexico. We run late, of course, and swing by don Fernando's just as he is going out for the evening. His eyes are bright and he is in excellent spirits. He is off to play dominos with old friends and the way he says it tells me that there might be more going on than just putting well worn tiles together.

We caught him as he was about to get into the Mercedes. He stands next to the open door and says goodbye to us, a clear message that even our parting will not deter him from his night's activities. The car is parked between his mansion and an almost identical building next door. This building is uninhabited.

"The story of the other house is quite different," Fernando had told me earlier. Ernesto Camara's brother had asked to hire the same architect to build an identical home next door. Ernesto gave his blessing and the second house was built—almost. Ernesto's brother had a wife and she and others in the family constantly interfered during the design and construction of the home. "The house was never completely finished," don Fernando had told me.

Now, standing outside as the cool evening breezes blew between the two giant mansions, I gesture to the other building and asked why Fernando had not bought it.

"I have not been able to convince them to sell it to me," Fernando says, adding with a laugh, "--yet!" And with that he is in his car and off. And so are we.

**Casas Camara,
left is owned by Fernando Barbachano G. Rul.
(Lori S. Albright photo)**

THE PAST

THE FIND OF THE CENTURY

THE 'SCEPTRE' WAS THE FIRST OBJECT with gold found in Cenote Sagrado, but it would not be the last. When Tozzer returned to Chichén Itzá a year later for his third season he learned that Thompson's dredge had recovered much more. The hyperbole came fast and thick when the young archaeologist wrote his family about the find:

> *I cannot begin to give you any idea of the magnitude, the importance both intrinsically and scientifically of the collection. There are gold plates, gold bowls, gold figurines and gold bells, all as bright and as polished as the day they were made. There is one gold bowl weighing far over a pound. And as for the jade, there is no end to it. There is probably more of this precious stone taken from the Cenote than all the museums in the country have in their united collections. The carving beggars description and there are hundreds of pieces: And copper bells by the cup full, many with heads of animals on top or in the shape of animals. The find is the one of the century, nothing like it has ever been taken out of Mexico.*

Tozzer then scrawled a prophetic line: "It will be famous the world over and I dread to think of the complications which may result."

The dredging of the Cenote Sagrado also reversed Thompson's fortunes. Stephen Salisbury and Charles Bowditch were now subsidizing the operation, paying not only the annual expense of the dredging (which came to $2,850), but also paying a healthy stipend ($1,999.99 per year) to Edward Thompson and his family. Tozzer saw that the Thompsons had spent the money on improvements to the hacienda, adding a second windmill that pumped water into a large tank on the roof of the main house, which was now plumbed to accommodate running water, including a new shower. The front of the hacienda's main building was now adorned with a fountain and several small, decorative gardens.

Thompson also repaired the old chapel on the rise overlooking the hacienda. When Tozzer arrived, the ancient building sported a brand new roof and a priest was coming from Valladolid to rededicate it. "The huts of the natives have been freshened up and a more general air of prosperity pervades the place," wrote Tozzer.

The cheerful surroundings did nothing to assuage the growing feeling of unease that was mounting in the anthropologist. He was not at Chichén Itzá to assist in the dredging; he was there to carry the artifacts out of Mexico to the United States. "My responsibility will be great," he writes. "I dread the idea of being the bearer of such priceless treasures."

But how to get the artifacts out of Yucatán? All cargo in and out of the state went through Progreso. Customs agents enthusiastically searched the belongings of every foreigner. Thompson's predecessor as consul, Louis Aymé, nearly had caused an international scandal when an inspector in Progreso opened three boxes bound for New York and found pieces of stucco removed from Maya temples. Taking the objects out using "normal" channels also was not possible. When Le Plongeon petitioned the Mexican government to remove the chac-mool he excavated from Chichén Itzá in 1875, the Yucatecan government illegally seized the statue.

Only a few months before Thompson started dredging, the Mexican government had come to Chichén to examine several painted statues that had been uncovered in the Upper Temple of the Jaguar above the Great Ball Court. The figures had been discovered by Le Plongeon decades earlier, but he reburied them and so they had remained hidden, until rediscovered by Adela Breton. The Mexican government confiscated the carved figures to ship to Mexico City.

How, then, to get the treasures of the Sacred Well out of the country?

In early spring 1905, Tozzer boarded a steamship in Progreso dressed in what appeared to be a typical Edwardian waistcoat. It was not unusual for gringos to wear their clothes from the north, but this vest was more than a little unconventional as it was not padded with cotton tacking but carved Mayan jades from the Sacred Cenote. Tozzer's regular host in Mérida, an American, June F. James (although no one ever called her by her first name. She was simply referred to as "Mrs. James"), had spent several days sewing the jades into the lining. Tozzer also carried a large suitcase filled with cigar boxes packed with the rest of the carved jades. He carried it past customs without incident. No one stopped him, or for that matter expressed even the slightest interest in searching the suitcase. One reason may have been that Tozzer was not leaving the country and thereby requiring an inspection. He was steaming to Veracruz.

Tozzer still had to be more than cautious, for as bad as Progreso's officials could be, customs inspectors and luggage porters at Veracruz were far worse. "Never let your baggage out of your sight at Veracruz," one writer warned. "The contents are often stolen in the very Customs House." Luggage porters were known to "loan" their official badges to thieving accomplices who would accept bags from unwary visitors with the promise of taking them to the train station, only to never show up. When the tourist calls the police, the real porter would appear and, of course, would know nothing about the stolen bags.

Tozzer was well travelled in Mexico and knew all the tricks, so he got through the port of Veracruz without incident. He took a train to Mexico City where he met Adela Breton and then returned to Veracruz to rejoin the ship back to Progreso. The young archaeologist did not go ashore when the ship anchored off of Yucatán. Instead Thompson's wife and Mrs. James met him on board with a suitcase packed with the gold artifacts from the cenote. Customs inspectors never searched the bag because the ladies were not leaving the country. William James also made a trip out to the steamship, his pockets full of artifacts. After transferring the treasure, Mr. and Mrs. James and Mrs. Thompson said their goodbyes and returned to shore. Tozzer sailed for Cuba and from there the United States without incident.

Carved jade from Cenote Sagrado

THE PRESENT

THE THOMPSONS LEARN THE TRUTH

MAY ON CAPE COD has yet to shake off spring and usher in the bloom of summer. The day is gray and somewhat raw, but for Cape Codders it's perfect weather to be at the seashore.

Once again I'm driving to Black Beach, the former home of Edward Thompson. It's been a month since I left Yucatán. In the car it occurs to me I've come full circle. Several months ago I drove out here and learned from Heleni Thayre, Edward Thompson's great-granddaughter, that the family had Maya cousins in Yucatán. Now I am returning to the Thompson homestead to confirm that fact. I have no idea what to expect, other than the assurance by Edward Thompson's granddaughter, Ginny, that she wants to know the truth, regardless of what it is.

The cottage has a six-pack of Edward Thompson descendants when I arrive. Ginny, the only one I had met before, had come down with her son, Gary Foulke, who is ailing from some unspecified illness. There are a bunch of Thompson cousins: Randy Thompson, Kathy Thompson, Wendy Soderlund, and Janet Sawyer. Most of the assembled clan descends from through Ginny's father, Edward Josiah Thompson, second child of Edward H. and Henrietta. Wendy is the only one descended from another son of Edward Thompson, Ernest Hamlin Thompson.

We gather in a circle in the cozy living room of the beach cottage, sitting on furniture typical of Cape Cod cottages, none of it matching yet all with same musty smell. I ask where Heleni is, as she was the one who started me on this quest. Ginny assures me her daughter will be there shortly. Everyone is anxious to hear what I have to say, so I enthusiastically launch into my tale of Yucatán and of finding Thompson's Maya family.

I start from the beginning, how I first became interested in Thompson and Chichén Itzá. How he had dredged the Sacred Well. And how he had left behind a Maya family in Yucatan. I tell them how I went to Yucatan to find Thompson and discover if it was true that he had a Maya wife.

I play a recording of don Fernando talking about don Eduardo. "He sounds just like my father," Ginny marvels. I point out that both men had grown up in the same place, in Mérida and at Chichén Itzá. Fernando describes how Thompson had a son named Carlos Marrufo by a Maya woman, Victoria. I stop the recording and describe how I found the Marrufo family and had visited the home of Carlos Marrufo's widow, Maria Luisa.

Ginny chuckles and recalls how her aunt, Margarita, had once met some of the "Mexican Thompsons" when she was living in Florida. "She was shocked. It was just embarrassing for her," she says. While Edward Thompson's daughter may have been aghast, there was no such reaction among the Thompson descendants. Ginny says she understands completely. Henrietta, Thompson's wife, "weighed less than a hundred pounds and had had eight children, and the last two died," adding, "She was tired." Everyone laughs.

City shoes clomp on the weathered boards of the porch. Heleni rushes in with typical dramatic flair. She scolds me for showing up early, although I argue there was no set time, just that I would show up in the late afternoon.

I play some of my interview with doña Maria Luisa and the translations by her son-in-law, Bibiano. Before coming, I had thought about keeping back the part about how Edward Thompson had left Victoria with nothing and how Fernando Barbachano Peón had evicted her from Chichén Itzá. But I leave it all in.

Not surprising, they take it all in stride. Heleni recounts her trip to Chichén Itzá twenty years ago. "The hacienda when I was there wasn't being used," she says. I explain that it was a seasonal hotel in those days.

"We stayed there twenty-six years ago," Wendy says. "We only stayed two nights because we didn't how wonderful it was."

"I remember the elegant hotel where I had dinner," Heleni continues, and I tell her that must have been the Mayaland next door. Of the hacienda, she only remembers an empty, abandoned building. "I have pictures of the most adorable Maya family that I thought were caretakers of the hacienda. I can't seem to remember the details. I think I have to go back."

"It sounds like everyone should go back," says Janet.

Heleni laughs. "We should go back as a *horde*!"

"I've never been," Ginny says quietly.

Heleni stops. "You haven't been there, mother?"

"I've never been there," she says. She was in Yucatán once, in Cancún, but never made it to Chichén Itzá.

"Oh, we should go while mother is still perambulatory," Heleni says. "We should go *soon*." Everyone laughs again.

I pull out pictures of the Marrufos. I also share the e-mail address for Ariel, one of doña Maria Luisa's sons. I herd the Thompsons out on the deck and take their picture in the same style as the one I took of the Marrufos.

"So what's going to happen?" I ask.

"We need to go to Chichén," Heleni says firmly. "That would be an ideal time for us to have a big family reunion."

"Who wants to push a wheelchair?" asks Ginny.

"Let's plan on next February," Heleni says, ignoring her mother. Someone asks me if I would be willing to go. At that moment, I realize that contrary to what I had been thinking when I arrived, I had not, in fact, come full circle. Or if I had, I was getting ready to take another turn on Fate's big wheel. I was going back to Mexico.

U.S. descendants of Edward H. Thompson

Photograph from brochure promoting Thompson lecture, circa 1911

PART TWO

In Mexico, nothing happens until it happens.
　　　　　—*Attributed to Mexico President Porfirio Diaz (1830-1915)*

THE PAST

REVEL IN THE GLORY

THE ARTIFACTS ENROUTE to Harvard, Thompson could take a breath and plan his next move. He had proved that Diego de Landa's claim was no myth. The Cenote Sagrado had been a scene of sacrifice, of artifacts of gold, copper, and jade, and of human beings. The time had come to reap the glory.

He requested a leave of absence from his consul post beginning Aug. 1 so he could attend the October meeting of the American Antiquarian Society. There Stephen Salisbury and other hoi polloi of Boston society would fete him.

On the day of his departure from Yucatán, Thompson received a letter from the State Department Auditor of the Consular Service, complaining that the Yucatán consulate had not turned in required vouchers, receipts, and accounts. For Thompson, charges of this type were old hat. The auditor was new and apparently not familiar with the obstacles of running a consulate in Mexico's most remote state. Thompson, however, was willing to educate the new man. His letter in reply, written not long after his arrival at his Cambridge, Mass., home, was soaked in exasperation. "In my previous letters to the Hon. Auditor...I have given as clearly and as fully as possible the reasons why owing to circumstances beyond any human control I have been unable to furnish all of the receipts and vouchers required," he wrote. "Within the period mentioned in the communications of the Hon. Auditor this Consulate has been three times violently driven in the streets by fires that have destroyed whole blocks around it. It is almost by miracles that the Consulate has not been utterly effaced."

Despite these disastrous fires, Thompson said he has been working at night and on his days off attempting to restore the files. The strain on his eyes, he wrote, requires "immediate, painful, and expensive treatment." Making plain the breadth of his sacrifice, Thompson recommended that "justice requires I have more time to straighten out matters and in asking for it, I only ask for fair play and justice."

In the past, a response such as this would keep the State Department away, at least until a new auditor was appointed with the next administration. But Thompson already had received more than "fair play and justice." For the past two years, he had been a phantom presence in the consulate office in Progreso, only showing up when he absolutely had to be there. His communication with the home office in Washington, D.C., was spotty, sometimes going months between reports. His neglect of his duties did not escape his superiors at the Consular Service. Thompson continued to draw his $2,000 full-time salary, plus a percentage of the fees he collected, but he was spending half his time, if that, on the job.

This was the second time in two years that Thompson's performance had come under scrutiny. In the early weeks of the dredging, the State Department had received a letter of complaint about Thompson from representatives of the Isaac Kubie Company of New York, an importer of cattle hides from Yucatán. The company charged that Thompson was neglecting his duties in favor of his "archaeological and botanical studies," and as such, failed to properly supervise his clerk at Progreso who was charging the exorbitant sum of ten dollars to inspect bundles of hides to insure they had been properly disinfected. Thompson defended his clerk at length and then launched into a lengthy diatribe detailing how Isaac Kubie was out to get him. "He made the threat that if he 'could not move me, he could remove me,'" Thompson reported. The consul offered to press formal charges against the company on the grounds they attempted to evade inspections of their hides by falsely claiming that there were no infectious diseases in Yucatán, even though it was well known that anthrax was killing whole herds of cattle in the Campeche region.

As far as the charges that he was neglecting his job in favor of his other pursuits, Thompson countered that part of his duties were to roam the region gathering information for reports to Washington, such as his recent article on the henequen industry which was later reworked and republished with great fanfare in the National Geographic magazine. "I have never understood that it is a misdemeanor for a Consul to be interested in scientific subjects," Thompson replied. "Neither my investigations of the subject matter for my official reports or my interest in scientific work are allowed to interfere with my regular Consular duties." A more accurate statement may have been that his consular duties frequently interfered with his scientific interests, but now was not the time for blunt honesty. Thompson was on a roll and he justified himself further by stating, "I have absolutely no business other than my Consular duties and in this foreign land a man must have something outside of routine work to interest him or else take to drink or worse."

Thompson had by 1905 served more than fifteen years as the American consul in Yucatán. He had seen presidential administrations come and go and had powerful friends in Washington and elsewhere who protected him. Although never arrogant, he was confident in his ability to keep his employers at bay and thwart any criticism of his duties or of his office. But the current president, Theodore Roosevelt, was not like his predecessors.

He had traveled the world and had seen the work (or lack thereof) of America's consuls. When he addressed Congress in December 1904, he called for reform of the consular service. No longer should consuls be dependent on fees and they also need to be professionalized, he said. While he stopped short of demanding that they take an examination, he did say they should be required to speak the local language. This was not a problem for Thompson who not only spoke Spanish but Maya. Roosevelt, however, was opposed to consulate officials spending too much time in one location. And in the minds of many, Thompson had overstayed in Yucatán. Whether he realized or not, Thompson's days were numbered.

By fall 1905, Thompson was back in New England and among the archaeological community, a conquering hero. Not the State Department auditors, nor even the president of the United States, could stop him from getting his due. He accepted the congratulations of the American Antiquarian Society at a meeting that included Stephen Salisbury and Edward Everett Hale, two of the three men who had been at the fateful dinner in twenty years earlier when he accepted the assignment to go to Yucatán. Thompson also pontificated about his discoveries to budding archaeologists at Harvard's Anthropology Club. One of the members, Sylvanus Morley, paid a visit to Thompson at his home to discuss spending a season in Yucatán, including a stint at Chichén Itzá. Neither man could have foreseen that in twenty years Morley would replace Thompson as the king of Chichén Itzá.

Thompson had made the most important archaeological discovery in North America, even if few knew about it. He was on top of the world, but then that world collapsed. A few days after his return to Yucatán, Thompson received word of the death of Salisbury. The implications did not become clear until after the first of the year, when Thompson received a letter from Lyman Ely, executor of Salisbury's will. Thompson owed more than $20,000 to the Salisbury estate, which held the deed to the Hacienda Chichén as collateral. Ely demanded that the debt be paid in full.

Ely was not a bureaucrat like a State Department auditor who could be kept at bay with a litany of excuses. The executor would have had Thompson's full history with Salisbury in front of him: The numerous loans, of which nothing had ever been repaid; the broken promises of scientific reports that never arrived; and the never-ending pleas for additional funding.

Thompson wrote what had to be the most important letter of his life. "I feel…that I must now, in justice to my own interests, write plainly and speak clearly of things that I am greatly disinclined to even mention in writing lest the facts reach the knowledge of those that might make improper use of them," Thompson wrote the executor. The unfair demand by Salisbury executors had placed Thompson under the greatest pressure a man can face, that of the need to provide for his family. He revealed to Ely, in case he did not know, that only a few months ago he had found "*the sacred treasure of the ancient Mayas.*" The words were so important, Thompson underlined them for emphasis. He provided a list of what had been recovered from the Sacred Cenote. For the first time, there was something resembling an inventory of the most valuable items (emphasis Thompson's):

"A *strange weapon*, hitherto only known by legends and rock carvings [an *atlatl*, a stick with a hook at one end used to propel spears and darts great distances];

"The skeletons of sacrificed maidens;

"*Jewels of jade* covered with wonderful carvings in great number of priceless scientific value;

"Vessels of strange patterns filled with incense and sacred symbols of unknown meaning;

"*Great quantities of gold*, portions of gold disks, pure gold beaten out and covered with incised work;

"*Plates* of *pure beaten gold*, some of which *weigh over a pound*;

"*Large disks of pure gold*, beaten out and covered with strange symbolical figures in *repoussé*;

"*Many idols, amulets*, and *figurines* in *solid, massive gold*...priceless;

"Symbolical carved figures, basins and bowls *in gold, solid* and *plated*;

"Bells in great variety and shape of *solid gold* and *very massive*."

In case there was any confusion, Thompson made clear his point. "All these and an infinite variety of copper and other articles of great intrinsic and inestimable scientific value were taken by me from *off my plantation* and by direction of Mr. Salisbury and Mr. Bowditch, who furnished me with the funds *with which to take them out* were turned over by me to the Peabody Museum in whose care they now are." For this, Thompson wrote, shouldn't the mortgage be annulled and title to Chichén Itzá given back to him? He claimed Salisbury had promised that he could cease his labors in Yucatán by 1908 and would receive a paid position at some unnamed institute endowed by the millionaire (though no record of this promise existed). "He was the last person in the world to desire me to take all these priceless treasures from my plantation and then strip from me even the ownership of the plantation itself," he wrote.

The long wait—for the letter to arrive in Worcester, for Ely and the executors to weigh the demand, and for their answer to travel back through the mails to Yucatán—must have been excruciating for Thompson. But his gambit worked. The executors annulled the debt and turned the deed to Chichén back to him. He had been given a clean slate. But Thompson being Thompson, it would become another squandered opportunity and one that would result in his banishment forever from Mexico.

THE PRESENT

OTHER EXPEDITIONS TO THE SACRED WELL

WHILE MY TRIP to Mexico provided many answers, it spawned even more mysteries, the biggest coming, appropriately enough, from a bathroom wall. Outside the restrooms at Chichén Itzá the Mexican government had placed Thompson's dredge. Next to it was a sign, mounted between the entrances to the washrooms for men and women, which reads, in large type, *"Desde 1904, Edward H. Thompson rescató gran cantidad de ofrendas del cenote sagrado, que posteriormente sacó ilegalmente del país."* Even if you don't understand Spanish, the word "ilegalmente" gets your attention.

The sign continues at length Spanish but there is an English translation that summarizes it in one sentence: "Already in the sixteenth century, there were reports of treasures to be found in the sacred cenote, but it was not until 1904 that Edward H. Thompson undertook explorations which produced remarkable quantities of material that illegally left the country and were finally donated to the Peabody Museum of Harvard University."

The Spanish section of the sign contains more information, including repeating that Thompson illegally had sent the artifacts to the Peabody, but then adds, "Unfortunately most of those treasures received some damage in the way they were taken out from the bottom of the well." There was no inventory of exactly what was taken from the cenote, according to the sign, but those items that are known today included objects made of ceramic, stone, metal, wood, shell, and textiles, as well as the remains of humans and animals. "Part of that what was taken out by Thompson was returned to the country, which at the present time they are in the museums of Mexico City and Mérida, capital of the state of Yucatan."

Mexican archaeologists, who must have been responsible for the sign, have had a hard-on for Edward Thompson since the 1920s. But it was the last couple of sentences that caught my attention: *"En las temporadas de 1960-61 y en 1967-68 se hicieron renovados intentos de arrancar al Cenote el resto de las ofrendas, pero ni con las técnicas más modernas se pudo evitar que el 'Pozo de los Itzaes' siguiera guardando muchos de sus secreto."* Translated it reads, "During the seasons of 1960-61 and 1967-68 there were renewed attempts to extract from the cenote the rest of the [Maya] offerings, but despite using the most modern techniques, the 'Well of the Itzaes' continues to protect many of its secrets."

I had not been aware that anyone other than Thompson had excavated the well. Fortunately the local library proves once again to be my friend. The second expedition was the subject of a book, *The Well of Sacrifice*, by Donald Ediger. Ediger had been a young newspaper reporter in his twenties when he was plucked from the Miami Herald to write about the 1967-68 expedition. The great thing about writers is that they end up on the internet, which makes them easy to find. I track down Ediger in France and we exchange e-mail. He promises to talk to me once he returns to the United States.

In the meantime I devour *The Well of Sacrifice*, a very readable account of the second expedition that also includes a lot of detail about the first. Both were the brainchild of Mexican Pablo Bush Romero, who was the quintessential hyphenate—a newspaper recently refers to him as an "impresario-hunter-archaeologist-diver-explorer." According to Ediger's book, Bush played the part to the hilt. "[He] looked like a hero...the classical picture of someone who goes on archaeological expeditions. His shoes were...white, and so were the socks that covered his legs to the knees. His shirt, too, was white, and he wore a pith helmet."

Bush Romero was born in Mexico City in 1905 and had made his fortune by building one of the largest Ford dealerships in Mexico. In 1958, he organized the *Club de Exploraciones y Deportes Acuaticos de Mexico* (CEDAM), a loose organization of explorers and divers—"men of goodwill"—to search the waters of Mexico for treasure and turn it over to the Mexican federal government. CEDAM's purpose, as Bush saw it, was to thwart the modern day pirates who came to Mexico to "avail themselves of treasures from the ancient Maya and Aztec civilizations." CEDAM, he said, "places the sport of diving and the talents of its members at the service of country, science, and humanity."

Bush's CEDAM searched for shipwrecks, primarily in the waters around Yucatán and recovered many valuable artifacts. But much of what they did smacked of publicity stunts. CEDAM claimed to have found the long-lost grave of the pirate Jean Lafitte, the hero of the Battle of New Orleans, on the northern coast of Yucatan; in the late 1980s, he was the subject of a *New Yorker* story when he tried to recover the skull of the hero of the Mexican Revolution, Francisco "Pancho" Villa, which the Yale Skull and Bones society reportedly was using in its arcane rituals.

Even before he founded CEDAM, Bush always had his eyes upon the treasure of the Sacred Cenote. In 1954, he and a team of divers attempted the cenote but recovered no artifacts because the water was too thick with algae to see. One of the divers dropped his flashlight and even though it cast a bright beam, it disappeared out of sight within seconds in the murky water. Despite that failure, Bush Romero was certain that the secrets of the well could be cracked. After consulting with other diving enthusiasts, he decided the best way to excavate the cenote was with an underwater vacuum cleaner known as an airlift.

In the late 1950s, Bush persuaded the National Geographic Society and INAH, the federal agency with oversight over the ruins of the Chichén Itzá, to fund a joint expedition. The INAH man assigned to Chichén Itzá to oversee the project for INAH had the improbable name of William J. Folan. According to Ediger's book, he went by the name "Willie" and was from the United States. Folan is alive and I find him in Campeche, capital of the state by the same name south of Yucatán, where he is the director of the *Centro de Investigaciones Historicas y Sociales at the Universidad Autonoma de Campeche*. His name in the university directory is listed in the traditional manner in the Latin world as Dr. William Folan Higgins, the latter being his mother's maiden name.

Folan speaks to me from his office in the Román Piña Chan Center at the university. He's seventy-five, an age when most gringos are retired and has been director of the center for the past twenty-five years. An expatriate of the United States, in 1961 he was the INAH archaeologist in charge of the Cenote Sagrado project. "I was the field director," he says. "When I got there, they made me the director," he adds and laughs. Although he is suspicious of my motives for interviewing him, he throws himself into it with relish. I can't get over the fact that he is an American and has been involved in Mexican archaeology in leadership roles for longer than I have been alive. He reminds me of Peter Schmidt, a German-born archaeologist who has been working for the Mexican government at Chichén Itzá since the 1970s—another survivor, a stranger in a strange land. Folan has found a home in Mexico.

Folan says he had problems with the Cenote Sagrado project from the beginning. The airlift was too big. "They were misusing what could have been a useful tool," Folan says. "Smaller diameter hoses would have been more effective, particularly when it comes to gathering certain types of artifacts and skeletal material. It was an experiment," he says, and one that decided for Folan that airlifts should not be used for underwater archaeology.

Pablo Bush had no expertise with an airlift, so he enlisted an expert, Virginia diver Norman Scott who had learned to use the airlift during the excavation of the sunken city of Port Royal in Jamaica. At Chichén Itzá Scott's team recovered thousands of artifacts, similar to what Thompson had found more than fifty years previous: human bones, carved jade figures and beads, copper bells, copal incense, and pottery, whole and in shards.

There were some unusual items that turned up. A contorted figure of a dancer made of rubber, believed to be one of the oldest items of that substance ever found. Five matching rings, made of copper covered in gold foil; and a bone knife with a handle of carved glyphs and covered in gold foil. The only solid gold items were two tiny beads. The airlift also recovered the flashlight that had been lost in the 1954 dive. The excavation of the Cenote Sagrado ran for four months, "and then, unexpectedly and at the height of our enthusiasm, we received orders to suspend work," according to an account by Bush. INAH staff "believed that the airlift procedure was damaging the fragile pieces and made it difficult to assess the correct historical stratigraphy of the salvaged objects," he wrote. Folan concurs, stating he and others at INAH believed the airlift was harming the recovered artifacts.

The expedition ended earlier than expected, but Bush was not discouraged. "I am of the same opinion as Thompson that what we salvaged represents less than ten percent of the enormous treasure," Bush wrote. "We will return some day, God willing."

William Folan, right, and wife Lynda

THE PAST

WILLARD AND MORLEY

THOMPSON RESUMED DREDGING THE SACRED CENOTE within days of sending the letter to Salisbury's executors. Even though he had lost his patron of more than twenty years, life goes on, especially when you receive a fresh start. Thompson had entered a new phase of his life and he kicked it off by planting two seeds of friendship that would not come to fruit for almost twenty years: the aforementioned Sylvanus Morley and an "enthusiastic amateur," T.A. Willard.

Willard showed up unannounced at the Hacienda Chichén in 1906. He came bearing a letter of introduction from Thompson's good friend in Mérida, Mrs. James, so his arrival was welcome. Willard was from Cleveland and knew Mrs. James's husband, William James, who was one of the major importers of U.S. goods to Yucatán, including products from Willard's company. From Mrs. James, Willard had learned of the dredging of the Sacred Well and upon meeting Thompson, offered his assistance. Thompson instead offered Willard join him for lunch.

After the meal, Thompson brought out a small, cloth bag from which he produced a ring. He handed it to Willard and urged him to try it on. It fit perfectly. Thompson told him it was the first pure gold ring found in the cenote. The ring sealed some kind of deal between them. The next day Willard joined Thompson at the Sacred Well and slogged through the buckets of mud brought up from its bottom.

Thompson let Willard wear the ring the entire time he was at Chichén Itzá. Willard loved it so much he went to Mérida and had a copy made. When it came back he was delighted to see the jeweler had made an exact replica. It was so exact that neither he nor Thompson could tell which was the original and which was the copy. The owner of Chichén Itzá gathered the rings up in the cup of his palms and shook them like dice. He let one of them fall on the table. "That one is yours, since I know of no better way to decide the question," he said. To his dying day, Willard never knew if he had the original or its modern duplicate.

After a few weeks, the time had come for Willard go back to the United States. But he had found his life's passion. He returned to the Yucatán every year for the rest of his life, usually spending more than a dozen weeks, many of them at Chichén Itzá.

Thompson and Willard had much in common. Both were storytellers. Both were independent in thought and action. Both were dreamers and visionaries, particularly when it came to business schemes. There was one, overriding difference: few of Thompson's ideas made money; Willard's record was somewhat better.

"When I made my first trip there...I was employed as an electrical engineer," Willard recalled several decades later. "Due to certain changes being made by the company I was granted a two months' leave of absence and naturally went to Yucatán." Willard, for some reason, was understating his role and just exactly who he was. To say he was "employed as an electrical engineer" was like saying Thomas Edison was head of research and development at the Edison Company. Since 1902 Willard had owned his own company and his business was batteries. He had to return to the United States because he was preparing to introduce his product into a completely new industry—the "automobile," and Willard was certain that his battery could not only light the night lamps, but even replace the crank to start the engine.

Willard and Thompson became lifelong friends; Thompson's relationship with Sylvanus Morley, the Harvard-trained archaeologist, was a friendship, yet it was far more complicated than that. Each man would use the other to further their careers and bring worldwide fame.

Morley, known as "Vay" to his friends, arrived at Chichén in 1907. He was a small, furtive young man, who would later earn the nickname, "The Little Hummingbird," for the way he would flit around an archaeological dig. He spoke in a high-pitched, nasal bleat that would scare birds in the trees when he got excited. Thompson was away from Chichén when Morley showed up, but Vay settled in quickly, helped by one of Thompson's daughters. The two of them hit it off and one evening even enjoyed a supper of pickled onions and crackers while watching a romantic sunset from the top of the massive Las Monjas.

When Thompson arrived at Chichén, he led the neophyte archaeologist on a tour of the site, spinning one story after another. Morley joined Thompson at the lip of the cenote as the dredge retrieved loads of mud, rocks, leaves, branches, and artifacts. During one of his watches, he found the handle to a dagger, carved in the shape of two entwined serpents. The year before Thompson had recovered a blade of chert, a flint-like substance typically found in limestone, that had traces of red pigment and copal. The two pieces matched perfectly. Like Tozzer before him, Morley spirited the artifacts out of Mexico and to the Peabody Museum.

Thompson was a man in charge of his destiny. He had made one of the most important discoveries in the Americas. He owned Chichén Itzá free and clear for the first time. And he now had an ample cash flow, thanks to his consul salary and his contract to dredge the cenote, both of which paid him $2,000 per year. There was no way it could last. By 1908, there were discussions going on at the highest levels of the State Department about replacing Thompson and he would have been fired if not for the personal intervention by Massachusetts Senator Henry Cabot Lodge and Charles Bowditch. The State Department sent an agent to perform a surprise inspection of Thompson's consulate offices in Progreso who, predictably, found them to be in "deplorable condition," and Thompson nowhere to be found. Thompson's superiors reprimanded the consul for his neglect, but allowed Thompson to retain his position. The reprieve was short-lived and it was only a matter of time before he would be replaced. It did not bode well that within a few months there would be a new presidential administration and neither of the two candidates had the strong Harvard affiliation that Theodore Roosevelt had.

Also in 1908, Bowditch decided that the Peabody Museum had received enough artifacts, so he declined to renew Thompson's contract to dredge the Sacred Cenote. It didn't help that the vein appeared tapped out. "At last the dredge bit only on rock and boulders, against which the steel jaws made no headway," Thompson wrote in his autobiography. "Again and again the bucket came up empty and with its jaws twisted and bent."

Bowditch did not abandon Thompson completely. He hired him to do some minor archaeological work at Chichén Itzá, creating moulds of lintels, but for a far smaller stipend than he had been receiving to do the dredging. With his consulate salary now at risk, Thompson's future prospects for supporting himself looked grim.

Just when circumstances were their most desperate, Thompson stumbled across a solution that he saw would solve all his problems. And as usual, it would be one that would leave him in a deeper hole than he had been in before.

Thompson had been dipping from the same financial well for two decades. The time had come to find a new patron and, as luck would have it, one showed up almost on his doorstep. In September 1908 Thompson was back in New England, enjoying the last vestiges of summer at his cottage on Cape Cod overlooking Buzzards Bay. One of his neighbors, Boston lawyer Walter Austin, attended a party where Thompson mentioned that he was putting together a private expedition to continue exploration of the cenote, one he swore would net more gold and carved jade than his previous forays. And all he would need was $4,000, for which he was seeking investors.

Austin was intrigued and asked Thompson not to seek any investors until they could speak privately. A couple of weeks later, Thompson contacted the lawyer and told him he had managed to scrape together enough of his own funds to bring down the required investment total to $2,800. "Under the peculiar circumstances that you and Mrs. Austin understand perhaps better than anybody else it is a somewhat delicate matter for me to personally undertake," Thompson wrote Austin. He did not elaborate upon those peculiar circumstances, but went on to write, "In case we do succeed in arranging the matter I shall ask you to allow me in due time to present Mrs. Austin with the necklace made as she designed but from 'material' taken from the Sacred Well itself. It will thus be one of the only three necklaces of the kind in the world. The other two of different make and pattern belonging to my daughters." Thompson also agreed to send Austin any gold, copper, flint, and jade he recovered "as a guarantee that the funds so kindly provided shall be returned in case of my death meanwhile."

That Thompson could die exploring the cenote was not some boilerplate legal language. His intention was to risk his life in search of artifacts. Thompson was certain an untold number of smaller, heavier artifacts were passing through the giant jaws of the dredge. "There must be hands at the bottom of the well—not the dead hands of pitiful maidens, but live hands of sturdy men to explore every inch of the uneven rocky bottom," he wrote in his autobiography. He would dive the cenote and even though he was more than fifty years old, he planned to do it himself.

Norman Scott

THE PRESENT

SACRED WELL, ROUND TWO

AFTER THE CONTROVERSY OF THE 1961 EXPEDITION, one would assume that the last person who would be allowed anywhere near the Sacred Cenote would be Pablo Bush. But as he promised, seven years later Bush returned once again with Norman Scott and this time with a bigger, more ambitious plan to coax the cenote to give up its artifacts.

I'm thrilled to learn that Scott is also among the living and still in the treasure-hunting business. When I catch up to him at his home in Florida, he is on his way to Austria to search for Nazi gold in a mountain lake. Scott was one of the principals behind the 1961 and 1967 cenote projects. He considers those two expeditions into the Sacred Well the crowning achievements of his career. In some respects, they pioneered new approaches to running treasure-hunting expeditions, he tells me.

Although Pablo Bush was wealthy, he had no intention of using his own money to explore the Cenote Sagrado. He appointed Scott to find funding for the first expedition and Scott says it was he who convinced Melvin Payne, vice president of the National Geographic Society, to underwrite the first project's expenses. Unfortunately Payne and Bush did not get along. "Mel Payne's attitude was that the Society was putting up the money, so they wanted to have control of the operation and get the credit," remembers Scott. "Pablo Bush Romero, a staunch nationalistic Mexican, said 'No.'" The struggle of wills strained Bush's relationship with the National Geographic Society for years. Even the article that appeared in *National Geographic Magazine* was split—one half written by Eusebio Dávalos Hurtado, director of INAH, and the other half written by National Geographic.

Folan agrees that Bush was a source of friction. "I liked certain aspects of Bush Romero's personality," he says diplomatically. According to Folan, another source of conflict was Norman Scott. Scott agrees there were clashes, but says they were not between him and others, but between the U.S. and Mexico. Before the diving began on that first expedition, Scott's team sat down to dinner with the divers from the Mexican Navy who were participating in the expedition. The Mexican divers explained that for the first week they would converse in English, but after that they would only speak and answer in Spanish. They left no doubt that this was to be a Mexican expedition.

Yet despite all the troubles and hurt feelings from the first expedition, Bush managed to convince authorities to let him have another shot at the Sacred Well. I e-mail don Fernando about what he remembers and he tells me that Bush Romero in 1967 knew better than to involve the National Geographic Society again. The first expedition had destroyed that relationship. He still needed the permission of INAH. The federal agency would not approve his request of a permit unless the property's owner said it would be okay. The owner of the Sacred Well at that time happened to be my friend, don Fernando, who inherited it upon his father's passing. "INAH instructed Pablo to acquire, in writing, permission from me to explore the well at Chichén," recalls Fernando. Bush, he says, was incredulous. *Seek the acquiescence of the Barbachanos? Impossible!* "He could not believe he had to come to my home and request my permission."

But come he did—reluctantly. He opened the meeting with don Fernando by launching into a tirade about how unnecessary he thought it was. "Pablo, I want to do some archaeological digging in back of your Ford dealership in Mexico City," Fernando recalls telling him. "Would INAH authorize me without your permission? Be sensible, Pablo. Chichén is my private property, including all of its ancient buildings. The well is no different."

Fernando says he agreed to allow Bush to explore the Sacred Well again on one condition: "I want the majority of the finds to remain at Chichén and be lodged at the museum my mother intends to build there," he told him. Bush Romero agreed and with that began what has been called the largest archaeological expedition in North America.

On Sept. 18, 1967, a caravan of twenty-one trucks crawled through the archaeological zone at Chichén Itzá. The air was wet with rain, the remains of Hurricane Beulah. More than one person noted the irony that an exploration of the subterranean home of the Maya rain god Chaac had begun with the mother of all rainstorms. The trucks crept along the ancient sacbe, which although a millennium old still provided sure footing for the giant tractor-trailer trucks. Donald Ediger described the scene in his book: "The vehicles now parked amid the ruins, the tons of equipment which they carried and the men who drove them, were here for one purpose—to break the seal that nature had imposed and to excavate the Sacred Well, thereby opening the time capsule of the Mayas."

Ediger calls me upon his return from France. He is impressed that Scott is still alive, for the last time he was in contact with him, the diver was battling a brain tumor. Ediger tells me he remembers much about the expedition. Once again, Scott had been called upon to raise funds for it. "To finance an expedition like that he needed a lot of money and he did what had to be done to get it," Ediger says. The cost was in excess of one million dollars U.S., making it the most expensive underwater expedition in the Americas. The bulk of the financing came from a thirty-nine-year-old Texas oilman, F. Kirk Johnson. Johnson and Norman Scott had been partners on several treasure-hunting expeditions in the Bahamas. Johnson liked to chase the fantastic and the unusual. In the 1950s he had financed several expeditions in search of the Abominable Snowman in the Himalayas.

According to Scott, Johnson did not have to foot the entire bill. Bush and Scott managed to find sponsorships for every part of their plan. The trucks and other vehicles were donated by the Ford Motor Company; chemicals came from the Purex Corporation; cameras and lenses from the Nikon-Ehrenreich Photo Optical Company. Even don Fernando kicked in for housing and fed members of the expedition at the Hacienda Chichén and the Mayaland Hotel. These sponsors got plenty of publicity, for in addition to Ediger's book, several magazines—*Look*, *Argosy*, *Saga*—all planned articles on the expedition. Doubleday agreed to pay $75,000 for the rights to publish Edger's book, Norman Scott tells me, which at the time reportedly was the highest advance paid for a non-celebrity book. A film crew had also come along to shoot a television documentary.

"I decided I could sell an expedition in advance to the media," Scott recalls. "I'm the one who pioneered that in this country. That's the only way to do expeditions. Unless you've got a Bill Gates behind you, someone puts up the front money with the expectation that they have a chance to get it back. The one security is the media. Especially in Mexico, because we knew going in we weren't going to get the artifacts."

Scott says he found an investor who was willing to put $125,000 into the expedition in exchange for whatever Scott could collect from the media. Doubleday, Look magazine and all the others paid handsomely for the privilege to report the story, to the tune of a quarter-million dollars. "He essentially doubled his money," Scott says.

Since Scott's team could not use the airlift, they come with two strategies for getting to the well's artifacts. The would first attempt to pump it dry; failing that, they would clarify the water with chlorine so divers could find artifacts as easily as if they were on the bottom of a swimming pool. What made approvals from INAH easier this time was that there were approaches that originally had been proposed by a Mexican engineer, Edgar Espejo Evie, in 1954. The concept had been further refined by Willie Folan, who had not been invited to be part of this expedition. "I got back on the project," Folan tells me in our interview. "I had a lot of people backing me up." According to Folan, INAH director Roman Piña Chan and other officials wanted him at Chichén Itzá, including at least one who threatened to resign. Pablo Bush was dead set against Folan joining but he had no choice. When Norman Scott arrived in Merida the first thing Pablo Bush said to him was, "You kept the governor waiting for a whole day and Willie Folan is in town." Folan and I laugh.

The expedition brought a crane weighing thirty-five tons to lift equipment in and out of the cenote. They set up a pump and several hoses to draw water from the cenote and expel it into a length of aluminum pipe that terminated at a shallow depression some thirty meters away. The operation hired more than a hundred of the local Maya, many of whom believed there was no way the well could be pumped dry. The Maya, according to Ediger, believed that Chaac, the water god, would return the water to the well. It may not have been superstition but common sense.

The pump initially worked. The first day the water level in the cenote fell by a foot, exposing "Thompson's Bank," a muddy ledge where Thompson had disposed of some of the tailings from his dredging sixty years before. Folan and INAH field director Victor Segovia Pinto, along with Scott, explored the bank and found a stone carved with a Toltec design. It was the first artifact of the expedition. The INAH archaeologists thought that Thompson had missed a lot of treasure during his dredging and that by excavating the bank they would find what he had left behind. That was until the ground started to boil.

Water bubbled up next to the well. Scott ordered the pump halted, but he was too late. A wave of brown water exploded out of the brush and nearly carried one of the crew over the side into the cenote. The pump water had saturated the water table and the excess flowed to the lowest ground it could find—the cenote. The pumping was halted until pipe could be laid to a new discharge site, a former cenote 250 meters away.

Pumping resumed, but the long discharge pipe sagged at some of the joints. INAH's Segovia and a crew of Maya were charged with leveling the pipe. With every new task, the Maya were in high spirits, even though they did not understand what the crazy gringos were up to. They laughed and joked as they worked. That was until Segovia, while adjusting one of the pipe joints, received a blast of water in the face. "*Mejen kisin, Chaac!*" he cursed, the Maya equivalent of calling the god Chaac an asshole. Segovia instantly regretted his epithet, for the mood of the Mayan workers soured. From that point forward they went through their labors sullenly.

A few days later a pipe carrying chlorine froze and burst, spewing deadly gas into the cenote where a dozen men were working. The expedition had been pumping the chemical into the cenote to clarify the water. As clorine began to replace oxygen in the air above the cenote, the crane operator began hauling men as quickly as he could. Just as the last man was brought to the top, the engine in the crane stopped. It had run out of gas.

Several men were hospitalized, but none died. After that incident, the Maya refused to work in the cenote. "So I took two of the prettiest girls we had, Ann Campbell and Doris Dowd, lowered them into the cenote and had them frolic in the water and shame the Maya Indians," Scott recalls. "They went back to work and after that I didn't have a problem."

The expedition resumed excavating Thompson's Bank and feeding chlorine into the water. Within days the green, murky waters of the cenote became as transparent as glass. The divers brought up artifacts from the cenote bottom. Scott and his team recovered a great mass of treasure, but there was nothing that surpassed the finds of Edward Thompson or of the 1961 expedition. Divers found more skeletons, hyperbolically estimated to come from 400 individuals, and jade pieces, gold rings, vases, and thousands and thousands of sherds. Everything was readied for shipment to Mexico City where it was to be catalogued by INAH.

On most days, Scott had to walk by the guardhouse at the main entrance to the archaeological zone. There, rusting in the bushes, was the orange peel bucket dredge and winch Thompson had used sixty years before. Scott told Ediger that seeing that dredge every day was the hardest part of the expedition for him, because it reminded him how much Thompson accomplished with only a fraction of the equipment, personnel, and funds.

I tell Scott that like Thompson before him, archaeologists today think the techniques he used damaged artifacts, especially the use of the airlift in the first expedition. "That's bullshit," Scott says. The airlift only removes detritus from around the artifact "and the artifact is brought up by the diver," he says. No artifacts ever went up the airlift, because there was a screen over the intake hose. "The archaeologists didn't like it because they didn't understand it and they were jealous of it because it could cover an area of excavation faster and more thoroughly than divers blowing the sand away by fanning.

"Look, there are two schools of thought in archaeology and they still prevail today although they are getting closer," Scott continues. "You have the treasure hunter and you have the archaeologist. The archaeologist is of the opinion you remove the artifacts *in situ*, regardless of how much money it takes, and if you don't have the money, you let it sit for another 200 years. The proper treasure hunter says, you should always have an archaeologist on hand, but you bring the material up so you can learn from it and preserve it and let the general public observe it in museums.

"The archaeologist is very jealous of the treasure hunter because the treasure hunter usually has more money than the archaeologist. Archaeologists depend on funding and grants, whereas the treasure hunter gets the businessman to finance his expedition. I've always advocated and spoken around the nation that the archaeologist and the treasure hunter should work together so they can accomplish the end result."

Of all his accomplishments, Scott is most proud of the Chichén Itzá expeditions. A few years ago, he took his girlfriend to Yucatán. There, at the lip of the Sacred Cenote, next to a small temple, he got down on one knee and proposed. His future wife knew how important the expedition into the Sacred Well had been. "She had seen the film made by CBS, seen the articles, seen the pictures of the objects we removed," Scott says. "But when we got down there, there wasn't one, single mention of the expedition. And the only picture from the expedition was in the men's room."

To Norman Scott, it isn't enough. "It's their country and their cultural heritage, but when someone comes in there to do something for them where they don't have to pay a penny...the fact is, that had I not gone down there, I doubt it would have been done to this date. I got paid, but the only thing that matters to a man in my position is recognition for the work I did."

I tell Scott that during my recent visit to Chichén Itzá I had learned that one of the INAH researchers was looking for photographs of the artifacts taken from the cenote during the 1961 and 1967 expeditions. "I have sixteen thousand photographs," Scott says. "Tell these people you are in touch with I would be happy to make available, free of charge, a representative sample of photos of the artifacts. If they want to send someone up here, they can sit here in the film room and go over them. But what I want is recognition for the Chichén expedition, recognition for us and for the Mexican divers."

That recognition was not forthcoming. At the end of Ediger's book, he describes the last night of the expedition. Segovia of INAH shares some good news. The Barbachano family, he says, has agreed to donate a sum to construct a museum at Chichén Itzá that would exhibit the artifacts they had recovered. "The Yucatecans were especially happy over the news because they had become tired of seeing relics of their past shipped off to Mexico," Ediger recalls. "Now these would stay in Yucatán and the treasure from the well would become an attraction to both students and tourists. When Scott heard the news about the museum, I think he began to become aware of the true value of what he had found."

Today there is no museum of artifacts at Chichén Itzá. I ask don Fernando what happened to it. "The items taken from the well were supposed to be sent to Mexico City for classification," says an exasperated Fernando. "It was a lie. Most of the items were stolen. The museum was never built—to lodge what?"

I ask archaeologists in Mexico if Fernando's accusation is true. The pottery fragments were the subject of a paper by archaeologist Eduardo Pérez de Heredia Puente, but beyond that, little has been published about the rest of the artifacts found and there has never been an exhibition of the artifacts from either 1961 or 1967. No one I speak with seems to know where they are stored.

Then I find my smoking gun. During an Internet search I stumble across a newspaper article profiling one of the American divers from 1961. In a photograph he holds one of the five gold/copper rings recovered in the first expedition. Later one of the rings (or possibly the same one) shows up on an online auction site, although the sale mysteriously is cancelled.

I confront Norman Scott, who tells me one of the Mexican archaeologists let the dive team have the rings. The journalist part of my nature is jubilant, but the human being part of me is more than a little sad and disappointed that the only rings found in the 1961 expedition were spirited out of the country. Five nearly identical rings, crafted with a level of skill previously unknown of in the Maya world. I've seen pictures of hundreds of items taken from the Cenote Sagrado, including rings and none can compare to the workmanship of these five rings—

And then I laugh. The expedition just happens to find *five identical rings* of superior craftsmanship? And these were some of the few gilded artifacts recovered? *Puh-lease!*

THE PAST

TO THE DEPTHS

PABLO BUSH ROMERO AND CEDAM were not the first to dive the Sacred Cenote. Edward H. Thompson from the beginning had wanted to go underwater. "With Thompson, in our opinion, underwater archaeology was born," wrote Pablo Bush in a later memoir. "His work was deduction and precise prognostication and planning, and he found what he was seeking."

Months before he began dredging, Thompson sought out a professional diver in Boston to teach him how to breathe beneath the depths using diving equipment. Thompson learned how to put on the rubber-lined, canvas diving suit, the shoes with heavy iron soles, the heavy lead necklace, and the oversized, copper diving helmet. He learned how to operate the equipment underwater and, more importantly, how to teach others to operate the pump on the surface that provided fresh air to the diver.

At the end of the first season of dredging, Thompson had approached Salisbury and Bowditch about diving the Sacred Cenote. The two men agreed to finance another season of dredging, but implored Thompson to abandon the idea of diving. The explorer agreed, but only if he could apply the savings from the submarine work to bolster the crew working on the dredge. Thompson had postponed what he figured would be inevitable, and the inevitable arrived in 1908, thanks to Walter Austin. Thompson had finished his work for Charles Bowditch in July and Bowditch ordered Thompson to sell the dredge. Thompson pleaded that Yucatán was in the midst of a recession and therefore he could not get a fair price for it. While that may have been true, it also provided Thompson with a convenient excuse to continue using it on behalf of Walter Austin.

Before Thompson returned to Yucatán, he sent Austin a contract. In exchange for $1,500, Austin would receive one-third of the proceeds of the sale of the cenote collection. Thompson would get to keep any pottery sherds or broken jades that he found for his own "scientific purposes." In a show of good faith, Thompson sent Austin two boxes of "fine worked jades," six gold bells, two gold idols, two gold masks, gold fragments, a box of flints, and a box of "various amulets."

Thompson hired Nicolas, a Greek diver from Florida who had relocated to Cozumel to work the burgeoning sponge industry. When Nicolas tested the diving suits and equipment that Thompson had acquired, he found "dangerous defects" that would have failed at the depths of the Sacred Cenote. The diver returned to Cozumel to acquire sturdier diving gear. By April everything was ready. The diver and all the apparatus arrived safely at the Hacienda. Thompson also imported a flat bottom scow and managed to get it over the side of the cenote and into the water without sinking it.

Nicolas was an experienced diver and had in his youth had dived for statues and other antiquities off the shore of Greece. However, diving the clear, warm waters of the Aegean did not prepare him for the murky and frigid waters of the Cenote Sagrado. After several dives, he told Thompson he could not reach the bottom for it was littered with tree trunks and boulders. Thompson ordered the Maya to dredge the dive area to clear the debris, but this made the footing treacherous, and Nicolas reported mini-avalanches of loose boulders and stumps. After several days of failure, Nicolas announced he was quitting. Thompson suggested an alternative plan: Why not share the load and work a three-hour shift with another diver—Thompson. Together they would guide the dredge so that it was no longer blindly scooping at random, but instead focusing on areas that appeared most productive. Nicolas thought Thompson was crazy. The job was not safe for a professional diver—what chance did a fifty-year-old inexperienced man have? Thompson was "rather obstinate" and refused to take no for an answer. "I soon proved to him that I was as much a man underwater as on the surface."

On the morning of the appointed day, Thompson, Nicolas, and two Maya workers "rode" the dredge's orange-peel bucket down to the scow that carried the diving suits, hoses, and pump. Thompson and Nicolas stripped, soaped their wrists, and slid into the diving suits. They fitted the helmets, thirty pounds each, over their heads and peered out of the goggle-shaped eyeholes. Last came the weights and the canvas, iron-soled boots. "I waddled to the edge of the craft and clambered down the rope ladder about as gracefully as a turtle falling off a log," Thompson wrote in his autobiography.

He released the last rung and floated down into the void. The surrounding waters glowed yellow, darkened to green, and then a purplish black. "After that, I was in utter darkness," Thompson wrote. At the bottom of the cenote, the water became a black slurry. Particulates were so thick that Thompson's undersea flashlight was useless—he could see nothing. The cenote was approximately eleven meters deep with another nine meters of mud, tree debris, and stones. The dredge had removed the mud and organic waste, but many of the stones were either too heavy or too slippery to be raised. Thompson thought the rocks had come from the ruins at the lip of the cenote and they had either tumbled or had been pushed over the side. Their first task as divers was to chain these stones so the derrick could lift them out. The men worked together, unable to see the rocks or each other. When they needed to communicate, they would touch their helmets together so they could speak. One after another, the crane lifted the heavy rocks, which as Thompson had suspected were quarried stones, many covered with carvings.

The divers then focused their attention on finding treasure. Wrote Thompson:

> *I remember distinctly my sensations as my fingers touched upon curious small objects like coins, small nuts, and rings. I could hardly contain my curiosity as I tucked them into my pouch, and my eagerness to get up to light and air to examine them was almost irresistible. When I had collected perhaps twenty or thirty I gave the signal and started upward. Before my diving-dress had been more than half removed I plunged my chilled fingers into the dripping pouch and drew out beautiful embossed rings, small bells of copper, and several bells of pure gold. There were bells and ornaments and medallions of gold repoussé and gold filigree, of exquisite design and craftsmanship. There were lovely carved jade beads and other objects of jade. Just as truly as any mining prospector, I had struck gold, but gold tremendously more valuable than raw nuggets; for, whatever might be the mere intrinsic value of my golden finds, each bit was in reality beyond price.*

The greatest dangers facing the divers were the cold and the water pressure. The two men could only dive for a couple hours at a time and when emerging from the cenote "our lips were blue and our bodies covered with goose-flesh and trembling with chill." The ill effects from the cold water could be cured by blankets and hot coffee, but the injuries from the press of water would cripple Thompson for the rest of his life. During one dive, Thompson, distracted by some object he had found, forgot to exhaust the air pumped into his suit. He became buoyant and shot to the surface. His helmet banged against the bottom of the scow, startling the crew that was working the pump. Thompson scrambled out from under the craft and managed to raise his helmeted head over the gunwale. The Maya yanked off the helmet and were relieved to see don Eduardo was alive and was laughing. That part of the story seems doubtful, for Thompson says that when he shot to the surface, the change in pressure blew out his eardrums, resulting in a loss of hearing that would plague him for the rest of his life.

Working in tandem, Thompson and Nicolas guided the dredge to a small treasure trove of gold—dart shafts and points, bells, circlets, a mask and amulet, and more. Thompson estimated their combined value at $15,000 and a similar amount for the items already in Austin's safekeeping. "If we hold them until the right one appears as a purchaser they are very liable to bring a sum much in excess of these figures." Thompson wrote.

After several days, Thompson was satisfied that his collaboration with Austin was over. The "Austin/Thompson Collection" had 100 gold objects, thirty carved jade figures and pendants, and fifty artifacts of copper. The archaeologist wrote Austin of his future plans. He intended to continue diving, calling it a "divinely given chance." A recent increase in his consular salary now gave him the resources to continue on his own, "but I feel that it would be ungrateful for me not to allow you to continue with me to the end of the last chapter if you so desire."

Austin smelled a rat. He believed Thompson was cutting him out as a partner. Thompson reassured him that was not the case, just that the work Austin had paid for had been completed. There was now another phase ahead. Thompson explained that he wanted to install a steam-powered dredge, one that would not collapse the walls of the cenote, and use it to remove the debris blocking access to the bottom so divers could get to it safely.

Austin continued to be apprehensive about this new development, despite Thompson's assurance that the banker's initial investment was safe. When the entire collection was sold, Thompson promised, Austin would get back his money off the top; the profit would be split between the two men as they had earlier agreed.

What Thompson had neglected to mention was that he had convinced his longtime patron Charles Bowditch to finance the next round of diving. Bowditch also paid for the steam engine to power the dredge. Thompson also withheld the news that the ax had come from the State Department and in June he was fired as consul.

Then the Bowditch contract went sour. Thompson reported to Bowditch that the vibration of the steam-powered dredge threatened to collapse the edge of the cenote. Diving with Nicolas had been dangerous, but diving alone proved foolhardy and only resulted in a small number of artifacts recovered. Thompson soon abandoned the practice and returned to working the hand-cranked dredge, with the same poor results. The time had come to call it quits. Except there was that little matter of the Austins.

Walter Austin continued to pressure Thompson to sell the collection. In late 1910, Thompson wrote Austin that he had an offer of $6,000 for the collection from the Peabody Museum. He invited the Austins to visit Chichén and, no doubt to Thompson's dismay, they took him up on it and began making preparations to visit in early 1911. Walter Austin asked

Thompson what kind of guns he should bring. "Rifles are almost useless here," Thompson told him. "A good shotgun, your Mauser pistol, and suitable ammunition for both will be what [you] will need." Thompson asked Austin to purchase a couple of cheap, single-barreled, breech-loading shotguns and ammunition. "I would like them to give as presents to some of my native hunters," he said. "By the time that you get down here we will have the trunks and stones that have drifted in out of the way and we will be able to let you see how things look as they come up out of the mud after a sleep of a thousand years."

The Austins arrived in Progreso in early 1911, but Thompson was at Chichén so he sent an associate to meet and entertain them. The couple visited Uxmal and enjoyed Carnaval in Mérida before heading to Chichén Itzá. Thompson had his personal volan, the one with the initial "E" on the front and back, meet them when they got off the train in Dzitas. He warned them to make certain their belongings were secured, otherwise they will "fly up in your face." Thompson promised to meet them at the wide gate entrance with liniments and lotions. "Then prepare, oh audacious man! Prepare for what is coming to you."

When they reached the hacienda, Thompson made them comfortable, then took them on a tour of the ruins. At the Cenote Sagrado there was no diving, but the dredge was working, so the Austins watched Thompson's Maya workers haul up several loads and then helped sort through the mud.

During breakfast on one day of the visit, a rider thundered up the road to announce that the railroad outside Dzitas on the way to Valladolid had been blown up by sublevados who "were marching down" upon the Hacienda Chichén. Thompson's face grew serious, but he told the Austins that if indeed they were coming he would take them mules and grain for their horses. The rebel Maya would accept the items, Thompson said, and in return issue a receipt that, unfortunately, "is not worth the paper it is written on." But the Hacienda Chichén would not be molested, Thompson promised.

As the Caste War had been declared officially over seven years earlier, it must have seemed unsettling to the Austins that rebel Maya were still wandering the lands near Chichén Itzá. The Austins remained on edge for several more days, but there was no sign of insurgents. Nonetheless, when they departed Chichén in the volan, Walter Austin lay on the thin mattress with a loaded revolver hidden beneath him.

Back in the United States, Walter Austin awaited word of his share of the sale of the Austin-Thompson collection. Several weeks passed and, after hearing nothing, he contacted the Peabody Museum. The director, Frederic Ward Putnam, told Austin that he knew nothing about any purchase of the collection, much less for $6,000, but he was aware that Charles Bowditch had given Edward Thompson $500 toward the collection, which the museum was holding in good faith.

Austin had had enough. He explained to Putnam that the collection belonged to him and he would come to collect it from the Peabody, unless he received his half of the $6,000 he had been promised. It took almost a month, but Peabody or Bowditch scraped together Austin's share of the Austin-Thompson collection and sent him a draft.

For Thompson, $500 is all he received.

THE PRESENT

THE FATE OF THE TREASURE

DID THOMPSON KEEP ANY OF THE ARTIFACTS from the cenote? If there was treasure in the Thompson family, they were doing a pretty good job at hiding it. During my interview with grandson Edward Thompson, there was one point where I thought I was about to have a deep family secret revealed. "Something keeps flitting in my mind," Edward says. "I remember being at my sister's cottage [formerly owned by Thompson]...I was downstairs and looking at some treasures." My ears perk up.

"Treasures?" his wife Priscilla says, sounding surprised.

"Oh, it was an accumulation of nuts and bolts," Edward explains. "He was a practical man, he wasn't esoteric."

We laugh. "Well, I'll tell you this," Priscilla says. "The family never got rich on anything. No sign of money in any of the six children. One of the brothers, whose main interest was inventions, was poor as a church mouse. I never saw the least sign of any money."

Not only is there no treasure among the Thompson descendants, they don't have much in the way of any kind of wealth. While Edward Thompson the senior had been paid to dredge the cenote, as near as I could determine, he was not compensated based on the value of what he recovered. Also, the money he made from the dredging was plowed back into the hacienda or into his family's upkeep. But not all the artifacts ended up in the hands of museums.

Thompson, as promised, had made for Mary Austin a necklace of jade beads recovered from the cenote, one of three that he gave away. Ginny Kuykendall, Thompson's granddaughter, told me that she inherited one of them, but that it was stolen several decades ago. Teobert Maler, Thompson's archaeological nemesis, possessed several artifacts from the Cenote Sagrado that he had purchased from Thompson's Maya workmen, according to T.A. Willard. "Thompson steals from the Mexican government and I steal from him," Maler reportedly was fond of saying.

I scour an online auction house every day for items related to Chichén Itzá. Most of the stuff is crap: Cancún timeshares, trinkets purchased by Aunt Edna from souvenir vendors, or video games that use the ancient city as a setting. But on this day a baker's dozen of auctions pop up. A seller has pulled out all the stops. Each item has its own elaborate page, with flashing lights, graphics cribbed from other web sites, and paragraph after paragraph of background about the ancient Maya. The seller also added a soundtrack as each page plays a romantic piano solo on my computer. What is he selling? Maya artifacts, all supposedly recovered from Chichén Itzá in the late nineteenth century.

Every sentence in the auction advertisement comes with typewriter smiley faces: "This is an extremely rare prize! :)" or "This piece probably belongs in a Mayan cultural museum, but until then perhaps it can remain in your gentle care ;) "

Three of the items, according to the seller, came from the Sacred Cenote, "which were sacrificed to Chac! :(" There is a head from a clay figurine, a jade ear spool, and a small, clay bowl. Bidding starts at $25, but I am willing to pay any price to get them. I win all three: The figurine head for $43.55; the bowl for $76; and the jade spool for a whopping $102.50. For a little more than $200 I am the proud owner of my own treasures from the Sacred Well.

After each auction I receive a cheery e-mail from the seller: "YOU'VE WON! : o) *happy roar*" I arrange payment for the artifacts and several days later receive two small boxes in the mail.

I unwrap my treasures with the tenderness objects older than 500 years deserve. The Maya figure head has pinched features: pinched lips, pinched eyes, and a pinched nose, as if angry at having been removed from the cenote. The clay contains large particles of sand. The back of the head is scorched, either during firing or as part of some ritual. At the tip of its hooked Maya nose is a chip of quartz, which looked more like a pus-filled pimple than a decoration. In its right ear the artist molded a spool, identical in shape and form to the jade spool I just purchased.

That spool, unlike the other two items, is undamaged—still alive in Maya eyes, as they ritually killed everything tossed in the cenote. The stone does not appear of very good quality, more jadeite than jade. There is some dried dirt in the inside, possibly from the cenote itself.

The bowl is a tiny treasure. It fits neatly in the palm of my hand and holds little more than a quarter cup of water. The Maya knew nothing of the potter's wheel, so the bowl had been pressed by hand and formed into its concave shape with fingers. Although undecorated, the glaze gives it a metallic shine of a color somewhere between gold and copper. The bottom has been blackened, not from sacrifice but from firing where the clay form had once rested upon coals. And there is a small chip in the lip, the only damage to what is a perfect artifact.

The seller sent along copies of the notes he took when he purchased the items in the late 1960s. The person who sold it to him had bought the objects from a private party in New York on April 27, 1936, someone with the initials "J.C.T." "T" may stand for "Thompson." Possibly one of his children or grandchildren sold the items after Edward Thompson's death in 1935.

I get a wild idea. What if I take these three objects to Yucatán and throw them back into the Sacred Well? Thompson and all the other explorers devoted their lives to taking artifacts out of the country. I want to be the first person to smuggle Mayan artifacts back into Mexico.

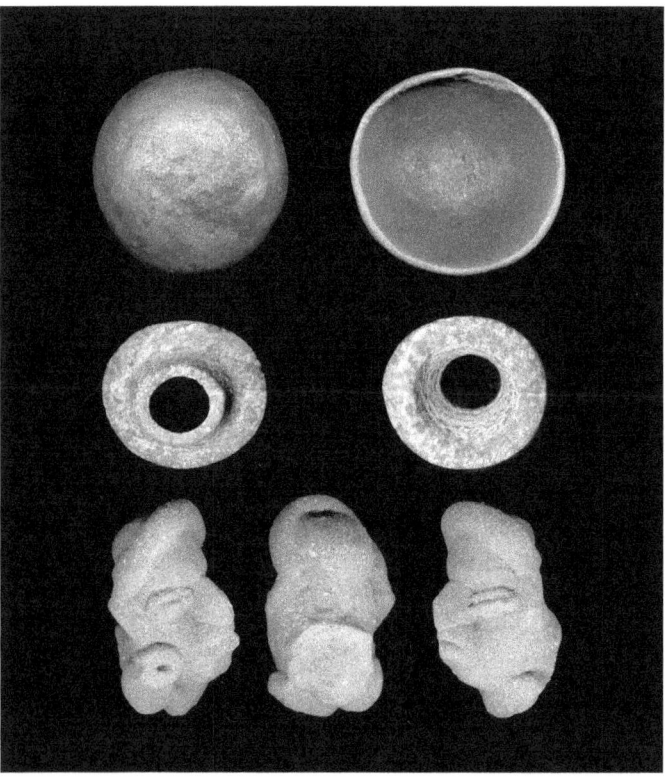

Unprovenanced Cenote Sagrado artifacts

THE PAST

EDWARD THOMPSON, HACENDADO

EDWARD THOMPSON OPENED the second decade of the twentieth century unemployed. His contract with Walter Austin had been a debacle, but he at least had escaped without owing anything. He owned, free and clear, Chichén Itzá. As assets go, that wasn't bad.

He didn't tell people he had been fired as U.S. consul. His standard story was that he had resigned "to carry out certain archaeological undertakings of importance at Chichén Itzá, the once great capital in Yucatán of the ancient Maya civilization." The truth was his archaeological work at Chichén was done. He had run out of patrons. Everyone who had hired him in the past was either dead or dying, and anyone else that had money to explore the ruins wasn't interested. His final, large project hearkened back to his giant casts of Uxmal and Labná erected at the 1893 Columbian Exposition in Chicago. The American Museum of Natural History in New York commissioned Thompson to take paper moulds of the Upper Temple of the Jaguars at Chichén Itzá, which would be reconstructed to adorn the museum's new Columbus Avenue entrance. The project became another farce. To acquire the moulds required substantial excavation of the much-collapsed Temple of the Jaguars, which gave Thompson's nemesis, Teobert Maler, another opportunity to launch an attack in the Mérida newspapers. Maler charged that Thompson was ruining the ruins, so the Mexican government shut down Thompson's moulding operation. It required several weeks of negotiation and arm-twisting before he could resume. The delay cost Thompson dearly, not only financially, but also on his health as the work was pushed into the moist heat of July, August, and September, when Thompson normally would back home on Cape Cod—"all because of the spiteful envy of a half-crazed person," he later wrote

To add insult to injury, the New York museum never built the entrance. Instead it cast a mold of one of the feathered serpent pillars and placed it in the Mexican/Central American wing. Thompson proposed to the Smithsonian Institution to make moulds from carvings in Chichén Viejo, a relatively unexplored section of Chichén Itzá, for $3,600. His old friend, W.H. Holmes, was director, but had to give Thompson the bad news: There wasn't any money for such work. Thompson reduced his request to $500, but the answer was still "no."

In an ultimate display of *chutzpah*, Thompson attempted to interest the Mexican government to pay him to dredge the Sacred Cenote so that he could, he said, exhume "large idols of stone" that the Bishop de Landa had described when he had visited Chichén in the 1500s. The Mexican government politely declined and in its letter to him included a copy of the section of the Mexican Constitution regarding protection of antiquities.

Without an institution or individual to pay for archaeology, Thompson gave it up and devoted his life to more capitalistic pursuits. His aim: To transform Chichén Itzá into a hacienda that would rival the working plantations owned by the Casta Divina. This time he wouldn't gamble everything on one get-rich scheme as he had with the papaya plantation scheme. He called upon his experience as American Consul, which had put him in regular contact with the most successful businessmen of Yucatán and their counterparts in the United States. He knew now he had to diversify and do so in industries that had a proven track record in Yucatán: cattle, timber, and henequen.

As far back as the 16th century cattle had been raised at Chichén Itzá. When Thompson bought the property in 1894, he established a small herd, which by the turn of the century had grown, he claimed, to 300 head. His cattle soon had great renown, not only for their quality but also for their bravery. Justo Sierra Méndez, the founder of Mexico's national university, on a visit to Chichén in 1906 had marveled at a steer that was grazing near the top of the pyramid, El Castillo. "Is it possible that there are cattle in the world able to climb similar heights?" he asked.

Thompson had replied, "Oh, my cattle are so good, so magnificent, so brave, that regardless where it wants to climb, the cattle of Thompson know no fear."

Thompson also began cutting timber, another popular Yucatecan industry. Large companies harvested the vast forests of Campeche to the west, Quintana Roo to the east, and Belize to the southeast. The Hacienda Chichén had groves of zapote and other hardwoods from which Thompson had lumber cut to manufacture doors and windowsills.

Most of all, Thompson wanted to join the henequen kings. As American consul, he wrote no fewer than five reports on the henequen industry and had studied numerous plantations firsthand. In the first decade of the twentieth century henequen agriculture was expanding outside of the Mérida zone and into the west. Several plantations well beyond the Hacienda Chichén were abandoning cattle and sugar cane for henequen.

A few years earlier Thompson had tried to lure the United States' largest consumer of henequen, International Harvester, into a partnership. He proposed to put 5,000 acres of Chichén Itzá into henequen cultivation and sell half-interest in the enterprise for $75,000 gold. Half interest or full, International Harvester was not interested. Sometime before 1912, Thompson decided to go it alone; he purchased a sizable parcel north of the Hacienda Chichén and planted several large fields of henequen. As the plant requires seven years to mature, it was a gutsy move on Thompson's part to tie up capital for that long. But it was all part of his diversification strategy that he believed at the end would pay huge dividends.

While any other hacendado would have been satisfied to have hundreds of cattle ranging through the ruins, forests tended and carefully harvested, and hundreds of henequen plants under cultivation, not so Thompson who looked to expand in one more industry—tourism.

This was not an untried scheme like the papaya debacle that nearly ruined him in the 1890s. He had been carefully crafting a plan to convert the ruins of Chichén Itzá into a worldwide attraction. Tourism was an industry whose time had come, of that he was certain.

One of his last projects as American consul before getting fired was a report promoting the region as a tourist destination. Tourist agencies and steamship lines for many years "have cast longing eyes on a certain Mexican State, *Yucatán*," he wrote. Previous attempts to build a tourism industry had been a failure because of three significant challenges: outbreaks of yellow fever, a lack of accommodations, and "the apathy of the inhabitants of the state, who could see in the possible influx of tourists, no special gain to themselves." Times were changing, Thompson continued. Streets had been paved and sanitary systems installed to thwart yellow fever; a new hotel had opened in the center of Mérida; and an awareness was growing among locals that tourism brings dollars. As evidence that Yucatán was open for business, Thompson enclosed a brochure prepared by Henry

Case, the local agent of the Ward Line steamship company, titled "Yucatán, the Egypt of the Western Hemisphere." The pamphlet expounded on the wonders of the region and recommended three tours to passengers who stop in Progreso on their way to Veracruz: a short visit of a few hours lasting the duration of the vessel's stay in port; a week's stay, in which one would get off the Ward Liner, tour Mérida and Campeche, visit the ancient Maya city of Uxmal and then be back in Progeso in time to catch the next ship out; and longer stays, that would include a visit to Chichén Itzá.

Thompson exaggerated the opportunities and his report was more visionary than prescient. Others were neither so optimistic nor enthusiastic. *Terry's Mexico*, at almost 600 pages, was in its time the most detailed and useful guide for travel in Mexico. In its inaugural edition in 1909, Yucatán merited only ten pages at the back of the book. One of those pages was devoted to Chichén Itzá and, while Terry raved about it, he was less passionate about the journey to get there ("The roads are execrable") and the accommodations one found when they arrived ("a so-called Guest-house, unfurnished, in which travelers are at liberty…to swing their hammocks"—if, of course, they knew enough to bring one). "It is the highest degree unfortunate that better accommodations are unobtainable, and that the tourist interested in archaeology should have to bear the privations to which a visit to perhaps the most interesting group of ruins in America exposes him."

Terry's Mexico was bad publicity, a very poor beginning upon which to build a Yucatecan tourism industry. Thompson set about countering Terry. He tackled his own promotion of Chichén Itzá and did it in the most prominent medium of the day: *National Geographic Magazine*.

It wasn't the first time something he had written had appeared in the publication. In 1903 an article on Yucatecan agriculture, which had for the most part been a reworking of one of his consul reports, appeared. This time he submitted an original work and, in 1914, "The Home of a Forgotten Race," appeared as the lead article of that issue.

National Geographic Magazine was a publishing phenomenon. Circulation in 1903 had been fewer than 3,000 copies; by 1914, the publication was well on its way to becoming a cherished American institution. Membership in the society (which came with a subscription to the magazine) exploded during the second decade of the twentieth century and Thompson's article went into more than 300,000 homes, businesses, and libraries. There was no secret to the publication's success. "The National Geographic Magazine has found a new universal language that requires no deep study," Associate Editor-in-Chief Oliver La Gorce wrote in a promotional brochure of the time. "The Language of the Photograph!"

Thompson's article included fourteen photographs, all full-page save one. Every picture was credited to Thompson and depicted all the significant monuments: El Castillo, the Ball Court, the Nunnery, the Observatory, and the Sacred Cenote. The article, which even today is considered one of the most comprehensive and readable accounts of the ancient city, still managed to leave out one or two significant details. It never mentioned that Thompson was the owner of Chichén, nor did it cover his archaeological investigations, namely the dredging of the Cenote Sagrado. Thompson did mention the legend of sacrifice, but concluded by writing, "Could this deep old limestone water pit, the Sacred Well, be given a tongue and made to tell what it had seen, what world romance could equal it?"

Not only was "The Home of a Forgotten Race" distributed to a third of a million subscribers, but it was summarized and sometimes quoted verbatim in newspapers around the world. You couldn't buy better publicity.

THE PRESENT

HURRICANE WILMA

TOURISM TODAY is the Yucatán Peninsula's biggest industry. In the 1970s the Mexican government saw the same advantages Edward Thompson had envisioned sixty years before and invested hundreds of millions of dollars to create the resort area of Cancún on the peninsula's northeast coast. There are now dozens of hotels that served millions of visitors each year. The region also has become a popular destination to hold business meetings, which is what brought my CEO into my office. Would I be willing to fly to Cancún on behalf of the company? he asks. One of our clients was throwing a swanky conference, directed at CEOs of Fortune 500 companies, and we have been invited.

My next trip to Yucatán (with the Thompsons) is several months away. Now I can return to Mexico and, what's more, do it on my company's dime. I can't believe my luck. But luck can turn, and at that moment it was turning in the Atlantic, a hurricane that the experts thought likely to strike Yucatan about the same time as my visit. I had witnessed such a storm almost twenty years before on Cape Cod, a hurricane with the most unassuming name, "Bob." I remember sitting on a loading dock at one of the local schools, watching a sheet of plywood slice like a Frisbee through the air across one of the athletic fields at just the perfect height for decapitation.

Hurricanes are more common in Yucatan and also more intense. Hurricane Isidore in 2002 had pried up a section of the metal roof of don Fernando's mansion and the rains damaged two floors and much of the antique furniture contained therein. He still hadn't repaired the damage. Always *mañana*.

This year has been the most active hurricane season in recorded history. A few months before, Hurricane Emily had ripped across the peninsula. It started at Playa del Carmen on the east coast, then bisected the peninsula, exiting as a tropical storm near Mérida. To Yucatecans it was little more than an inconvenience. This next hurricane was shaping up to be a doozy. Even its name scared me: "Wilma." Every time I see "Wilma" in the news, I hear Fred Flintstone screaming it in my head.

Wilma is on a collision course with the Yucatán Peninsula, into the tourist area known as the Riviera Maya, from Cancún south to Cozumel. I e-mail don Fernando asking if he is prepared. His family owns a high-rise hotel on Cozumel Island, and he and Maruja have the penthouse. "Cozumel is ready to receive Wilma if she cares to come in," he answers. His own house will be safe, he says. "Mérida is out of reach, a few drops of rain and some wind to cool the evenings."

A couple of days before I am to leave I receive an e-mail from the conference sponsors, telling us not to worry, that the authorities in Cancún are prepared should the hurricane hit. The next day they cancel the conference. Someone has come to their senses, aware that there will be little positive P.R. value in hosting a conference where dozens of the world's top CEOs are carried away by 150-mile-per-hour winds.

When Hurricane Wilma slams into Cancún and Cozumel, it is a Category

5 storm and doesn't budge for *thirty hours*. The winds blow out the windows of the hotel where I would have been staying. At the same time they pick up sand from the beaches and blast paint off buildings. From Cancún, Wilma skirts the north side of the Yucatán Peninsula. As Fernando had predicted, Mérida is spared, but Cozumel is not. When Fernando is able to get the hotel on the telephone, his daughter-in-law tells him that, "Damages are greater than you may imagine. Your penthouse is totally destroyed. Nothing left but bare walls." Maruja had several first edition books in the penthouse's library and she is beside herself that they are now gone forever.

"We are now matching New Orleans," Fernando writes. "We are in bad shape. Forget the comparisons. Never thought I would experience again what has happened to us now. The first reports are shocking." Still, he remains philosophical. "Nature is nature," he writes. "One must take it on a stride. I have been in worse shape before, more than once. So be it. My family survived the ordeal, safe and sound. What more can I ask?"

Hurricane Wilma did more damage than any other storm in recent memory. During Hurricane Gilbert in 1988 the eye of the storm passed over Cozumel. The winds and rain damaged only twenty of the suites in Fernando's 180-unit hotel; Wilma, by comparison, destroyed more than 100 units. Fernando says he does not have the money on hand to fix the entire property. He will have to sell his private airplane, which cost $3.2 million, and maybe sell some undeveloped property on Cozumel. "I will be devoid of cash for a while," he says. Still, "we have always managed to survive, even when my airline was taken over by the government, inflicting a $40 million loss...[that] took almost twenty years to recuperate." The recovery from Hurricane Wilma will not occur in his lifetime, he says. "I have faith my family shall manage, too."

Above, Chichén Itzá, circa 1913.
Below, Sylvanus Morley and one of many articles about his disappearance

ALARM FELT FOR THEM.

S. G. Morley, a Harvard Student, and J. H. Nusbaum May Have Died on Visit to Cozumel Island.

SANTA FE, N M, April 17—Alarm is increasing over the fate of Sylvanus Griswold Morley, Harvard student and recognized authority on Central American history, and Jesse H. Nusbaum, photographer, who have gone to explore the old temple ruins on Cozumel Island of Yucatan.

Both are with the School of American Archeology of Santa Fe. They accompanied Gen Guin Luiz of Yucatan, who went to Cozumel on a peace mission, as the Indians on that island have refused to permit any whites to land.

Letters received here today indicate

THE PAST

THE RETURN OF MORLEY

GIANT WAVES AND GALE-FORCE WINDS battered a tiny sailboat that bobbed a few miles off Cozumel Island. In the hold the archaeologist Sylvanus Morley and his photographer, Jesse Nusbaum, were tossed about. They had been exploring the Maya ruin of Tulum on the east coast of Yucatán in the spring of 1913 and as they had sailed back to their base in Cozumel the storm had whipped up almost out of nowhere. Tons of water crashed repeatedly on the deck, drenching Morley and Nussbaum below, and threatened to overwhelm the boat's tiny bilge pump. The craft was at risk of capsizing or being smashed to pieces against the reefs off the shore of the Yucatán Peninsula.

The headline a few days later in Morley's hometown newspaper in New Mexico told the tale: "Grave Danger in Visiting Isle of Cozumel. Peril of Morley-Nusbaum-Luis Expedition in Facing Cannibals. Mrs. Morley Alarmed over Husband's Fate."

Morley had come to Yucatán a few weeks earlier in a brand new role: motion picture director. Morley and Nusbaum were shooting a movie for the Panama-California Exposition, a "world's fair" to open in San Diego in 1915 to celebrate the city's newfound importance as the US gateway to the soon-to-opened Panama Canal.

In the six years since his first visit to the region, Morley had fulfilled his promise and become a dynamic force in archaeology, a little man who chased the mysteries of the ancient cultures that once thrived in the southwest United States and in Latin America. He had hit the ground running after graduating Harvard, winning a position as a fellow in Central American archaeology for the Archaeological Institute of America based in Santa Fe, N.M.

His personal life also had found a rhythm. None of the countless women he dated at university took root, but he found what he believed was his life partner, Alice Gallinger Williams, the granddaughter of a U.S. senator. The couple had married in 1908 and moved full-time to New Mexico. With a steady job, Morley's life had entered a familiar routine: Exploring Mexico and Central America in the winter and spring, and spending summer and fall at the Institute's headquarters, teaching classes and writing field reports. It was during this period that he emerged as the "Little Engine That Could" of American archaeology.

"He never let up," his colleague (and future boss) Alfred Kidder once noted. Kidder had joined Morley in the American Southwest not long after the little man's first visit to Chichén. "Heat, cracking sunburn, thirst, saddle soreness, rock bruises, cactus stabs, nothing discouraged him," Kidder wrote. "I can see him now, a quick, small figure in high boots and khakis and an enormous straw hat that was always falling off, stumbling about among the fallen walls and along the rimrocks, perilously close to nasty drops. Why he never broke his neck...is a mystery—he never looked where he was going. He'd trip and go down, then pick himself up and keep on, cheerfully whistling."

No matter where he explored or what he saw, Morley returned to Chichén Itzá. "It seems to have been the most holy shrine of the Maya people, comparable only in importance to the Mohammedan Mecca and the Christian Jerusalem," he once wrote. And like those Maya pilgrims who travelled to Chichén to pay tribute to the Maya gods, Morley kept coming back with a new plan, each grander than the next. He knew from that very first visit in 1907 that he wanted to devote his life excavating Chichén Itzá.

He published his first article on Chichén in 1911 and it appeared in newspapers around the country. "Chichén Itzá, the Holy City of the Itzas," would frame Morley's public perception of the ancient city. It was the version Morley always returned to when he explained Chichén Itzá to others.

> *Long before the discovery of America there flourished in southern Mexico, Guatemala, and parts of Honduras a great civilization, which has been called the Maya. It may be said at the outset without exaggeration that this civilization had reached a height equaled by no other people of the western hemisphere prior to the coming of the white man. In architecture in sculpture, and in painting the Mayas excelled. Their priests were astronomers of no mean ability, having observed and recorded without the aid of instruments of precision such as are known to us the lengths of the Solar and Venus years, and probably the lengths of the Mercury and Mars years. In addition to this they had developed a calendar system and perfected a chronology, which in some of its characteristics was superior to our own.*

On this most recent visit to Yucatán, he returned to Chichén on behalf of the Archaeological Institute of America to shoot a movie. Morley's film was to be about contemporary Maya life, intercut with reenactments of the ancient Maya civilization as photographed amidst the ruins. He cast actors and shot footage of Maya villagers and of the crumbling monuments.

But the movie never made it to the theater because Morley's life changed direction upon his return to Mérida.

Wife Alice and their daughter True were waiting for him. This was the second time Alice had joined him on the road and, according to Morley, their relationship had become strained. The continued absences required of his profession and Alice's occasional ill health either meant she was unsuited to be the wife of an anthropologist or, more likely, he was poorly suited to be her husband. Two years later Alice would file for divorce on grounds of desertion and Morley would not challenge it. It is more than possible she saw that her husband was going to be even more remote, courtesy of a single letter he received while in Mérida.

The missive was from Robert Simpson Woodward, president of the Carnegie Institution of Washington, D.C., who wondered if Morley would be interested in submitting a proposal to establish a department of anthropology. The Carnegie Institution was a relative newcomer in the world of scientific research. In 1902 Andrew Carnegie had endowed the institution by donating $2 million with the direction that it be an independent, self-supporting organization to explore the principles of science. The Carnegie Institution started out by funding the research of others, but in 1904 decided to bring everything in house by creating departments of "exceptional" individuals within their respective disciplines. One area that had been ignored was archaeology and anthropology, which were new disciplines compared to biology and astronomy. That changed thanks to one of the members of the Institution's board of trustees, William Barclay Parsons. Parsons had been the engineering genius behind the New York City subway system and the Cape Cod Canal. He also was an amateur Mayanist, having stumbled onto the mysteries of the ancient civilization after making a stop in Yucatán during a break from his official duties as a member of the Panama Canal Commission. He toured Maya ruins, possibly even Chichén Itzá, which would have put him there during the period Thompson was dredging the Sacred Cenote. A few years later, in 1909, Parsons got Hiram Bingham (who would discover Macchu Picchu two years later) to write a proposal to the Carnegie Institution Board of Trustees to fund a department of Central American anthropology. The board rejected the proposal, but the idea refused to go away. In early 1912 rumors began to swirl that the Carnegie Institution was again entertaining the idea of forming an anthropology department.

Morley had gotten wind of the project and although he had no direct connection to the Carnegie Institution, he knew several people in Washington, D.C., who did. In a letter to Frederick W. Hodge at the Smithsonian Institution, Morley laid out his plan to excavate Chichén Itzá and more importantly, why the Carnegie should put him in charge of the project. He wrote that he had the education and five years experience in the field of Maya archaeology, as well as the management skills to run an expedition, as he had done at the Maya city of Quirigua in Guatemala. He could do it on the cheap, for an annual grant of $5,000 per year from the Carnegie. Also, he had the contacts, among them Edward Thompson, with whom he had already discussed a lease for Chichén Itzá.

Thompson, in the midst of his own tourism plans at the Hacienda Chichén, could not believe his great fortune. Once again he would receive an annual stipend, but this time to do nothing: no dredging or other archaeological work. He and Morley agreed on an annual sum, around $3,000 per year, but of course that was contingent upon Morley convincing the Carnegie Institution of his proposal.

Morley's was to be one of three proposals considered. The others were by William H.R. Rivers of St. John's College, Cambridge University, and Albert E. Jenks of the University of Minnesota. Rivers had been instructed to propose a project in Europe, Asia or Africa; Jenks in North or South

America, exclusive of Central America and Mexico, which was to be Morley's area of focus.

Rivers's advocated an anthropological study of the peoples in Melanesia and Polynesia in the South Pacific, places where aboriginal culture was disappearing. Jenks took a Chinese restaurant menu approach, listing several places on the two continents that would be suitable for study. Morley, of course, wanted to excavate Chichén Itzá. But before he could write his proposal, he had a commitment to explore Tulum. Which is how he found himself being thrown around in a small sailboat during a gale off the shore of Cozumel.

A few days after the initial report of his disappearance, the *Boston Globe* got word that Morley was safe in Mérida. Somehow the little boat had made it to open sea, where the swells were still large, but not so violent. The boat and crew were tossed and turned through the night, but the next day they were able to strike out for shore and made it to San Miguel on Cozumel Island.

Apparently none of the movie film Nusbaum shot at Tulum survived the rough voyage. It didn't matter. Morley abandoned the movies for a chance to excavate and rebuild a Maya city. He returned to New Mexico where he corralled his friend Hodge at the Smithsonian to help write a winning proposal that would persuade the Carnegie to spend its money in Mexico.

His competition certainly knew what they were up against. Rivers designed his proposal so that it was less a recommendation than it was an attack on anything he thought Morley would suggest. Jenks spent little time forming his proposal, as if he knew he was a distant third. Morley's proposal, by comparison, was a revelation. His focus was razor sharp—excavate, study, and restore the city of Chichén Itzá, building by building. Unlike the other two scholars, he wrote his proposal for the layman as well as the academic. He filled it with colorful detail, as well as practical logistics on how to dig up an ancient city in the Yucatán.

Morley even included a vague reference to Thompson's dredging of the Cenote Sagrado. In describing the Sacred Well, he wrote, "Recent archaeological investigations substantiate the sacred character of this cenote and the fact that human victims were thrown into it." In case anyone knew what he was talking about, Morley wanted to reassure Mexican authorities that this expedition would be different:

> *This question of the ultimate disposition of objects found during the course of excavation has been the rock upon which many an archaeological expedition has foundered, not only in Mexico but also in other parts of the world. The stand herein taken, that archaeological objects belong to the country in which they are found, rather than to the finders thereof, it is confidently expected, will enlist the active interest and sympathy of the Mexican Government in this particular project. The antiquities at Chichen Itza, whether they be in the form of statuary, reliefs, wood carvings, vases, metal ornaments, or what not, were the product of a Mexican civilization, and for that reason, originals should in all justice remain in the custody of the Mexican nation. For exhibition in museums and for scientific instruction, casts would serve as well.*

The Carnegie executive committee reviewed the proposals on Oct. 16 but failed to reach a decision. Not long after the meeting Morley heard from Parsons, who was on the executive committee, that his proposal was greeted favorably and that from all appearances would be selected. While this was excellent news, Morley began to hear whispers that there were those who supported the Chichén Itzá project, but not if Morley ran it. One supposed ally was preparing to stab him in the back. Edgar Hewett, Morley's boss at the Archaeological Institute of America, was furious that his protégé was about to get a $20,000 grant from the Carnegie Institution, the same organization that had rejected his proposal years before. Hewett had even travelled to Chichén Itzá with the intention of locating his own research center there.

Hewett, who many found to be a difficult and stubborn collaborator, realistically had no shot at the job, but there was another candidate to run the Chichén project who was a bigger threat. Carnegie Institution Board Director Parsons, at the request of the Carnegie Executive Committee, had approached Charles Bowditch and Frederick Putnam, patron and director of Harvard's Peabody Museum, respectively, about the project. Both agreed it was an excellent idea, but said that Alfred Tozzer would be better suited to run the project. When Morley's friend F.W. Hodge learned of Tozzer's candidacy he wrote Morley to let him know. Morley then revealed to what lengths he would go to get the job—he sacrificed his friend Tozzer, a man who had mentored him at Harvard, into the Sacred Well. Morley telegrammed Hodge that if Tozzer's role in the dredging and transporting artifacts from the Cenote Sagrado ever became public, Mexico would never allow him anywhere near Chichén Itzá.

Morley left out one small, but crucial detail, in his telegram: He failed to mention that he, like Tozzer, also had carried artifacts from the Cenote Sagrado out of Mexico to the Peabody Museum. Apparently Hodge knew nothing about Morley's involvement, because the stratagem worked. Tozzer's candidacy to run the new Carnegie program disappeared, just like the men and women thrown into the Sacred Well a millennium before.

On Jan. 15, 1914, the Carnegie Executive Committee selected the Chichén Itzá project and named Sylvanus G. Morley to run it.

Three months later, almost to the day, the US Marines invaded Veracruz. It would be almost a decade before the Carnegie would put a shovel in the ground at Chichén Itzá.

THE PRESENT

PYRAMID DEATH DIVE

AS I WALK PAST A COWORKER'S OFFICE, she asks me excitedly if I've met our newest employee, Meghan. "Have you asked her about Chichén Itzá yet?" she asks. Her eyes are bright and she has a wide smile. "You have to ask her," my colleague says. "She saw someone killed there."

A few seconds later, I'm in Meghan's office. She's a little older than a lot of the new hires, most of whom are fresh out of college. After a quick introduction, I ask her about Chichén Itzá. "I saw an old woman fall off the pyramid," Meghan says. "It was one of the worst things I'd ever seen in my life."

You were there on Jan. 5? I ask.

That stops her. "How did you know?" she asks.

Serendipity, I think. I tell her I know all about it. All about Adeline Black and the day she died. That was the day they closed the pyramid, El Castillo, possibly forever.

HURRICANE WILMA HIT the tourism industry of Yucatán hard. Many tourists who had booked tours cancelled or had to cancel because their hotel was gone or in ruins. Not Adeline Black. She had turned eighty-three months earlier and, according to friends, was in excellent, if not vigorous, health. She was a member of the Canyoneers, the volunteer arm of the San Diego Natural History Museum that helped manage the Tecolote Canyon Nature Center. "She was the heart and soul of the Canyoneers," according to Bill Howell, who manages the volunteers. Adeline regularly led hikes through Tecolote Canyon.

Adeline had joined the Canyoneers a quarter-century before after the death of her only child. Her son, Tony, had been killed in an accident involving a drunk driver. She dealt with her grief by throwing herself into volunteering. It proved a good thing, because there was more tragedy to come. Two years after losing Tony, her husband John died. "Canyoneering is a way of restoring your soul," Adeline once said. "It's a lot better than vacuuming or doing the laundry."

In 1994, she began traveling the world. A longtime friend, Bill Barbour, had lost his wife the year before and the two became travel partners. "She always had to go one more place, one step higher, and to know one more thing," Barbour recalled in an interview with the *San Diego Union*.

The two seniors left San Diego before Christmas for a three-week adventure on the Yucatán Peninsula. They had saved the best for last. On the last day they visited Chichén Itzá. The timing was perfect. The day had begun with clear skies and the direct sun made it hot, if not uncomfortable, but by the time Adeline and Bill arrived, fleecy clouds had begun to fill the sky. A few were soaked with a threatening gray that normally indicated rain, but instead it cooled the air and made temperatures comfortable.

Like hundreds of other tourists who visited that day, Adeline decided to climb the ninety-one steps to the top of El Castillo. She never made it.

MEGHAN TELLS ME that she and her boyfriend were in the middle of a vacation week at the Iberostar resort at Playa del Carmen, south of Cancún. They had signed up for a tour of Chichén Itzá at their hotel. Early that morning a shuttle picked them up and took them to a central location, where they joined tourists from other hotels and boarded a bus for Chichén Itzá.

"We were such tourists," she says. And so was everyone else aboard the bus. She remembered talking to one woman who she thought might have been crazy. "She said she wasn't traveling with her husband because the last time they took a trip on a train, he tried to strangle her."

"I guess you could understand why they didn't travel together," I say, and we laugh.

I ask her what she knew about Chichén Itzá before the tour. "I knew nothing, zippo," she says. Everything she learned came from the two "amazing" tour guides on her bus. She thought they were Maya, but didn't know. They were full of interesting information and kept the bus entertained during much of the ride to Chichén, which took a couple of hours.

When the bus arrived at Chichén Itzá, one of the two men continued the tour inside the archaeological zone. "We were standing at this tree and he had just started talking when all of a sudden I hear screaming, like 'Oh my God!' I look over and I see it, clear as day, this woman toppling. She was falling, slowly tumbling, hitting each step. It looked like they had tossed down a rag doll."

According to witnesses, Adeline was about two-thirds of the way up the pyramid when she fell. "I was praying she was okay, but the tour guides were like, 'She's dead,'" Meghan recalls.

The guides let their charges know that they wouldn't be allowed to go up the pyramid. "There was no way I was climbing it after that," says Meghan. "Everyone that was on it had to get down, they all looked horrified…and were going down on their butts, they were so scared. Then they shut it down and roped it off. We proceeded to the Ball Court, where I thought I was going to cry.

"It was a blur for about forty-five minutes. I wasn't paying attention, I was thinking about life, how life was short, how someone just died in front of us. I was questioning life. You could tell no one was paying attention."

"But you continued the tour?" I ask.

"We continued the tour. They told us to keep going, to think good thoughts about her."

I asked her if after it was over, did she tip the tour guide?

"We did." She looks down and lets out an embarrassed laugh "We gave him an extra tip."

ADELINE BLACK DIED at Regional de Valladolid Hospital four hours after she fell. They held a memorial service for her a month later at the Natural History Museum where she devoted so much of her time. A memorial hike in her honor was scheduled for late spring.

Following the death of Adeline Black, INAH prohibits anyone from climbing El Castillo. Her accident is not why INAH closed the pyramid (it had been discussed for years), but it gave them an excuse to finally do it once and for all. Every day new tourists arrive at Chichén and are heartbroken to learn that climbing is no longer permitted. That's okay by Meghan. She thinks the pyramid is too dangerous to climb for anyone, not just eighty-year-olds.

After she tells me her story, Meghan and I find we don't have much more to say to each other even though I see her almost every day. Our offices are only a few feet apart, but even though we share the tale of Adeline Black, we don't become close. We exchange pleasantries in the hallway. After a few months she leaves our company and I never see her again.

Every once in a while her name comes up in conversation at the office. And if I happen to be involved, I tell the story about how she was at Chichén Itzá the day Adeline Black died. Many find it to be a bizarre coincidence that a woman who witnesses an event that I am writing about "just happens" to be hired at my company. I explain that it was even stranger than that. The reason I knew about Adeline Black to begin with was because I had read an account of her death that someone had posted on an internet travel bulletin board. Meghan had been the author.

What do you suppose the odds are that someone I work with happened to be at Chichén Itzá that very day, the very hour, the very minute, this woman died? On any given day, Chichén Itzá gets five thousand visitors, but since Hurricane Wilma, that number has fallen by half. To my knowledge, only two people who were present that day posted information on the Internet about what they saw. What are the chances that one of those people, the very one who led me to the story of Adeline Black in the first place, would come to work for my company, which has only 100 employees?

Some people I work with don't think it was a coincidence. They believe there is something else at work. If there is, then He, She, or It is working pretty hard, because I can list a half dozen other "coincidences" since I began researching this book.

I've talked with other writers and they all have the same kind of stories to tell. Amazing coincidences that lead them to major breakthroughs in their research. Or how someone they met on a bus happens to know the brother of the person they are writing about, a person they had thought long dead. These type of stories lead me to think that it is not so much divine intervention, but rather the entire world is within reach of anyone during their lifetime.

El Castillo, before and after. Above, a photograph of Chichén Itzá's pyramid minutes before Adeline Black fell to her death (photo courtesy Teresa Wojohowicz). Below, a photo of the empty pyramid minutes after the accident (photo courtesy Luke Plonsky).

THE PAST

FLIGHT IN THE FACE OF REVOLUTION

THE MEXICAN REVOLUTION OF 1910 skipped Yucatán, at least at the beginning. When the Carnegie Institution agreed in early 1914 to proceed with the Chichén Itzá project, Yucatán was quiet, even though other parts of Mexico were engaged in an unofficial civil war. The region appeared insulated from the conflict, but the first indication that that status quo would change occurred when the U.S. military invaded 400 miles across the Bay of Campeche at the port of Veracruz on April 21, 1914.

The reasons or justification behind the invasion mattered little to Mexico and Mexicans; the villain always would be the United States. Rumors began to spread across the nation that the American military had slaughtered women and children to take the city. Mexico President José Victoriano Huerta Márquez telegrammed his military governor in Yucatán warning of a possible U.S. invasion there. This spurred anti-American demonstrations throughout the region. In Mérida a mob crying "Death to the Americans!" attacked the "home of a well known and well liked American businessman," no doubt William James and his wife June. They destroyed a car parked outside the casa, then fired shots into the house. Police arrived just the mob was about to break down the front door. Another mob (or possibly the same one) traveled to Progreso and attacked the U.S. consulate and tore down the U.S. flag. Any Americans who appeared on the streets were jeered by the mobs.

U.S. Consul Wilbur Gracey had seen enough. It was not safe to stay in Yucatán. The State Department warned Americans it was time to get out of Dodge. According to official sources, they did, all except for two: Miss Kellogg, a music teacher; and the former American consul and owner of the Hacienda Chichén, Edward Thompson.

Thompson was alone in Yucatán. Most of his family had moved to the United States. That last holdout was Thompson's eldest son, Edward Josiah, who had been helping him at the hacienda and had escaped on the first ship out of Yucatán after the U.S. invasion. Thompson the senior refused to leave and instead went into seclusion away from the Hacienda Chichén. His instinct to remain proved correct, for the fires that raged in the hearts of Yucatecans soon burned out, particularly after word reached the peninsula that Huerta's inflammatory telegram and the related rumors had been a pack of lies. But what the Veracruz incident demonstrated that the Yucatán peninsula was not immune to the forces of the Mexican Revolution. In late winter 1915 the revolution arrived in full force.

By that time Venustiano Carranza de la Garza had wrested power from Huerta and to maintain his control he knew he needed money. He turned to Yucatán and its healthy and wealthy henequen industry to support his government. Carranza installed General Toribio de los Santos as military governor of Yucatán, who pressured the region's wealthy hacendados to provide the federal government a sizable "loan." The hacendados responded by backing their own revolutionary, Colonel Abel Ortiz Argumedo, who rallied Yucatán's military forces and drove Gen. Santos from power.

To maintain control, Col. Argumedo tried to secede Yucatán from Mexico and sought a loan from the United States to support a newfound sovereign nation. Instead all he managed to do was irritate Carranza who sent federal troops into Mérida to crush the rebellion. "HUACH, HUACH squeaked the soles of their muddy boots on the newly paved stones," José Monseral told historian Gilbert Joseph in an interview decades later. "*Huach*" is Yucatecan slang for someone from Mexico City. "HUACH, HUACH, HUACH, as if to identify themselves to us as they marched through our city." After several minor skirmishes, Carranza's forces drove Argumedo from power. The colonel and his supporters fled to the farthest end of the state, El Cuyo, a village on the northeast coast of Yucatán. Argumedo's secretary of state, Manuel R. Yrigoyen-Lara, was a good friend of Edward Thompson, and he dispatched a plea to Chichén Itzá wondering if the ex-consul had any influence to find transportation for him and nine friends off the peninsula and out of Mexico.

Thompson met with Col. Argumedo and Secretary Yrigoyen-Lara at El Cuyo. The village was home to 250 souls, it's two major features were a wharf of more than 100 meters long that projected into the Gulf of Mexico and a new lighthouse, set a few hundred feet back from the beach on top of a free-standing hill that, upon closer inspection, also was manmade—a ruin of an ancient Maya temple. El Cuyo was a company town for *Compañía Comercial de Fincas Rústicas y Urbanas*, a conglomerate controlled by many the hacendados who had backed Argumedo's rebellion. The deposed governor announced his intention to make the little community his exile-in-residence. Yrigoyen-Lara asked the deposed governor if he was certain that he wanted to remain while his followers fled the country. "If all the people here should desert me, I will remain here, like Robinson Crusoe on his island," Col. Argumedo replied.

But how to escape? Thompson told Yrigoyen-Lara that he had heard "that some natives were building a schooner at San Felipe, about fifteen miles from their hiding place," Thompson recalled later, "and I decided that then was a good time to go fishing." When he got to San Felipe, his heart must have sunk. The schooner wasn't finished. The hull was complete and there were two rough masts and some sails, but much of the rigging was missing. There was but half a deck and no rudder. Further complicating matters was that the ten men Thompson had been asked to spirit out of Mexico had now grown to twenty-six men, women, and children, including a woman late in her pregnancy.

Provisions for a voyage were hard to come by in the poor fishing village, which had a population of fewer than 100. All the fugitives could scrounge was a half-barrel of crackers, some flour and corn, and a few dozen eggs. Certain that Carranza's military was closing in, the half-completed ship headed for Cuba, 200 miles across the Yucatán Straits from San Felipe. "We had to sail by dead reckoning and at once encountered a line storm so that it was only by the grace of God that we survived," Thompson recalled.

Once at sea, Thompson revealed to Yrigoyen-Lara that when he was at El Cuyo, he had happened to peek into a crate, one of many in Col. Argumedo's camp. It contained gold coins. As Yrigoyen-Lara later learned, the brave Col. Argumedo was not so much Robinson Crusoe as Long John Silver. Before fleeing Mérida, Argumedo had robbed the state treasury, estimated at more than $300,000 U.S. While Yrigoyen-Lara and the others floated helplessly in the Gulf of Mexico, the colonel spent part of that fortune to purchase a steamship, which he commissioned to become the sole vessel in the newly created Yucatán navy. With a few trusted guards, Argumedo abandoned El Cuyo and sailed for the United States.

Back on the schooner there was Yrigoyen-Lara could do with the knowledge of Argumedo's deceit, because by that time he, Thompson, and the others were lost at sea. For more than a week the tiny ship floundered in the gulf, never sighting land or another ship. The limited water they carried had to be rationed to a few ounces per day.

On the eleventh day, the boat-that-almost-was encountered an American fishing schooner, the Francis V. Sylvia. "They gave us all the water they could spare and several cakes of ice so that we could save the drippings to drink," Thompson said. "Best of all, we got directions from them and headed toward Cuba." Two days more sailing and they reached Havana, where, according to Thompson, they were afforded a hero's welcome. Once back in civilization, the ex-consul then went to Washington, D.C., where he conferred with his former bosses in the State Department and with Massachusetts Senator Henry Cabot Lodge. He also spoke with the *Washington Star* newspaper:

> *These people so near to us in every way are now threatened with practical annihilation. The bands of warring Mexicans of the north, and especially the bands of brigands, have fixed their eyes on Yucatan as a rich prize, and their clutching hands have already followed the gleam of their eyes. They have tasted the blood of the brave young men who sought to defend their homes, their mothers and their sisters, and thirst for more. Angered by this resistance, they have openly proclaimed their intention to overcome all opposition by the use of fire and the sword.*
>
> *Driven to it by their continued acts of rapacity, and worse, the people of Yucatan arose as one man in an effort to rid themselves of this nightmare by means that all the world should regard as lawful.*

"I do not expect to go back to Yucatan for some time, for no doubt I should be shot full of holes if the Mexicans got hold of me," he told a reporter. As always, though, he remained upbeat and was philosophic about what had happened. "To have had part in saving twenty-six lives is recompense sufficient to me for anything I have suffered myself, including loss of my plantation, which has probably been confiscated," he said. The reporter asked him his next step. "Boston," he said; to renew friendships there and "try to get the bloodshed out of his eyes."

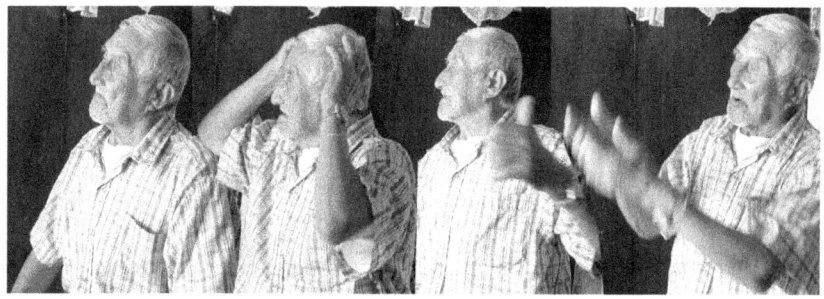

Juan Duran Coral, the last eyewitness from San Felipe

THE PRESENT

99 YEARS OF MEMORIES

JORGE DURAN CORAL HAS SPENT HIS ENTIRE LIFE in San Felipe. He was there when Edward Thompson arrived in his village, but he remembers it differently.

Duran Coral lives with his family in one of the small houses that crowd together to ward off the winds from the ocean. Although the town is sheltered by a sand spit and long cove, these offer little protection from the occasional hurricanes that strike the coast. His house has a temporary feel, as if all its possessions could be loaded up in a truck within minutes. Calendars and other papers hang from the stained panel walls with electrician's tape.

Duran Coral spent his life as a *pescador*, a fisherman. On the day of this interview he is *noventa nueve*—99 years old—and he recalls the events of 1915 with crystal clarity, the kind that comes from having told a story many, many times. Age has not slowed him, at least when it comes to relating the history of his village. As he recounts the tale of Thompson's escape from Yucatán, he jumps up from his chair and has to be coaxed to sit down. He waves his arms emphatically in the air to make a point.

From his vivid descriptions, one gets the impression that this was the only thing that ever happened in San Felipe. But, as he reveals, it actually was several events that happened all at once.

The first was that a rich man, Ruperto Lucero, came to San Felipe and Panaba, the neighboring town to the south, to set up a business. Lucero was from Campeche, which was famous for its trees and the many types of wood harvested from there. Lucero thought the trees of Panaba were equal to those of Campeche and that San Felipe could serve as a port from which lumber could be shipped to Europe. At first, Lucero hired ships from Campeche to transport his cargo, but he did not like the service. He decided to build his own clipper to sail his product across the Atlantic. It would be the first and only ship ever built in San Felipe.

He hired eighteen carpenters from Campeche, Duran Coral says, who built an eighty-ton barque with two masts. When the ship was finished, it required 100 men from Panaba to launch it, and even then it could only be done at high tide during a storm, a norte, when waters are at their deepest. To keep it upright, the ship required 600 bags of sand as ballast.

Duran Coral tells his story with a cadence of numbers: *eighteen* carpenters, *eighty* tons, *two* masts, *100* men, *600* bags. The tale is remembered by its numerals and the numerals in turn give the story weight and credence. The building and launching of the boat was the biggest thing to ever happen in San Felipe, at least the biggest thing to happen until Edward Thompson came to steal the boat.

The old fisherman does not recognize Thompson's name and or that a gringo had been present. All he knows is that men related to Gov. Argumedo came to San Felipe and demanded the boat and provisions. And they needed one more thing: a captain. There was one pilot in all of San Felipe, Concepcion Diaz. One of the former governor's men produced a *pistola* and ordered Diaz to take them to Cuba. What choice did he have? So he took them. According to Duran Coral, the ship was left in Cuba and never returned to San Felipe.

THE PAST

THE FIRES OF SOCIALISM

AS ONE MAN, EDWARD THOMPSON, FLED MEXICO, another man returned. Not long after President Carranza's forces retook Mérida and established military rule in 1915, a tall, light-skinned Mexican with penetrating green eyes stepped ashore after a year's exile.

Felipe Carrillo Puerto had been born forty years earlier in Motul, a small city east of Mérida. His family was what passed for middle class in Mexico; far from privileged, but not peons, either. His early life seemed unremarkable. Like other men of his generation, he married and raised a family, working a wide series of jobs, mostly manual labor. That changed in the waning days of the Porfiriato, when politics fired his imagination and he launched a newspaper in his hometown. This earned him the wrath of the powers-that-be, who imprisoned him for his journalistic impudence. Thus began a recurring life pattern: Carrillo Puerto would politick and attract the ire of someone in power who would then either imprison him, banish him or, on three occasions, attempt to assassinate him.

He was in a self-imposed exile from Yucatán when Carranza's man, General Salvador Alvarado, rode into Mérida in 1915. That summer Carrillo Puerto returned to Motul and had been home for a short time when Alvarado's men threw him in prison, accusing him of acting as an agent for one of President Carranza's political enemies, Emiliano Zapata. Carrillo Puerto had spent the past several months with Zapata in southern Mexico and had seen firsthand how the rebel leader had successfully appealed to the disenfranchised peons and indigenous peoples in the region to build a powerful political base of support. Carrillo Puerto offered to do the same for Carranza and soon he was freed to organize the Socialist Party in the hinterlands. Carrillo Puerto went from pueblo to pueblo, forming branches of the Socialist Party called *Ligas de Resistancas* (League of Resistance), with the stated purpose of creating "a system of associations where people organized to help each other." The Ligas enabled laborers and small farmers to "help themselves through education, collective bargaining, cooperative associations and the pooling of their political clout." By 1922 there were 417 Ligas across the Yucatán Peninsula with membership topping 72,000. They became the foundation of the state's socialist movement. As one observer noted, Felipe Carrillo Puerto had "converted the Socialist Party into a camp."

In the midst of Carrillo Puerto's coalition-building, Edward Thompson returned to Yucatán. It was, to say the least, an *odd* decision. He had hijacked a ship, illegally transported fugitives out of the country who, one presumes, still were wanted by the government. Europe was at war, and the U.S. had joined the conflict, so traveling by sea had become dangerous. He had no archaeological work to conduct. So why come back?

According to Thompson, he returned "by request of the authorities at Washington," he wrote cryptically in a letter to friend, "to ascertain certain facts much to be desired and to make certain investigations equally desirable." Reading between the lines, Thompson was a spy. Although his name does not appear on a published list of spies for Office of Naval Intelligence, the list may be incomplete or, possibly, Thompson was working for his former employer, the State Department, in the agency's

Bureau of Special Intelligence. If he was a spy, as we will see, he was not the only one.

Once his commitment to "Washington" was over, Thompson remained in Yucatán to address what he described as his "personal interests." According to Thompson, powerful unnamed interests attempted to take the Hacienda Chichén from him in the courts, and friends were warning him that, should the legal route fail, they would take it by force if necessary. Thompson indicated that the threat was personal, aimed at him, but what is more plausible is that he became swept up in a land reform crusade brought by the Mexican Revolution. And the instigator was Felipe Carrillo Puerto.

Southeast of Chichén Itzá, Thompson owned property around a small cenote, X'Katun. Carrillo Puerto and others from his party began visiting the region, promoting socialism and telling the Maya that large property owners such as Thompson no longer controlled their own lands. A group of newly minted *socialistas* invaded X'Katun, kicking out the families that had been renting from Thompson for years. Thompson had purchased the land in part for the valuable trees that grew upon it; the squatters cut them down and burned them to plant their *milpa* (corn fields).

Thompson and his caretaker, Juan Olalde, visited X'Katun on Oct. 18, 1918 to negotiate with the squatters. "Upon arriving ... we were received in a war-like mode by the Indians living there, who, without listening to Mr. Thompson's reasons, tried to murder us savagely," the caretaker later reported. It was only because of the timely intervention of another group of Maya friendly to Thompson and the fact that Thompson and his caretaker were armed, that they were able to escape with their lives, he said. The attempt to retake X'Katun failed. The land around Chichén Itzá now belonged to the socialistas.

Felipe Carrillo Puerto's movement spread, and often by violent means.

The village of Pisté, a short distance from Chichén Itzá, was loyal to the Liberal Party, but after socialistas (reportedly from Yaxuna) cut the throat of Fecundo Mex, knifed Juan Marquez and threw his body into a well, and set Pablo Martin's house afire (among many others), no one dared stand up to them. That was, according to Thompson's caretaker, when they made their power felt. "Mariano Hau gave them fifty pesos not to kill his favorite milk cow; they took [the money] and also robbed him of his cow, and they would have killed him if he had not escaped to the town of Dzitas with his family." Angel Mex fled town to prevent his daughter from being raped. Many of the established families (an estimated half of the population) fled Pisté, leaving behind their homes, cattle, and crops. It was the biggest exodus from the town since the Caste War seventy-five years before.

For his part, Thompson took his battle to the courts, or so he claimed in a letter to a friend, and prevailed. "The Government has formally acknowledged that my...titles are impregnable and my land-rights must be fully respected," he wrote in early 1920. "All persons occupying or cultivating my lands must hereafter pay rental according to the law or be dispossessed of their holdings and buildings." The same applied to any archaeologists looking to do work at Chichén Itzá. "No person, individual or expedition, can venture upon or do work within the land area belonging to me without the given permission of the Mexican government *and of myself* [emphasis Thompson's]."

Thompson finally could see a conclusion to his struggles to protect his property. "The end is just not yet," he wrote. "But the light is ahead and not far off." In this Thompson proved prescient, except the light ahead turned out to be raging bonfire.

On April 17, 1921, a period when Thompson was living in Mérida, caretaker Olalde left Chichén to visit one of his children who had taken ill.

He left behind his eighteen-year-old daughter. One of the local socialistas visited the hacienda on the pretext of looking for Olalde. His daughter let the man into the house and left him alone briefly, which gave the visitor the opportunity to find the caretaker's guns and steal them. Fortunately he did not find all of them; almost two weeks later, Olalde woke in the middle of the night to find two men skulking around the hacienda corral. The caretaker and his son, armed with a rifle and a pistol, fired two warning rounds and the intruders returned fire. After exchanging a dozen or more shots, the intruders fled.

In April his daughter mysteriously disappeared. On May 18 Olalde's wife took ill, so the caretaker took her to the home of another daughter. While he was away some person or persons set fire to the hacienda. When Olalde returned four days, he found the main casa "total ruined," along with everything inside, and all the ancillary buildings destroyed. Only the school had been left untouched. The greatest loss was Thompson's library and museum, which included many artifacts he had exhumed from the Sacred Well. "Everything was burnt and destroyed on purpose in a criminal and treacherous manner," Olalde said.

Felipe Carrillo Puerto

THE PRESENT

'WE GO TO CHICHÉN ITZÁ'

THE GREAT MEXICAN REVOLUTIONARY ZAPATA died at the hands of assassins on April 1919, but others arose to take up his mantle. Today his political descendants have their eye on Chichén Itzá.

The site has become a political hot potato. Tourists complain about the local Maya vendors who have lain siege to the archaeological zone, but they now are joined by legions of salesmen of cheap, foreign-made trinkets. Many of these salesmen are not from Yucatan or even Maya. They harass tourists to buy their trinkets, which many believe have been manufactured in China and smuggled into the country.

Quetzil Castañeda, an anthropologist who writes extensively about Chichén Itzá and the vendors, describes it thus: "Tourists typically experience an overwhelming swarm of obviously poor, dark skinned Indians aggressively hawking handicrafts carved in ancient iconography, shouting in the tourists' faces, 'One dollar! One dollar, lady!'" According to Castañeda, this style of selling is called *tiich'*, Maya for "to offer."

In the weeks leading up to Hurricane Wilma, tensions between government officials and the vendors reach a peak. Brigadier General Audomaro Martinez Zapata (no relation to the revolutionary) calls the vendor situation a *"bomba de tiempo"* (time bomb). Several officials demand the military sweep the vendors out of the archaeological zone, just as had been done twice before, in the late 1980s and late 1990s. Others demand that Mexico expropriate Chichén from the Barbachanos. Only with total control of the land can the government exercise full control, they argue.

All the scenarios point to a removal of the vendors from the archaeological zone, by force if necessary. But the vendors are organized (or, many believe, not independent but working for much larger interests). The leader of their union is Vilevaldo Pech Moo, INAH's former director at Chichén Itzá. When he was ousted from that job, he turned his skills as a lawyer to defending those opposite INAH's interests, and he now represents the vendors, the very group that as director he had kept out of Chichén Itzá. In August, Pech Moo announces that the vendors have found a powerful ally—the Zapatistas in Chiapas.

Ten years earlier the *Ejército Zapatista de Liberación Nacional*—EZLN— led an armed revolt against the Mexican government in their home state of Chiapas, southwest of Yucatan. Although stopped by the Mexican Army, they did not give up their revolutionary struggles, but instead put down their arms and turned to organization and propaganda to push for their ends. The leader of the Zapatistas is Subcommandante Marcos, whose visage is well known throughout Mexico and around the world—a faced covered by a ski mask with his ever-present pipe, which he smokes through a slit cut for his mouth.

As part of the Zapatista campaign aimed to influence the Mexican national elections to be held next year, Marcos announces that he will tour the other states of Mexico to hear the complaints of the people against their government. He calls it "the Other Campaign," to distinguish it from the mainstream presidential campaigns. Marcos is not running to be president; he is running to bring awareness to his cause.

Six weeks before Hurricane Wilma, Pech Moo had announced that

Marcos and the Zapatistas were coming to Chichén Itzá to "demand respect of the constitutional and human rights of the artisans." Several of the craftsmen had traveled to Chiapas and meet with Marcos, Pech Moo reports, and Marcos had agreed to make Chichén Itzá one of the stops of his tour. This sent the powers-that-be into a panic. A few weeks later several legislators showed up at Chichén Itzá to negotiate with representatives of the vendors. Then Hurricane Wilma strikes and for a few weeks the problems of the vendors fade into the background.

But now, in the fall, the chess game resumes. The national director of INAH tells newspapers that he expects a resolution within two weeks, even if it means using force to evict the vendors, but it is an empty threat. Nothing happens. The vendors grow even bolder and by the end of the month they are marching in protest, burning the INAH director in effigy. The Zapatistas announce they will come to Chichén Itzá after the first of the year. Concurrently, the Mexican military announces that it coincidentally has transferred 800 troops from Chiapas to Valladolid, a few kilometers away from Chichén Itzá. The government claims the troops are there de vacaciones (on vacation), but no one is fooled. These soldiers have been brought to Yucatán because they are very familiar with the Zapatistas and their tactics.

After New Year's, the media goes into overdrive covering the anticipated visit of Marcos. The *Diario de Yucatan*, the region's leading newspaper, writes story after story, and no detail is too insignificant. They even uncover and publish the address where Marcos will be staying in nearby Valladolid, something that must distress the security-conscious Zapatistas.

A few days before the visit, the EZLN cancels. "Commandante Ramona," one of Marcos's closest compatriots in the EZLN, dies of cancer on Jan. 6. By all reports, Marcos is devastated by her death. She was one of his principal organizers and her death stops the "Other Campaign" in its tracks. Marcos withdraws to Chiapas. He resumes his tour five days later, but with an abbreviated schedule in Yucatán; one of the stops he drops is Chichén Itzá.

On Jan. 20, Marcos is in the middle of the second day of meetings with disaffected groups, including the vendors from Chichén Itzá. One of the artisans declares, "We invite the Subcomandante to visit us. We are waiting for him to come and experience our problems. The Maya are here. We are present. How is it possible that the government says we don't live there [in the Chichen Itzá archaeological zone] when we have lived there for generations? We are humble people, artisans. We make hammocks. I earn my living by making hammocks. How is it possible that the government wants to take away from me what is mine? But we will not leave our lands. We are going to fight even though it is impossible."

At the end of the day, Marcos stuns those assembled. "We all have fears," he says. "We fear losing life, or the people we love, but there are also other fears. There are fears of entering something bad or that has dark interests behind it or that will go in another direction, or of entering something badly organized. It is a legitimate fear. One must have a clear view of where one enters before going there. There are always causes whose leaders take another path and what always happens is that somebody uses a movement for his own benefit. This is already happening. But there is also this restlessness in many humble and simple people—I'm not speaking just economically, because there are people who live comfortably but who can also be humble and simple—who feel something should be done.

"Tomorrow we are going to Chichen Itzá," he says. "We invite everyone to go there, to go together with us to listen to the word with these *compañeros* and *compañeras*." There is strong applause, but according to one correspondent, it is far from unanimous.

The next day, Marcos and his supporters stride into the archaeological zone of Chichén Itzá. He speaks briefly, explaining that it was Commandante Ramona who insisted he come. A crowd of 300 vendors gather around him to hear the Zapatista leader tell them, "*No se rindan, no se vendan.*" "Do not surrender, do not sell out."

Capitalism, combined with a corrupt government, is trying to convert Mexico's archaeological sites into great commercial centers, Marcos says. Mexico City wants to make money on the backs of the dead. An indigenous person of Mexico only serves a corrupt government once he is dead; if he is alive, the government persecutes him; if he rebels, the government represses him; if he works to live, the government takes the work away from him.

The wealth of the country is not in dead stones but in the people with history and culture, and what the foreign visitors look for is culture, he concludes. And after posing for pictures, he leaves. No one will be removing the vendors anytime soon, that is certain. For the next few months on the grounds of Chichén Itzá one can hear the familiar cry, "One dollar! One dollar, lady!"

Commandante Marcos (photo courtesy Jim and Ellen Fields, Yucatan Living)

THE PAST

THE DREAM OF GOMEZ RUL

FELIPE CARRILLO PUERTO, who learned his organizational tactics at the feet of Zapata, was enjoying a meteoric rise in both Yucatecan and national politics. Except for a brief hiccup in 1919 when President Carranza turned on the socialistas and briefly exiled him out of Mexico, his political power increased exponentially. He could even get away with the occasional exuberant blunder, such as the labor rally in Mexico City where he dramatically waved a black and red flag and called for workers to loot businesses and blow up government buildings if it would put food in their mouths.

He ran one of his stooges for governor of Yucatán in 1920, and in the fall of 1921 he ran for the job himself, winning handily. He consolidated his power by turning to the one group he could trust—his family. Within months of taking office, almost 150 members of his extended family could be found working in state government. He also put his faith into a group long ignored by Yucatecan politicians, the Maya.

Carrillo Puerto, who claimed to be part Maya, was said to have descended from Nachi Cocom, the last great Maya leader of the 16th century whose territory included Chichén Itzá, and whose people put up one of the most spirited defenses against the Spanish conquerors. One of the central planks in Governor Felipe Carrillo's platform was to promote the reputation of the ancient Maya civilization. In this he set aside his persecution of the rich and influential, and instead cooperated with them and anyone else who could help bring back the luster of the civilization that controlled the peninsula before the arrival of the Spanish.

He became intrigued by a proposal that was circulating: Build roads to the ancient Maya cities so the public can see them. One man was working tirelessly to achieve that dream, Francisco Gomez Rul, one of Yucatán's true Renaissance men. Gomez Rul was a photographer, frequently shooting for Edward Thompson (many of the photographs that appeared in Thompson's article in *National Geographic* had been taken by Gomez Rul). He shot one of the first movies in Mexico, a 1906 short called "El Tobaco." He was one of the founders of Yucatán's first university. And, most importantly, he believed that the ruins of the ancients were the most valuable resource in the region, more important than henequen or sugarcane.

To achieve his goal, Gomez Rul helped to form an organization to promote archaeology in Yucatán, the *Asociación Conservadora de los Monumentos Arquelogicos de Yucatán* (Association for the Preservation of Archaeological Monuments of Yucatán). The group recruited some of Yucatán's most prestigious citizens, including Felipe G. Cantón, considered to be the richest man on the peninsula. Somehow, Gomez Rul appealed to Carrillo Puerto and got him to cooperate with Cantón, who had provided muckraker John Kenneth Turner with the most damaging quote regarding Maya "slavery" in an exposé published in the United States, *Barbarous Mexico*:

> *"It is necessary to whip them — oh yes, very necessary,"* [Cantón] *told me, with a smile, "for there is no other way to make them do what you wish. What other means is there of enforcing the discipline of the farm? If we did not whip them they would do nothing."*

The Man Who Owned a Wonder of the World

Asociación Conservadora de los Monumentos Arquelogicos de Yucatán. In front, Carrillo Puerto in center in white, Canton next to him. In back, third from the right, is Gomez Rul

Gomez Rul also needed the cooperation of Edward Thompson. Whatever issues that existed between Carrillo Puerto the socialist and Cantón the capitalist were only political. In Thompson's case, men acting under the umbrella of Carrillo Puerto's socialist movement had burned his hacienda and destroyed his library and collection of Maya artifacts. Rather than hold a grudge, the two men became fast friends. Construction on the new road began on Sept. 4, 1922, in Dzitas, the closest train station to Chichén Itzá. Edward Thompson began building the road at his end, from the Hacienda Chichén.

Gomez Rul, or at least, his organization, was not done. It convinced a group of Americans to form a foreign chapter. Some of the most prominent men in the United States were members: Oil man Edward L. Doheny, whose founded the company that controlled 1.6 million acres of oil fields in Mexico; Minor C. Keith, founder and vice president of the United Fruit Company; Col. Cornelius W. Wickersham, who served in the trenches of World War I but also had renown as a New York lawyer on Wall Street; and several of the leading archaeologists and anthropologists of the day, such as Marshall Saville, Clarence Hay, and Benjamin Gates. R.A.C. Smith, former Commissioner of Docks for New York City was elected president.

The group announced its intentions shortly after forming. "With the return of peace and stable conditions in Yucatán, Mexico, an effort will be made to restore and preserve the world-famous Maya Ruins, and to attract tourists to Uxmal and Chichén-Itzá, the two most accessible of the cities which have intrigued scientists and archaeological students from all parts of the world," according to a statement by the organization. "These ruined cities, with their magnificent carved stone temples and public buildings, pyramids, &c., flourished hundreds of years before the Christian era and tell of an advanced civilization which existed on the American Continent at a time when Europe was steeped in barbarism."

While the purpose of the organization was to spark scientific investigation into the ancient Maya of Yucatán, it appeared the real motivation behind its members was to spark the Carnegie Institution, that is, to get the lumbering organization off its arse and begin the Chichén Itzá project. Barclay Parsons was president of the New York chapter of the Americas chapter of the Association; Sylvanus Morley was also affiliated. The Americans announced that they would visit Yucatán early next year to identify opportunities for exploration.

If it was a dodge, it worked. John C. Merriam, the new president of the Carnegie Institution, soon announced his intention to see Chichén Itzá himself and determine if the region's governor, Felipe Carrillo Puerto, had given up his radical politics, and if Yucatán was stable enough to launch the project.

Edward Thompson, 1920s

PART THREE

"Ghosts come in troops at Chichén Itzá."

-- Hudson Strode

THE PRESENT

RETURN TO YUCATÁN

ALMOST A YEAR HAS PASSED since our family was in Yucatán. I'm more than ready for Round Two. Hurricane Wilma only delayed my inevitable return, which has been months in the planning. This time I am returning with the Thompsons. I almost can't bear the anticipation. For the first time in more than seventy-five years the two families will reunite and I will be there when they do.

The only thing that tempers my excitement is that I don't know these Thompsons. Ginny, the matriarch, made good her word and chose not to go. Heleni, her daughter, also had to pass. In their place will be Heleni's sister, Alexandra "Alex" Thayer; Ed and Priscilla Thompson's son, Warren; a great-great granddaughter of Edward Herbert Thompson, Elizabeth "Lizzy" Sawyer, and her mother, Janet Sawyer, who I met at Ginny's cabin, but didn't get to know.

For this trip only my daughter Sarah will be along. The itinerary will be as packed, but I've allowed for some downtime. This time we will fly into Cancun, the tourist destination hotspot, instead of Mérida. From there we'll rent a car and drive to Holbox, an out-of-the-way coastal community where we'll meet a friend. Then on to Mérida to spend a couple of days with don Fernando, followed by Chichén Itzá where we will hook up with the Thompsons and the Marrufos.

Don Fernando and I produce a blizzard of e-mail in the weeks leading up to the trip. I share with him the latest results of my research. In one e-mail, I write about his grandfather, Francisco Gomez Rul, and his campaign to bring the Carnegie to Chichén Itzá and to have the Yucatán government improve the infrastructure to get there. Fernando writes that the road to Chichén was one of his grandfather's greatest achievements, although he did not live to see it completed.

We also discuss politics and upcoming presidential election in Mexico. "I do not support any one of the three candidates," he writes. "I shall not cast a vote this time. I shall go to vote, yes, only to scrap the ballot and express concern for Mexico during the next six years." He believes Andrés Manuel López Obrador (better known in Mexico by his initials, AMLO), a member of the radical third party in Mexico, would win. "The PRI party is crumbling and there is no way its members would vote PAN. AMLO and his PRD party will benefit."

A few days before we are set to leave, there appear a series of news stories about Chichén Itzá in the Mexican press. Yucatán Governor Patricio Patrón Laviada declared Chichén Itzá a priority for the state. Representatives of the federal archaeology agency INAH announce they are pursuing *expropiación* of the ancient city. "Expropriation" is what Mexico did to the U.S. oil companies in 1938 when it nationalized the oil industry. This is the first time I've heard that the federal government has become involved and intends to *take* Chichén Itzá, so I ask don Fernando about it. His reply? It's all true, he writes, and worse, the Barbachanos have been backed against a wall:

> *We are at an impasse. The following is highly confidential. We offered to donate [Chichén] in exchange for permission to build a commercial compound and a hotel, with museum and entertainment towards*

enhancing the visitors' comprehension of the great Maya civilization, plus help in restoration of some important structures.

They said no.

There are major interests that we be out of Chichen, except for what already exists—the Mayaland Hotel, my sister's Hacienda Chichen hotel, and the Villas Arqueologicas [not owned by the Barbachanos]—only!

We then asked if the federal government was after an outright sale.

They said no.

What do you want of us, then? The reply was to expropriate. Why? we asked, that would be an embarassment!

No, they said, and explained:

To buy would take approval after approval of various and complicated instances. Expropriation would be expeditious without any bureaucratic encumbrances.

Bureaucratic encumbrances.

There is nothing we can do. What we are after is a prompt payment, God only knows how much, but the law permits payments over fifteen years. A hell of a law! But such are some Mexican laws.

Please be very careful with this info for the time being. Please, please.

Fernando

He adds a postscript, explaining it is not the government that is the source of the family's troubles, but the powerful men behind the government. According to Fernando, there are two groups fighting over Chichén. The Barbachanos are like a boat caught between two hurricanes. He urges me to say nothing, he is only telling me this "for history." Fernando writes:

> *If any member of my family knew I had given out the above information, I could be shot in the head; the situation is very delicate. Powerful, conflicting forces are working against each other...hoping to do us in... creating negative turbulence to acquire beneficial footing over everyone, including us. The invading vendors at Chichen are inconsequential in the shuffle. They do bother the visitors and they shall be expelled. They were the ones used to explode into a national public confrontation the fact that I own Chichen, so predators [could move in] and take us out for their own benefit, and we know who they are.*
>
> *Thus we tread lightly in a battle to survive the best we can, knowing we are the losers, trying to salvage the most we can from our once very important possessions, Chichen Itza, the object of your research and study.*
>
> *We are not crying, we are fighting, though...Chichén Itzá...shall no longer be owned by the Barbachano family, after sixty years of being the guardians. Against all odds, the federal government shall take over. Perhaps this is the best that could happen, but the inward pride of being the owner of Chichen Itza shall not pass lightly, nor joyfully, no matter if we are compensated properly.*
>
> *These thoughts are not aspirins to hide the pain, but true reasoning of facts that surface in my mind, or at least they are what I truly think...*

THE PAST

FROM SPY TO SOCIALITE

AS EDWARD THOMPSON BATTLED the socialistas for control of Chichén Itzá, there was one man who was more anxious at losing the ancient city: Sylvanus Morley. "Morley was so manifestly frightened at the prospect that I had to laugh," Thompson wrote to a friend. "It was to be a mansize fight and one that he evidently had no relish for. In other words the little fellow got cold feet and I don't blame him."

Thompson, perhaps, had once again fallen into hyperbole regarding Morley's mental state, but it would not be outlandish to say Morley was deeply concerned. Even though the Chichén Itzá Project had been put on hold as Yucatán was swept into the chaos of the Mexican Revolution, it had not been abandoned. The Carnegie Institution kept Morley on its payroll and his bosses tried to keep him busy, sending him on expeditions to Mexico and Central America. Possibly because there wasn't much for him to do, he added a second job: spy. War had broken out in Europe and the U.S. military had intelligence that the Germans were attempting to establish a secret submarine base in Central America or the Yucatán Peninsula. The Office of Naval Intelligence recruited Morley to survey the region posing as an archaeologist, not a difficult cover story as he actually was one. Morley and his team of "agents" traveled over 2,000 miles of coastline and, while they found no German fifth columnists, the little arcaheologist identified a future threat to the United States, which, based on his reaction to Edward Thompson almost losing Chichén Itzá should come as no surprise: socialism. In Morley's opinion, it was destroying the Yucatán.

"(The Socialist leadership) liberated the peons; dismantle[d] the churches; drove out the priests; closed the cantinas; prohibited the sale or manufacture of liquor in the state; abolished bullfighting; opened schools; fixed an eight-hour working day and minimum wage scale," Morley wrote in one of his reports. "An enlightened program you will say. Yes, but as in Russia, one that is ruining the country."

By requiring increased wages, Morley explained, the government inadvertently encouraged the labor population—mostly Maya—to work fewer days. Henequen requires constant attention and without it, the plant goes to flower or worse, the forest overtakes the field. Morley estimated that since the socialist regime had taken over more than half of all the henequen fields in the nation had been lost. The state had exported a third less henequen fiber (almost all of it to the United States) the previous year than it had the year before and the trend was getting worse. "In short, the present condition here constitutes the most scathing arraignment of socialistic governmentary control that I ever knew of anywhere and except for Russia is the blackest case against socialism on record."

After the war Morley returned to more traditional archaeological pursuits. His intelligence reports and activities were slapped with a Top Secret tag and buried in Defense Department archives, where they remained for more than eighty years. But Morley was not one who could keep a secret and his espionage career was nearly made public six months after the signing of the Treaty of Versailles. A fellow archaeologist, Franz Boas, published a letter in *The Nation* denouncing the use of archaeologists by the intelligence community. Although he never named Morley and his team, Boas was explicit enough that anyone in the profession would have known who he was talking about. Boas wrote that such activities "prostituted science" and were diametrically opposed to the essence of the profession's code of morality, which was "the service of truth."

Boas's professional colleagues, instead of rising in support, turned on him. His letter appeared ten days before the annual meeting of the American Anthropological Association, which used the gathering to censure Boas and remove him from its executive committee. Nothing further, either explicitly or implicitly, was said about Morley the Spy.

In early 1923, the Carnegie Institution sent Morley the Archaeologist to Yucatán as the advance man for an official visit, which would include the Carnegie Institution director John C. Merriam. Merriam was relatively new, having been named to the office in 1920. Based upon how this visit went, he would decide whether or not the time was actually right to begin work at Chichén Itzá.

Morley's ship arrived in Progreso at Feb. 7. As always, the liner anchored well off shore. A sailboat arrived to transport Morley and company to the shore. Mindful that Yucatán was not only hot, but "dry," Morley snagged a bottle of scotch and two of cognac from the Ward Liner stores. There were some American henequen men on the ship who offered to take Morley and friends into Mérida on their special train. Morley was home. "It was the same flat adorable old Yucatán as ever, flat, flat as a pancake, as far as the eye could reach in every direction." He thought it was looking a "little down-at-the-heel" as well. "The plantations through which we passed looked ill-kept and many, many of the sisal-plants I saw had thrown up their lofty single stalked flower, always a bad sign in a hemp field as it meant the end of such a plant."

Waiting for Morley and his companions was Mrs. James, who brought her automobile to take the party to their hotel. Morley reacquainted himself with his old friends. He had not seen Mr. James in more than three years and Mrs. James' hair was now a glowing, snow-white cap. The party then paid a formal visit to Governor Felipe Carrillo Puerto. Morley predictably was put off by Carrillo Puerto's politics, but seemed surprised to find common ground with the governor thanks to their deep interest in the Maya ("a strong bond of sympathy between us, probably the only one in fact," Morley remarked in his diary).

Two days later Morley met with Edward Thompson and the two men mapped out the next week's itinerary for Dr. Merriam and company. Carnaval was in full swing. The celebrations in Mérida were almost world famous. And because Morley was in town, he was obligated to work every day and attend Carnaval parties every night. On Sunday, the wealthy held a costume ball. The theme for this year was decidedly American for invitees were asked to dress as a member of the Ku Klux Klan. The abuses of the Klan in the United States were being widely reported in Yucatán, but apparently the rich and powerful were not so disgusted that they couldn't throw a ball of dancers dressed in sheets.

Morley didn't don a costume for the event, but instead wore fine evening clothes. He loved to dance and, even though he was at the time in a committed relationship, his diary revealed that he was not without a wandering eye. He especially was proud of his pickup line. "Pardon me," he would say. "I am Dr. Morley of the Carnegie Institution of Washington and one of the United States' delegates to the Twentieth International Congress of Americanists. Would you care to dance this fox-trot?"

The people of Mérida, rich and poor, would celebrate Carnaval for the next two days, but for Morley it was over. The Carnegie was coming and with it, the future of Yucatán.

THE PRESENT

TRAPPED IN CHIQUILA

THE WEATHER IS BRISK and, typical for March, punctuated by gusty blasts of wind. Traffic on the Massachusetts Turnpike is light and the roads are clear, despite the occasional flurries of snow that materialize from the mostly clear sky. I pick Sarah up at her dormitory at the University of Massachusetts in Amherst. She has been waiting for me, looking out the window of her room so I wouldn't have to get out of my car.

"We're going to Mexico," she says to no one in particular when she gets in. It becomes a mantra, something she repeats until we arrive the next day. She tells me how excited she is about the trip, that she has relished telling her friends about her adventure and how she is going to help her father with his book. I tell her that I am somewhat less enthusiastic because, frankly, I am ambivalent about her coming along. Writing is a self-centered and selfish activity, and not to be shared, except on the printed page. There is a lot I have to get done and I fear that my attention will have to be split between my research and my role as father. Sarah assures me this won't be a problem.

And there is the little matter of the artifacts from the Cenote Sagrado that I bought online. I have them secreted in my luggage. I did not mention this to Sarah, but the scenario did run through my head of my luggage being searched at customs and me being hauled away in chains, leaving my daughter to fend for herself in Mexico. I knew if I said something, she would probably be more nervous than me.

The next day we fly into Cancún. Our objective for this trip is to continue my interviews with don Fernando, meet a few more members of his family, and then rendezvous with the Thompson descendants at Chichén Itzá, who would meet for the first time their Maya cousins.

First, though, we are going to spend a couple of days on Holbox, an island off the northeast coast of the Yucatan peninsula. We are meeting a friend, Paul "Pablo" Harding, who works in the film industry in Toronto. Pablo has been going to Holbox for decades and has invited Sarah and me to join his family for a short vacation before I have to get down to work.

We clear immigration and customs and no one bothers to inspect my luggage. We get a ride to the rental car company and make arrangements to have a car for the week. While we wait for an attendant to bring out a car, I ask the overly friendly fellow behind a podium for directions to Chiquila, the landside port for the ferries to Holbox. I pronounce the name like the banana company, "Chi-KEE-lah." I get a puzzled look in response. On the counter of the podium, under a plastic transparent cover, is a map of Yucatán, I find Holbox and drag my finger south to Chiquila. "Ah, CHEE-kee-lah," he says, and looks at me with eyes that convey the pity he regards my gringo-ness. "Getting there is very easy," he says, and from under a counter he produces, with great flourish, a tourist map of Yucatan. His directions are simple: Take the Cuota (the toll road that runs between Cancún and Mérida) halfway to Nueva Xcan and then strike out north for Chiquila. I will be there by five o'clock, he tells me.

Sarah and I set out from the airport. It has been five months since Hurricane Wilma, but the devastation can be seen everywhere: Power poles down, buildings destroyed, and worst of all, signs missing everywhere. We pass the turnoff to the Cuota and have to backtrack to find it. The highway leading to the Cuota has flooded and washed out, leaving only a gravel bed.

As we drive, I explain to Sarah that we have to reach Chiquila before sunset so that we can catch one of the last ferries to Holbox. The one thing we didn't want to do is to be caught out after dark. Driving in Yucatan after sundown is a big no-no. Friends have warned me of this time after time. You never know what is going to pop out at you: Drunks passed out in the roadway, livestock emerging from the jungle, or potholes as big as cenotes that would flatten a tire. Most dangerous of all are the men peddling the three-wheeled cycles, which frequently are without reflectors, making them nearly invisible in the gloom until you are upon them.

At Nuevo Xcan there is a tollbooth, but I don't see an exit. I ask the toll taker, but he only speaks Spanish and I can only pick out a word or two. He keeps repeating something that sounds like "Libra." Like the astrological sign? A road scale maybe? Or did it mean "book." I ask Sarah, who I had thought would be my translator thanks to her schooling in Spanish. "How would I know?" she says. So much for my translator.

We drive on, hoping the exit is ahead. When we are almost to Valladolid, sixty-five kilometers away, we give up and drive back to the Nuevo Xcan tollbooth. I find another tollbooth operator, this time one who speaks some English, who explains what I already knew: There is no exit. We must either go back to Cancún or ahead to Valladolid and take the "Libre" (free) road.

It is after five o'clock when we make it to the turnoff to Chiquila via the free road. We have another seventy kilometers to go and the sun is already low. I figure if we race, we can make Chiquila a little after sunset, probably too late for the ferry, but maybe we can get a private boat to take us to Holbox.

The road, like most in Yucatan, is straight and flat. There is one lane in each direction and no shoulder; where the blacktop ends, the forest takes over. We zip along at about 120 kilometers an hour and only slow when we hit the first village, Kantunikin, and the inevitable speed bumps known as topes. Just as we get through the town, we come upon the single biggest piece of road equipment I've ever seen, a giant road grader, taking up more than a lane and a half of the highway. There was no way around it as it crawls forward at less than ten kilometers an hour. We fall in behind and wait for an opportunity to pass. The sun is only a few degrees above the horizon. I look at Sarah, she looks at me, and we both don't even need to say anything. There is no way we are going to get to Chiquila to make any boat. Sarah then says, "You know, if mom was here, she'd be dead by now."

I nod. "We'd have to pull over, prop up her up against a tree and hope somebody finds her," I say.

We don't get to Chiquila until well after eight. The sun is long gone and the town is pitch black. It smells of sewage and bad cooking. We can't find a boat to take us over to Holbox; a young boy offers to lead us to the sole motel in the town, which we find is surprisingly cheap at 200 pesos a night. There are beds, with matching coverlets, no less. But the sheets are stained with a brown, crusty substance, so we sleep on top of made beds. I swear something chews on me throughout the night.

It really can't get much worse, I think, but I'm wrong. Unbeknownst to me, as I drift fitfully off to sleep, I've locked the keys to the rental car in the trunk.

THE PAST

MRS. ALMA REED

TWO DAYS INTO LENT, the Ward Liner Mexico chugged into the waters off the coast of Yucatán. Aboard was a delegation from the Carnegie Institution—Dr. John Merriam and Gen. Barclay Parsons—as well as an assortment of other dignitaries and a group of what Morley disparagingly called "tourists."

One of those tourists was an apple-cheeked woman in her early thirties, wearing the trendiest fashions of the day. She was fond of cloche hats, which fit snugly to the contours of the head and slid down over the eyes, giving her a coquettish gaze. Alma Reed—Mrs. Alma Reed—was, in her own words, a "tall, slender young woman with an oval face, chestnut brown hair, classic features, fair skin, and very large, dark blue eyes." Her greatest asset was the ever-present smile on her face, but a smile that belied a seriousness of purpose. She was not, as Morley sniffed, a "tourist," but a writer for the *New York Times*, and although no one, including her, knew it at the time, she nearly would derail the Carnegie Chichén Itzá project before it got off the ground.

Reed lived in San Francisco where she had built her reputation writing for one of the daily newspapers about juvenile murderers on death row. Her most famous case was Simon Ruiz, a seventeen-year-old from Mexico who had been sentenced to hang for killing a railroad foreman. Reed wrote articles protesting his execution and she assembled an ad hoc association of women's groups (such as the California Housewive's League) to petition the governor of California for clemency. A month before Ruiz's execution, the governor commuted his sentence.

For her campaign, Reed received a platinum vanity case inscribed, "Respectfully presented by the Mexican Government to Alma Sullivan Reed, in high appreciation of her altruistic efforts." With the gift came an invitation to visit Mexico by the nation's president, Alvaro Obregón. Not one to waste an opportunity, Reed contacted the *New York Times* and offered to write for them while she was south of the border. Reed spent three months in Mexico and got to know many of the movers and shakers of government, including those who oversaw archaeology. She traveled throughout Mexico in a semi-official capacity. Communities she visited threw fiestas in her honor and over time she became known as *la niña periodista*.

Through the connections she made in Mexico she learned of the Carnegie visit, and once again she offered her services to the *Times*. According to Reed, the newspaper's owner Adolph Ochs personally assigned her to tag along with the Carnegie group and file dispatches from Yucatán. Reed approached her new assignment with the same gusto she employed to fight for the lives of the teenagers on death row. "I have determined to work today as never before," Reed wrote in her diary while at sea on her way to Yucatán. "My one desire now is to prove myself worthy of the confidence that Mr. Ochs placed in me. I will not, must not, let him down."

When Reed disembarked at Progreso, she was introduced to Morley and a delegation that included distinguished members of Yucatán's Casta Divina: Felipe G. Cantón, who would be her host, and José Raphael de Regil Casares, another wealthy hacendado and possessor of one of the best private collections of Maya artifacts. Governor Felipe Carrillo Puerto had made available his private train to whisk the visitors into Mérida once they cleared Progreso customs. As the train pulled into the Mérida station, the official band of the state of Yucatán struck up a medley of American college fight songs, beginning with the University of California's, where Dr. Merriam had long been a professor. From there the group piled into several automobiles to the Parque del Centenario for a luncheon of tortillas, tamales, and beer.

After the meal, a driver took Reed, Merriam, and Parsons to Cantón's mansion on the Paseo de Montejo. That evening they were feted once again, this time at a banquet held in the foyer of the Peon Contreras Theater. A long table had been erected with more than 100 place settings. As guests entered, they were introduced one-by-one to Gov. Carrillo Puerto and his sister, Elvia, who served as the unofficial First Lady of Yucatán.

After dinner, there were three speeches of welcome, in Spanish, English, and in Maya, the latter delivered by the governor himself. Reed could not understand a word Carrillo Puerto said, but she was swept up in his aura. She described him in messianic terms as the "deliverer, protector, and infallible guide" of the Maya. Someone later translated his speech for her. The governor told the archaeologists, "High up there in their sculptured halls they are waiting. The ghosts of the Maya are waiting for you. They have been silent through the centuries. You will be the first to hear their story. Hear it and tell it to the world."

The next night the governor had Reed seated next to him. Reed noticed that she was getting more attention from everyone else because of it. "I realized I was sharing his limelight," she noted later. "I was tranquilly conscious that the collective gaze not only was embracing me but was taking detailed note of my personal appearance. My French blue satin dinner gown, my simple, classic hairdo, and my every movement were under close and, I sensed, approving scrutiny."

The next day, Carrillo Puerto accompanied Reed and the other "tourists" to Chichén Itzá. His private train carried them to Dzitas, where they boarded several *fordingas*—Model T's modified into passenger buses. Carrillo Puerto's new road was now twelve kilometers long, but still short of reaching Chichén. At the end of the finished highway, the vehicles had to crawl along the old road, which was corrugated by sharp ridges of limestone.

Alma sat next to the governor. He spoke of how no one would ever again have to ride the volan, the infamous flatbed wagon that bounced visitors about. "That's all in the past now, like the hacienda floggings of our Indios," he told Reed. "By July, the last layer of macadam will be laid, and the motoring time between Dzitas and Chichén Itzá will be cut to less than a half hour." He told Reed of his plans to invite Maya from all over the peninsula to Chichén Itzá to dedicate the new road, the first official reunion of the Maya people in several centuries.

At Pisté, the road resumed. Edward Thompson had spent $7,000 to connect to the new highway. The visitors gasped as, one by one, the fordingas turned a corner, revealing the crest of the great pyramid, El Castillo, as it loomed over the treetops. The road cut through the south end of the Great Ball Court, which had been cleared of trees and brush, and then passed along the south face of the pyramid. There the caravan stopped and four Maya musicians struck up a traditional song. Carrillo Puerto hopped out of the lead car and embraced Edward Thompson, who was awaiting their arrival. Someone pulled out a white ribbon and the governor symbolically cut it. Several women and many of the men had tears in their eyes.

The governor introduced Thompson as "don Eduardo." The owner of Chichén Itzá took over and guided the party around the ruins, the entire time spinning colorful tales of the ancient Maya. Reed commented that Thompson moved like a man much younger, but she must have seen that he had a noticeable limp. While trying to repair the hacienda after socialistas torched it, Thompson had attempted to move a heavy stone carving that had been damaged in the fire. His grip slipped and it crushed his foot. It would be years before he would return to the United States to have surgery that would abate the pain, but not correct the damage.

The Hacienda Chichén was in no better shape than Thompson's foot. After the tour, the group took luncheon at the main house. The grounds were choked with brush and only one of the out buildings had a roof. Thompson had tried to repair his casa, but it was not fit for guests. A makeshift dining room had been set up on the terraza by hanging heavy henequen curtains across the arches.

After dinner, Reed found a quiet spot to review her notes from the day. Thompson drew up a chair next to her. He told her that she reminded him of a girl he once knew on Cape Cod. He asked her about her newspaper work and wondered if she would be interested in hearing about the "greatest archaeological adventure of the New World." Intrigued, Reed pressed him for more details, but Thompson demurred and told her to return on a day when there were not so many around. What he wanted to tell her was in the nature of a confession, he said, "and I'd rather 'confess' to a pretty and ambitious young journalist like yourself, especially since I find you so simpatico." He would say no more, other than that there were rival archaeological groups—one group would like the story to remain quiet and another would like it to have the widest possible release. Reed promised to return at the earliest opportunity.

Over the next few days Reed experienced more of the wonders of Yucatán and its handsome governor. The Carnegie team was likewise enamored by Chichén Itzá. They stayed at the archaeological site for several days, inspecting the ruins and attempting to determine which should be excavated. Eventually they selected the so-called "Court of a Thousand Columns."

After Merriam, Parsons, and Morley departed Chichén Itzá, Reed returned to hear Thompson's "confession," which, as promised, was a doozy. He told her everything—how he had dredged the Cenote Sagrado for years, recovered countless artifacts of gold, copper, jade, and pottery, and how he had shipped those artifacts to the Peabody Museum at Harvard University.

Thompson had given Reed the story of a lifetime. Later that night she attempted to write the article, but no words would come. She was too distracted with thoughts of Felipe Carrillo Puerto. Instead she scrawled at the bottom of her notes of her interview with Thompson the following: "Love, beyond my every hope or dream, has come to me at last!"

Alma Reed

THE PRESENT

LOVE AT THE END

LOVE, ACCORDING TO DON FERNANDO, is one of the last things human beings can enjoy as they near the end of their days.

Sarah and I sit with him in the cool basement of his mansion. We had arrived in Merida the night before after our adventure in Chiquila and Holbox. I told him about the crusty sheets at the hotel and how I could not find my car keys the next morning. I remembered the last place I had seen them was when I opened the trunk the night before to get our bags. A search of our room came up empty and I knew in my heart where they were. After several anxious minutes, I remembered that I could get into the trunk by lowering the back seat. Fortunately I had forgotten to lock the car. I spent several minutes blindly reaching into the trunk through an opening behind the backseat until my fingers snagged the keys.

Sarah and I hired a boat to take us to Holbox, where we enjoyed a pleasant day with friends. They were only slightly worried that we hadn't shown up the day before. They had been coming to Mexico for years, so they well knew that things just happen. We spent the night and then left the next day for Mérida to meet don Fernando.

I'm keen to hear an update on the Barbachanos' fight to keep Chichén, but I cannot find time with Fernando alone. Hans is always around and I am certain to keep an eye on me.

I ask Fernando about his health. "My quality of life is restricted," he says, but without bitterness. He requires monodialysis three times a week to clean his blood because his kidneys no longer function. He is in constant discomfort and, to my eyes, even more pain since we saw him a year ago, before his car accident. He is all but confined to a wheelchair. "But I am able to work. Write. Love," he says. "And it is a love that returns. My wife and I are in love. We've been married fifty-six years. She still hates my jokes, but she's always hated my jokes." Sarah laughs.

Maruja, joins us for breakfast. I had told Fernando that I wanted to interview her and take her picture. As Hans wheels her in, it occurs to me that she must spend a long time getting dressed and coiffed. That attention pays off, for she always looks perfect.

She was born to Spanish parents and christened Maria Magdalena Herrero García, but to all she is Maruja, the name she received from her mother and one that has been passed down to her eldest daughter, granddaughter, and great-granddaughter. Her family long has been entwined with the Barbachanos, which makes perfect sense as the histories of the two clans are similar. Maruja's parents were from Spain, immigrants to Yucatán in the first half of the 20th century, just like the Barbachanos, although they had arrived a century earlier. Her sister Teresa also married a Barbachano, Manuel Barbachano Ponce, a cousin of don Fernando. Her brother Eugenio, who for many years worked in the Yucatecan government overseeing its highways, also collaborated with Manuel who became a famous Mexican filmmaker and with Fernando running his short-lived airline, Aeromaya. As a boy Eugenio had been sent to boarding school in Cuba where he became friend-for-life with Fidel Castro. When one of Eugenio's children was diagnosed with a life-threatening cancer, Castro had him brought to Cuba where physicians cured him, Maruja says. The relationship also must have come in handy in 1968 when an Aeromaya plane was taken at gunpoint to Cuba by not only the first female hijacker in history, but the first hijacker to go from Mexico to Cuba since Edward Thompson absconded with the boat in 1915. One reason such actions were so rare is that there were daily commercial flights to Cuba from Mexico.

Maruja and Fernando have six children: Fernando, who owns the Mayaland resort; Maruja, who owns several businesses in Valladolid, the largest city near Chichén Itzá; Carmen, who is launching a vegan-style restaurant in Mérida; Christina, who I hear had just moved back from Miami; Isabel or Belisa, who runs the Hacienda Chichén for don Fernando's sister; and Juan, who runs the hotel in Cozumel. Her first three children were born at home, the second trio in hospitals. Her father, she says, had warned her never to give birth in a hospital.

"They exchange the babies there, he told me," Maruja says with a big smile.

"Well that's what happened with me," Fernando announces. "Or so my sister says."

Maruja and Fernando have several grandchildren and Maruja mentions that she had been talking with one of them just that morning. "They all have relations before they get married, which was unheard of in my day," she says. She looks at Sarah. "Do you have a boyfriend?"

I want to put my fingers in my ears, because there are things a father is not supposed to hear. "I have a boyfriend," Sarah says. Maruja asks if they are planning to marry. Sarah says no. Thankfully the line of inquiry ends there. Maruja returns to her granddaughter. "They don't get married so young," she says. "Forget about family, it's all about two cars."

When she was a child growing up in Mérida, "we had a home and one car," she says. She walked to school, she says, although admitted that during the hottest times of the year her father occasionally would drive her. School was held daily in two sessions, from eight to noon, and then you returned at two and went until five. Students returned home during the two midday hours for lunch.

"And siesta?" I ask.

Maruja chuckles. "My father had a siesta, the children had to work," she says. Her father, she explains, "was easy," while her mother was the strict one in the family. Her voice takes on a wistful quality as she speaks about her father, the affection he would show her, the kindnesses he would do for her. She bemoans that her father had been there for her until his death. But the need for your parents extends long after their passing. "The sad thing about dying, there are so many things I would have loved to talk with my father now," she says. "It's very sad that when you're ready for things you want to know, your parents are no longer there. I really miss my father every day."

Maria Magdalena 'Maruja' Herrero Garcia

THE PAST

SCOOP

FELIPE CARRILLO PUERTO TOOK ALMA REED to his hometown of Motul to introduce her to his mother. Adela Puerto de Carrillo was a diminutive woman, but erect with a spine of steel, who gave birth to fourteen children. Adela Puerto de Carrillo spoke of her family's history, how she was descended from Spanish-descent merchants, and how her husband was mestizo, descended from Spanish and from Maya.

Reed had in her possession a story that would make Adolph Ochs of the *New York Times* proud, but there was little she could do with it. It didn't make sense to mail the article to New York, because the mail boat was the same ship she would be taking when she departed Yucatán in a few days. Instead she passed the time with Carrillo Puerto. She spent an afternoon with him at a ceremony in the village of Suma where the governor provided the local Maya with land where they could grow their crops. The slogan of Carrillo Puerto's socialist leagues was *"Tierra y Libertad*!"—"Land and Liberty!" To acquire land for the campesinos, the governor seized large swaths of haciendas that belonged to the Casta Divina. One of Carrillo Puerto's favorite targets was Felipe G. Cantón, Alma Reed's host in Mérida.

Reed also spent several evenings with Carrillo Puerto and a pair of

Yucatecan songwriters, Luis Rosada de la Vega and Ricardo Palmerin. The governor commissioned them to write a song that captured their new relationship.

A couple of days before she was set to leave, the Carnegie group decided to explore Loltun, a spectacular cavern south of Mérida that had been used by the Maya for centuries. Once again, the governor's private train was pressed into service. By this time, Reed and Carrillo Puerto were inseparable and it was obvious to everyone that he was smitten. At the end of the rail line, the group mounted horses to take them the six miles to Loltun. When the party got to the cavern, the couple wandered off by themselves for a little privacy. They later rejoined everyone inside the cave.

At Morley's suggestion, the group set off to view several figures that had been carved into one of the cave walls. The path was treacherous and at one point required everyone to creep along a narrow ledge that overlooked a deep hole—certain death should anyone slip. Everyone managed to cross the chasm without incident, but then the guide became lost. Soon everyone was wandering in all directions, trying to find a way out. The governor roared out an order in Maya and everyone stopped (according to Morley, the governor shouted, "The first man that speaks I will shoot!"). He then directed the guide to quit looking for an alternative exit and instead lead everyone back out of the cave the way they had come in.

Once outside, everyone remounted the horses and rode back to the train. Morley recalled that next to the station lived an elder of the Xiu clan, a direct descendant of the family that once ruled Uxmal and southwest Yucatán. Morley asked the governor if he wished to be introduced. Felipe Carrillo Puerto spit out a no and called the Xius traitors to the Maya people. He did not explain, but the Xius were the first Maya clan to collaborate with the Spanish in their conquest of Yucatán. The governor was reported to have descended from the Cocoms, who had to be conquered by force.

Two days later, Carrillo Puerto and Reed said their goodbyes and she departed by ship from Progreso. When she arrived in Havana, she telegrammed the *New York Times* with her story of Thompson's dredging of the Cenote Sagrado. The paper ran a few paragraphs on the third page the next day.

Upon her return to the United States, Reed visited the Peabody Museum at Harvard in the company of Roberto Casas Alatriste, a former member of Mexico's Chamber of Deputies, who happened in New York to negotiate relief for Mexico's national debt, and a woman from the nation's Ministry of Foreign Relations. The party asked to see the artifacts from the Cenote Sagrado and was admitted to an upstairs storage room with glass cases filled with artifacts, exactly as Thompson had described to her.

Reed expanded the story for the *New York Times*' Sunday magazine, which ran a month later. She wrote the article "as tactfully as I knew how... fully aware that the revelations it contained could provoke an international incident." Tact, however, did not exclude hyperbole. Reed began the article by noting that the recovery of the cenote artifacts, as discoveries go, is "the most important in the history of American archaeology."

In her autobiography, written years later, Reed claimed the article created a furor. "In less than sixty days after the disclosures—which, due to Mr. Thompson's status as American consul in Yucatán, had created a scandal—the government of Mexico, demanding return of the whole collection of ancient objects or an indemnity of two million dollars, instituted a lawsuit against the Peabody Museum," she wrote. But Reed's recollection was like Thompson's. There had been no furor. Sylvanus Morley, who was in Yucatán when the story broke, feared that Reed's article would derail the Carnegie project, but nothing came of it. He met with José Reygadas y Vertiz, the federal inspector of Mexico's pre-Columbian monuments, to feel him out about whether the *New York Times* article would affect the

Carnegie's ability to get a long-term concession to excavate Chichén. To Morley's relief, Reygadas y Vertiz indicated that because the Carnegie was turning over all the artifacts it found to the Mexican government, he did not anticipate any problems.

Morley's involvement in the Cenote Sagrado dredging remained a secret. Reed mentioned Morley in her *New York Times* article, although not by name. She quoted don Eduardo who described how "scientists" had been present when the dredge recovered a sacrificial knife. There was only one scientist present at that event and that was Morley, who was also the person who carried the knife from Mexico to the Peabody Museum.

While in Mexico City, Morley successfully negotiated the concession to excavate Chichén with the Mexican government. Reygadas y Vertiz's instincts proved correct, for Morley came away with a ten-year permit to excavate Chichén Itzá. But the dredging of the Cenote Sagrado always loomed over the Carnegie project and Morley, despite his canny political skills, would not escape from under its shadow, as he would soon learn.

The archaeologist returned to Yucatán and spent several days at Chichén Itzá with his sister. While poking around the domed El Caracol, he uncovered what appeared to be a large, round stone about the diameter of a wagon wheel, covered with carved figures and glyphs. Mexican authorities gave him permission to excavate the stone and in June he unearthed it along with what turned out to be an altar almost two meters wide by one meter high and thirty centimeters thick. It would be his last discovery before officially beginning his duties reconstructing Chichén Itzá. Morley had been planning to excavate Chichén since he first laid eyes upon the ruins at twenty-two; he was now forty and was ready to begin what he believed would be his life's work. When he returned in July it would be as the director of one of the largest archaeological digs in the history of the Americas.

No one was more enthusiastic about the Carnegie project than Felipe Carrillo Puerto. The governor believed that Yucatán had reached a "golden hour," and that the truth about the Maya race and the ancient peoples throughout Mexico was about to be fully revealed to the world. He directly linked efforts such as the Carnegie Institution's with his social programs to make life better for the Maya of today.

Upon the completion of his highway to Chichén Itzá, Carrillo Puerto formally announced the dedication celebration, the first great gathering of the indigenous people since the Spanish Conquest. In the midst of the extensive preparations for the massive fiesta, Carrillo Puerto received word from Alma Reed that she would be returning to Mexico. The *New York Times* had assigned her to spend three months in Mexico City to report on developments there. The governor tried to persuade her to lay over in Mérida on her way to the nation's capital, but Reed declined. Instead he promised to visit her in Mexico City once his celebration at Chichén Itzá was over. He later wired her that he would meet her on board her Ward Liner when it anchored off the coast of Progreso.

In early July Reed departed New York for Mexico. When the ship arrived and anchored five kilometers from the shore of Yucatán, a power launch met the ship. But there was no Carrillo Puerto. Instead, he had sent his chief of staff, Manuel Cirerol Sansores, and a small group of musicians. As they pulled up to the ship, the group sang a song that Reed instantly recognized as the composition Carrillo Puerto had commissioned for her. It was the first time she heard the completed song, "*Peregrina*," and although she did not know it at the time, it would become the unofficial love anthem of Yucatán, a song so powerful that even today only a few notes will moisten the eyes of Yucatecans. Cirerol Sansores tried to persuade Reed to jump ship and join Carrillo Puerto at Chichén Itzá, but she would not budge. So instead he gave her letters and documents from the governor and from

Edward H. Thompson. The note from the former said she would be seeing her love in a week or so in Mexico City.

The governor could not come, Cirerol Sansores told her, because Maya were arriving hourly to Chichén Itzá for the celebration. Carrillo Puerto anticipated that almost 100,000 Maya would fill the ancient city. The governor was using the occasion to spark awareness in the Maya of their "noble cultural heritage."

On July 15, 1923, Carrillo Puerto officially opened the new highway to Chichén Itzá. The state government bussed Maya in from all over Yucatán to see the ruins and the governor gave a brief, but moving speech in their language. He recalled his first visit to Chichén, long before his involvement in politics, and how he had been moved to tears by the grandeur of the ruins. He praised the men who built the road, telling the crowd that while it had been paid for by the government, the money meant nothing without the collective labor and collective wills of the workers who had built it. He concluded by reminding the audience that while governments past had cheated them, his administration supported and helped them.

After the ceremony, Carrillo Puerto left Yucatán for a month in Mexico City with his love, Alma Reed.

THE PRESENT

FAMILY MATTERS

I ASK FERNANDO what he knows about Felipe Carrillo Puerto. He shrugs and says he knows nothing. This strikes me as odd, as the late governor was so important in opening Chichén Itzá to the world. Furthermore one of Fernando's good friends, he once told me, was Manuel Cirerol Sansores, who was Carrillo Puerto's chief of staff. And finally, Fernando's grandfather, Francisco Gomez Rul, not only knew the late governor, but apparently knew him well enough to dedicate a book to him. Fernando brushes it off, reminding me that he never knew his grandfather, who died a week before he was born.

Sarah and I arrive at the Mayaland Resort just after dark. The Thompsons are staying at the Chichén Itzá Hotel in Pisté, a couple of kilometers away. I haven't quite figured out how I am going to meet up with them to take them to meet the Marrufos. In fact, I hadn't even told the Marrufos I was coming, although my understanding was that at least one of the Thompsons has been in touch with them via e-mail. My plan, if you can call it that, is to check in, drop off our luggage at our room, and then drive to Pisté to find the Thompsons. But as we register, the clerk asks us out of the blue if we are with the Thompsons.

"The Thompsons are here?" I ask. The clerk tells me that they are staying in one of the bungalows. I ask if someone can direct me to them.

After depositing our luggage in our room, a bellboy leads me, serpentine, through the grounds of the resort to a bungalow. I knock on the door and it is answered by a short woman with a shock of gray hair and a confident, almost defiant, gaze. She introduces herself as Alex. She is precisely as her sister Heleni described her. She's one of the great grandchildren of Edward Thompson.

The door to the adjoining suite is open and from it emerges two more Thompsons. One of them, Janet Sawyer, I had met several weeks before at Thompson's old camp on Cape Cod. Janet introduces me to her daughter, eighteen-year-old Elizabeth, or "Lizzie" as she is called. There is one more Thompson, cousin Warren Thompson, who is as yet unaccounted for. Warren is the son of Edward Thompson, the grandson of the original who I interviewed back on Cape Cod.

Janet and Lizzie appear to be in a daze. I recognize it as the decompression that everyone goes through when they first arrive in a foreign country. Alex, on the other hand, does not appear to be fazed at all. She flits about the room, unpacking, chatting the entire time. I ask her when they are planning to meet the Marrufos and she says that one of the sons is coming to pick them up in a few minutes. "Where are you getting together?" I ask, telling her I have my own car and can drive over.

She looks at me quizzically, but there is no confusion in her eyes. "You're not going," she says. "This is only for family."

THE PAST

RED TIGER WITH EYES OF JADE

ALMA REED WAS IN SAN FRANCISCO. Carrillo Puerto had been planning to join her later that month and the two were to be wed. Around her neck she wore a small copper bell, a Maya artifact from Chichén Itzá's Cenote Sagrado. Carrillo Puerto had given it to her and had inscribed upon it, "Remember the Maya, lovely Alma Reed."

But in January 1924, her thoughts were not with the Maya, but with the man she had left behind in Mexico. The couple had spent a romantic month in the capital city in late summer. While he was there, Carrillo Puerto took time for a little politicking, announcing his support for President Obregon's handpicked successor, Plutarco Elias Calles. The choice did not sit well with everyone. In September, a member of Calles's cabinet, Adolfo de la Huerta, resigned and, with the support of the military, launched a coup on Dec. 6.

One of de la Huerta's supporters, General Guadalupe Sanchez, telegrammed Carrillo Puerto (and other governors), demanding to know, "Are you with us or against us?" Carrillo without hesitation declared his support for Obregon and Calles. The next day he issued a public statement, reiterating his allegiance. On Dec. 8, the Yucatecan Congress in a vote also backed the president. Carrillo Puerto then began a flurry of telegrams with his counterparts in the southeastern Mexican states of Campeche, Chiapas, Tobasco, and the territory of Quintana Roo, and received their support as well.

However, Carrillo Puerto failed to win over the federal troops stationed in Southeast Mexico and worse, he failed to gauge how influential they actually were. On Dec. 12, the Yucatán government received a request for aid from Campeche to put down a mutiny by a handful of federal troops. Yucatán responded by sending a federal battalion under the command of Carrillo Puerto's man, Col. Robinsón. The mutiny, however, had been a ruse, for all the federal forces in Campeche were backing de la Huerta. They captured Col. Robinsón, added the Yucatán federal troops to their own and turned the train around to return to Mérida to seize the government. As they sped toward their destination, someone sent a telegram to Carrillo Puerto pretending to be Col. Robinsón, advising the governor that the "rebel forces have fled in disorder," and to meet the victorious troops at the train station to discuss the situation. The governor smelled a trap and decided it was time to get out of Mérida and live to fight another day.

He escaped in his personal train, heading east. He stopped in Motul, his hometown, and briefly flirted with making a stand there. But while his family, friends, neighbors, combined with thousands of campesinos from neighboring towns would have the numbers to repel the federales, their hunting rifles and machetes would have been no match against trained troops. Carrillo Puerto instead instructed his followers to not resist and, along with his personal police force and his closest followers, struck out for the northeast coast where he hoped to find a boat to take him across the Straits of Yucatán to Cuba and from there to the United States. They rode the governor's special train as far east as the tracks would take them, to the cattle town of Tizimin. From there he continued past San Felipe, where Edward Thompson had found a boat eight years before. His party acquired mules and wagons and pressed farther east.

The farther Carrillo Puerto got from Mérida, the less support he found. With federales closing, the governor's special police began to feel none too special. They griped about their wages, as they had not been paid in two months. As the group forged ahead, the governor and his followers sought donations from the locals along their route but only managed to raise a few pesos here and there. They had to sell their side arms to pay the police so they wouldn't turn him in. At Solferino, a few miles from the coast, the governor released his police escort and most of his supporters, save for three of his brothers and a few close followers. And then, at least as far as the federal forces pursuing him were concerned, he disappeared.

Had he found a boat or ship to take him to Cuba? Or Maya sympathetic to his cause who guided him overland to British Honduras? The governor had no such luck. He and his men had pressed on to Chiquila, the easternmost village on the northern coast of Yucatán. From there they traveled several kilometers east along the coastline to a remote cornfield (milpa in Maya), which became their hideout. The owner of the milpa had built a simple shed to ward off the elements and a crib that held the harvest corn. There was also a stand of banana or plantain trees nearby and, most importantly, a small spring for fresh water. They obtained the services of a young man from Chiquila, Mariano, who scrounged food and other supplies and paddled them out to their hideout.

Hiding in a milpa had to be uncomfortable, if not miserable, with little protection from the elements or insects, especially at dusk and dawn when marsh mosquitoes swarmed by the hundreds to feed. Carrillo Puerto sent one of his men to Cuyo, a small port community, to see about getting passage to Cuba. Days passed and he never returned. Then young Mariano stopped bringing supplies.

What the governor and his men did not know was both men had fallen into the hands of the federales. First they captured the associate at Cuyo and, with the knowledge that Carrillo Puerto was still in the area, focused their manhunt in that region. When they received intelligence that a young man had been roaming local villages seeking food, they arrested him, correctly guessing he was helping Carrillo Puerto.

Neither man revealed where the governor was hiding, but in the end, their loyalty did not matter. The fugitives, coming to the realization they were on their own, attempted to escape Yucatán. Returning to Chiquila they acquired a boat and sailed for Cuyo, where they hoped to catch a steamship. Instead the prevailing winds drove them across Laguna Conil where they ran aground not far from the village of Holbox, where federal forces captured them. There would be no escape to Cuba, the United States, or anywhere. Instead, they were taken back to Mérida, tried and convicted. Three days into 1924, Felipe Carrillo Puerto, three of his brothers, and several of his supporters were removed from the state prison to Mérida's largest cemetery, then lined against a wall and executed by firing squad. So that there would be no question as to their fate, the bodies were placed on display like sides of beef.

Sylvanus Morley and Edward Thompson rarely agreed on much, but on Felipe Carrillo Puerto, they were unanimous: Archaeology in Yucatán had lost a great friend. He had done more for to promote investigation into the ancient Maya than any governor over the past four centuries.

The delahuertistas quickly went to work erasing any evidence of Carrillo Puerto in the peninsula. History, however, was not on their side. By April 18, federal troops under President Obregon retook Mérida and the delahuertistas fled south and east (looting and pillaging along the way). One of the first acts of the restored government of Yucatán was to declare henceforth that Jan. 3, the day of Carrillo Puerto's execution, would be a day of mourning.

The wall where they executed Carrillo Puerto became a shrine, a symbol of his martyrdom. In 1925, the governor was disinterred and his remains placed not far from the wall where he had been shot, at the center of a monument devoted to socialism.

Alma Reed spent her last years in Mexico, ostensibly as a writer, but more as a hero of the nation. She wrote for an English language newspaper in Mexico City. In 1961, the Mexican government awarded her its highest civilian honor, the Orden des Aguila Azteca, for her longtime contribution to Mexican arts.

She died in 1966 and although she outlived Carrillo Puerto by more than forty years, she carried a torch for him her entire life. She had wanted to be buried next to Carrillo Puerto, but the closest she could get was across the street. Even after four decades, Carrillo Puerto's children would not have it. Alma Reed, they said, was not family.

Alma Reed's burial site

Above, the Rotundo of Socialists,
where Felipe Carrillo Puerto is interred.
Below, a 1931 magazine illustration celebrating the life
of Carrillo Puerto.

THE PRESENT

WHAT IS FAMILY?

'NOT FAMILY?!' I FUME. "Not family!" Sarah and I sit on the dining patio at the Mayaland Hotel, waiting for someone to take our order. I'm so aggravated, I don't think I can eat.

Less than an hour earlier I had been stunned into silence. After Alex announced that I would not be allowed at the Marrufo/Thompson reunion, I had no idea what to say. I mumbled a goodbye and returned to my room. From our balcony overlooking the Mayaland parking lot, I had watched the American Thompson descendants pile into a van driven by one of the Marrufo brothers. More than a year of work, months of planning, and now at what I saw as a climax of all my work, I'm kept away. They wouldn't even be here if not for me.

I mutter through dinner, not even tasting the food I'm shoveling into my mouth. Sarah has heard enough.

"Dad, isn't this what your book is all about?" she says. "Family?"

That stops me. She's right. The book really isn't just about Chichén Itzá anymore. It's about families—the Thompsons, the Barbachanos, even my own family.

How did a nineteen-year-old get to be so smart?

The anger begins to subside, but resentment still burns in my gut. I had promised to take the Thompsons on a tour of Chichén Itzá the next day to show them what their ancestor, Edward Thompson, had done there. I had assembled some fifteen pages of a script from my research. There is no way that is going to happen now. I'm going to focus on my work and not worry about them. After dinner, Sarah and I visit the reception desk at the Mayaland, and arrange for a guide to take my place. I'm going to let them pay for it.

Even though we have a busy day tomorrow, I'm too wound up to sleep, so I suggest to Sarah that we walk over to the Hacienda Chichén next door. It's a beautiful evening and the cool breezes stir the palm trees creating a pleasing natural static as the long leaves rub together. As we approach the broad stairway at the entrance to the main casa, who should be there but Bibiano getting ready to serenade the guests. We greet each other with a warm abrazo and it turns out we are thinking the same thing at the same time, but Bibiano says it first:

"Why are you here?" he asks. He thought I would be at Maria Luisa's with everyone else.

So did I, I think. But instead I explain in polite terms how the Thompsons felt it would be more appropriate to have only family present for the big meeting.

Bibiano is aghast. This meeting would never have occurred if not for you, he says. *Tell me about it*, I think. "This is not right," he says.

I shrug and say something like, "What can you do?" In my mind, what's done is done. Bibiano excuses himself and Sarah and I chat with one of his sons.

A few minutes later Bibiano returns. "It's all arranged," he says. "Tomorrow night we will have a fiesta in your honor."

THE PAST

REBUILDING CHICHÉN ITZÁ

ALTHOUGH HE WAS BUT A TEENAGER, Carlos Marrufo went to work for the biggest employer in central Yucatán. And at this moment, in 1927, his neighbors were laughing at him.

Marrufo was at one end of a Rube Goldberg device the men from the Carnegie Institution had dreamed up on the spot to move ahead on the years-long project rebuilding one of the giant temples at Chichén Itzá. The boy sat on a block of stone that a millennium ago Maya artists had chipped away to create elaborate bas-relief carvings. Young Carlos dribbled water from a tin can as a two-man buck saw, almost two meters across, scraped back and forth across the stone. What prompted all the laughter was what powered the saw. Instead of two men, it had ingeniously been connected to the stripped axle of a Model T pickup. Maya from all over the area had gathered around the contraption. They stared at the saw, then for reasons unknown to the Carnegie men supervising the project, burst into laughter, followed by excited chatter in Maya.

For the Carnegie men, it was just another day at the office. They were doing something no one had ever done before, transforming a mound of rubble back into a glorious Maya temple, and they were often forced to improvise. The solution to today's challenge was the result of a fortuitous accident. One of the Carnegie men, Gustav Stomsvik, had wrecked the pickup truck the previous day while swerving to avoid one of the Maya workmen who had wandered into the middle of the road after "celebrating pay-day on credit." Rather than take the truck out of commission, the archaeologist in charge of the project, Earl Morris, converted the accident into a solution and now the bareback wheel powered the saw as well as provided free entertainment to Maya men and women from kilometers around.

Misfortunes and disasters, big and small, had plagued the Carnegie Institution's excavation and restoration of Chichén Itzá from the beginning. Just as Sylvanus Morley was about to kick off the first season of exploration in 1924, the assassination of Carrillo Puerto plunged the state of Yucatán into chaos. The Carnegie Institution's advance man, J.O. Kilmartin, was at Chichén Itzá mapping the ruins and had been expecting Morley and the rest of his team to join him; instead he spent several months with only the occasional company of Edward Thompson and a group of local Maya workmen. It was not until spring that General Huerta was deposed and order restored.

Once Morley got the all-clear signal, he tried to get to Yucatán as soon as possible, but got held up in New Orleans awaiting a ship to Progreso. There he happened to run into Felipe Cantón and other hacendados who were in exile. There were rumors they had conspired with the delahueristas to murder Carrillo Puerto, rumors that Cantón denied. But according to Morley they indicated that some of their subordinates might have been involved. The idea that Cantón, who had sat across the table from the governor during numerous archaeological meetings where they debated the future of Chichén Itzá and Yucatán, had at the same time been planning Carrillo Puerto's murder seemed unthinkable, but Morley had been around Mexico enough to know that the boundaries between friends and enemies can be paper-thin.

On May 18, Morley arrived at Chichén Itzá. With him was Earl Morris, an experienced field archaeologist who had supervised many excavations in the Southwest United States and who would direct most of the work at Chichén. Another archaeologist, Monroe Amsden, and Morris's wife, Anne, were also present. The first priority was to make the hacienda habitable. Morley's team hired local Maya to repair the casa principal and several of the outbuildings, including the hacienda chapel, which was secularized into a photographic darkroom, and later into living quarters for Morley.

In that shortened first season there were a few visitors. The highlight for Morley had to be hosting President Plutarcas Calles; the low must have been a stop by Alma Reed. Morley must have been horrified to read her article, which mentioned the Carnegie project and Augustus Le Plongeon's wild theories, almost in the same paragraph. Even worse, the story was syndicated to newspapers around the country with a prominent photograph of Edward Thompson.

Thompson also was an occasional visitor that first season, usually when he needed money. He pestered Morley for advances on the rent and, according to Morley's biographer, had failed to pay the taxes on the property, forcing the Carnegie Institution to spend an extra $400 to bring them current.

The Carnegie, however, was not paying to make the staff comfortable, entertain guests, or placate the landlord, but to excavate ruins. Because of the late start that first season lasted less than a month so the only archaeological work consisted of clearing brush from the area known as the "Court of One Thousand Columns" and doing some cursory exploration. "As might be expected in this class of excavation, the minor objects recovered were few; a fair quantity of potsherds, two nearly complete vessels, a few shell beads, a jade celt, and several flaked blades of obsidian," Morris reported, sounding almost apologetic.

Re-erecting the Court of the One Thousand Columns was not going to make the splash the Carnegie Institution desired, generating only as much excitement as watching an infant stack wooden blocks. For the following season in 1924-25, Morley and his team decided instead to excavate the large mound that loomed over the Court of One Thousand Columns, which they estimated was more than half as tall as the nearby pyramid El Castillo and covered two-thirds of an acre. Under the mound was a temple long collapsed and buried by the forest, so that its sides resembled "rock slides on a mountain peak." What attracted the archaeologists to the mound were the features that were visible—two giant feathered serpent columns at the top similar to El Castillo and, in the middle, a chac-mool statue. They named it "The Temple of the Warriors."

To accomplish their work, they needed a large and local labor force.

The Temple of the Warriors pre-excavation

Morley turned to an old friend, Juan Olalde, who Ann Morris described as "a dignified old Mexican, foxy as a serpent—

> —who had served as major-domo on a Chichén plantation for forty years [not true, but Olalde certainly could have told Morris this]. Through an admirable wiliness, Juan had managed to steer clear of entangling alliances with either of the two factions of the Chichén neighborhood. The near-by village of Pisté was a hotbed of banditry, and the whole district was divided along cleavage lines which embraced every imaginable social and economic subject, but which in the end might be said to boil down to a case of bandits who were in versus bandits who were out of power.

Among those Olalde hired were his old nemeses, the Tuns of Pisté. When Ann Morris wrote of Pisté's "hotbed of banditry," she was referring to the Tuns, who had aligned themselves with the socialistas during the political troubles of the early 1920s that resulted in the burning of the Hacienda Chichén. They may have been the very ones who had taken pot shots at Juan Olalde in 1921, or the ones who had threatened his family. If so, Olalde did not hold a grudge, for he hired many of them, including Faustino Tun, Bernardino Tun, and Pablo "Tigre" Tun, the barrel-chested patriarch of the family. The story told amongst the Carnegie crowd was that during those unpleasant times of the socialistas, Pablo Tun murdered one of his enemies and, as the man was perceived as quite intelligent, Pablo reportedly ate his brains to acquire his wisdom. "Thus it became a regular password among the staff whenever we met him to say, 'Pablo Tun, he eats brains,'" Anne Morris wrote.

The Carnegie project was to be big and, over the course of its twenty-year history with Chichén Itzá, hired anywhere between fifty and 100 laborers (and at one time the foreman, who may have been Olalde, managed to sneak it up to 215 while Morley was away). The work was dirty and grimy, but every day the Maya workers showed up in clean clothes: "white vest, trousers rolled to the knees, a kilt-like apron of striped material like pillow ticking, straw sombreros, and leather sandals."

Most of the laborers came from Pisté and other nearby communities. Even though their ancestors may have been the people who had built the ancient ruins, the skills and techniques to construct giant monuments of stone had been lost. The Maya knew how to build their traditional huts and for centuries had relied on the machete, the adze, and sticks with points hardened by fire as their primary tools of survival. To excavate the ruins, they had to work with shovels and wheelbarrows. "Some of the workers acquired an early dexterity with our civilized tools and others appeared hopeless in their clumsy fumbling," Ann Morris noted. "There is an art even in ditch digging." One of the most difficult tools to master was the pick and only a few of the workmen became proficient at its use.

The Maya were resistant to many new techniques. When removal of the tailings from the excavation was going too slow, the Carnegie men built a ramp from the ruins that the workmen could push their wheelbarrows up and then unload them into a hopper. When the hopper was full, it was dumped in turn into the bed of a truck. At first none of the Maya would use the ramp. "Are you men or old women," Gus Stomsvik, a Norwegian foreman, yelled at them, and he grabbed a wheelbarrow, pushed it up the ramp and dumped it. "Tigre" Tun, the patriarch, shouted, "I am as good a man as a Norwego!" and then ran his wheelbarrow up to the hopper and emptied it. As an added flourish, he flipped the barrow on his head and sauntered back down the ramp.

There was plenty of work for everyone, even those not inclined to the backbreaking labor of excavating ruins. For them, there were day-labor jobs that paid based upon the amount of work completed, although sometimes these backfired on the Carnegie staff. One of the piecework tasks was to break large stones into spalls, smaller pieces of rock, for which those of low motivation were paid by the bucketful. One brilliant fellow, Localio Balaam, figured out how to crush rocks more efficiently by sledging them against Edward Thompson's long-abandoned dredge. Balaam was so productive that by the time all the stone had been crushed, he had earned four times the wages of the other men and with his newfound wealth took two weeks off.

Even though the work was hard and the tools unfamiliar, there was never a shortage of labor. The Carnegie must have been the largest employer in the region and every two weeks it paid its workers in cash. Every other Friday, Morley sent two of his archaeologists, one armed with an old Winchester shotgun, to Dzitas to pick up the payroll from the train. On the next day the laborers would queue up at the hacienda and one of the Carnegie men would hand out a stack of coins. At the end of the day, whoever had gotten stuck with the job of paymaster would have to scrub the black stain of Mexican silver from their hands.

Many of the archaeologists held condescending attitudes about the Maya workers, but those opinions did not keep them from occasionally slumming with the locals. Some of the young archaeologists would slip off to Pisté to attend dances where they could get beer (the Hacienda Chichén was a no-drinking zone). Eric Thompson described how he danced the traditional *jarana* with a local girl and at the urging of some of the Maya men, placed his hat upon her head. "At the end of the dance I took it from her and put it back on my head, thereby unwittingly bringing shame on my pretty partner." According to custom, the male dancer only retrieves his hat once he demonstrates his gratitude and affection by giving the girl dancer a small token of appreciation, usually in the form of pesos. "When I learned of my faux pas, I tried to remedy things by an overpayment. That wasn't too good, either, for though to us gringos it was a small sum, to the

Maya it indicated a passion that had swept me off my feet."

Such cultural blunders were common. It did not take much to offend, anger, or hurt a Maya. "A word, a phrase, an action, that to one of us would seem utterly trivial, may in him touch a chord as deep as his very being, and bring forth an emotional response altogether bewildering in its intensity and inexplicability," noted Earl Morris.

He related the story of two "houseboys," José and Gonzalo, who worked at the hacienda. José became the favorite of the Carnegie crowd, "because of his willingness and speed in obeying requests that were made of him." A jealous Gonzalo decided to take José down a peg by planting gossip that he was interested in another man's wife. This blew up into a violent confrontation where José's wife cracked the alleged home-wrecker over the head with the local version of the shillelagh and would have killed her except for the intervention of one of the gardeners. As a result, José and his wife were fired. "Gonzalo, more crafty than his smile would indicate, cheerfully did the work of two, refusing extra pay, until we could secure another house-boy."

Morris, however, leaves out the epilogue—all the Maya servants at the hacienda were fired and replaced with Koreans.

And while Maya performed most, if not all, of the backbreaking labor excavating the ruins, they were supervised by mestizos. The decision may not have been racially based, but more one of language, as mestizos were more likely to speak Maya and Spanish, versus the local Maya who for the most part spoke only their indigenous language. Most of the Carnegie archaeologists, however, learned only a rudimentary Maya vocabulary, preferring instead to learn Spanish.

Morley fancied himself fluent in Spanish and Maya, but in truth he butchered both languages. One could fill a book with stories of his poor pronunciation, mixed-up vocabulary, and mangled tenses. There was the time he returned to Chichén Itzá to find eight new Korean workers waiting for him when he expected just one because his instructions had sounded like *"ocho chinos"*—"eight Chinese" as Koreans were called—instead of *"un otro chino."* As one of his Mexican friends once commented, "I don't see how Dr. Morley manages to get every word in a sentence wrong." After one speech that included an especially pungent set of linguistic miscues, the Mexican archaeologist Alfonso Caso y Andrade cracked that it had been a "memorable evening" because "we have had addresses in three languages: English, Spanish, and Morley."

No one seemed to mind his careless language skills. Morley was one of those people who communicated by sheer force of will and enthusiasm, the very same dynamism that had persuaded the Carnegie Institution to spend $20,000 per year on Chichén Itzá and then increase that expenditure to $100,000 per year throughout the Maya region. At Chichén Itzá alone the Carnegie excavated and/or reconstructed more than a dozen Maya monuments. No obstacle was too big. When they discovered that the Temple of the Warriors had been constructed on top of another monument, they restored that one as well, reconstructing a temple within a temple. When locusts consumed the maize crops of their Maya workers, Morley arranged for a giant shipment of the grain from New Orleans and for several weeks they paid their crew in silver and in corn.

The most spectacular near-disaster occurred midway through the second season. April in Yucatán is one of the hottest months and on one of the most stifling, humid days, a wall of black, ominous clouds formed in the southern sky. Other clouds began to coalesce and soon the entire sky was dark. At 3:50 p.m. a heavy rain began to fall and the archaeologists and workers at the Temple of Warriors took shelter inside an ancient corridor that ran through the Court of a Thousand Columns. It was a *turbonada*, a sudden storm that appears to come from nowhere. The rain turned to hail the size of BBs, to the wonder of the archaeologists. "Sooner would I expect ice to fall in hell than here," one of them thought. The storm grew in intensity, as gale-force winds blasted the countryside and hail the size of walnuts began pounding every exposed surface. Before it was over, every tree in the forest was denuded, deer and turkeys caught in the open were pounded to death, cabbages and tomatoes in the hacienda garden exploded as if shot by a rifle. Fortunately it was too early for the Maya to begin planting their maize for the crop would have been decimated. At the base of El Castillo, the hail had been blown into drifts more than a meter deep.

The storm had damaged some of the exposed architecture on the Temple of Warriors, but it could have been much worse. There was one major benefit. The forest had been "beaten down so that one could see the surface of the earth," Ann Morris wrote. "We were startled to find old mounds that we had never dreamed of, not ten feet from constantly traveled paths." In the days following the storm, Carnegie archaeologists roamed the countryside around Chichén Itzá and were able to create detailed maps of most of the significant structures left behind by the Maya. The "Carnegie Map," as it is known today, was in its time one of the most detailed of any of the ancient cities and towns in the Maya world. When printed it was four feet by two feet. "One could do something with a map like that," one lucky recipient of a copy gushed.

THE PRESENT

IGUANA LOVE

THE NEXT MORNING I still am not over my perceived lack of appreciation the Thompsons had shown the night before. Sarah and I meet them for breakfast and I explain that I have arranged for a guide because I have a lot of work to do, especially since the spring equinox is upon us. For the next few days Chichén Itzá swells with tourists from all over the world who come to see the Maya god Kukulcan crawl down the side of the great pyramid, El Castillo. The pyramid is oriented so that at a certain time on the day of the equinox the sun glances off the northwest corner of the pyramid and projects a jagged shadow against one of the balustrades on the north stairway. It resembles the feathered serpent, Kukulcan, wriggling down the pyramid.

The actual day of the equinox is tomorrow and on that day the number of visitors to Chichen Itza swells into the thousands. The light-and-shadow effect occurs for a couple of days before and after, so there will be a smaller, but large crowd today. I explain to the Thompsons that I want to conduct interviews with the people who have come to see the event and I have so few opportunities to be in Yucatan, I can't afford the time to give them the tour. Instead I will give them a tour of the Hacienda Chichen in the evening, which I explain is more appropriate anyway since that is where Edward Thompson lived.

I am only being partly truthful. The thought of spending two or three hours with them puts a knot in my stomach. I still hurt from the night before. I don't even want to see them until the evening. This poses a challenge, because I am sure to run into them in the archaeological zone. I need a place to hide and I decide the perfect place to do that is the Cenote Sagrado.

In my knapsack is the bowl, jade spool, and figurine head from the Sacred Well. This may be my chance to toss one or more of the artifacts back into the well.

Not long after parting with the Thompsons, Sarah and I find ourselves at the Sacred Well. I want to be like Edward Thompson and sit and ponder on the little, ruined shrine next to the cenote, but tourists are no longer allowed near it. Instead I perch my butt uncomfortably on a rock a few meters away. Sarah wanders off to take pictures.

Somewhere below a frog squawks. A flock of small birds dives into the pit, swoops over the water in a clockwise pattern three times, chasing insects, and then flies off. A few minutes later, they return. One, two, three times around the inside of the cenote and then away. I pull out my journal and decide to just observe. My attention is attracted to a motion in one of the trees overlooking the cenote. A large iguana sits on a branch where it is jerking its head up and down in a violent motion. He repeats this several times. I can't figure out what he's doing. I spent the entire fifth grade year in a classroom next to a large cage where my teacher kept a pet iguana. The lizard didn't do much more than sit and if he did move, it was slowly, deliberately. This fellow in the tree would jerk his head every couple of minutes.

Then I notice in the tree a second iguana, much smaller, slowly creeping up from below. Its natural camouflage and slow movements had prevented me from seeing it. I now understand. The large one has to be the male and the head jerking is a mating dance, showing off its puffed neck to attract the much smaller female.

Once she is close, the male crawls up her back and gently licks the side of her neck, a gesture that seems almost tender, until he sets his teeth into her loose flesh. Once she is firmly in his grasp, he forces up her tail and copulates with all the poetry of a used tire sale. Another virgin sacrificed at the great well.

THE PAST

'THE CITY OF THE SACRED WELL'

MORLEY MAY HAVE BEEN CROWNED the new king of Chichén Itzá, but he lived in the shadow of the former lord of the realm, Edward Thompson—at least as far as the press was concerned. Newspapers covered the progress of the Carnegie project, but most of the stories lacked the sizzle to capture the public imagination. Edward Thompson's discoveries from the Cenote Sagrado, even though they were more than twenty years old, always made for good press. And thanks to Alma Reed's 1923 "exposé" of his exploits, he now felt free to talk about them. So he went on the lecture circuit.

Alma Reed became Thompson's de facto press agent. For years she continued to rewrite and republish her article about Thompson's discovery of treasure in the Sacred Well, but she wasn't the only one. Drew Pearson, long before he became the most widely syndicated newspaper columnist in America, wrote a profile of Thompson that was circulated widely in newspapers of the day. But the biggest publicity boost was yet to come, a full-blown biography, published by Century books, one of the leading publishing houses in the United States.

The author was Thompson's old friend, T.A. Willard. Since that initial visit in 1906, when he had helped Edward Thompson exhume artifact after artifact from the Cenote Sagrado, Willard had become a regular visitor to the region. He spent three months of almost every year in Yucatán, primarily in the company of archaeologists and explorers, or investigating his own theories about the Maya and their ancient civilization.

According to Willard, he had hounded Thompson to write about his exploits. Thompson relented but only if "you write the book, Willard—I'll help." One wonders if Thompson ever thought Willard actually would do it, because the two men did not spend much time together during its writing. Willard wrote it based on his recollections of Thompson's tales, from notes he had taken over the years and that Thompson had lent him, and from their two decades of correspondence.

In spring 1926 Willard's *The City of the Sacred Well* hit bookstores. The ponderous subtitle—*Being a Narrative of the Discoveries and Excavations of Edward Herbert Thompson in the Ancient City of Chi-Chen Itzá with some Discourse on the Culture and Development of the Mayan Civilization as Revealed by Their Art and Architecture Here Set Down and Illustrated from Photographs*—underscored the depth which Willard examined his subject. The book ran almost 300 pages and contained seventy-two photographs and drawings.

Accounts differ as to how much participation Thompson had in the book. Willard calls him his "companion and co-author," and years later said that every quotation came from Thompson, although a few were "jazzed up" at the demand of the publisher. Thompson claimed that most of the embellishments were Willard's, although anyone who knew Thompson to any degree was well aware of his tendency to over-dramatize and exaggerate.

Of all the romantic hyperbole in the book, Willard outdid himself in the descriptions of the artifacts taken from the cenote. He went on for pages about objects being pure gold when they were, in fact, mostly copper with gold plating. He ascribed their value as almost priceless, in the hundreds of thousands of dollars, when as bullion they were worth a few thousand dollars at most. He included more than a dozen illustrations of artifacts. For three years the public had been reading about the discovery; now for the first time they could see what all the excitement was about.

When an archaeologist asked Thompson about Willard's overstated appraisals, he replied, "I did tell that the scientific value was priceless." The rest was Willard, he said. But it wasn't as if Thompson objected. "The book is readable," he admitted. Thompson knew that *The City of the Sacred Well* was going to bring him some kind of trouble. "As a re-creation. O Lordy! What he makes me say and do. May heaven help me."

Willard was justifiably proud of the book. He not only sent an advance copy to Thompson, but also to Mayanist Juan Martínez Hernández in Mérida who he thanked in the acknowledgements. Shortly after receiving the book, Martínez wrote an article about it for the *Diario de Yucatán*, which accompanied the story with many illustrations of the Cenote Sagrado treasures from the book. The article, neutral in tone, ran on page two above the fold. And that is when the shit hit the dredge.

Three weeks after Martínez Hernández's article appeared, the Mexican Secretary of Public Education, José Manuel Puig Causaranc, demanded his counterpart in the federal department of justice investigate Thompson on charges of robbing the Cenote Sagrado and illegally shipping artifacts rightfully belonging to the nation of Mexico to the United States. Thompson knowingly violated Mexican laws, the secretary charged. Puig Causaranc said not only should Thompson be brought to justice, but the government also needed to move quickly to seize Thompson's holdings in Mexico in compensation for the stolen artifacts.

The story exploded in newspapers across Mexico, containing a level of vituperation expressed against a single American as had not be seen since Gen. Jack Pershing's invasion ten years earlier.

Willard was horrified at what his book had wrought. He wrote his old friend Martínez Hernández about the controversy, no doubt unaware that the Mexican Mayanist had been the inadvertent source behind much of it. "If I may be permitted to express my opinion of this matter, I should say that the measures taken are not in the right direction and that they can only succeed in creating many and unnecessary difficulties," Willard wrote. "I never thought it right for the said Peabody Museum to keep those objects hidden away because they belong to the whole world, but I suppose they did so foreseeing the very difficulties which now appear."

Willard pointed out that had the cenote treasure remained in Mexico, it would not have survived the turbulent times following the Mexican Revolution. Now that Mexico is entering a period of stability, would it not make more sense to send a friendly delegation to Cambridge, Massachusetts, and politely request the directors of the Peabody Museum to split the collection? "An appeal to the law leads nowhere when the matter can be settled amicably," Willard wrote. "The prosecution of Mr. Thompson will not give satisfactory results. The gold is not in his possession. He delivered it to the persons for whom he was working and who paid him a salary to obtain it. He is as guilty as I might be myself.

"The plan which your countrymen are following will bring upon them the hatred of all the scientific men and women of the world," Willard concluded. "Therefore why not go in by the door instead of breaking in?" What Willard did not know was that the Mexican government had already kicked the door down. His letter arrived in Mérida as the hearing into the Thompson case was coming to a close. Even though the prosecution listed him as a witness, no one from Mexico, apparently, had approached him to testify.

Three weeks later, in early October, Judge Castillo Rivas ordered Thompson stand trial on the charge of robbery and the Hacienda Chichén, including the city of Chichén Itzá, confiscated.

Thompson no longer controlled his hacienda, property he had owned for thirty-five years. He would be arrested if he set foot in Yucatán ever again. How had he miscalculated Mexico's response to the Willard book so badly?

The truth, it turns out, was that it was not a mistake, but a gamble, the biggest of Thompson's life. He calculated the odds, knew the risks, and no doubt saw he was down to his last chance.

He always knew that there was a risk the Mexican government could take action against him as a result of Willard's book, but that was far from a fait accompli, because the dredging of the Cenote Sagrado was old news and had been the worst kept secret in Mexico. Three years had passed since Alma Reed had broken the story in the *New York Times*. Representatives from the Mexican government had accompanied Reed when she viewed the artifacts at the Peabody Museum and had taken no official action. One reason may have been that officials in Mexico had known of the dredging for much, much longer. While Reed's 1923 *Times* article was the first time the cenote dredging had been reported in the U.S. press, Mexican newspapers had published accounts of it years before that. Thompson's archaeological nemesis, Teobert Maler, had authored articles that appeared in Mérida newspapers attacking the owner of Chichén Itzá and his dredging project in 1911 and 1914; nothing resulted from those very public pronouncements.

In 1911, when Thompson had approached the post-revolutionary government about dredging the cenote, one of the reasons the government denied his permit was because they knew about his past operation and feared his request was a subterfuge to ship artifacts out of the country—again.

But the Mexican government's knowledge of the dredging went back even further. During the case presented against Edward Thompson in 1926 the Mexican prosecutor never revealed that the government had been aware of Thompson's dredging from the beginning. Santiago Bolio, the Inspector of Ruins in Yucatán and the leading federal official in charge of watching Chichén Itzá, had tried to stop Thompson. Bolio had visited Chichén and seen the dredge in operation. In May 1904 Bolio filed a denunciation against Thompson in court to halt it. Bolio dropped the case not long after Thompson put him on the cenote-dredging payroll, but he continued to report Thompson's dredging activities to his superiors.

Bolio was not the only federal official who knew about the excavation of the Cenote Sagrado. President Diaz's Secretary of Public Education, Justo Sierra Méndez and a large entourage had seen the dredge during a visit to Chichén Itzá in 1906. Among those in the secretary's party was Maler, who made sure the secretary knew what Thompson was doing. Much to Maler's disgust, Sierra Méndez didn't care.

There had to be another reason why members of the federal government rushed into action in 1926. No one, even the government itself, engages the Mexican legal system if they can avoid it because it is so laborious, complex, and expensive. Additionally, despite the promises of the Revolution, the courts still favored landowners and the rich.

There were even those in 1926 who wondered what the sudden rush was all about. There were some who speculated at that time that the Mexican government was moving quickly to prevent Thompson from selling Chichén Itzá. However, the only buyer ever discussed in these rumors was the state of Yucatán, which wanted to turn the site into a state park—why would the federal government want to stop that? Did the federal government know of Thompson's lease agreement with the Carnegie Institution, which included an option to purchase?

No, there was another reason why the Mexican government took such drastic action, and that was at the heart of Thompson's gamble: He was suing the federal government for $175,000 U.S., the equivalent of almost $350,000 Mexican. The Mexican government, Thompson charged, had conspired to burn the Hacienda Chichén in 1921 and under a recent treaty with Mexico, he was entitled to compensation for his loss. In early 1925, the U.S. and Mexican governments created a joint commission to hear and decide claims by U.S. citizens who had lost property as a result of the Mexican Revolution and the turbulent decade that followed. In May that year Thompson filed a claim, charging that the burning of his plantation had been politically motivated by the socialista government of Yucatán. He included several affidavits from witnesses, including one by his superintendent Juan Olalde that named names of those who had been behind the burning. According to Olalde, the perpetrators included the very same members of the Tun family who a few months later would testify against Edward Thompson in the cenote dredging case. During that hearing Bernardino Tun testified that shortly before the burning of the hacienda, he "had the opportunity" to look in the warehouse and see several crates containing artifacts from the Cenote Sagrado. What Tun had failed to mention was that he happened to be in the warehouse because he was the one setting the fire.

Thompson's claim came to the attention of Mexican officials at almost the same time as news of Willard's book and the retribution came swiftly: If Thompson wanted to sue the Mexican government for $350,000, then the government would sue him for $1,000,000—a Mexican standoff. To insure its position, the federal government would take Chichén Itzá as collateral. Even if Thompson won his claim, he would lose.

Thompson was not, however, willing to lose Chichén Itzá without a fight. On Nov. 29, 1926, he sent his attorney, José Casares Martínez de Arredondo, to plead his case before the judge. "Mr. Thompson has enjoyed in this city a good reputation and his standing is well known," Casares told the court. He asked that the court interview three witnesses who could testify to the government's knowledge of the dredging: June F. James ("Mrs. James), the expatriate American member of the Archaeology Institute of Yucatán; Luis Rosado Vega, director of the local archaeological museum; and banker Alberto Garcia Cantón. The government, however, was in no hurry to act on these requests as it already had what it wanted: Chichén Itzá.

The *Boston Globe* caught up with Thompson at his home on Cape Cod, several weeks after Mexico seized the Hacienda Chichén. The ex-consul wasn't angry; he was, if anything, upbeat and philosophical about Mexico's actions. "In doing as I have done, I feel that I have protected Mexico against herself," he said. "When the proper time comes, I can prove this fact so patently that none can deny it. Until that time does come I am content to bear what comes to me with fortitude and patience."

He then told the *Globe* reporter, "I am today as poor as when I first landed in Yucatán more than forty years ago. But I did my duty as I saw it and am proud of what I have done. If, as I am told, Mexico has seized my plantation, 'Chichén,' in reprisal for what I have done for science, so let it be. I am ready to make this sacrifice."

THE PRESENT

INAH

ONCE THE IGUANA LIVE SEX SHOW is over, I lean out as far as I can to look into the depths of the Cenote Sagrado. All I can think about is how Edward Thompson sacrificed Chichén Itzá here. Certainly politics did him in. That's just the way it is in Mexico. But if he had not dredged the Sacred Well and made his discoveries so—so *public*—I suspect he would not have had it stripped from him.

In my knapsack are my Cenote Sagrado artifacts—the molded clay head from a figurine, the small clay bowl, and the jade hoop. I have them at the ready, prepared to re-sacrifice them to Kukulcan. To do it right, I must poke a hole or break the little clay bowl, ritually killing it. As I hold it in my hand, I hesitate.

What a stupid idea. What had I been thinking?

I sheepishly repack the artifacts, feeling a little like Frodo before the fires of Mount Doom.

Enough with the Sacred Well. I don't want to walk back via the broad, ceremonial sacbé that takes us to El Castillo because we might run into the Thompsons on their tour. I notice behind don Fernando's palapa there is an unpaved road through the forest, which must be how staff brings in new stock. I have no idea where it goes, but it appears to head in the general direction of the main entrance.

Sarah and I set off on a little adventure. The road turns out to be not too bad and relatively well traveled. A pickup approaches and we move to the side. I nod to the men inside and act like I belong here. It's an old newspaper reporter tactic, almost as good as carrying a clipboard. We walk for about a quarter-mile before the road terminates at a compound. There are equipment sheds, pickup trucks, and a low, flat-roofed building with several cars parked in the front. I figure this must be the local headquarters for the Instituto Nacional de Antropologia e Historia (National Institute of Anthropology and History, better known as INAH). A man works outside the main building and I approach him. I had read that there was a new director at Chichén Itzá, Eduardo Pérez de Heredia Puente, and figure this is as good a time as any to meet him. Maybe I can introduce myself by donating the artifacts? That might win me some goodwill. The INAH employee doesn't speak English, but somehow we manage to convey that we desire an audience with Sr. Pérez. Alas, he is not in, we are told. I leave behind a business card.

Sarah and I decide to head back to the Mayaland, because now seemed to be a good time to move our stuff over to the hacienda. We spy an unpaved road leading from the INAH headquarters to a broad wall of an ancient Maya ruin. It takes a second to orient myself, but my guess is that this is the rear of the west wall of the Great Ball Court. We start walking.

The road passes between two short pillars. I almost walk past them but something about them catches my attention and when I look closer I see they have old, worn metal plaques upon them. I can't be sure about all the words, but it reads something like this:

> *La Liga de Resistencia "Edmundo C. Canton" de la Ciudad de Merida, commemora la inauguracion de esta Carretera ex Dzitas y Chichen-Itza Portante mesoamerican por el ciudadano Felipe Carrillo*

Puerto gobernador constitucional del estado Y presidente del partido socialista del sureste of Mexico Julio 14 de 1923.

The plaque dedicates Felipe Carrillo Puerto's road to Chichén Itzá. On July 14, 1923, Governor Carrillo Puerto brought in Maya from all over Yucatán state, said to be the largest gathering of indigenous people in Mexico in modern history. I remember reading accounts of how the governor wept at the conclusion of his speech.

The famous highway, the one that opened Chichén Itzá to the world, is now little more than a dirt path. The road formerly cut through one end of the Great Ball Court and then deposited visitors in front of El Castillo. It probably wasn't much of a road back in the day, as the space between the two pillars barely has room for a single car. The pillars, like the road, have been neglected and are returning to nature. The north facing one is illegible, with letters worn away in places. There is a certain irony, I suppose, that archaeologists today bemoan the loss of Maya hieroglyphs to erosion and other forces of nature and here is the modern equivalent of a Maya stela, one that archaeologists walk by every day and they couldn't care less.

Then we almost walk by it. Not far off the path something draws my eye, a small obelisk resting on a concrete platform. This was not Mayan, but clearly of modern design, and as it is short and stubby, it is about as impressive as a thumb. Standing a little over a meter high, the obelisk has four sides, each covered with arcane symbols that I recognize as belonging to the Masonic order. One side has a grid containing roman alphabet letters and what appear to be corresponding parts of a cypher. At the top is a legend, *"Clave de las Letras"*—"key to the letters." This appears to be some kind of Masonic Rosetta Stone. I can't figure out why it is sitting here behind the Great Ball Court where no one can see it. Then I remember

Felipe Carrillo Puerto's road. This had been the entrance to Chichén Itzá, so instead of being hidden from public view as it is today, this was at one time a place of prominence. I can't tell who built this little monument, or what it represents.

Not all the mysteries at Chichén Itzá are ancient.

The mystery obelisk

THE PAST

THE BIG FIND

THOMPSON'S LEGAL TROUBLE with Mexico never resulted in so much as a hiccup to the Carnegie Institution's work at Chichén Itzá. José Reygadas y Vértiz, one of the lead Mexican government officials with oversight over the nation's Maya ruins, called the Carnegie Institution "reliable," although he was quick to point out that the concession to excavate had been executed by his predecessor, long before the action against Thompson. "I do not defend the Carnegie Institution," Reygadas y Vertiz told a reporter, "but I do say that if any person would present me with concrete proof that object of the ancient civilization were being taken out of our country, in less than twenty-four hours the respective concessions would be nullified." The hearing against Thompson had taken place when the Carnegie operation suspended operations for the rainy season. Work resumed at Chichén Itzá that winter as scheduled.

In all it took three years to finish excavation and restoration of The Temple of the Warriors. A celebration was scheduled for March 10, 1928 to turn it over to the Mexican government. After that date the Carnegie would no longer be allowed to explore that part of Chichén. Earl Morris, who had spent three field seasons on the project, was certain they had missed a great find and in the days just before turning over the keys he knew right where to look.

The ancient Maya buried offerings under their altars and ceremonial spaces, and the Temple of the Warriors had four that the Carnegie had never explored. Morris persuaded Carnegie president John C. Merriam, who had come to Chichén for the ceremony, to allow one last excavation.

Morris, Merriam, and a workman named Danyél, slipped away to the Temple of the Warriors. They first investigated a large dais with an intricately carved riser in the Northwest Colonnade that Morris described as a "spectacle of almost incredible magnificence." There they made a rude discovery—someone had beaten them to it. The ancient red mortar floor had been torn up and whoever had done it must have found something, because only a small portion of the floor had been disturbed. The looters had gone to the trouble to re-plaster over their hole to disguise their crime. The excavation must have occurred during the months the Carnegie was not working at Chichén Itzá. And who but an archaeologist would even know where to dig? Neither Morris nor Merriam speculated as to who committed the crime. But the looting did give Morris the confidence that his hunch was right, as long as the thieves had not searched under the remaining three ceremonial spaces.

Morris, Merriam, and Danyél, excavated the other three locations but found nothing other than some broken pottery and the bones of a bird. Morris was ready to give up, when Danyél reminded him of one other sacred spot—in the temple within the temple.

There was no altar in what was now called the Temple of the Chac Mool, inside the Temple of the Warriors, but there had been, Ann Morris had proven that. At the top of the Temple of the Warriors was an altar held up by several carved men, called atlantes. What had puzzled archaeologists was that each of the atlantes had been counter-sunk more than twenty centimeters into the floor. Not long after the Temple of the Chac Mool had been discovered and excavated, Ann Morris had studied a section of the wall that had markings at a height of seventy-five centimeters. She then intuited that it corresponded to the height of the atlantes and the altar, meaning that when the ancient Maya constructed the Temple of the Warriors, they had recycled the altar, but had been forced to "cut the table legs" to make it fit in its new location.

By tapping with picks at the floor where the altar had once stood, the men identified what sounded like a void. Breaking through the floor, they found what appeared to be the lid of a large stone cylinder. After a break for lunch, they returned and removed the lid. Inside, staring back at them from the bottom of the cylinder, was the profile of the feathered serpent, Kukulcan, in the form of an elaborate circular mosaic crafted from hundreds of individually shaped fragments of turquoise. Each piece had been affixed to a wood backing, which over the centuries had disintegrated. The mosaic rested intact at the bottom of the cylinder, but the slightest jar would turn the work of art into a worthless pile of turquoise chips.

Once again, necessity proved the mother of invention. Morris devised a scheme whereby he gently applied a thin layer of cement to the mosaic as it lay. He managed to put on several coats until he was certain not a single piece of turquoise would shift position, at which time the stone cylinder was removed from the hole and carried to the hacienda. Later a specialist from the American Museum on Natural History in New York, Shoichi Ichikawa, reconstructed the mosaic and made a copy of it.

The Kukulcan mosaic arguably was the most beautiful and the most elaborate example of Maya art found up to that time at Chichén Itzá. Turquoise is found only in the northern reaches of Mexico, thousands of miles from Chichén, an indication of how precious this mosaic must have been to the people who had buried it centuries earlier.

The excitement over the mosaic certainly must have overshadowed the ceremony transferring the Temple of the Warriors to Mexico. By that time the Carnegie Institution was already at work excavating and restoring three other monuments, including the Maya observatory, the round Caracol.

Above, Temple of the Warriors post-reconstruction. Below, the excavated mosaic disc, now in the National Museum of Anthropology in Mexico City.

THE PRESENT

EQUINOX

SARAH AND I SLIP THROUGH a gap in a fence and emerge into the Great Ball Court, which is packed with tourists. It is so quiet on the other side of the Ball Court wall that I forgot today is the day before the equinox, one of the most crowded days at Chichén Itzá. Over the next few days tens of thousands will come to witness the feathered serpent god Kukulcan slowly take shape and "crawl" down the side of El Castillo, the giant pyramid. Or so I've been told. In a few hours the sun will achieve an angle where its rays glance off one corner of the pyramid and project seven diamonds of sunlight on the side of a staircase, the one with heads of serpents carved at the base. According to what I've read, at around 4:30 the sun-and-shadow will resemble a snake frozen in mid-slither down the pyramid.

It's not even noon and the flat expanse around the pyramid is swarmed. The best spots to sit out the heat are under the trees, but vendors have snagged those areas. Any tourist seeking respite beneath the foliage must endure a continuous sales pitch.

I guide Sarah through the crowd. The equinox event is not going to occur for another five hours and there is no way I am going to have my daughter stand in the sun until then. I'd learned my lesson about children and sunstroke on the last trip. Time for lunch and a siesta. We head out of the archaeological zone to the Mayaland to pack our bags and relocate to the Hacienda Chichén.

Later, while enjoying a delicious meal on the hacienda terraza, a lanky man approaches to our table and asks if he can join us. It's Warren Thompson who I only had met that morning at breakfast. I invite him to sit down. "How was your tour?" I ask.

Warren shrugs. Much of what the guide said had sounded like a bunch of crap, Warren thought. And he didn't know a lot about Edward Thompson, in fact got him mixed up with the archaeologist J. Eric Thompson.

I want to ask him about his meeting with the Marrufos last night, but stop myself. If it was a magical evening I will be crushed. Instead we talk about the gathering crowd for the equinox. "Did you notice all the people who had staked out shady places next to some of the ruins?" Warren asks. He points out that once the sun crossed the meridian those choice spots would become like mini-ovens as they not only would get the direct sun but also the rays that reflect off the ancient bleached walls. "We're supposed to be so advanced, but the Maya a thousand years ago knew more about the movement of the sun than your average tourist," Warren says with a smile. I laugh. I like this guy and now I'm feeling a little guilty about sticking him with a guide.

I explain that the crowds coming for the equinox are a recent phenomenon. A Mexican lawyer, Luis E. Arochi, wrote a popular book in the 1970s where he described the light-and-shadow effect at length. He became famous as the man who "discovered" it, which drew the ire of a countryman, José Díaz Bolio, who claimed he had published about it in the 1950s.

There also is an unconfirmed story that Arcadio Salazar Nava, one of the men who worked on the restoration of the pyramid in the 1920s and 1930s, was the first to notice the sunlight-and-shade snake. He supposedly mentioned it to a government artist/archaeologist in 1928, who in turn published an article about it—or so Salazar claimed, but the article has never turned up.

Scholars today point to a picture of El Castillo taken by American Southwest photographer Laura Gilpin in 1932 (but not published until 1948) as the first time the light-and-shadow appeared in print. Gilpin's photograph, titled "Sunlight and shadow on the balustrade of the north stairway," makes no mention of the equinox.

"Here's how obsessed I am," I tell Warren. "I checked every claim." Arochi, who became famous from the equinox phenomenon, was a Johnny-come-lately (although he was the first to publish about it in a popular format). Diaz Bolio, contrary to his boast that he was the first to publish, never mentioned it even though he wrote at length about equinoxes at Chichén Itzá. There's no evidence that Arcadio Salazar discovered it in the 1928 because El Castillo was still being reconstructed and the north façade, where the effect occurs, was only half finished at the time of the spring equinox. Also, the archaeologist he reportedly told about the effect, Miguel Angel Fernández, was no longer directly involved in work at Chichén Itzá at that time.

"And the photograph by Laura Gilpin?" I say. "She didn't arrive at Chichén Itzá until April, long after the equinox." If you examine the photo carefully, you can see the serpent is not quite right, appearing thicker at the bottom then at the top.

"The first one to write about the shadow-and-light was a guy named Jean-Jacques Rivard," I tell him. In 1971 he published in an academic journal a brief but thorough article, with illustrations, describing the phenomenon.

I tell Warren how it became my mission to find Rivard, who disappeared without a trace not long after his article was published. I searched Internet databases, university directories, and distant telephone books. I asked everyone and anyone if they knew him or had met him. Except for that article, Rivard did not exist.

"I finally found him," I tell Warren. "You know where?" He shook his head. "A half hour from my home. I'd been driving by his house every day on my way to work in Boston." It was pure luck I stumbled across his name listed among the mourners in a *Boston Globe* obituary.

Serendipity.

I contacted Rivard, who was living in a suburban community between Boston and Cape Cod. He agreed to meet me for an interview at the Robbins Museum of Archaeology, one of those small museums that every town seems to possess. Jean-Jacques was almost ninety, a gnomish man who moved easily without the need of a cane or other help. I shouldn't have been surprised to learn that he had little formal education beyond high school. But he could draw and in the 1960s worked at the Massachusetts Institute of Technology as an artist. His life in those days centered around drawing for M.I.T. and taking care of his mother, who was senile. "I had no time for marriage or women," he told me. "Finally my mother died. I was fifty." Freed of his care-giving responsibility, he began traveling with M.I.T. scientists. "That's when I started going to Mexico," he said, then adds, "That's why I never amounted to anything. I look in the mirror and I know what I am."

But didn't he know he was famous? I ask. Thousands come to Chichén Itzá every equinox. He's the man who "discovered" the shadow-and-light phenomenon. Jean-Jacques scoffs at the notion that he discovered anything. "All the guides and all the visitors who were there at that time saw this, but no one ever made anything of it," he said. "And I, stupidly, made something of it."

Jean-Jacques Rivard

Jean-Jacques said the guides were the ones who had told him about it. When he was at Chichén on behalf of M.I.T., he didn't stay in hotels but with the local people. "They just took me in," he said. "I made a hit with them or something." One night over dinner a guide mentioned the equinox shadow and intrigued, Jean-Jacques asked him to take photographs of it and send it him in the United States. At the same time University of Northern Colorado's Museum of Anthropology was seeking articles related to Mesoamerica for one of its publications. Rivard offered to write about the serpent on the balustrade. When he returned the Chichén Itzá the next year he received permission from the Mexican government to take photographs of the equinox and of the position of the stars from the top of El Castillo. His article was published in 1971 and the rest is history—almost.

How was the article received? "There was no reaction...for *years*," Jean-Jacques said.

He learned of the impact a few weeks before we spoke. John Carlson, an archaeoastronomer, "has been looking for me for thirty years," and had found him a few weeks before I did. According to Carlson, Jean-Jacques' article was not only the first about the equinox phenomenon; it was the very first published article on what would become the discipline of archaeoastronomy.

While Jean-Jacques was proud of his achievement, he had no illusions that he would profit from it. "I'm a pauper," he told me. "I have no money. Never been able to hold onto money. But I'm surviving."

I tell Warren how much I liked Jean-Jacques. He was an "enthusiast," like Warren's great grandfather Edward Thompson. How sad that it took so long for professional archaeologists in academia to recognize his contribution. "That's typical of the Ph.D.s," Jean-Jacques told me. "They have a clique and if you don't belong to that clique, you are mud. I found that out many times." He told me about the archbishop of Toledo who challenged Queen Isabella of Spain to her face. When the queen pulled the "Do you know who I am?" the archbishop responded, "Lady, I know who I'm talking to, the queen of Spain, Isabella, a handful of dust in the hand of God like me." Jean-Jacques chuckled and said, "That shut her up beautifully."

Chichén Itzá during the equinox (Pereira photo)

THE PAST

THE MAYALAND

FERNANDO BARBACHANO PEON today is the acknowledged founder of the Yucatán tourism industry, but its gestation and birth was as intricate and complex as any Yucatecan family.

Barbachano's father-in-law, Francisco Gomez Rul, deserves at least some of the credit, for in the early 1920s he hatched a series of schemes to bring tourists to Mexico. In 1921, he formed *Compañía Impulsora del Turismo a las Ruinas de Yucatán S.A.* ("Company Driving Tourism to the Ruins of Yucatán"), a corporation dedicated to building facilities and providing services for visitors. The company offered for sale 1.7 million pesos in stock to finance its plans.

Gomez Rul also published a guidebook to Yucatán and its ruins, sold postcards, and published articles on tourism. He helped convince an association of henequen producers, made up of the cream of Yucatecan society, to revive the bi-lingual magazine *El Agricultur* to not only promoted Yucatán's biggest industry, henequen fiber, but also its newest industry, tourism.

Gomez Rul correctly predicted a future in which tourism would become Yucatán's largest industry, but he was far ahead of his time. His tourism business ventures failed to attract a single visitor to see Chichén Itzá or spend a vacation in a Mérida hotel. Gomez Rul was a visionary, for he could see that the future of Yucatán was in tourism and he did everything possible for when that future arrived. But his plans crumbled in early 1924 with the assassination of Gov. Carrillo Puerto and then his own accidental death in April. It would fall to someone else to open Yucatán to tourism and, according to local legend, that person would be Fernando Barbachano Peón.

Barbachano Peón's father was in the liquor importation and distribution business, and it made sense that his son would follow suit. But upon entering adulthood he chose another path. One reason may have been that the state of Yucatán, like the United States, had entered into Prohibition. The state was dry, so there may not have been any business for young Barbachano Peón to enter.

Barbachano Peón married Gomez Rul's daughter, Carmen Gomez Rul Castillo, shortly before her father's death. According to Barbachano family lore, he picked up his father-in-law's mantle and went into tourism. The young man met steamships from New York and New Orleans that stopped in Progreso and attempted to wheedle passengers on their way to Veracruz to lay over for a week in Yucatán, see the sites, and then catch the next ship on to their original destination. In his first year, he did better than Gomez Rul, but not by much, as he only managed to convince seven passengers to jump ship.

At least that was the story, one that Barbachano Peon told his entire life, long after he became the king of tourism. But was it true? As with all stories, yes and no.

Barbachano Peón had the smarts and chutzpah to bring Gomez Rul's vision into reality and to start his own business. He would have understood that he could not wait for tourists to appear, that he had to get out and hustle. But to say he started the Yucatán tourism industry is not quite accurate, for by the time he entered it, it was already there. By 1924 Yucatán had become a magnet for a very specific form of tourist: divorce seekers. When Felipe Carrillo Puerto's administration liberalized Yucatán's divorce laws in 1923, it unwittingly created a Yucatecan visitor industry and one entrepreneurial American capitalized upon it. John W. Germon had come to Yucatán in 1909 to serve as assistant to Henry Case, the Progreso agent of the Ward Line steamship company. Only twenty, Germon's previous work experience had been two years as a reporter for his hometown newspaper, the York (Penn.) Dispatch. His U.S. citizenship won him an appointment as vice-consul at the end of 1911, a post he held throughout the tumultuous years following the Mexican Revolution. In the 1920s, he left government service and the steamship company to pursue his own dreams, including a foray into the developing tourism industry. In 1924, a few months after Felipe Carrillo Puerto's assassination, he sent out the following flyer to US newspapers, announcing a new kind of vacation:

> *Of importance to Tourists and Travelers to Mexico. Divorces obtainable in the state of Yucatán on basis of thirty days residence.*
>
> *NO GROUNDS REQUIRED and no service of summons involved. Secrecy and confidences observed. Write or telegraph for information or details. Many Americans availing themselves of Yucatán divorces.*
>
> *AN OPPORTUNITY of visiting the famous pre-historic Maya ruins of Uxmal and Chichén Itzá, which are attracting world-wide attention, will be yours.*
>
> *YUCATÁN, the land exotic, a treasure-trove for the scientist, anthropologist, and archaeologist, where the ancient Maya civilization vies with the recent Egyptian explorations.*

MÉRIDA the capital of Yucatán, is a modern city of 100,000 inhabitants, well paved throughout, dotted with numerous tropical parks, where the comforts and demands of the most fastidious can be supplied.

It may have been Barbachano Peón who provided the opportunity to visit "the famous pre-historic Maya ruins of Uxmal and Chichén Itzá," although according to family lore and other anecdotal sources that began in 1927. It is also possible that Germon worked in concert with Barbachano or even Edward Thompson, who was living in Yucatán during this period. But while the possibility of a quickie divorce may have brought visitors to Yucatán, the interest to see the ancient ruins was sparked by the publicity surrounding the Carnegie Institution excavations at Chichén Itzá.

If the legend is correct and Barbachano Peón began a tour business encouraging steamship passengers to leave the ship behind in Progreso for a week or more in Yucatán, he must have been doing it at the behest or in concert with the Ward Line. By 1927 the steamship company was promoting trips to Mérida, Uxmal and Chichén Itzá to its passengers, although with no mention of either Barbachano Peón or Germon.

Despite all the publicity about Chichén Itzá, persuading someone to go there was a hard sell. The completion of Felipe Carrillo Puerto's road to Chichén helped, but it was still not easy or pleasant to get there. There was a single train that left Mérida at 5:30 in the morning—if it ran, that is. Once aboard, it was five hours to Dzitas. First-class passengers were entitled to a single seat upholstered in breathable wicker; others sat on sweat-collecting, butt-numbing planks. The wood-burning locomotive occasionally blew ash into the passenger compartments. There was no dining car, but the train stopped every few kilometers at the tiny villages along the way where locals swarmed the cars with food to sell: fruit, vegetables, and, of course, the omnipresent tortillas, either plain or sometimes slathered in refried beans, goat cheese, and chopped turkey or venison, and then rolled like a canapé.

When passengers got off in Dzitas they found it much the same as it had been for decades—a dusty, dirty town, one that travelers to Chichén wanted out of as soon as they got off the train. If they were lucky, one of the Model T fordingas that served the archaeologists and workers from the Carnegie Institution or the Mexican government was there; if not, you either took the infernal mule-drawn volan wagon or, more likely, waited, uncomfortably, until motorized transport arrived—or not. Once there you only had a few hours to see Chichén Itzá before you had to be whisked back to Dzitas to catch the train as it made its return trip to Mérida.

If getting to Chichén Itzá was arduous, a trip to the other prominent ruin in Yucatán, Uxmal, was worse, because the only regular train to the vicinity left Mérida in the afternoon, requiring one to stay overnight. The only accommodations in the area were at the Hacienda Uxmal, owned by the Peón family, where one could obtain lodging and meals for five pesos per person.

The biggest challenge of any tour operator in Yucatán was not getting customers to Chichén Itzá or Uxmal, but finding them a decent room in Mérida. There was only one hotel of reasonable quality that tourists found acceptable, the Gran Hotel in the center of the city. If the Gran was full—not an unusual condition considering the number of divorcees that were coming to Mérida to spend the required residency of thirty days—there was no other place to put tourists, as other hotels were primitive by comparison.

Only the most adventurous tourist would endure such privations to see the ruins. That Barbachano Peón had managed to persuade seven passengers aboard the Ward Line steamer to spend a week in Mérida and from there visit Chichén Itzá is probably true. But one of those passengers would change his life.

Percy Childs Madeira Jr. had come to Yucatán in the late 1920s not to seek a quickie divorce, but to see the Maya ruins. Madeira, born in 1889, had spent twenty years in the family's Pennsylvania coal business but then abruptly changed his life course to chase a dream—he went back to school to become an archaeologist. He became interested in the ancient civilization of Yucatán, probably from the head of the University of Pennsylvania anthropology department, noted Mayanist George Gordon Byron. Madeira wanted to see the ruins for himself and he hired Barbachano Peón to give him the grand tour and take him to Chichén Itzá and Uxmal. The two men were kindred spirits in search of their life's goals and, fortunately for Barbachano Peón, Madeira had money enough to make all their dreams come true. Madeira loaned Barbachano Peón ten thousand U.S. dollars to launch a full-service tourism business.

The centerpiece to this new venture was to be a hotel next to the ruins of Chichén Itzá. Barbachano Peón understood that with an inn at Chichén, he could keep visitors there for more than an afternoon, increase their respective comfort, and maximize his revenue. Also, someone would build accommodations for travelers, that was certain, for the new governor of Yucatán, Bartolomé García Correa, announced shortly after taking office in February 1930 that his administration would construct a highway between Mérida and Chichén Itzá, making getting to the ruins far more convenient for tourists.

Barbachano Peón wanted to be the first and he wanted to be the best. It was an excellent plan, except for one minor detail—from whom would he purchase the property to build the hotel? Ownership of the site was in dispute. Edward Thompson owned Chichén Itzá but the Mexican government had seized it. Thompson was contesting the government's charges, but as is typical for Mexico, the case slogged through the courts and would take years to resolve. Barbachano Peón came up with a gutsy solution. Rather than buy the land from Thompson or attempt to deal with the government, he chose a third course: He squatted, building his hotel without any permission at all. "Hotel" may not quite describe that first iteration of the newly named "Mayaland," which consisted of what appeared to be a group of Maya houses. "Who cared to do anything [about] the construction of some thatch-roofed buildings," said Barbachano Peón's son, Fernando Barbachano Gomez Rul, in an interview. "My father's lawyers were shrewd. If you build on someone else's land, the owner either pays for the construction or sells you the land."

In later years workers at the Mayaland Hotel would tell customers that no less than Sylvanus Morley picked the location of the hotel, where the main building's entrance offers a majestic view of the Maya observatory, the Caracol. This is unlikely considering the Mayaland's illegal nature. The Mayaland Hotel also did Morley and the Carnegie no favors as there were rumors circulating that "at least one of the well housed American archaeologists at Chichén Itzá owns stock" in the Mayaland.

Barbachano Peón began construction in 1930. However, the class of clientele who could afford to travel to Yucatán would not tolerate typical Yucatecan accommodations. His inn would have to be first class. He spared no expense. Even though from the outside it resembled a Maya village with "the same oval white houses, thatched with palm leaves, bound with vines," the interiors were plush. Comfortable beds replaced the traditional hammocks, with headboards and furniture hand-carved in a "modernistic" style with Maya themes, and plenty of electric lights. The wow factor was reserved for the bathrooms, which were covered in gleaming white tile and fully plumbed.

Building a hotel at Chichén was an important piece to solve the Yucatecan tourism puzzle, but it was not the only one. Early on Barbachano Peón understood that to be successful, his tours had to be as seamless as possible. Not only did that mean a hotel at Chichén Itzá, but also a similar base of operations in Mérida. That was solved when one of his cousins had fallen on hard times and converted his home into a hotel. José Rafael de Regil Casares—better known as "Rafael de Regil" or don Rafael —had been a wealthy hacendado who in 1915 had been one of the primary backers of Colonel Abel Ortiz Argumedo and his ill-fated attempt to wrest control of Yucatán from invading federal forces. During Argumedo's brief reign, don Rafael co-signed a note for almost $500,000 to arm the revolution, but the guns arrived in Yucatán too late and instead were seized by the federal government. For Regil's involvement in the failed coup, the federal government seized his hacienda in Campeche.

Regil then involved himself in tourism and was one of the major partners along with Edward Thompson, William James, and others in Francisco Gomez Rul's failed tourism venture. By the late 1920s, he owned only a single hacienda south of Mérida and in the city a forty-room mansion—an "old rambling Victorian barn," as one travel writer described it—stuffed with European furniture and Maya relics that he had collected. Not long before Barbachano Peón opened the Mayaland, Regil renamed his mansion "The Hotel Itzá" and recast himself as the most genial host in all the Yucatán.

While the Maya ruins were seen as an economic driver to Barbachano Peón, to don Rafael they were a marvel to be revered. He had been exploring the ancient cities of Yucatán for decades and had collected what many considered one of the best private collections of Maya art in the world. The Barbachanos were relative newcomers to Yucatán, having emigrated in the early 19th century; Regil was descended from the original conqueror Francisco Montejo, but his roots in Yucatán went much deeper. Once when asked about the purity of Mexican stock, he replied, "Let us forget for a moment the superficial and polite reports...Look at me—closely." After his guest had examined his features and said he could see nothing other than a man descended from Spanish gentry, don Rafael chuckled and said, "I am what you Americans call a half-breed—or something like it. To be sure, I have my genealogical pedigree in documentary form dating back to before the Moorish Conquest of Spain. But my Mexican records have significant blanks. The Indian! We ask no questions."

Although Regil and Barbachano Peón were cousins who shared a great-great grandfather, they were miles apart in Yucatán's social hierarchy. Regil was a member of the Casta Divina and Barbachano Peón was not. Ironically, Regil was considered more of a member of the Peón family, even though he did not carry the name. That came with a very special advantage with regard to tourism, for he was closely related to the branch of the Peón family that owned the Hacienda Uxmal, which Regil had upgraded into a more acceptable inn for guests. Now, by partnering with Regil, Barbachano Peón could offer tourists a full tour, with days and nights at Chichén Itzá at his new Mayaland hotel, and at Uxmal at the hacienda there.

In 1930, with the new hotel in Chichén Itzá under construction, Barbachano Peón published a two-color brochure offering by the end of the year six different "all expense tours" ranging from a single day to two weeks, priced from $30 to $160—far from cheap. When the Mayaland Hotel at Chichén Itzá opened that fall, full-service tourism in Yucatán was truly born.

When one purchased a tour from Barbachano Peón, visitors no longer had to rough it. To eliminate many of the headaches common to travelers, Barbachano Peón assigned each group of tourists a "guide," who accompanied them from their arrival by steamship (assisting with customs) to their departure. When those inevitable problems erupted during a tour, the guide was there to solve them or smooth them over. Somehow

Barbachano found several personable, English-speaking Yucatecans who were willing to give up several days at a time to respond to every tourist's need and keep a running patter about a wide range of subjects—the ancient Maya, Yucatecan customs and food, the local flora and fauna, contemporary Maya village life.

A typical tour of Chichén Itzá meant getting up at 6 for breakfast, into the ruins by 7; back to the Mayaland around 10:30, before the heat of the day became too oppressive, for ice-cold beer. Perhaps there might be a lecture before lunch, after which a siesta for couple of hours, and then back to the ruins by 4 until dusk.

To make the visit to Chichén Itzá and Yucatán as smooth as possible for tourists required a tremendous amount of coordination between Barbachano Peón's Mayaland Tours company and travel agencies, the steamship line (and by the mid-1930s Pan American Airways), and his cousin Regil. It also meant splitting a share of the proceeds from each tourist. There was nothing Barbachano Peón could do about travel agencies and transportation providers, but his relationship with his cousin was contentious almost from the beginning. The fracture may have been purely business, but it also may have been personal. Everyone liked don Rafael, who came across as a combination of genteel uncle and rumpled professor. Barbachano Peón, although not without his own personal charm, was viewed as a man who was all business, even ruthless. He became known as *El Tigre*, the Tiger, for his bare-knuckled approach to commerce.

While Regil was far from a dilettante at business, he was not as single-minded as Barbachano Peón. But despite the setbacks to his personal fortune that resulted from the Mexican Revolution, Regil was still a man of means and a member of the Casta Divina. Barbachano Peón was on his own.

The inevitable break occurred in 1932. Barbachano refused to allow

From left, Carmen Gomez Rul Castillo, Fernando Barbachano Peón, José Rafael de Regil Casares. At right, the first brochure of Mayaland Tours.

guests of don Rafael to stay at the Mayaland. Regil attempted to build his own hotel at Chichén in nearby Pisté. While he slogged through the permissions from the government to make that happen, he placed his guests in two substitute locations: in the Chichén Itzá quarters of the federal Inspector of Ruins Eduardo Martínez Cantón, who was a friend; and in a small inn just outside the walls of the Hacienda Chichén run by Edward Thompson's former cook, Victoria Manjarrez. In the case of the latter the lodgings were fairly primitive, with only hammocks and an outdoor privy. Regil convinced Manjarrez to make several improvements, such as furnishing the rooms with beds and installing bathrooms.

Barbachano Peón defended his turf in sly ways. Upon learning that Regil was sending tourists to the federal encampment, he asked permission to lodge one of his guests, an American, there. The owner of the Mayaland also offered to bring over a bed. When that request was granted, Barbachano Peón "sent over a half dozen beds" and began lodging the overflow from the Mayaland there, which resulted in federal officials closing the federal encampment to all visitors (which may have been Barbachano Peón's plan from the beginning).

If the relationship between Barbachano Peón and Regil was contentious, it must have become outright hostile after the 1935 edition of *Terry's Guide to Mexico* was published. The guidebook lavished praise on don Rafael and his Itzá Hotel without mentioning Barbachano Peón. In fact, the guide went so far as to state that Regil was the operator of the Mayaland Hotel at Chichén Itzá. By that time Mayaland Tours had vacated its desk at the Hotel Itzá (eventually moving into the Pan American Building). Barbachano Peón lodged his tourists when they were in Mérida at the Gran Hotel and not the Hotel Itzá, and he continued his prohibition of Regil's guests from the Mayaland Hotel. Turnabout was fair play and Barbachano Peón's customers were not permitted rooms at Regil's new hotel at the Hacienda Uxmal.

In 1940, the Carnegie Institution completed its work at Chichén Itzá and left the Hacienda Chichén. Barbachano Peón began paying rent to the Thompsons so Regil "cannot have the Casa Principal as headquarters for his tourists." Rather than expand his operation into the hacienda, Barbachano used it for storage and let the forest once again take back the other buildings.

The battle between Regil and Barbachano Peón was never in doubt. Barbachano Peón even won control of the Hacienda Uxmal, purchasing it (and the ancient city of Uxmal) in the 1950s. Other competitors came and went and always Barbachano Peón remained victorious. "As a business adversary, he was formidable," one acquaintance described him. But his battles with competitors were nothing compared to his biggest challenger—the governments of Yucatán and Mexico.

THE PRESENT

MORE BARBACHANOS

BELISA BARBACHANO HERRERO is the youngest daughter of Fernando and Maruja. She manages the Hacienda Chichén, which is owned by Fernando's sister, Carmen Barbachano y Gomez Rul. Belisa sits in front of me, looking very uncomfortable as I wave a large microphone in her face.

She is one of two Barbachanos I am slated to interview. I will meet her older brother, predictably named "Fernando," at the Mayaland. All I know about Belisa is what don Fernando has told me and at the time he was very angry with her for some perceived slight involving doña Maruja. I don't understand what it is all about, but what I do know is that Fernando is or has been angry with almost all of his children at one time or another. Most of the time, at least from my perspective, it is because they never seem to do what he wants.

Belisa has managed the hacienda resort for more than a decade. How she came to earn this position, according to members of the family, goes back to when Aunt Carmen (who has no children) asked her nieces and nephews what she could give them from her various businesses and properties. Belisa, unlike her siblings, didn't want anything. "I want to work," she said. And so tia Carmen gave her a job running the Hacienda

Chichén, which at the time was a small seasonal inn.

Today, the hacienda is open year-round. "It's been ten years," she says. "The hotel was pretty simple ten years ago. My mission has been to make this a place I can live, where I can have my friends and my clients (and my clients also become my friends)," she says. Running the hacienda is about balancing the old with the new, she explains. The buildings that surround the main house were once home to the Carnegie archaeologists and "I take care that each room stays within that heritage" and that it reflects the heritage of those archaeologists. "I have tried to minimize the changes as I have added the comforts."

The gardens, she says, are not artificial in a landscaping sense, but are closer to tended jungle gardens, hence why they attract so many birds and butterflies. The native trees are filled with birds of every description. Some 150 of the 250 species known to Yucatán have been seen on the grounds, she tells me. "It is a very rich area for wildlife," she says. "We're training our workers to understand the importance of even the iguanas—people do eat the iguanas, so we tell them, 'No, these are not going to your kitchen.'"

She runs the hacienda like a community, she says. They say in business one should eschew nepotism, "but we are one hundred percent focused on nepotism: Cousins working with cousins, brothers with brothers. My two most important reservation directors are sisters." Jobs are handed down, father to son, just as the management of the hacienda has been handed down to her. It also means there is a commitment to the communities that surround Chichén. Belisa talks about projects they have done, from installing potable water systems to repairing ancient churches.

She pauses, as if she can't go on, then says, "I'm getting very emotional about the hacienda because it is a treasure."

I tell her how much I love the hacienda. "It's a very strange place," she says. "I think it has a soul of its own. It takes some people at their heart."

The business attracts archaeologists, researchers, Maya lovers, and those who love travel. Most who come feel how alive it is, that it is not a cold hotel, she says. "Ninety percent of the people will tell you they did not expect the feeling of the place."

At that moment her husband Bruce Gordon walks in on the interview, but he's bringing gifts. In his hands are some chocolate—Maya chocolate made local by Belgian chocolatiers who came to Mérida because they wanted to be in the land where cacao originated. The candy is almost eighty percent cacao, which means it's like dark chocolate on steroids.

Belisa resumes talking about her employees. "The workers are from generation to generation, transferred from my grandfather to me," she says. "A lot of these old, old ladies remember my grandmother and they kiss me. It's very emotional, very family-oriented, very much the soul of my grandmother. I miss her very much."

I confess that while I've done a lot of research on her grandfather, Fernando Barbachano Peón, I knew little about her grandmother Carmen Gomez Rul Castillo. "To me she is the grandmother of my life," Belisa says. "She taught me without words the work I am doing today. She taught Maya people to make beds when they didn't know. She took a bunch of farmers that came from very limited possibilities and—I don't know how to talk about this, it's very painful—"

She can't go on. Bruce picks up the thread while Belisa composes herself. Over the years he has come to learn the impact the hacienda has had on the people of the surrounding communities and much of that was because of doña Carmen. Bruce describes how he has been out in the bush and run into old *milperos* working on their corn crops. "They remember your grandmother," he says.

"My grandmother was, to me, far more important than my grandfather," Belisa resumes. "My grandmother thought of people. She was not doing a business, she was doing a way of life. She taught people how to serve in the hospitality industry when that was not understood. Teaching the protocol of how to serve a meal to a person who has always worked as farmer, who has roughness and strength as qualities instead of delicate movements, was not an easy task. I cannot imagine the barrier of the language because in those days people spoke far more Maya than Spanish," she says.

"The more I do this the more I absolutely admire her. A very bright and very tender woman, and yet very strong. She must have been very tough raising two children in the jungle. The more I know about my grandmother, the more difficult it is for me to quit. I do get very tired and I do at times want to quit, but that is impossible. Sometimes you want to scream and that's when I think about my grandmother."

Later, when I interview Fernando Barbachano Herrero, the eldest son of Fernando and Maruja, he tells me the same thing. Sarah and I meet him at the Mayaland, the hotel his grandmother ran for decades, which he now owns. He possesses the Barbachano charm like his father, but is much taller and, according to my daughter, is handsome. He is as emphatic as his sister Belisa when it comes to his grandmother. "If you are to be the judge, she was really the head of the woman's movement eighty years before their time in this country," he says. "She was an amazing, amazing woman. A woman who was not only an inspiration and a very hard worker, she was a designer, she helped the people and saw to it that the people's needs were met," he says.

"My grandfather is credited with being the pioneer of tourism in this country and I urge you in your book to do some research into my grandmother, who deserves equal credit."

THE PAST

THE WOMEN OF CHICHÉN ITZÁ

FERNANDO BARBACHANO PEON may get the credit for building Yucatán's tourism industry, but he did so in partnership with his wife, Carmen Gomez Rul Castillo. And hers arguably was the hardest job. She ran the Mayaland Hotel—trained and managed the staff, planned the menus, supervised any new construction—and did it all while caring for her five-year-old son, Fernando, and a newborn baby girl, Carmen Barbachano y Gomez Rul. While her husband was in Mérida building that end of the business, she was at Chichén insuring that her customers had every luxury and more importantly, were insulated from the reality of living in the bush—thriving scorpion populations, the occasional poisonous snake, and at least once, the majestic jaguar, whose wet paw prints were once found leading away from the hotel fountain.

For such a remote area almost exclusively inhabited by Maya and mestizos, white women called the shots. Not only Carmen (assisted by her aunt) at the Mayaland, but Sylvanus Morley's second wife, Frances, was the true power next door at the Carnegie Institution's headquarters at the Hacienda Chichén. "Vay" and Frances had met in Sante Fe in 1926 and, even though she was fifteen years his junior, Morley knew instantly he wanted to marry her. In March 1927 he brought her to Chichén Itzá and at sunset proposed to her atop El Castillo, twenty years to the day after he first visited Chichén Itzá. Frances became Morley's guardian and micromanaged his life. During meals she would hover over her husband and hand him his napkin, put food on his plate, salt it, and even butter his bread. The two were the source of local gossip, the result of their non-stop public displays of affection—a taboo in conservative Yucatán where men courted women without even speaking to them or looking directly at them. "They often pull ears and sometimes kiss!" one observer noticed. The couple was so amorous, it became a bit of a joke by some of the archaeologists and visitors to Chichén Itzá. At one meal Morley leaned over to buss Frances and on cue all the other couples at the table simultaneously turned and kissed their partner. The table roared at its prank on Morley, but according to one of the witnesses to this event, "I do not remember that it reformed him."

Between the Mayaland and the Hacienda Chichén was doña Victoria, who fed the Carnegie workers and later took in visitors. Her husband, Carlos Marrufo, and her sons frequently were away, leaving her run her little inn.

These three women had little interaction with each other; even though they lived within a few hundred feet of each other, their lives did not appear to intersect with any regularity.

Of the three, doña Carmen had the greatest challenge. While the Carnegie Institution refused to hire Maya as servants in the main house (considering them unfit for domestic service), doña Carmen had no such luxury. She depended upon local labor to clean the hotel rooms, work in the kitchen and laundry, and maintain the grounds. Few, if any, of those she hired had any experience at all. Her workers were farmers who grew maize or laborers who rebuilt the ancient Maya temples for the Carnegie.

**Left, unidentified woman, Fernando Barbachano Gomez Rul and his mother, Carmen Gomez Rul Castillo in the archaeological zone of Chichén Itzá.
On right, Victoria Manjarrez and daughter Ofelia.**

Or they were young girls hired from the villages and who wore huipils. They lived in Maya *nas* with packed dirt floors and hammocks in which to sleep. They had no experience cleaning buildings with tile floors and modern bathrooms. They had to be taught the proper way to strip a bed and then make it, even though they themselves would probably never spend a night in one over the course of their entire life. They had to be trained how to serve drinks in glasses filled with ice even though they drank from hollowed dry gourds. They learned to set a table with silverware, plate, and napkin, even though they had no use for such things for in their homes the tortilla served all those purposes and was edible to boot.

The biggest training challenge no doubt had to be to get the local men to accept orders from a woman, although at Chichén Itzá this may have been less of a problem because there had always been unusually empowered white women. For more than fifty years Chichén Itzá had attracted strong-willed gringas, such as Alice Le Plongeon in the 1870s and 1880s, Adela Breton after the turn of the century, and Edward Thompson's wife Henrietta. These women endured the same hardships as their male counterparts, but it is the men who received most of the credit for the discoveries and accomplishments. It is a tradition that reached back to the ancient Maya of Chichén. The oral history of Maya regarding Chichén is filled with exploits of men, such as man-as-god Kululcan, or the three brothers who legend had it together ruled the ancient city, or of the king of Mayapan, Hunac Ceel, who conquered it. But the hieroglyphs found on some of the walls at Chichén Itzá refer to women. There are glyphs in Akab Dzib which describe at one prominent woman, the mother of a dynastic ruler, although in her case the world of men still intrude as her name has been translated as "Lady Penis."

The only oral legends that mentioned women at Chichén Itzá were about those who were sacrificed into the Cenote Sagrado, but there was one well known story of the woman who said, "no." Like the other sacrifice victims before her, this woman was led into the little shrine at the lip of the Sacred Well where the priests explained that she would be lowered by a long rope into the cenote thirty meters below and dunked repeatedly until she encountered the gods, or until she died, whichever came first. If the gods came to her, they told her to ask for rain. "I will ask no such thing," she said. Instead she would tell the gods to send no maize or anything at all. "The boldness and assurance of that virgin in her speech had so great an effect that they left her and sacrificed another in her place," according to a Spanish monk who documented the tale.

A millennium later, another strong-willed woman Ann Axtell Morris ventured into Sacred Cenote, not as a sacrifice but of her own free will. She lived at the Hacienda Chichén for several years assisting her husband Earl with his excavations of the ancient monuments for the Carnegie. She eventually became a skilled excavator in her own right, in addition to her work as a staff artist. According to Axtell Morris, there were two types of archaeologist wives: Those who stayed at home and those who joined their husbands on their expeditions. Of the latter, acceptance among the husband's archaeology colleagues had to be earned. "The poor newcomer who presumes to break into the sacrosanct circle must stand trial by fire, till it is decided she is all right," Axtell Morris once observed.

Axtell Morris possessed those ephemeral qualities that made her "all right." Crazy, but not too crazy; hard-boiled about facts, but still retains a "will-o'-the-wispish flair"; unbothered by ants in the oatmeal or other discomforts; perceives indigenous people, past and present, as something more than the stereotypical savage; "finally it is imperative to consider a skeleton as a very lucky find, and not as a dead human being."

One afternoon in the late 1920s, Axtell Morris, her husband, and two other men wanted an adventure to escape the tedium of archaeology. They found they could reach the cenote waters by climbing down a tree that was growing on a ledge about halfway down the cliff. They made it the rest of the way by shinnying down one of the tree's thick, exposed roots that stretched to what Axtell Morris described as a "small beach." She apparently did not know the beach was man-made, the tailings left behind by Thompson's famous dredge two decades earlier. As they stood on Thompson's Beach, the quartet marveled at the thought that under the jade green waters was a fortune in Mayan treasure.

The four spent the afternoon lazily swimming the cenote. When the sun disappeared over the lip, the shade gave the appearance that twilight was only a few minutes away. The party hurriedly dressed on the beach and one by one the men climbed up the root, then up the tree and out of the cenote. They threw down the end of a rope and instructed Axtell Morris to tie it around her waist as a safety harness. Morris, unaccustomed to ropes and knots, put too much slack in the loop around her body. As she crawled up the tree root, the oversized noose began to slip over her head. She panicked, let go of the tree root and grabbed the rope with both hands. The three men had no choice but to haul her up, unceremoniously banging her repeatedly against the wall of the cenote.

Morris wrote that she remembered nothing of the ascent. She could not let go of the rope once she was topside and the men had to pry it from her fingers—not unlike those women of centuries past who were also pulled from the cenote. Once she regained her senses, she found the world above the cenote was now "beautiful beyond anything I had ever imagined," she wrote. "For those few minutes, the scales of the commonplace fell from my eyes, and I saw the earth and loved it, in the manner one should."

Tatiana Proskouriakoff was another woman whose impact on Chichén continues to be felt today. Although spent only a few weeks at Chichén Itzá but her impact on archaeology of the site, not mention in Maya studies overall, was tremendous.

Morley hired her to draw reconstructions of Maya cities. In 1940, as the Carnegie project at Chichén was winding down, she spent several weeks at the Hacienda Chichén. Her drawings would become some of the most famous renderings of Chichén since Frederick Catherwood had been there a century before.

One drawing in particular received wide distribution. She drew the Cenote Sagrado from a perspective at the far northern side and looking south toward El Castillo and the Great Ball Court. She did not know it at the time, but the Cenote Sagrado would become her life's work. In the late 1940s, she joined the Peabody Museum. Alfred Tozzer introduced her to the artifacts Edward Thompson dredged from the Cenote Sagrado. Tozzer asked her to draw the crumpled golden disks Thompson had recovered. "They are magnificent," she wrote "worked in repoussé with figures and scroll work...I will probably be very foolish to take it on, but don't know who else could do them...[a] pencil drawing of mine might be better than what they would otherwise do."

Proskourikoff would devote more than a decade of the last years of her life on the cenote collection. In the 1950s she went to work full-time for the Peabody Museum at Harvard where she had a little office in the basement. From there she worked on a giant jigsaw puzzle, reassembling the shards of broken jade that Thompson had dredged. Her efforts resulted in a book, *Jades from the Cenote of Sacrifice*, which contained photographs and drawings of the reassembled jades and reconstructions of those jades that had pieces missing.

Another woman soon arrived who arguably would have more impact on the locals then any before her. In 1937 Elva Legters moved to the small village of Xocempich, a few kilometers north of Chichén Itzá. She and her husband David were Presbyterian missionaries from the United States. David was the son of L.L. Legters, famous in missionary circles for his travels through Central and South America. David had accompanied his father on one of his missions to the Amazon and, from that experience, received a calling to spread the Gospel in the Yucatán, a place he had read about extensively. In 1934 he married Elva and by the next year the two were in Mexico City, learning Spanish. In 1936 they moved to Mérida, eager to find a community that would serve as their base of operations in Yucatán. They tried east of Chichén Itzá in Ebtun, but found the town too hostile to Protestants. They also looked south of Chichén at Chankom, the village where Robert Redfield had conducted his groundbreaking anthropological studies for the Carnegie Institution, but found the well poisoned, reportedly because Redfield or someone working for him had given the locals alcohol, possibly in exchange for their cooperation with the study.

The two selected Xocempich, in part because it was home to another evangelical, the Rev. Ezequiel Lango, who had met David Legter's father, L.L., during one of his missions to Yucatán. The Rev. Lango offered his home to the Legters until they could find a place of their own. The house turned out to be a traditional Maya na, a small hut with a palm-thatched roof and mud-wattled oval.

The couple had decided before even coming to Mexico that they would employ an indirect approach when it came to preaching the Gospel, for not only did they consider it ineffective, Mexican authorities considered it against the law. Instead they decided that they would be of service to the local Maya and by doing so would gain their trust and an opportunity to introduce them to their brand of Christianity. It was Elva who gave them that opportunity, because she had a valuable skill to share: she was a nurse, trained at Johns Hopkins.

Infant mortality rates in rural Yucatán were high, as much as sixty percent, so Elva began an educational program, traveling from village to village to explain to local midwives and future mothers techniques that would increase a baby's chances of living. "Malarian, hookworm, and various intestinal complaints could be thwarted through proper know-how and medicines," Elva's biographer wrote. " Accident cases, including snake-bite victims and those injured by machete cuts and the falls of trees, responded better to modern treatment than to incantations and useless unguents. Little by little, the word spread through the bush communities that a miracle woman, who charged nothing for her services, could be found in Xoecempich."

When Elva became pregnant, she went to the United States to have her child, a boy. She soon returned to Xocempich to resume her nursing practice while at the same time raising her son. His first languages were English, spoken in the home, and Maya. "All my friends were Maya,"

David Legters Jr. recalled in an interview. "I didn't know I wasn't Maya."

The Legters had been at Xocempich for some time before they ever received an invitation to dine with the Morleys at the Hacienda Chichén. David was too busy at the time to accept, but Elva, who thought she needed a break, decided to accept on her own. Like so many before her, she enjoyed an exquisite dinner with the Carnegie crowd prepared by the Morleys' Korean cook. Afterwards Sylvanus led everyone out to the Great Ball Court to play records on his phonograph. Elva was taken to the guest cottage with a bed, which must have seemed the height of luxury. Her reverie was short lived, interrupted by shouts of a man who had run over from the Mayaland Hotel. "Quick, quick!" he shouted. "Don Fernando's aunt is dying!"

Elva grabbed her medical kit, which traveled with her always, and went to help. The elder woman was in convulsions and Elva knew almost at once that unless she got to a hospital she would die. Someone scrounged up an old truck and they placed the patient in the open bed, with Elva along to hold her down so that neither the bouncing truck nor the woman's convulsions throw her over the side. Hours later the truck was in Mérida and the sick woman was able to get the medical attention that saved her life. Elva, meanwhile, took a bus to Pisté and instead of returning to the Hacienda, she walked home, arriving as her husband was cleaning a rifle. "I thought you would like a good rest and would stay a while," he said, surprised to see her. "Did you get lonesome?"

"No, I had unexpected company," she said, and sank into a hammock.

The Thompson descendants at the home
of Bibiano Uh Tun and Victoria Marrufo Nah

THE PRESENT

FIESTA!

LATE IN THE EVENING Sarah and I drive up to Bibiano and Victoria's home, a few hundred feet from doña Maria Luisa's house where we first met the Marrufos. A carport on the side of the house had been converted into a makeshift banquet room by installing a long table and plastic chairs sporting logos for cervesa. Latin music blares from a P.A. system that Bibiano and his family must use when hiring out as musicians.

The party is already underway. Victoria is cooking a giant pot of spaghetti for the children, who are scurrying around in every direction. Even though we were told to bring just ourselves, Sarah and I stopped at a store along the way and purchases several large bottles of Coca-Cola. I also bring along copies of the photographs I took last year and a couple of surprises. I give Victoria a photograph of four small children posed on a staircase.

"Carlos Marrufo," I tell her, along with his two brothers and sister. She does not understand what I am saying, but Bibiano comes over and translates. I had found the photograph in the archives of the Carnegie Institution. I ask if she knows which one of the four is Carlos, as the children were not identified except as belonging to Victoria's grandmother, doña Victoria. She points to the boy on the far left.

One of Victoria's brothers breaks out a bottle of tequila and pours a shot into a small glass. He mixes it with grapefruit soda and then slams the glass onto a short wood plank. He hands me the glass to drink. I pour it down and the concoction tastes familiar (much later I remember my grandfather's favorite drink was a grapefruit soda mixed with Canadian Club whiskey).

It turns out that the visitors from the United States--Alex, Janet, Lizzie, Warren, Sarah and me--were not the only featured guests. It is also the birthday of Bibiano and Victoria's youngest son, Joseu. Bibiano leads everyone in a song, which wanders around for a couple of verses before it settles into the instantly recognizable "Happy Birthday," albeit in español. A cake appears and all the children start screaming, "*Mordida*! *Mordida*! *Mordida*!" I knew the term, but in the context of bribe one pays to police. Joseu bends down to the cake and someone pushes his face into it. "Mordida," someone tells me, means "bite." As police put the bite on you, Joseu puts the bite into the cake. Everyone laughs and claps.

"Everything is about family," I say to no one in particular. "Without family, everything falls apart."

"Family is very important," someone says, then adds, "You are very important."

I make a face. "Naaaaaaah," I say.

Someone else asks if I know Spanish. I shake my head. "Maya?" they ask.

"*Poquito*," I say. I hold up one finger and say the one Maya word I know. "*Ma*! (which means 'no')–That's it." Everyone laughs, and they decide I need to learn more Maya.

"*Ko'ox*," someone says, which to my ear sounds like "Koh-OHSH," with barely a pause between syllables. That means vamanos–let's go!

"*Ko'ox wenei*" ("Koh-ohsh we-nay")–Let's go to sleep.

"*Ko'ox meyaj*" ("Kos-ohsh may-yah")–Let's go to work.

And the most important variation--"*Ko'ox janal*" ("Koh-ohsh hah-nah")–Let's eat. And we do.

"Take a seat, please," Bibiano tells us. Victoria and doña Maria Luisa bring out plates with a local variation of the tostado called a "*panucho*"–tortillas with beans, lettuce, pickled onion, and other vegetables, topped with chicken. I look at Sarah, who is a vegetarian. She shrugs. When in Rome…

None of Bibiano's family or the Marrufos join us at the table, which I thought was odd. I had a slight panic that there wasn't enough food to go around, but I later learn that guests are always served first.

After dinner come the speeches, from Bibiano, the Marrufos, the Thompsons. "I hope this day is not the first or last," says doña Maria Luisa says in Spanish. "I'm happy to know you to today."

Bibiano and his sons pull out their guitars. "We hope that you will like the music," he announces. "This is the kind of job we do at the hacienda. Hacienda was a very important place for us for this was a way we can work together. As soon as I taught them to play, all my sons play guitar. So when I have a day off, they go for me. That's very important. While I'm not a teacher, not rich people, I am a musician. We have no more to give you. Thank you very much." With that, the trio launch into their mini-set.

I am asked to say something. "Eduardo Thompson, when his wife went up to United States he found comfort with a woman in doña Victoria. Tell you what I feel right here. Family is family, it doesn't matter who your parents are, who you are married to, it doesn't matter. The Marrufos are family to the Thompsons, regardless of what Edward Thompson did or when he did it, everybody is family."

One of Victoria's brothers, Guillermo, approaches and asks a question in Spanish. I only understand two words, "Eduardo Thompson." Bibiano shows up to translate. "He wants to know if his father was Edward Thompson's son," he says.

"As best I know, si, he was," I reply. "Fernando Barbachano of Chichén Itzá, he says Carlos Marrufo was the son of Edward Thompson." After Bibiano translates my answer, I ask when Carlos died; 1975, when Guillermo was twelve. Carlos was sixty-three at the time. I do quick arithmetic in my head. That meant he was born in 1912, which was after Edward Thompson's wife and much of the family returned to the United States.

THE PAST

MORLEY FALLS, MEXICO RISES

UNTIL THE CARNEGIE INSTITUTION committed to Chichén Itzá, the Mexican government had demonstrated minimal interest in the Maya ruins of Yucatán. In the early 1920s, it had dispatched Miguel Angel Fernández to make models and draw plans of the monuments, but once Sylvanus Morley's men began digging, the Mexican Ministry of Education's Department of Archaeology came up with a budget for its own archaeological program at Chichén Itzá.

For the most part, the Mexican Chichén project was left to its own devices. The jefe at the site was the Inspector of Ruins, Eduardo Martínez Cantón. Martínez Cantón had gotten the job the old fashioned way: He had inherited it from his father, the Mayan scholar Juan Martínez Hernández, upon his retirement in 1916.

Martínez Cantón also inherited a distrust of men who came from large colleges or foundations. "All Institutional men are humbugs to a certain extent," his father once wrote. "They have to show up something, for the time and money spent." Many times they take credit for discoveries that someone else had made years earlier. When he learned that a famous, publicity-seeking archaeologist was on his way to Yucatán, the elder Martínez Hernández remarked sarcastically, "You will see how many new things, untold of, they will discover."

His son, Martinez Cantón, had been a critic of the Carnegie project from the beginning. According to Earl Morris (who had left the project in 1928), the Inspector of Ruins "had picked flaws in every step of the excavation and reconstruction that I was directing." One day in May 1927 Morris happened to be at the top of the Temple of the Warriors when Martinez Cantón rushed up the broad staircase to meet him. "He gave me a bear-like [hug] and said 'I congratulate you.'" Morris recalled. He wondered if the inspector had come to appreciate the job the Carnegie was doing, but it turned out that he was instead congratulating Morris because, he said, "your countryman, Lindbergh, has made a solo flight across the Atlantic."

Even when the Carnegie performed good deeds it backfired. The hacienda had its own medical clinic with a trained nurse that it opened to anyone from the surrounding communities. In 1929 more than 500 people came through its doors. Martínez Cantón told anyone who would listen that the nurse was a seditionist, propagandizing the Maya to turn against the government. The Carnegie let her go.

By 1930, the bloom was off the rose of the Carnegie Institution project, not only in Mexico but in the United States. The source of most of the problems was Sylvanus Morley, who made a series of political missteps. His good friend, Dr. Thomas Gann, had purchased the jade in Mexico City and sneaked it out of the country by sewing it into his vest, the same method Thompson had Tozzer use to ship the carved jades from the Cenote Sagrado in 1905. Morley knew nothing of the purchase or its concealment until after the two men crossed the border into the United States. Somehow the head of the Dirección de Antropología (Mexican Department of Anthropology) found out and, furious, contacted the head of the Carnegie Institution, J.C. Merriam. Merriam had returned from Mexico only a few weeks before and had promised that the Carnegie would not take any artifacts. Here was Morley's good friend, someone who had been recommended to serve as physician to the Chichén Itzá project, caught almost red-handed. Merriam never forgot what he perceived as a betrayal by Morley. "I can't have Morley running this organization anymore," Merriam later told archaeologist Alfred V. Kidder in the late 1920s. He offered the job to Kidder, who became "Director of Historical Research," which, among other duties, gave him oversight of all the archaeological work in Central America and Mexico, including the Chichén Itzá project.

Morley also was coming into criticism from many Mexican archaeologists, who in the past had supported him. In 1930 Kidder asked his old professor, Alfred Tozzer, to go to Mexico to get his own sense of how the Carnegie Institution was being regarded. Tozzer, in the years since losing the Carnegie Chichén Itzá Project job, had done well. He was chair of Harvard's Anthropology Division and his influence in the world of archaeology was immense. By 1930 it seemed as if everyone who entered the field of archaeology had, at one time or another, been mentored by him. Tozzer also assumed curatorship of Middle American Archaeology and Ethnology at the Peabody Museum, which meant he now managed the treasures from the Cenote Sagrado. For years he had been preparing a series of volumes on the collection, but until Thompson's legal troubles with the Mexican government were resolved, little if anything could be published.

Tozzer arrived in Mexico and in short order was able to sniff out the troubles facing the Carnegie Institution. Few Mexicans, Tozzer concluded, could understand how a foreign institution like the Carnegie "can spend all this money with no hope of visible financial returns." According to Tozzer, "practically all" believed the Carnegie was not searching for the secrets of the Maya so much as they were looking for oil, or worse, spreading propaganda to turn the people against the government to enable a takeover by the U.S. "I don't know any country in world so different in their mental processes from us than Mexico," complained Tozzer. The Carnegie had spent nearly $100,000 on the Chichén Itzá project "and not a word of thanks...only knocks."

But the Carnegie's troubles did not stop there. When Tozzer got Chichén Itzá, he saw that the Carnegie was doing its job too well. It had been almost two decades years since he last set foot on the hacienda and everything was different. The hut where he had stayed during those visits was gone, replaced by comfortable guesthouses. "No garrapta-eaten cattle, no stinking pigs, no mud, everything very nice and most comfortable," he noted. The grounds were beautifully landscaped, the main casa spic and span, with four servants around to cook, maintain, and clean. And that was exactly the problem.

"The main trouble is the *lujo*—grandeur at Chichén," Tozzer observed. When Mexicans not affiliated with the Carnegie project arrive at Chichén Itzá, they stayed in crude huts and ate poor food; the Carnegie team had electric lights, running water, and even an ice plant. To add insult, around the hacienda were signs warning people in Spanish to stay out. Tozzer called it "bad psychology," adding, "What would we do and think if a foreign institution camped down on some important site in U.S.A.?"

But Tozzer's biggest issue with the Carnegie's project at Chichén Itzá was not its relationship with Mexico, but with advancing the archaeological knowledge. While the work on the ruins was "spectacular" and "remarkable"—at the time of his visit some thirty-five structures had been excavated, restored, or cleared of vegetation—Tozzer believed so much more could be done but doubted whether the Carnegie was up to the task. In the end, he would prove prescient.

There were great discoveries yet to be found at Chichén Itzá, but they would not be made by the Carnegie, but by the Mexican archaeologists led by Martínez Cantón.

Over the years at Chichén, Martínez Cantón had formed a warm relationship with T.A. Willard—"Tom," as he was known to friends. Even though his old friend, Edward Thompson, could not return to Mexico, Willard continued his annual visits. Even though Martínez Cantón helped the prosecution of don Eduardo, Willard sought his friendship and Martínez Cantón reciprocated. Perhaps it is more accurate to say they had a mutual respect for each other and felt free to use each other. Willard relied on Martínez Cantón to keep him up to date on developments at Chichén and Martínez Cantón relied on Willard for money, goods, and access to the media.

After the Mexican government charged Edward Thompson with theft, Willard needed a new place to stay at Chichén, so for several years he bunked with Martínez Cantón at the federal encampment. The federales operated out of a small compound of Maya huts and buildings on the opposite side of El Castillo from the Temple of the Warriors. While the Carnegie was transforming a plain mound into the majestic Temple of the Warriors, Mexican archaeologists set about "replacing the fallen parts of the Maya monuments." Most of their effort focused on the Great Ball Court, reassembling the collapsed sections of the Upper Temple of the Jaguars and the eroded giant walls that bounded the playing field.

In the evening Willard and Martínez Cantón would sit around the fire. The Inspector of Monuments would play his violin while Willard smoked and listened. The two men gossiped about the Carnegie archaeologists and would dream up their own archaeological projects. One subject that often came up was the possibility of a smaller pyramid buried under El Castillo, just as the Carnegie had found one beneath the Temple of the Warriors. "You can be sure that 'El Castillo'...has something very important inside," Martínez Cantón's father predicted in early 1931 shortly before Willard made his annual trip to Yucatán. "Most assuredly there is another smaller building under with paintings, bas-reliefs, and probably a shaft with plenty of bones."

Shortly after Willard arrived that season at Chichén Itzá, Martínez Cantón ordered two of his men to begin digging into the base of the decrepit southern face of the pyramid. "I sentimentally set aside the first stone removed and marked it 'No. 1,'" Willard wrote. "But as no one else around me seemed to have any sentimental feelings for the block, it was discarded with the rest."

The two men burrowed more than nine meters into the pyramid before striking pay dirt—the wall of another pyramid. Unlike the outer shell, the interior pyramid did not have a staircase on its south wall. Emboldened by the discovery, Martínez Cantón had his men tunnel down from the top. Willard had to leave, but upon his return to the United States he received word that the vertical wall to a temple that rested atop the smaller pyramid had been found, which according to Martínez Cantón was "beautifully ornamented." Willard had apparently bet his friend that if he did find a temple, it would be in a state of ruin. "Tell Tom to get ready with the one hundred dollars," Martínez Cantón wrote Willard's wife not long after his crew unearthed the temple. "It is complete with façade and ornamented with serpents and tigers. It is something unusual for the archaeologists. Seems to be very old…the outside was so well preserved the inside should be intact."

Martínez Cantón's excavators did not find a doorway to the temple on the south side so they carved a shaft from the top of the north face. They had guessed correctly, for they found an entrance blocked with rubble. The also uncovered the top of a staircase, which they believed to be the only one on the interior pyramid.

This was the discovery that presumably would make Martínez Cantón famous the world over. News of the pyramid-inside-the-pyramid broke at the end of May 1931 in the Diario de Yucatán. It soon hit the newspapers in the United States. A reporter in Los Angeles, where Willard was currently living, contacted him about the find. Willard admitted he had been present during the excavation and when word of that article got back to Mexico, officials were outraged to learn that a gringo had been present and may have even participated in the excavation.

"I am sorry to tell you that my Eduardo has lost the confidence of his superiors through the instrumentality of your indiscretions and, very probably, will have to resign in the near future," Juan Martínez Hernández wrote Willard in June. "It will be the case of Mr. Eduard Thompson, but he will not be able to find his living by giving lectures." Martínez Cantón's superior in Mexico City, Ignacio Marquina, ordered the excavation halted and sent a representative to take over the work. "Eduardo has rivals who have profited [from] the opportunity to denounce him," Martínez Hernández explained. "The impression is that you are allowed a free hand in Chichén, for excavating and for publishing the results of the excavations carried out by the Mexican government in the press of the United States." Willard was henceforth cut off from receiving intelligence from the Martínez family.

Willard wrote back to Martínez Hernández apologizing for any misunderstanding, but said he had not claimed to have participated in the excavation or possessed any knowledge beyond what had already been published in Mexican newspapers. "I'm very sorry to have this matter come up to cause trouble, for it is well known in this country that I am a solid friend and a defender of Mexico at all times," he wrote. "Furthermore I am not interested in such petty happenings as seem to have been magnified to a gigantic scale ... I don't intend to become the purveyor of gossip but I think that if you look deeper you will find some other more prominent contributing causes for this."

Those "other prominent causes" included almost everyone with a stake in Chichén Itzá, among them Mexican archaeologist José A. Erosa Peniche, the entire Carnegie Institution senior staff including Sylvanus Morley, and hotel entrepreneur Fernando Barbachano Peón. Martínez Cantón had made enemies of all of them and although he and his father believed that the enmity was undeserved, the Inspector of Monuments, during the conduct of his official duties, appeared to have gone out of his way to antagonize everyone.

The flap with Willard blew over, but Martínez Cantón's superiors put him on a short leash. He was forbidden from speaking with Willard or any member of the press and reports of all his excavation were to now be channeled through headquarters in Mexico City. The next year excavation resumed. The Mexican team decided to tunnel from the base of the north face of the pyramid to reach the staircase from the bottom. However, unlike the southern exterior of El Castillo, which was much eroded with exposed interior stone, the north face had in recent years been consolidated and was now beautifully restored. Instead of tunneling in from the staircase as they had on the south side, Martínez Cantón's men cut in from the side of the staircase's balustrade. The men excavated a shaft to the center of the staircase, then made a right turn directly at what they figured to be the corresponding center of the staircase of the interior pyramid. It was exactly where they expected it to be, but with a surprise. Buried at the foot of the staircase they found a large stone box, 120 centimeters long, eighty centimeters wide, and twenty-five centimeters tall. Inside were not one, but two turquoise mosaics. There also were two large, flint knife blades, hundreds of turquoise beads, carved jade plaques, a small piece of finely woven cloth, and the skeleton of an iguana or other lizard. This was a find to rival anything discovered by the Carnegie Institution. The turquoise mosaics were of a similar style to the one found under the altar in the Temple of the Warriors by the Carnegie, but both were larger.

The discovery should have strengthened Martínez Cantón standing with his bosses, but instead it made his position far more precarious. "Sr. Erosa got very jealous and wanted to get [Martínez Cantón's] work," one of Willard's informants in Yucatán wrote him. The relationship between the two men became so toxic that Marquina asked Juan Martínez Hernández to step in, "for Marquina wants both of them working as before, otherwise, he will put away both of them."

The intervention was not enough to save Martínez Cantón. His conflict with Erosa was only the tip of the iceberg: Everyone at Chichén wanted him out. "Now about ten politicians are working to put me away from Chichén," he wrote Willard at the end of the year. In 1935 he was replaced as Inspector of Ruins, the post given to more popular Manuel Cirerol Sansores, the former secretary to the late Governor Felipe Carrillo Puerto. The timing of Martínez Cantón's dismissal was unfortunate, because the inner pyramid under El Castillo was about to give up its biggest secrets.

The Mexican engineers finally were confident they could excavate the smaller pyramid's temple without causing the entire top of the pyramid to collapse. By the end of the year the Maya laborers had cleared out the first of two rooms. Inside they found an almost perfect chac-mool statue with all the adornment intact. The eyes, teeth, and fingernails were covered with bits of seashell, as polished as ivory. Some of the original paint on the statue had survived.

In 1936 the team excavated the back room and found the biggest prize of all, a handsome throne carved in the shape of a jaguar. It was painted a bright red, with seventy-three green spots of inlaid jade. Resting on the back of the jaguar, where one would sit, was another mosaic disk.

Sylvanus Morley was prompted to call it "the most outstanding archaeological object ever discovered in the New World." Years later Mexico would claim that someone had offered to buy the jaguar throne for one million dollars, but without even a hint of irony said it had told the potential buyer that it was not for sale.

Today credit for finding the inner pyramid is usually given to Erosa Peniche, who gave a paper on the discovery in 1939 and who mentioned it in a guide book to Chichén Itzá that was translated into English by John Germon, now the Mérida manager for Barbachano Peón's travel service. In some literature, Manuel Cirerol Sansores is listed as the man who found it. Rarely, if ever, is Eduardo Martínez Cantón given credit and, if so, it is usually in a list with Erosa Peniche and Cirerol Sansores.

Never mentioned at all are the names of the Maya workman who risked their lives by excavating the tunnels and room.

THE PRESENT

BACK AT BIBIANO'S

ALEX IS TALKING TO ME, but I'm not listening. We're in the car, heading to Mérida. I'm taking Alex to her hotel. Behind me Bibiano's son Jaime is chauffeuring the other Thompsons, Janet Sawyer and daughter Liz. Warren Thompson left yesterday. He'd had a good time, but he was more interested in diving reefs than visiting newfound family. Before he left we promise to stay in touch.

I'm not ignoring Alex, but I am preoccupied. All is good between us, although I never mention how upset I got at her "You're not family" statement. It's been a whirlwind couple of days and I need some time to digest it all.

The fiesta was two nights ago. Before the party broke up, I took Bibiano aside and asked him if I could come by his *casa* tomorrow morning, because I want to speak to him. When I pulled up the next day, he was waiting for me. Before I can tell him why I have come, he thanked me for the last night. In a strained voice, he told me that last night was the first time Victoria's family had come to his house. "It was because of you," he said.

I'm not sure I understood him correctly. Victoria's brothers had not walked the couple hundred meters down the street from their mother's to Bibiano's? That can't be what he means. I don't ask him why. I have no idea what rift could exist between the branches of the family, but if my time in Mexico has demonstrated anything, it's that families fight.

"It wasn't because of me," I said. "It was because of Edward Thompson."

We chat for a few more minutes. And then I did something stupid.

I don't know if it was guilt or gringo arrogance, but I gave Bibiano a thousand pesos. The fiesta the night before must have cost them a pretty penny and I knew they were not rich. My pretense was I wanted he and his sons to sing "Peregrina," the love song Felipe Carrillo Puerto had written for Alma Reed, once a month at the hacienda and think of me.

"No," Bibiano said firmly. "No."

I told him I insisted and would not take no for an answer. And rather than insult me, Bibiano took the money. His eyes, wounded, his hand held the slick Mexican bills as if they were diseased. I knew then I had made a terrible mistake. But it was too late to take it back. I walked out to the car. We hugged and I drove off.

I saw him a couple more times over the next two days and we had regained some of the closeness I had felt in the moments right before I handed him the money. But as I speed across the Yucatecan landscape to Mérida, a piece of me wonders if my stupidity has killed something between us.

THE PAST

THE END OF THOMPSON

EDWARD THOMPSON DIED IN 1935, killed in no small part by the weight of a lifetime of questionable decisions. By the end, he had lost his health, his wealth, and his wits; but the worst was he lost his optimistic enthusiasm and the will to live.

Considering his advanced age, he was productive until the final few weeks. Only three years before he had published his own autobiographical account of his explorations of the Yucatán, *People of the Serpent: Life Among the Mayas*. The book received a warm critical reception and sold well.

But what was left of his career the Great Depression turned to ash. A few weeks after *People of the Serpent* hit bookstores, he and Henrietta moved in with one of his sons in Plainfield, N.J. "If the good Lord will but give me a few more years of lectures, I may be able to climb out of the hole," he wrote his friend T.A. Willard. He was well into his seventies and nearly penniless, the direct result of his legal battle with the Mexican government, a battle he was losing.

The government chipped away at his holdings. Thompson lost an adjoining parcel of several hundred hectares he called "La Esperanza" because he could not produce a clear title. Then, X'Katun, where Thompson had once had an armed confrontation with squatters after the

Mexican Revolution, was taken by the government and converted into an ejido, a large swath of property owned by the government but run as a cooperative by local villagers.

Somehow Thompson managed to sell the two hectares that the Mayaland hotel squatted upon to Fernando Barbachano Peón. The official price recorded sometime in 1932 was 200 pesos, but Mexico being Mexico, it is more than likely that the actual price was much higher, paid either in cash or in comparable services.

Neither Thompson's claim seeking recompense for the burning of his hacienda in 1921, nor the case against him by the federal government for excavating the Cenote Sagrado was moving ahead with anything that could be considered alacrity. In 1931 the treaty between Mexico and the United States that covered damages incurred by U.S. citizens during the Mexican Revolution had expired, so Thompson's claim was in limbo until the two nations renewed it. The federal government, meanwhile, was happy to let its case lumber through the courts, consuming every available penny Thompson had to maintain his defense.

If he could only find a way out of his financial troubles, then "after that, come what may, I shall be ready for the great change," he wrote Willard. But Thompson was to face one more heartbreak before his end would come.

At the end of 1934, Thompson decided to take a trip. "By the last of the week we will be on our way to Oklahoma," Thompson wrote Willard. His daughter Alice was either about to marry or had recently married a man from that town. Thompson was striking out west with his wife and another daughter, Abby, in tow. "I sincerely hope this trip will be of lasting benefit to my wife and daughter. As for myself, I can stump around and make myself a nuisance to my friends." But once he got to what he called "the wild and wooly west," Thompson found his ability to "stump around" limited. In his final letter to Willard, written from Oklahoma, he issued an ominous prognosis. "The trouble with my foot and leg has been changing into a numbness which relieves me of some pain, but I cannot mistake the symptoms," he wrote.

Because of his limited mobility and that of his aged wife, the couple had to be grateful their youngest daughter, Abby, had accompanied them. Of all Thompson's children, she was his favorite, and as she was unmarried, she lived with her parents in their later years, serving as her father's secretary and drawing illustrations for his books. No doubt because of her father's growing infirmity, it fell to Abby to light a fire in their temporary quarters in Oklahoma to ward off the December chill; something went wrong, her clothing ignited and she was burned to death.

Edward Thompson was inconsolable. He buried his daughter in Oklahoma. Within five months he was dead.

"Poor old don Eduardo," T.A. Willard wrote Alfred Tozzer. "I carried him along for years and just before he died he wrote me a wonderful letter in which he regretted his ability to pay me back. But he was very welcome for the first book sold eighty thousand and why, I cannot figure out, since it was full of mistakes."

Despite Thompson's passing, the legal machinations in which he was involved ground ahead. Not even death could deter the judicial system. Even though Willard spent months of each year in Yucatán, it was not until two years after Thompson's death that he was finally called in to testify on the Cenote Sagrado case. "They...hauled me before the judge whom I will say was a gentleman and after the trial he gave me a cigarette and apologized asking me to come and see him." The federal government did drop the criminal charges against Thompson after his death, but the civil case pressed ahead.

Whenever possible, the Mexican press loved to ambush American dignitaries about the Cenote Sagrado treasure. A few months after Thompson's death, the American ambassador to Mexico, Josephus Daniels, visited Chichén Itzá and a reporter for one of the Mexico City dailies wanted to know what was being done to return the artifacts to Mexico. Daniels replied that no one should run a side business while serving as consul, nor "should he take anything outside of the country that he has found without first having obtained official permission to do so." The ambassador, injecting a little levity, told the reporter, "I am delighted by all these things, particularly pyramids, that I should like to take them all home to North Carolina in my valises, but that would be as harmful an act for my country as for Mexico." In what would be a repeating pattern, the Mexican (and occasionally the U.S. press) would make a fuss about the cenote collection, but then nothing would happen.

Even Tozzer, who served as curator of the collection, got bushwhacked. For almost fifteen years no official from Mexico ever contacted the Peabody Museum about the Cenote Sagrado artifacts. In 1940, Tozzer happened to be attending a conference in Washington, D.C., when he was asked if he would to meet with Alfredo Caso, probably the finest archaeologist in Mexico at the time, who was in the midst of excavating sites in the Valley of Oaxaca of a pre-Maya civilization that would become known as the Olmecs. The two men got together on May 16 and, to Tozzer's complete surprise, all Caso wanted to discuss was the return of the Cenote Sagrado collection.

"Mr. Caso proposed that the Peabody Museum should hand over to Mexico the entire collection," Tozzer later reported. "Mexico would then return to the Peabody Museum one-half of the collection. He also said that he felt sure it could be arranged that various objects from the collections of the Museo Nacional might be given to the Peabody Museum as a gesture of friendship." Caso added that Mexico would not accept the collection unless all of the artifacts were returned.

Tozzer was taken aback by the request. For one, Caso already had been to the Peabody and personally viewed the entire collection; not once did he ever mention its return to Mexico. He could not understand why Caso at that moment was making "the first direct approach to a member of the Peabody Museum staff after waiting thirty-five years from the time the collection was made." Tozzer did not "approve the proposition to hand the entire collection over to Mexico...as this would be an admission that Mr. Charles P. Bowditch, who presented the collection to the Peabody museum, had done something wrong."

Tozzer told Caso that the fate of the collection was not up to him, but to the museum director. He added that from his perspective he could not imagine the Peabody would do anything with the cenote artifacts until the museum published its research about them. Once published, Tozzer told Caso "that he would like to see a final settlement regarding the cenote collection." Perhaps "a representative collection of all the different types of objects might be given Mexico." Or "the Museum might hand over the entire gold collection retaining all the jades." Caso replied he could not agree to any of these proposals. Tozzer then suggested that the Peabody might turn over half the collection. "With no hesitation Caso said yes."

Why was the Cenote Sagrado collection getting all this attention? There were thousands of artifacts from Mexico in scores of museums around the world. Why all the fuss? Caso told Tozzer, "If the collection had not contained gold, the question of its return to Mexico would probably never have been raised."

There it was. The gold. Or, to put it more plainly, Thompson's exaggerations about the gold. Despite Thompson's protest that he never told Willard the gold objects he had found were "priceless," his other statements from the same period and earlier demonstrate he loved to inflate the value of his find. Tozzer had the golden objects analyzed in the 1940s and the total value of gold in them was worth less than $5,000 U.S. But whether they were worth five dollars or five million dollars, they were gold, and gold was what Mexico wanted returned.

Tozzer and the director of the Peabody Museum, Donald Scott, met with the Harvard lawyers and president of the museum's to inform them of Caso's request to return the artifacts to Mexico. The men decided to do nothing, but wait and see how the litigation against Thompson resolved. On March 27, 1942, after sixteen years of litigation, a federal judge handed down a decision: There was enough evidence to prove that Thompson illegally obtained the artifacts and shipped them from the country. His estate would be forced to pay $36,410 Mexican, as well as come up with another fifty thousand pesos for indemnity against future claims.

Edward and Henrietta Thompson (center) and family

THE PRESENT

THE BEST THINGS IN LIFE

FERNANDO WANTS TO TALK MONEY. A lot of money. Money has been preying on his mind.

Sarah and I spend our last couple of days in Yucatán with don Fernando and doña Maruja in their mansion. Fernando asks if I will be willing to write an article about him and submit it to magazines. He wants to start another airline and he thinks it will be a good idea to start to get his name out there again, remind the world of who he was—the founder of the airline Aeromaya, which he believes was the first no frills airline in history.

His problem, though, is that his grandson Hans Thies Barbachano controls his money and has put Fernando on a strict budget. Fernando is furious, but, he says, there is nothing he can do.

Sarah is off with doña Maruja, who is taking her to meet a friend who is involved in a charity. One of my daughter's goals for this trip was to volunteer her time for some worthy cause and Maruja is facilitating that.

We relax in the cool basement of the mansion as Fernando continues his rant. His grandson's father, Hans, sits in a recliner. His face offers no expression, other than perhaps boredom, at Fernando's tirade about his son. He has heard this many times before.

The conversation then slides into a business deal with another of his children that in Fernando's mind had gone awry and cost him thousands of dollars. "Dollars!" he says. "Not pesos!"

I have known Fernando for a little more than a year and, like Hans, have heard this tale many times before. "Have you *ever* had a business deal with your children that worked?" I ask.

Fernando stops. He looks at me. He looks at Hans. "That is a hell of a question," he says. "That...is...a...*hell*...of a question."

"Why do you give your children your businesses if it never turns out the way you want?" I ask.

He has no answer.

Fernando goes up for a siesta and for the first time Hans and I are alone together. I have grown to like him very much. Although he says he is Mexican, he is German through and through, born and raised. I have German roots, although most of my ancestors immigrated to the United States in the nineteenth century. Like me, Hans can be blunt, and here in Latin America where everyone is so polite and circumspect, where no one wants to disappoint, he has remained true to who he is. He is never afraid to say what he thinks and, now that we are alone, he does not disappoint.

The problem don Fernando has with his children is that he gives them his businesses, but there is always a "string," Hans says. When they don't run them the way he wants or does what he says, he gets angry. I let Hans know I had already figured that out. Over the course of several months, Fernando and I have corresponded many times about his relationship with his children. At one point he told me he was estranged from three of them. "It makes me a little sad that a father [at the end of his life] is estranged from his children," I wrote.

"If it saddens you, imagine my pain," Fernando wrote. "Obviously I will forgive all, as I have always done after the wounds heal." In another e-mail, he wrote about Maruja's efforts to keep the family together. "My wife is and has always been the one that brings light where there is darkness, peace where there is struggle. She understands my problems, but would prefer that I forgive and accept."

Hans and I continue to talk about Fernando behind his back, but what we both know is that neither of us is afraid to say it to his face and, in fact, have done so numerous times. It is one of the reasons he likes us. Then Hans reveals what I had long suspected. He has been protecting don Fernando from me. "I thought you wanted Fernando's money," he says.

"I never wanted anything from him, other than what I said from the beginning—I'm writing a book," I say.

"I know," Hans says. He tells me that people approach Fernando all the time to fund their schemes. Fernando had told me of one gentleman who had stolen $50,000 U.S. from him—or so that was Fernando's perception, but I got the impression that it was more likely that Fernando invested and the business did not produce the results he expected.

I tell Hans I long had suspected that was why he never left me alone with Fernando. Apparenty Hans and I have just crossed a threshold. And when Fernando rejoins us, Hans leaves me alone with him. By this time Sarah has returned from her adventure with doña Maruja, who has now gone up to take her siesta. The three of us, Fernando, Sarah, and me, enjoy a quick lunch. Then Fernando tells us what is really on his mind. He begins with his favorite subject, the Maya. Of the hundreds of e-mails and conversations we have exchanged, the majority has been about his observations of Maya society today and of what he has learned about the Maya civilization of the past. I have told him that one day I will collect his thoughts and publish them and we have worked out an outline for a small book.

Today, he wants to talk about the Maya and money. The Maya were not concerned with material gains, unlike our society today. "The monetary system is the worst system to have because greed and jealousy become part of the equation," Fernando tells us. "When greed and jealousy become part of the equation, you have me."

Like his father—"El Tigre," Fernando Barbachano Peón—he is driven to find success in the business world. "It's an illness," he says. "I know I'm sick." He needs to be successful in the manner his father taught him. "I was made a businessman and I love the taste of success. It's in my blood, ever since I was a child."

Fernando looks at Sarah and I now understand he is talking to her, or to her generation, not to me. "I'm opening my insides, not just for you, but for me," he says. He clenches his fists in front of his chest. "I want to... *scrape*...and get out whatever I can get out. I know I need to succeed again."

His voice quiets, the passion drains. "Part of my despair is that I no longer have the opportunity. I don't have the [youth]. I don't have that which I would have had...forty, fifty years ago." What he had in the past was money. And now, he says, he has none. The Barbachano *family* owns Chichén Itzá, including the Hacienda Chichén and the Mayaland. It owns the Hacienda Uxmal and the land under the ruins of Uxmal. It owns hotels across Yucatán, from Mérida to Cozumel. But these are owned by other members of the family. The only asset Fernando has left in his name is the Casa Camara, the big mansion. "I will have to sell this house to have some base to start," he says. "My wife doesn't want me to sell this house. She wants to give it away to my four daughters. It's a goddam shame."

THE PAST

BARBACHANO VS. THE GOVERNMENT

FERNANDO BARBACHANO PEON had proved himself more than capable against his competitors. But now the full force of the Mexican government was being brought to bear in an attempt to wipe him out.

It was possible that the government was unaware that it was going up against Barbachano Peón. The government may have thought its opponent was the heirs of Edward Thompson. When in 1942 it won a judgment against Thompson's estate for almost $90,000 Mexican, the case was appealed to the Mexican Supreme Court. The man who bankrolled the appeal for the Thompson family was Barbachano Peón. Fortunately he didn't have to shoulder the entire burden, as the federal government had also appealed the case because it felt the judgment was too low. As far as Thompson's lawyer, Julius Aznar, was concerned, he compared it to a famous Spanish saying, *"Cuentas del Gran Capitán"*—the Costs of the Great Captain, referring to when King Ferdinand asked Gonzalo Fernández de Córdoba to present his expenses for the conquest of Naples. The conqueror supposed responded:

> *For picks, shovels and hoes, one hundred million ducats...*

> *For alms to monks and nuns to pray for the Spanish, one hundred fifty*

thousand ducats…

For perfumed gloves to give the soldiers to cover the stench of battle, two hundred million ducats…

For the replacement of bells damaged from ringing because we continued to win, one hundred seventy thousand ducats…

And finally, for the patience of having to lower myself to such pettiness of the king for whom I gave a kingdom—one hundred million ducats.

In one of those moments of karmic justice, Thompson's own "Cuentas del Gran Capitán," his somewhat exaggerated claim against the Mexican government for the burning his hacienda in May 1921, reached a settlement. The claim had been dragging along in one form or another for far longer than the cenote treasure case. It took the Mexican-American claims commission more than thirty-two years to render a decision. The good news for Thompson's heirs was that the claims commission found the Mexican government responsible for the destruction. Thompson's heirs, however, would not receive the quarter million dollars in damages their father had sought; instead the claims commission awarded them $7,500 U.S.—far, far less than the 90,000 pesos the family owed the Mexican government for the alleged theft of the cenote artifacts.

The Mexican government wanted more—a million pesos, in fact, the original valuation of the cenote artifacts, hence the appeal to a higher court. Within months of the claims commission decision, the *Suprema Corte de Justicia de la Nación*, Mexico's Supreme Court, issued its ruling: Thompson owed the government nothing.

In the years that followed the Supreme Court decision attained a mythic status and one wonders if those who comment on the case have ever read the decision. There are some who maintain that the court found

Thompson won on a technicality. Under Mexican law, the Nation owns all "ancient monuments." The problem for the prosecution was that ancient monuments were defined as: "ruins of cities, *Casa Grandes*, cave dwellings, fortifications, palaces, temples, pyramids, sculptured stones or those with inscriptions and, in general, all the buildings that under any aspect may be of interest for the study of the civilization and history of the ancient population of Mexico." The Cenote Sagrado, however, was a natural feature and not manmade at all. Some historians have speculated that because the Cenote Sagrado did not meet the definition of an ancient monument or that because the objects had been found underwater they were not protected by antiquities laws, this is why Thompson won the case. But what the Supreme Court found was that the artifacts taken from the Cenote Sagrado did not qualify as ancient monuments, regardless of from where they were taken. As Mexican law recognized that a private person could own artifacts—Rafael Regil, for example, owned an entire museum's worth of relics of the ancient past that he displayed at his Hotel Itzá in Mérida—the question becomes from whose property did he take them? The answer, of course, was he had taken them from his own. If Thompson was stealing the artifacts, he was stealing them from himself.

It was against Mexican law, however, to export those artifacts outside the borders of Mexico. The penalty for exportation during the first decade of the 20th century? A mere 500 pesos—maximum.

What the Supreme Court decision makes clear is that the federal government had no case and never had a case. It was the Mexican equivalent of the never-ending lawsuit Jarndyce v Jarndyce in Dicken's *Bleak House*: The prosecutors dragged their heels from the beginning, either to delay losing as long as possible or more likely hoping that Thompson would just go away.

The decision also confirms and lays raw the motives of those behind the prosecution. The federal government went after Thompson because 1) it felt public and political pressure; 2) Thompson had filed a large claim against them; and 3) the prize at the end was Chichén Itzá, which had become one of the most valuable pieces of archaeological real estate in the world. And now it fell right into the lap of Fernando Barbachano Peón.

There are historians today who believe that the Supreme Court decision was the result of backroom shenanigans. None interviewed by this book were even aware that Barbachano Peón had anything to do with the case, but when told, the immediate assumption was that the hotel entrepreneur had bought the decision. "Barbachano is a very wealthy and politically powerful individual…need I say more?" one of Thompson's biographers said in an interview for this book. "I know something about various lawsuits in Mexico and that's a time period I do a lot of research." He described the Supreme Court decision as "a crock of crap."

These historians only know of the Barbachanos as they are viewed today, as owners of a tourism empire in Yucatán. But during World War II, when the Thompson case reached trial, Barbachano Peón was fighting for his financial life. The war had wiped out almost his entire business and much of his staff. He had to pull his son out of Harvard because he needed help running the family business. He lost his hotel in Mérida and then his house. The family relocated to the only property they owned—the Mayaland Lodge at Chichén Itzá.

According to his son, Fernando Barbachano Gomez Rul, these business reversals were the result of the war economy and the actions of predatory competitors. But it appears just as likely that Barbachano Peón had liquidated assets for one giant roll of the dice: He bought Chichén Itzá—twice. He gambled his future and that of his family to purchase something that the government, competitors, and the neighboring communities appeared hell bent to take away.

Barbachano Peón purchased Chichén Itzá from the Thompson heirs for $10,000 U.S. According to his son, this figure had been agreed upon in advance of the court cases. Barbachano Peón would pay the Thompson family's legal defense in exchange for the right to buy the Hacienda Chichén should they prevail. The five surviving heirs of Thompson in the United States would each receive two thousand dollars, a substantial sum in the early 1940s. At least one member of the family expressed seller's regret. In the 1960s Thompson's daughter Margaret T. Diddel told an interviewer, "It was during the war and the family wanted to clear everything about the estate—taxes, lawyers, fees, etcetera. I was the only one for holding on and not sell it to this buyer especially but finally gave in. How father would have deplored what we did and rightly so." Apparently Diddel was unaware of the numerous occasions her father had attempted to sell the hacienda.

This turned out to be the second time Barbachano Peón bought the property. A few months after winning against Thompson in the lower courts, the federal government put Chichén Itzá up for auction. Barbachano Peón was the high bidder and paid $16,650 Mexican. When the Supreme Court reversed the lower court's decision, it appears that Barbachano Peón did not get his money back.

Over the years, the government would make motions to take Chichén Itzá, but Barbachano Peón held onto the property. President Lazaro Cárdenas did not include the Hacienda Chichén when the federal government redistributed the land of other haciendas to the people in the 1930s (according to one family member, Cardenas came to the Mayaland and struck a deal with Barbachano Peón). Surrounding the archaeological zone are several small pueblos: Pisté to the northwest, San Felipe to the north, X'calacoop to the southeast, X'katun to the south. These communities in the 1940s and 1950s attempted to expand their respective ejidos into Chichén Itzá. Barbachano Peón employed a variety of legal maneuvers to protect the integrity of the Hacienda Chichén. When the law changed to protect working cattle ranches from being converted into ejidos, Barbachano Peón bought a herd and kept it at the hacienda; when the law changed the limits to the size of haciendas, he split the Hacienda Chichén into several parcels and distributed them to his family.

"My father's lawyers were very smart," said Fernando Barbachano Gomez Rul. The end of the war also brought a newfound prosperity. People started to travel again and one of the places they wanted to see was the famous Chichén Itzá. Barbachano Peón's gamble would pay off many times over.

Fernando Barbachano Peón

THE PRESENT

THOMPSONS MEET THE BARBACHANOS

I HAVE NO IDEA if Fernando Barbachano Peón ever met Edward Thompson. Thompson could not have been at the real estate closing for Chichén Itzá as he had been dead for almost ten years at that point. The patriarch of the Barbachano tourism empire had not started his business until after Thompson was out of Yucatán. The two men may have met prior to Thompson's departure forever from Mexico in May 1925. Or they may have met during Barbachano Peón's trip to the United States in 1928.

Although they may not have ever shaken hands, they were in communication. According to Barbachano's son, my friend Fernando Barbachano Gomez Rul, his father had built the Mayaland on Thompson's land, property he did not own. My suspicion is that he did so with Thompson's permission, a promise of future remuneration. In 1932 Barbachano recorded that he had purchased from Thompson the two hectares that the Mayaland had been built upon. The price according to records was 200 pesos, although the actual amount that exchanged hands, off the official books, was probably more. Barbachano Peón had spent $10,000 U.S. to build the Mayaland and it is hard to swallow that all of that went into constructing the buildings. Also, Barbachano wanted to keep Thompson happy because his eventual goal was to buy all of Chichén Itzá.

It is more than possible that the two men never met and, if so, today may be the first time a Thompson has sat down face-to-face with a Barbachano. Alex, Janet, and Liz are coming over to meet with don Fernando. *This will be historic!* I think. In the end, it is anti-climactic. Fernando is delighted to be the center of attention and after the trio arrives and is seated in his study, he regales them with the story of his family and Chichén Itzá. They have already heard much of this from me, but they listen politely and ask appropriate questions. But unlike the meeting with the Marrufos, the Thompsons don't seem to be engaged.

After the session with don Fernando, I walk them out of the Casa Camara. We say our goodbyes and promise to be in touch once we get back to the United States. In my pocket I have the jadeite spool from the Cenote Sagrado that I had won in the online auction. Thankfully I wasn't so stupid as to throw it back into the Sacred Well. Instead I give it to Liz, who has been the most deeply affected by this experience. Her great-great grandfather had risked everything, including his life, to retrieve it. It makes sense to pass it to newest generation of Thompsons.

THE PAST

'SO WHAT?'

WALTER TAYLOR DIDN'T KILL the Carnegie Institution's Chichén Itzá project. He simply pointed out it had been in the grave all along but didn't know it. *Amaneció muerto*, as the Spanish expression goes—literally, "it woke up dead."

By all rights, Taylor should not have been the sort of man to denigrate the Carnegie's archaeological efforts in Mesoamerica. He was, if anything, the stereotypical archaeologist. Like others before him, he was wealthy (his father was a bond broker on Wall Street who escaped the crash of '29); he was a snob and an elitist; and he studied at the preeminent archaeological programs at Yale and Harvard. But those very qualities that made him the ideal candidate to join the exclusive archaeologist fraternity also were the very ones that made his critique so devastating. Only one of their own could hoist the Carnegie by its own petard, which Taylor did in his 1948 monograph "A Study of Archaeology." Over the course of seventeen pages Taylor eviscerated the Carnegie's Chichén Itzá project—in fact all its research in the Maya world—and demonstrated it was an abject failure.

Taylor charged that after all the careful excavation at Chichén Itzá and other Maya cities, after spending hundreds of thousands of dollars in research, the Carnegie Institution archaeologists knew little more about the ancient Maya and how they lived then when they had began. "Carnegie has sought and found the hierarchal, the grandiose. It has neglected the common, the everyday," Taylor wrote.

A bigger sin, Taylor believed, was that the Carnegie had conducted all its archaeology in service of nothing but digging and collection of facts. Excavation must test a theory, Taylor argued. But "theory" to the Carnegie men, was the same as "speculation."

Taylor's public display of archaeologist-on-archaeologist crime appeared in *American Anthropologist*, the scholarly journal of the American Anthropological Association. The book-length monograph critiquing other archaeologists was unprecedented, published as part of the American Anthropologist's "Memoir" series, which usually consisted of book-length research studies of tribes, cultures, and other peoples.

One reason that "A Study of Archaeology" found a home where it did was that Taylor was a close associate of the president of American Anthropological Association, which published American Anthropologist. The subject of the failings of the Carnegie project was near and dear to AAA President Clyde Kluckhohn, who had issued his own public critique of the Carnegie and its practices eight years earlier. In an article non-controversially titled "The Conceptual Structure in Middle American Studies," Kluckhohn drolly observed that many archaeologists "are but slightly reformed antiquarians." The difference between antiquarians of the past and archaeologists of today is that archaeologists dig for facts, not artifacts. Archaeologists, he wrote, are engaged in "obsessive wallowing in detail of and for itself." After all their excavation and collecting of data, they fail to answer the key question–"So what?" Kluckhohn's essay, though sharply written, had little impact. For one, as he stated in his article, he was not an archaeologist, but a linguist, or worse, as he called himself, "a layman." Also, he was Jewish and most archaeologists were WASPs.

If Kluckhohn was the father of Taylor's "A Study of Archaeology," the granddaddy who started it all was Alfred Tozzer. Both Kluckhohn and Taylor had been students of Tozzer's at Harvard and worked for Tozzer as a researcher. In the 1930s Tozzer had made his own attempt to right the ship of modern Maya archaeology. "The inductive approach has usually been entirely absent in archaeological studies," Tozzer wrote. That was not the case when archaeology began, when it was built upon wild theories and dogmas. "The Lost Tribes of Israel, it is true, have disappeared from current literature, but the sunken continents of Atlantis and of Mu are still objects of concern to some writers," he wrote.

The pendulum toward avoiding theory had apparently swung too far. "Our knowledge of details is often very great. We know pieces of the whole historical picture, but our failure to know how these pieces are to be fitted together is in contrast to the wealth of facts," Tozzer wrote. Despite some fifty years of archaeology in the Maya area, no archaeologist had managed to construct anything that resembled a "social history." Tozzer included himself among that number, adding, "May I be forgiven by my colleagues for exposing our ignorance."

Where Tozzer differed from former pupils Kluckhohn and Taylor was the regard he had for another ex-student, Kidder, and the Carnegie's program of work in Middle America. Twice in the essay he singles out Kidder for his excellence, although he may have been being polite as Kidder's essay on the Carnegie finds followed his.

Taylor's book contained no such niceties, nor did it mince words. Tozzer was a member of the archaeology fraternity and even though privately he enjoyed gossip and poking fun at colleagues, his published work, even when critical, was restrained. Taylor was a product World War II. He feared nothing from a group of angry archaeologists; he'd recently come back from the European theater where he'd served in the Marines, seen combat, been shot at and was nearly blown to bits by a German grenade. Having a group of collegial archaeologists mad at you was nothing to someone who had been caught behind enemy lines and spent months in a prisoner of war camp.

What impact did Taylor's monograph have on Kidder or the Carnegie project? It is impossible to identify. But within weeks after Taylor's "A Study of Archaeology" was published, Kidder announced a new plan for the future of the Division of Historical Research, one that could have come from Taylor's playbook. Kidder claimed he and others had been working on it all along, i.e., BT – Before Taylor. "Something should be said in this report concerning plans for the future as they have taken shape during the two years since [1945]," he wrote. The completion of the first phase of work, which included the massive Chichén Itzá project, has "made it opportune to assess past efforts, restudy the aims and methods of research and consider most effective orientation for the Division's future effort in that field." Kidder then proposed doing exactly the opposite of what he had proposed two years earlier. "There seemed to be danger that, in attempting to go farther with a program covering so long a span of time and so large an area, the interests of individual workers might become so channeled and specialized that the manifest advantages of team work might be lost. For these reasons and also because of the greatly increased cost of field work, it appeared that there should be a quantitative reduction in objectives and a shift from a general study of the Maya past to an attack upon some specific phase thereof." Kidder took his cue from Tozzer's suggestion a decade earlier, that the Carnegie should focus on Northern Yucatán, where Chichén Itzá is located, and attempt to verify or disprove the various Maya chronicles, as Edward Thompson had done fifty years earlier by dredging the Cenote Sagrado to prove Diego de Landa's 1566 claim that the Maya had thrown in gold, jade, and human sacrifices.

It was too little, too late. Kidder retired in 1950 and most of his proposal was ignored, although the Carnegie trustees did agree to one final archaeological project, that being the excavation of Mayapan, the city that according to Maya legend had conquered Chichén Itzá. Kidder never responded publicly to Taylor's charges, nor did Taylor's books appear to reduce his immense professional stature in the archaeological community. In the years that followed his retirement, he admitted that the Division and its projects were fatally flawed. "One of the great errors was that we bit off a great deal more than we could chew," he wrote in 1953. The Carnegie should have limited itself to north Yucatán where Chichén Itzá was and possibly the Petén Basin "instead of going wandering off into the Guatemalan highlands." The researchers who worked with the Carnegie did not help. They became specialists of a certain time period and therefore insisted on conducting their research horizontally all over Mesoamerica to pursue their interest instead of focusing on one region. "Naturally that was a great mistake," Kidder wrote.

All of these problems were compounded by events outside the Division of Historical Research's control, he wrote. "The depression came, the war came, the administration changed to one which was not interested in these problems..."

After the Mayapan project the Carnegie discontinued its archaeological program. Even by today's standards, the Carnegie's Chichén Itzá project, failure or not, remains one of the largest projects of its type ever attempted in the Americas. And when combined with the Carnegie's other work in Mexico and Central America

The Carnegie filled several bookshelves with its sixty volumes of research and hundreds of smaller reports. After Kidder's retirement, the Division of Historical Research became the Division of Archaeology, and it limped on until closing for good in 1958. The last report, of the Institution's final excavation in Mayapan, was published in 1962.

The Peabody Museum never had the resources to match the Carnegie Institution's archaeology program, but what it did have were the Cenote Sagrado artifacts free and clear. While the Mexican Supreme Court found that the relics had been illegally exported, they had not been stolen.

Alfred Tozzer studied the artifacts for almost a quarter century. The collection filled more than two large rooms and consisted of some 30,000 objects. The official requests to return the collection stopped after the Supreme Court decision, but every few years someone from Mexico would make a stink, although it resulted in no action from the Peabody. Tozzer and a small team pressed ahead with their plans to publish their analysis of the collection.

The Peabody published the first volume, *Metals from the Cenote of Sacrifice* by Samuel K. Lothrop, in 1952. Tozzer died in 1955, but the Peabody two years later published posthumously his massive volume covering all aspects of the collection, *Chichén Itzá and Its Cenote of Sacrifice*. This was followed fifteen years later with Tatiana Proskourikoff's *Jades from the Cenote of Sacrifice*, and in 1992 the final volume, *Artifacts from the Cenote of Sacrifice* by Clemency Coggins, reached publication.

The Peabody Museum respected Tozzer's pledge regarding return of the Cenote Sagrado artifacts to Mexico, at least in part. In 1960, three years after Tozzer's study was published, the Peabody returned ninety-four of the gold and copper artifacts from the Cenote Sagrado to Mexico (reportedly due in part to pressure from presidential candidate and Harvard alum John F. Kennedy) in exchange for artifacts in kind. Then, four years after the study on jades was published, the Peabody exchanged 240 of the carved jades with Mexico for more artifacts.

Still, the bulk of the collection remains buried in the vaults of the Peabody Museum, sticking like a bone in the craw of Mexican archaeologists even today. In 2008 Peabody Museum Director William Fash was ambushed during a trip to Mexico to honor one of his colleagues. According to the Mexican press, Fash had said he believed the time had come to return the artifacts. However, when asked about it a few weeks later, he said, "They heard what they wanted to hear. We're not in the position to do anything right now. Museums are not in the business of giving things back."

Fash must have suspected he would get questions about the collection for he hired a Harvard history student to research the records behind the Cenote Sagrado collection several months before his trip to Mexico. The student, Spencer D. Burke, later published an article in a student publication, the *Harvard Advocate*, on his research in which he blasted the Peabody for holding onto artifacts. "Though Harvard is under no obligation to repatriate the Peabody's Sacred Cenote collection…the records are clear: by removing the artifacts from Mexico, Thompson violated Mexican law and did so knowingly," Burke wrote. "The Peabody's reputation continues to be stained by its possession of these artifacts." Neither Fash nor the Peabody commented on Burke's story.

Mexico, on the other hand, comments on the Peabody collection every day at Chichén Itzá. If anyone wants to know what Mexico thinks, they only have to find Thompson's dredge. The answer is written on the bathroom wall.

One of the handful of artifacts from Chichén Itzá on display at Harvard's Peabody Museum

THE PRESENT

THE ARTIFACTS TODAY

AFTER SPENDING MONTHS on this project, the time has come to view the Cenote Sagrado collection at Harvard's Peabody Museum. I've seen hundreds of photographs and drawings of the artifacts, so many I can conjure some of the pieces in my head at will. I've been within a few feet of the collection, having visited the Peabody Museum and the Tozzer Library next door to go through their voluminous archives of letters, records, and books related to Chichén Itzá. I can't quite articulate why I haven't gone to see the collection before this. Perhaps I was afraid they wouldn't let me, but that notion is silly. My every interaction with the Peabody Museum has been one of openness and encouragement. Well, not with the scientists and professors, who have stonewalled or ignored my repeated requests for interviews and comment. For them I have had to resort to my old reporter's tricks, such as ambushing them at public functions where they could not run away. But the staff who oversee the collections have been nothing but helpful.

I reach out to my contact in the Peabody archives, Patricia Kervick, who forwards my request to Susan Haskell, the curatorial associate who oversees the Cenote Sagrado collection. I'm not even sure what remains in the Peabody, since much of the gold and carved jade was traded with Mexico in the 1960s and 1970s. The reply I receive from Haskell is encouraging. "We do indeed have many of the artifacts that came from the Cenote. In fact, there are over two thousand, seven hundred of them. I would be happy to spend an hour or two showing you some highlights of the collection," she writes. We make it a date.

Coincidentally, an old friend of mine, Ward Serrill, will be in Cambridge. He's a filmmaker in Seattle, but will be at Harvard to meet with a professor who will be the subject of a series of documentary shorts. We make plans to meet for a meal.

The Peabody Museum of Archaeology and Ethnology is in a large, u-shaped brick building at the edge of Harvard's campus. It takes up a wing, while the remainder is devoted to the university's natural history museum. I've been here many times since this project began, but this will be my first look behind the curtain at the massive collection of artifacts. After checking in at the front desk, Haskell comes out and introduces herself. She's a little older than me. I loom over her, but that's not unusual. She has a warm smile and, I discover, an infectious giggle that I can't tell if it originates from nervousness or amusement. We chat as she takes me up a flight of stairs and through a door that requires a code punched into a keypad. There are demonstrations of security everywhere.

She guides me to a room with several cabinets of large drawers. "This all came out of the cenote?" I ask. I had sent her a list of the artifacts I wanted to see and the first one she shows me is what Thompson described as the first gold found in the cenote. The "kneeling figure scepter" as it is called depicts a crouched figure with a headdress and the face is covered in what appears to be a gold foil. The photographs I have seen of this artifact do not do it justice. It is exquisitely carved at the end, about eight inches long. "Wow," I say, and repeat that word incessantly.

She shows me another staff, called a "diving figure scepter," which has pieces of jadeite inlaid in face that was carved at the end. Then she opens a drawer that contains the "sacrificial knife" that had been found in two different loads of the dredge, one-half of which had been recovered by Sylvanus Morley. It's huge, a foot long, clearly heavy and sturdy enough to cut through a human breast, hence its name. The handle has been carved to resemble two rattlesnakes intertwined, the blade projecting from the mouth of one. It's spectacular. "Wow," I say again. "Wow."

Haskell opens more drawers, many with gold artifacts (actually copper with gold leaf) and dozens of beautifully carved jades. She opens one drawer after another and there are surprises in every one. She pauses, looks at me. "It's a little overwhelming, isn't it?" I had to agree.

"There were rumors that Thompson sent all this by diplomatic pouch," I say. "This did not come by diplomatic pouch. It would have had to have been the biggest diplomatic pouch in the world."

I ask to see the incense and she explains it is stored in another room. After we lock up, Haskell leads me through labyrinthine hallways, to stairwells and elevators, through the bowels of the museum. As we walk, I ask her if she remembers when the Thompson family visited. Not only did she recall it, but she also showed other Thompson descendants. "There are two families," she says.

"The Maya family?" I ask incredulously.

"Yes, they came to see the collection," she says. "Representatives of them, yes."

She couldn't provide any more details than that other than she remembered they had been "blown away" by the collection. I knew there was no way that Carlos Marrufo's descendants had come to Harvard from Mexico, so who could it have been? Unfortunately, before I can ask, she takes me into a room with enough Maya incense to smoke up a football stadium. There are balls of copal, or *pom* as the Maya call it, filling shelf after shelf. Many are in ceramic bowls with three stubby legs. Some balls are impregnated with pieces of jadeite or other decoration. I marvel at what Thompson had recovered from the Cenote Sagrado. There was no way that any of this material was sewn into a vest to be brought to the United States. The Maya family is long forgotten and I would come to regret not following up.

I haven't even seen the ceramics dredged from the cenote. Haskell tells me they are in yet another room temporarily that is not open to non-employees. I promise to come back one day to see them. She leads me back out to the main entrance and after I thank I her profusely, I head out in search of my friend Ward.

I find him heading toward me about a block away from the museum. Even though it has been four years since we last saw each other, we pick up our relationship right where we left off.

We've been friends for more than a quarter century. We had met while living in Ketchikan, Alaska. I was fresh out of college, newly married, and was working as an advertising/marketing/public relations consultant; he had abandoned corporate life in downtown Seattle to become a controller for the Cape Fox Corporation, one of the several companies in the state owned by American Indian tribes. These corporations had been created as part of the Alaska Native Claims Settlement Act.

We became friends because of our shared interests: Bob Dylan, American Indian culture, and the arts. He had hired me for a few projects, including helping him promote a new subsidiary, Cape Fox Tours. The corporation created the Saxman Native Village, a location where the elders of the village could sew their traditional blankets and teach the younger generations the dances of the tribe. The corporation was funded by tourists who paid premium dollars to receive an authentic native experience. These days they call it "sustainable tourism," but back then Ward was a pioneer.

More importantly he created jobs for the tribe and gave everyone, young and old, pride in their heritage. Members of the tribe appreciated his work so much, that one of the elders, Martha Shields, had him inducted into her clan.

I had grown up in Oregon next to the Warm Springs Indian Reservation and had seen how tourism had helped there after the confederated tribes built a resort, Kah Nee Tah. This was before casinos, although those eventually found their way to the reservation, too. My father had been district attorney for a sparsely populated county in the desert of Eastern Oregon. My mother was never really a housewife. She worked pretty much the entire time I was growing up, although when I was young, it was only part-time. Even then she volunteered a lot.

My parents weren't color-blind, but they got along with members of the tribes. Recently one of my sister's childhood friends, Elizabeth Woody, wrote about how my mother had encouraged her when she was young. Mom had sponsored Lizzie, as we called her, for membership in Theta Rho, the girls auxiliary of the Oddfellows. Lizzie got blackballed and mom was certain it was because she was an Indian. According to Lizzie, mom went nuts. Even though we lived in a small town, my mother was not someone you wanted to cross when she had a head of steam, so I'm certain she let those who had done the blackballing know what she thought. "She told me I was going to be somebody," Lizzie wrote recently. "That is what mattered the most. She said I was going to be a major mind in this country on the history and status of the American Indians, even if I didn't know it at the time." Lizzie went on to become an award-winning poet, short story writer, and essayist. A true artist. Mom would have been proud.

My dad was the most principled man I know. Early in his law career, he opened a small office in our hometown. He had few clients, so he had to hire mom to be his secretary. Every so often, this fellow, an Indian, would stagger out of the only bar in town that served folks from the reservation, walk a couple of blocks to dad's office, and collapse on the bench in the waiting area. My mother was horrified, but dad wouldn't do anything. When she told me this story years later, it was one of the few times I ever saw dad get cross with her. "Max," he said sharply—her name was Maxine—"he saved a man's life!" For my dad, that explained it all.

I would tell Ward these stories when we lived in Alaska. I would tell him how in college I would spend days in the library researching Native American folk tales. He started calling me "Coyote," after the American Indian trickster god, and pretty soon all our mutual friends were doing the same.

Hanging out with Ward was usually an adventure and I almost always learned something. During one visit to his offices, he wanted to show me the shed his tourism company had built for totem pole carvers. We jumped into his pickup and he took me to a long building with plastic sheeting for windows. Inside was the preeminent carver in Alaska, Nathan Jackson, working a pole with a couple of assistants. I knew Nathan a little socially, but had never seen him carve. This was going to be the first pole raised in Saxman in more than fifty years. Nathan's a funny guy with a dry wit, but on this day he was all business, and from my perspective he was giving his assistants hell. Later on the drive back I asked Ward about that. "It's part of the culture," he tells me. "He never says "good job" or praises them. That's not why you become a carver. You do it because it's what you do." If positive feedback is what you crave, a carver probably is not the job for you.

That visit to the carver shed was a lifetime ago, but when we meet on the Harvard campus, it is like no time has passed. Our original plan had been to go get something to eat, but as long as he was in the neighborhood, Ward said he wants to see the Peabody Museum. Back in we go.

We start in the Latin American room and I point out the two pieces on display from the Cenote Sagrado—an ear ornament, a carved jade, a couple of other objects. I tell him briefly about my visit to the vaults to see the rest of the collection and I bring him up to speed on the progress of my research into Edward Thompson and the family I found in Mexico. He's interested, but he's also interested in the exhibits. Ward is a dawdler, while I like to zip ahead, which is how I find myself ahead of him. We're in the Hall of the North American Indian, a part of the museum I've never explored. I turn a dark corner and stop. I can't believe what is on the display. I read the placard and sure enough, I'm seeing what I think I'm seeing. I rush back and grab Ward. He turns the same corner and knows right away what it is: a Nathan Jackson totem pole.

According to a placard this new pole replaced a much older one that had been recovered by the Harriman expedition in 1899. A video plays from a screen next to the pole, describing how members of the Cape Fox tribe, descendants of the village from which the pole had been taken, demanded its return under the Native American Graves Protection and Repatriation Act (NAGPRA). The law, passed in 1990, required that museums around the nation to return certain artifacts—"human remains, funerary objects, sacred objects, or objects of cultural patrimony"—to families and tribes. In 2001 the Peabody returned the Cape Fox village pole and in exchange, the Cape Fox Corporation gave the Peabody a large cedar tree. The Peabody commissioned Nathan to carve a new pole.

I wondered what Ward must be feeling, what with the sudden juxtaposition of his past life in Alaska suddenly thrust into the present some 3,000 miles away. It had to be unsettling. In the video, representing the Cape Fox tribe was Irene Shields, the granddaughter of Martha Shields, who had adopted Ward. The totem in front of us had been carved in the shed that Ward had built for the tribe. I looked at him, but I couldn't read his face.

I knew what my reaction to the totem was. "I'll be damned," I say. "The Peabody Museum *does* give back artifacts."

THE PAST

BALANKANCHE

THE LAST GREAT DISCOVERY AT CHICHÉN ITZÁ was not made by an archaeologist. It was made by a guide.

José Humberto Gómez Rodríguez had been leading tourists around Chichén Itzá for only a few years when in 1959 he discovered the hidden cave at Balankanche. While there have been numerous other discoveries at Chichén, Gómez Rodríguez's find was truly groundbreaking, the biggest since Edward Thompson dredged the Cenote Sagrado.

Gómez Rodríguez's grandmother was related to the Barbachanos, so she spent the busy season of June and July working at the Mayaland hotel. From the age of eight Humberto would stay with her and spent his summers growing up among the ruins of Chichén Itzá. Knowing how much he liked to explore, old Bernardino Tun, the head gardener of the Mayaland, told Gómez Rodríguez of a cave not far away and gave him directions.

The entrance to the cave, though overgrown, was not difficult to find, some 300 meters off the road to the village of X'Kalakoop. At the mouth was a small group of ruins. In ancient times steps had been chiseled into the rock descending into the earth. "Maybe because I was very young and very small, the cave looked very, very big to me," he recalled in an interview more than a half century later.

At first he could only proceed a few meters into the cave before it became so inky black. No matter how hard he would try, he could not get his eyes to adjust. That Christmas he collected the little candles left over from the posadas. When he returned to the cave he explored its labyrinthine passageways, leapfrogging one candle distance at a time. "I could look back, see the candle, light another one…I started going into the cave farther and farther and farther in, little by little." Later he obtained a flashlight and was free to roam its passages for as long as the batteries would last.

Gómez Rodríguez had not been not the first to explore the cave. It was well known, at least to those who had spent time at Chichén Itzá. Edward Thompson had learned of it from the Maya who had helped him dredge the Cenote Sagrado. On Easter morning 1905, he explored it with the archaeologist Alfred Tozzer, who described it in a letter to his family in New England.

When the Carnegie Institution arrived at Chichén Itzá in the mid 1920s, there began several investigations of the cave and the exterior ruins, which had a name: *Balam Canche*, Maya for "jaguar throne." Researchers combed the floor for broken pottery and dug test pits. Others collected flora and fauna, or tested the groundwater that flooded the deepest parts of the cave. One was a teenager with a ten-dollar name: E. Wyllys Andrews IV. "Bill," the son of one of Chicago's leading surgeons, had grown up with the freedom and resources to pursue whatever intellectual interests caught his fancy. He was a regular visitor to the Field Museum in Chicago and through his parents knew some of the up-and-coming Maya archaeologists of the day, most notably J. Eric S. Thompson. It was only natural that he discovered a passion for Maya archaeology and anthropology.

Andrews arrived at Chichén Itzá a few days after his seventeenth birthday in December 1933 to spend six months as Sylvanus Morley's assistant at the Carnegie Institution's headquarters and to collect reptiles for the Field Museum. While exploring Balam Canche (today called "Balankanche"), Andrews saw what he thought was a white snake. He spent hours in the cave trying to capture a specimen for his collection, but never saw it again (later explorations found a blind eel, which easily could have been mistaken for a snake). He also encountered more dangerous creatures, such as a large centipede the Maya called *u dzudz milan* ("the kiss of hell") that, when cornered, scuttles forward or backward with a biting attack that injects a clear poison reportedly fatal to humans. The cave became most famous, at least in scientific circles, when in 1936 a scientist discovered a species of hooded tickspider (*cryptocellus pearsei*), a thick-legged arachnid previously unknown to North America except as fossils.

The renown of these archaeological and biological discoveries was minimal by the 1940s when Gómez Rodríguez began to explore it. He wandered its passages, his footsteps at times crunched in the dark as he stepped on the broken pottery left behind by prehistoric generations. The floor throughout the cave alternated between sahcab, a calcareous light-colored earth, and a dark clay that, once brought into the sunlight, turned out to be red.

Archaeologists from the Carnegie Institution returned one last time to determine when the cave had been occupied. They dug a test pit and recovered pottery from many different eras. In the end they determined that the cave had seen human habitation over a period of 3,000 years, right up through the Spanish Conquest.

Gómez Rodríguez knew none of this. He went to school to study anthropology, but the prospect of spending several years in a classroom held no appeal and he dropped out. Instead he became a licensed tour guide and went to work for the Barbachanos. In those days guides were more than founts of history, archaeology, flora and fauna about Yucatán. Typically a guide would pick a group up at their hotel and spend the entire day with them, driving them to ruins or churches or villages, making certain they got lunch and sometimes dinner, and attending to their every need, all with the hope of getting a big tip at the end of their visit. Gómez Rodríguez had an outgoing personality with a broad smile, which made him a natural when it came to being a guide.

Because he worked for the Barbachanos, Gómez Rodríguez returned time and again to Chichén Itzá and to the cave, where he spent much of his spare time. In early September 1959 Gómez Rodríguez had been guiding a couple from Ft. Lauderdale, Fla. "On the third day they said they were tired, that they didn't want to do any more climbing [of ruins]," Humberto recalled. "I said, 'Why don't we do something different. Let's go under the ground.'" So he took them to Balankanche. He gave them a flashlight and left them to explore while he went off on his own.

"I took one of the passageways that I was very familiar with and I went right to the end," he said. "I had been there I don't know how many hundreds of times." On this visit he noticed a wall that looked "a little funny," and in the glow of his flashlight it appeared to be of a different color. Humberto produced a large knife that he always carried and began scraping at the wall. "A section of it came off, like a big piece of stucco." Behind it was the same kind of man-made masonry one could find in any of the Maya ruins. Gómez Rodríguez was certain he had found a secret wall.

"Being twenty-three years of age at that time, the world was so small for me," he said. "There is no fear, there is nothing. Curiosity, yes, a lot. I wanted to see what was behind the wall. So I kept removing the stones, material, stones, material, and I opened up a hole that was big enough for me to crawl through."

Gómez Rodríguez managed to wriggle his thin frame through the opening and up an incline into a new chamber. He played the light of his flashlight along the walls, but it only could penetrate the gloom a meter or so ahead. "It was like having a blanket in front of me," he said. He went down several passages that appeared to be dead ends, but found one the appeared to go for quite a distance. He came to another small incline and could make out a large structure ahead of him. "I happened to find myself in front of an enormous stalactite and stalagmite," he said, fused together to make a giant column. "I started going around it very carefully." It turned out to be two stalactites and when he played his light between them he found a large vase in the shape of an hourglass. Half was painted red, half was painted blue. "And there was the Maya rain god staring at me and I was staring at the rain god, face to face."

Gómez Rodríguez began to back away and as he did, he shined his flashlight on the ground. He discovered to his horror that he had somehow stepped into an archaeological minefield. Surrounding his feet, in every direction, were dozens, if not hundreds of Maya artifacts: Incense urns of every shape and size, many with faces carved into the sides, as well as a wide assortment of metates, the grinding stones the Maya used to prepare maize. If his path had veered by only a foot or two, he would have knocked something over or stepped on a vase.

Once he had backed away, the stalactite/stalagmites did not look so much like a column as a tree. The roof of the cave was deeply pitted and gave the appearance of leaves. It was as if the ceiba, the sacred tree of the Maya, had been transported here into the underworld. Gómez Rodríguez knew that he had stumbled upon a very sacred place, one that had been kept secret for centuries. He did not have much time to think about it, because his flashlight was giving out. He retraced his steps, but had several moments of panic when he could not find the hole through which he had come. "Stupid of me, when I was crawling through the hole I didn't realize that I had been crawling up." The hole he had been looking for was low and hidden by an incline. His hand torch faded to a dull yellow, but before it was extinguished for good Humberto found the chamber exit. He squirmed back through the hole and raced to the entrance of the cave. On the way he ran into the couple he had abandoned. "They looked at me and they said, 'Where have you been?'" Gómez Rodríguez looked at himself in the light and saw his clothes were covered in clay.

"It was very, very difficult for me not to tell them. I wanted to tell somebody about what I had seen, but I was afraid that if I told them they would want to see and they would want to touch the things or move something or take something," Gómez Rodríguez said. He knew enough archaeology to know that you don't touch anything, "because the position of everything, the number of everything, the orientation of everything has a meaning."

So Gómez Rodríguez told them nothing, just returned his charges to the Mayaland hotel. "The moment I left them...I went to Pisté (the closest town to Chichén Itzá). I got a rope, extra batteries, another flashlight, and I went back in." He squeezed back through the hole and explored the rest of the cave. "I was able to find seven chambers, all of them with offerings," he said. "All of them." He lost track of time and when he emerged from the cave it was around 3 o'clock in the morning.

Sometime after sunrise Gómez Rodríguez picked up his guests at the Mayaland and returned to Mérida. He had another tour scheduled, this time to Uxmal. Before he left, went to talk to his boss and cousin, Fernando Barbachano Gomez Rul. Gómez Rodríguez told his cousin what he had seen. At first Barbachano was skeptical, knowing the cave had been explored many times before, but became convinced he was telling the truth. He instructed Gómez Rodríguez to take the guests to

Uxmal, leave them there and then drive to Chichén Itzá where Barbachano would meet him the next day. When Barbachano arrived he was not alone. Accompanying him was Yucatán Governor Agustin Franco Avilar, prominent physician Dr. Raul Cardenas, and Bill Andrews, who happened to be in Merida to conduct an archaeological investigation of the ancient Maya city of Dzibulchaltun.

It had been more than a decade since Andrews had been to Balankanche. He was dismayed to find that the ruins at the entrance to the cave were now all but gone, ground into gravel by the road crew that built the state highway a few years earlier.

The party spent hours in the cave. "After an entire night's exploration, it was clear we had one of the most striking archaeological finds of recent time," Andrews later wrote. The governor, upon emerging from the cave, went to the Mayaland and telephoned the army post at Valladolid. That night a detachment of soldiers showed up to guard the cave. A few days later, archaeological work began.

Fortunately there was an experienced team nearby. Andrews'

Balankanche (Bill Drennon photo)

Dzibulchaltun project was not scheduled to begin work for five weeks. "We applied for an emergency grant of $2,500 from the National Geographic and got it," recalled George E. Stuart, who worked for Andrews. Barbachano turned over the Hacienda Chichén to the investigators, fed them at the Mayaland resort, and provided additional labor and materials needed, including generators and electric lighting.

Andrews also requested the assistance of William J. Folan, the same archaeologist who later worked on the diving projects of 1961 and 1968 at the Cenote Sagrado. Folan was attending university in Mexico City when he got a telegram from Andrews asking him to join the Balankanche expedition, a project that kicked off a lifetime's work in the Yucatan Peninsula. Roman Piña Chan, the director of Monumentos Prehispánicos for INAH in Mexico City, flew in to take charge of the project.

Over the course of several days, the team carefully removed the artifacts, then took them to the Hacienda Chichén where they were recorded and photographed. The urns were especially fragile. How fragile? One night Andrews left a local man in his late teens/early twenties to guard the cave (the army had long since retired). There was a miscommunication about what exactly the young man was to protect and as a result someone got into the main chamber and, while examining the artifacts, broke several of them.

As Andrews's team removed the artifacts, there were discussions by Mexican archaeologists and officials about what to do with them. Would this project be like all the others in Yucatecan archaeology, where artifacts would be shipped to Mexico City for study never to return, just like Le Plongeon's chac-mool in the 1870s, the Upper Temple of the Jaguars atlantes in the 1900s, all the artifacts from Chichén Itzá during the Carnegie expeditions in the 1920s and 1930s, and as would occur with the hundreds of artifacts removed from the Cenote Sagrado in the 1960s? Not this time. Román Piña Chan, who was a subdirector for INAH, came up with a brilliant idea—turn Balankanche into an underground museum.

The artifacts would be left as they were in situ and the cave opened to the public once archaeology was completed. It would be the world's largest underground museum. For years to come, visitors would be able to discover the treasures of Balankanche again and again, just as Gómez Rodríguez had after crawling through the hole.

At least, that was the plan. But then the Maya showed up.

It began when one of the Maya workers mentioned to archaeologist Folan that a Maya shaman, called a *h-men*, from the nearby village of X'Kalakoop wanted to see the cave. Folan drove over and brought the h-men, Romualdo Ho'il, to Balankanche to meet with Andrews.

According to Barbachano, Maya in the region had known for generations that hidden somewhere was the home of the rain god. Once the residents of X'Kalakoop learned that the hidden cavern had been discovered, they knew what it was and were afraid that it was now defiled and would bring disaster down upon the Maya, such as drought or too much rain or damaging hail.

Ho'il explained in his native tongue that he and his men needed to perform rituals in the cave now that it has been opened "to protect those who have violated these sacred precincts," referring to all who had been in cave since its discovery. "It is necessary to do something so that nothing bad will happen to them. The *Yum Balames* who are in the cave are displeased and they must be pacified." One of the reasons, according to one member of the team, was that a woman had been allowed in the cave.

The Maya wanted to perform a ritual called *tsikul t'an ti' yuntsiloob* ("Reverent Message to the Lords") "to pray that there will be no danger for those who have penetrated these sacred places without permission of the gods," Ho'il said.

For Barbachano Gomez Rul, the arrival of the Maya changed his life. "One old man got close to me and said, 'Little Fernando, you may not recall me, but I was one of your teachers at Chichén.'" Barbachano was perplexed, because he did not remember any Maya teachers as a child growing up at the Mayaland. He only remembered a Yucatecan woman that his mother had hired to tutor him, but no men. The Maya continued. "I'm going to ask you something because I've never asked you for anything. I want you to give us permission to enter the cave of Balankanche and perform a ritual."

"I have no power to do that," Barbachano Gomez Rul replied.

"Yes you do. You can talk to the governor and the governor can give permission, so you can do it. So I will be back tomorrow at the same hour and I want an answer."

And in a rush, the memories all came back to him, the hours he had spent in the presence of the Maya workers at Chichén Itzá. Barbachano understood then he had been "indoctrinated into the Maya culture and the Maya religion by priests who worked as gardeners at the Hotel Mayaland." As he relates the story, now some fifty years later, his eyes moisten, his voice shakes. "At that time the whole memory came to my mind. At that moment I knew I had a mission. It was a very shocking moment and it is every time I recall the incident because I am living it at this moment. It brings very strong emotions."

The Maya received permission to perform their ceremony, but there was a catch—the ritual had to be recorded. At first Ho'il balked, according to Fernando, telling officials, "We are not movie stars, we are not playing a game; this is our religion."

Eventually the h'men relented and announced that he would return on Oct. 17 to perform the ceremony, which would require more than 24 hours in the cave. He calculated he needed 532 pesos for food and other supplies required by the ritual, including one large tom turkey, thirteen chickens, thirteen black candles, as well as incense, corn, leaf tobacco, honey, spices and two bottles of aguardiente or liquor. Rather than risk further provoking the yum balames or the local Maya, Andrews gave Ho'il 250 pesos and promised the rest once the ritual was completed.

At daybreak on the appointed day, Ho'il and his attendants began the day preparing *sac ha'*, a traditional drink made of maize. They also brewed up a batch of *balché*, a sweet, honey-based mead that is flavored with the bark of the tree for which the concoction is named. As there wasn't time to allow the drinks to ferment, they were spiked with the aguardiente.

To the archaeologists who had been working inside Balankanche, the idea of spending twenty-four hours inside the cave to perform a ceremony was somewhat disconcerting. Conditions in the cave were nearly unbearable. Not only was it hot, but the humidity ranged close to 100 percent. "Thick cardboard boxes brought in during the morning would be useless by afternoon for taking out specimens," Andrews wrote. "Even with [fewer] than fifteen men in the large inner chambers, the oxygen became exhausted in an eight-hour day, leaving the workers panting after a minimum of exertion, as if they were on a tall mountain peak."

To conduct the ceremony there would be more than double the number of people inside the cave at one time, and there would need to be burning of candles and possibly incense, all of which would consume available oxygen. But on the appointed morning at eight o'clock the archaeologists joined Ho'il and thirteen assistants (including several boys) to spend more than a full day underground. Andrews and two members of his Dzibulchaltun team, Folan and George Stuart, joined Mexican investigators Dr. Barrera Vásquez, Raúl Pavón Abreu, and Victor Segovia Pinto to witness the ceremony. Segovia (with Stuart's assistance) operated a tape recorder during the ceremony. Missing from the group was Fernando, who failed to arrive in time from Merida.

Over the course of twenty-nine hours, h'men Ho'il officiated over twenty-seven rituals which included sacrificing several chickens and one turkey, consuming sacred foods made of maize and honey, and drinking a lot of balché. A few hours into the ceremonies, Barbachano showed up and, by special dispensation of Ho'il, he joined the ceremony. Several hours later, Ho'il, possibly overcome by all the balché he had to drink, digressed from the ritual to eulogize Barbachano "as a protector of the community," even though he was very much alive and present in the cave.

The rituals continued until 2:30 in the morning, at which time Ho'il declared that that they had done all they could to placate the angry gods. All the food, drink, and accouterments required for the ceremony were packed away, save for thirteen candles that were left lighted on a makeshift altar in the main cavern. The h'menes ordered the cave sealed and instructed everyone to return two days hence.

The night before everyone was to return to Balankanche, the rain gods made themselves heard, unleashing torrential rains on Yucatan. On Oct. 20 at 7:45 in the morning, everyone assembled at the mouth of the cave. Ho'il recited a brief prayer and then led everyone into the bowels of Balankanche. At the altar they found four candles still burning. As thirteen is a sacred number to the Maya, so too, is four, and Ho'il declared this positive omen. But even more wondrous was the candles had remained lit even though the throne room was "raining." Water, percolating through earth, sprinkled from the hundreds of mini-stalactites that pitted the ceiling of the cave over the makeshift altar. The sacred cave, formerly defiled, now had been spiritually cleansed.

THE PRESENT

A DIOS DON FERNANDO

FERNANDO BARBACHANO GOMEZ RUL celebrates his eightieth birthday. He does not live to see eighty-one.

The last e-mail message I receive from him is to set a time for us to speak by telephone. When I call, Maruja answers and tells me Fernando is in the hospital. She is understandably agitated, slipping between Spanish and English, and I really can't understand what's wrong. Members of the family tell me later it was nothing serious, but within two weeks Fernando is dead.

Doña Maruja, in her grief, arranges for a funeral Mass for Fernando, which had he been alive probably would have amused him. Fernando always made a point of saying he was Maya, so his daughter Belisa arranges for Maya *h'menes* from Mérida to come to the Hacienda Chichén to perform a ritual for him. Even doña Maruja participates.

Fernando's ashes are divided; some are buried in Mérida. Others are scattered over the fire pit where the Maya funeral ritual was conducted. One of Fernando's granddaughters carries some of his ashes to the top of Las Monjas and lets the wind carry them over Chichén Itzá. And some are spread into the waters next to the hotel Fernando built in Cozumel, his favorite place on the planet. Fernando may have considered himself a Maya, but disposition of his ashes, appropriately enough, were in earth, air, fire, and water, the four elements of ancient Greece and European civilization from which his people sprang.

That was December. It's a new year and in February I'm back in Mérida, another research trip. I visit the Casa Camara to pay my respects to doña Maruja. When I arrive, I am introduced to three more generations of Marujas: in addition to the matriarch, I meet her daughter, granddaughter, and a baby great-granddaughter, all carrying the same name.

Maruja the daughter directs me to the billiard room where I had spent so many hours with Fernando. I have not met her before today and I imagine she doesn't know what to make of me. "Are you an archaeologist or a historian?" She asks.

"I'm just a writer," I say.

We make small talk while I wait for doña Maruja. I hear the stairway tractor in the background, so I know she is on her way down. I look in the doorway and there she is, standing! I have only seen her in a wheelchair. She accepts my hand and a kiss. With a cane, she makes her way to the leather sofa and I sit next to her in one of the chairs. She offers me water or tequila and I accept the latter. A servant brings in a tray with both.

Doña Maruja explains that she can no longer drink tequila, but she understands that the bottle sitting before us is of a private vintage and supposedly very good. I pour tequila for me, water for her, and we toast Fernando's memory. The tequila is delicious. Maruja tells me the story of Fernando's death. He had enjoyed a nice lunch of vegetable soup and was taking a siesta. Maruja was reading him the news when he gave a little cough. She knew immediately something was wrong and went to him. "He died in my arms," she says. Hans did not believe it, she tells me. "He kept shaking him, saying, 'Fernando! Wake up!'" But Fernando is gone.

"He never thought he was going to die," Maruja tells me wistfully. "Now

I must get used to my new life." Many decisions must be made. What will they do with the Casa Camara and, more importantly, the servants, many of whom have been with the family for years?

And, she confides, her children are with her all the time, which is a burden. I tell her of Fernando's distant cousin in the United States, Ben Muse, who once told me that since losing his wife one of the main reasons he visits Yucatán is to get a break from his children.

I ask about Hans. "Hans left two days ago," she says. In those final weeks, Hans's patience had become exhausted with Fernando's stubborn insistence on ignoring his doctors' advice, Maruja tells me. There was one incident where Fernando begged for water even though his doctors had warned him that consuming too much could kill him. That prompted Hans to pack up and move out, she says. Fernando wanted to call him to beg him to come back. "I told him, 'Fernando, you have to pretend you don't care.'" Sure enough, Hans returned in a couple of days acting as if nothing had ever happened.

This time, however, Maruja is certain Hans is gone for good. With her daughter (and Hans's ex-wife) Maruja around all the time, the household had become tense. Don Fernando loved Hans like a son, she says. That connection to the family is now gone.

But family can be far more than blood, including among the Barbachanos. When patriarch Fernando Barbachano Peón died in 1964, members of the family argued about what to do with the manager of the hotel at the ancient Maya city of Uxmal, who reportedly had been Barbachano Peón's mistress. At least one family member wanted to kick her out of Yucatán. But as the story goes, his wife, doña Carmen, would hear none of it. Whatever relationship the woman had with her husband, she would not tolerate any action taken against her. The woman, an American, later retired to Florida, and when she became seriously ill, doña Carmen flew to be by her side.

She wasn't family, but she was. It is not outside the realm of possibility that Hans will once more return to the fold.

Doña Maruja and I say our goodbyes and I promise to return, but I suspect this will be the last time I will visit the famous mansion on Paseo de Montejo.

I head for Chichén Itzá. When I get to Pisté, it is late afternoon and I'm bushed. It has been a draining day. I check into the Hacienda Chichén and fall into bed for what I think will be a quick siesta. I'm awakened by pounding on my door. My room is dark, which means my catnap has extended well after sunset. I open the door to one of the hacienda staff, who tells me in rapid-fire Spanish something I don't understand, but I make out one word: "*recepción*." I walk to the main casa where the reception area can be found and on the way I run into Jaime, Bibiano's son, dressed in his musician's uniform, which tells me dinner service at the hacienda has begun because he will be performing. We exchange hugs. "You look very tired," he tells me.

Inside reception I run into Bibiano playing around on his guitar. I give him a big hug and he is equally happy to see me. I'm relieved the money incident appears to be long forgotten. He invites me to his house after work and I promise to come after ten.

I shower and change, grab a late dinner in the dining room, then drive over to Bibiano's. As I pull up he's sitting on the porch and he's not alone. Next to him is on of the American Thompson's, Alex. I wasn't even aware she was in Yucatán. Although we've exchanged the occasional e-mail, I haven't seen her since we went our separate ways after visiting don Fernando in Mérida. As we hug, Victoria emerges from the house, which means more hugs. Then Liz Sawyer joins us.

Of all the U.S. Thompsons, for Lizzie the "reunion" with the Marrufos changed her life. When she got back home after the adventure last year, she immediately began to make plans to return, only this time for much longer. She originally had intended to enter university in the fall, but instead she raised money from family and friends and now was in the midst of spending six months in Pisté, living with her newfound relatives, and teaching English at a local school.

Even though I'm exhausted, I'm happy, almost ecstatic. Seeing these two branches of Edward Thompson's family together, swapping stories and sharing their lives, is exhilarating. Here in the shadow of Chichén Itzá these people from different backgrounds but similar heritage have found each other.

Above, Victoria and Bibiano.
Below, the Marrufo family on a typical Sunday afternoon.
(Pereira photos)

THE PAST

CHICHÉN FOR SALE

FOR DECADES Chichén Itzá has been controlled by no fewer that four different groups who every day engage in a delicate dance for mastery of the site. There are the Barbachanos, the tourism pioneers; there is the *Instituto Nacional de Arqueologica y Historia*, better known as INAH, the federal agency charged with the archaeology and management of the ruins; there is the state of Yucatán, which through its agency CULTUR collects tickets along with INAH; and there are the employees at Chichén who in many cases come from families who have worked at the site since the days of Edward Thompson.

The Barbachanos are no longer the influence they once were. After the death of patriarch Fernando Barbachano Peón in the mid-1960s, the family began to fracture, the holdings split among his wife, son, and daughter. Son Fernando Barbachano Gomez Rul had several children, and over the years he gave them pieces of the family business or set them up with businesses of their own until, by the time of his passing, he controlled nothing. The property within the Chichén Itzá archaeological zone is owned by three family members: Fernando's son, Fernando Barbachano Herrero, owned the Mayaland Lodge and surrounding property; Fernando's sister Carmen retained the Hacienda Chichén, which she leased to her niece Belisa

(Fernando's daughter) to run as a resort; Fernando's grandson by Hans and Maruja, Hans Thies Barbachano, received the main archaeological zone.

By the time of Fernando's death, the family had not worked in unison in years; in fact it was more likely for them to work against each other. These internecine skirmishes between family members were invisible to the public at large. The Barbachanos have become a public punching bag for the other interests at Chichén Itzá. When INAH or the state or the workers needed to stir up the masses, they played the Barbachano card, demonizing the family. In the United States, the Barbachanos would be considered the paragon of the family who made good, having built a wildly successful business out of almost nothing. But in Mexico, there is a distrust of the wealthy, regardless of how you made your money. By throwing the spotlight on the Barbachanos, others have been quietly expanding their influence on Chichén Itzá in the shadows.

As for Chichén Itzá, everything is about to change, thanks to Swiss entrepreneur Bernard Weber. Not long after the beginning of the new millennium Weber came up with a brilliant idea. Everybody had heard of the "Seven Wonders of the World," but what most people did not know was that all but one, the Great Pyramid of Cheops in Egypt, were gone. Weber decided to hold a worldwide contest to name a new seven.

He created the "New Open World Foundation" to manage the competition, which selected twenty-one famous sites from around the world. He opened voting to anyone who had access to the Internet or a telephone. It quickly grows into one of the biggest popularity contests in history. The government and large corporations in Mexico soon embrace the competition and spend millions of pesos promoting Chichén Itzá. Mexico's Coca-Cola Company emblazon every can of soda with a picture of El Castillo and a call to vote. PEMEX, the national petroleum monopoly, puts up posters in its service stations around the country. TelMex, the telephone monopoly, slaps the telephone number to vote on its ubiquitous phonecards.

The contest is not without its critics. UNESCO, the United Nations Educational, Scientific, and Cultural Organization, disavows any connection with the New Seven Wonders campaign. In 1988 UNESCO had named Chichén Itzá a "World Heritage" site, a designation designed to encourage and recognize that host countries "ensure that effective and active measures are taken for the protection, conservation and presentation of the cultural and natural heritage." The goals and objectives of the New Seven Wonders of the World, at least in UNESCO's collective mind, are different. "The list of the 'Seven New Wonders of the World' will be the result of a private undertaking, reflecting only the opinions of those with access to the Internet and not the entire world," a UNESCO statement reads. "Acknowledging the sentimental or emblematic value of sites and inscribing them on a new list is not enough…This initiative cannot, in any significant and sustainable manner, contribute to the preservation of sites elected by this public."

The rank and file at INAH, primarily the archaeologists, oppose the campaign to have Chichén named a wonder of the world, but the upper levels of management give full support. When Bernard Weber comes to Chichén Itzá to formally induct it into the contest, the INAH director of Yucatán, Federica Sodi, is among those to welcome him and in a speech says, "This archaeological zone is one of the biggest sources of pride in Mexico. We take great pride in the knowledge that people worldwide want to come to know this place."

Her opinion was not shared by one key subordinate, the new director at Chichén Itzá, Eduardo Perez de Heredia, who warns that increasing the awareness of Chichén Itzá in the world will be disastrous. "It is going to oblige us to implement restrictions because there is a limit of one and one-half million visitors per year which cannot be passed," he tells Reuters. To another news agency he says that the contest is "a discriminatory activity that foments competition and inequality." He decries Coca-Cola's promotion of the contest as "banal," especially for putting an image of "the sacred center of the Maya," El Castillo, on millions of cans of soda.

Perez de Heredia has been an archaeologist at Chichén for INAH for many years. In recent years he has done some of the best archaeological analysis ever conducted at Chichén Itzá. His study of ceramics excavated from the ancient city is accomplishing something that the Carnegie Institution with its vast resources could never seem to do: establish a historical timeline for occupation at Chichén Itzá. And, unlike most of his contemporaries at INAH, he published his research. Despite his acumen as an archaeologist, his selection as director at Chichén Itzá seems an unusual choice, for he is not Mexican by birth (born in Spain), nor is he politic in his public comments. His public proclamations of disapproval are not limited to the Wonder of the World contest. Of the tourists who come in droves on the equinoxes to see the shadow-and-light feathered serpent on El Castillo, he complains to a newspaper columnist, "Evidence does not exist that the Maya contemplated the shadows of the equinoxes. Chichén Itzá was not made to produce shadows."

His opposition and that of other Mexican archaeologists does nothing to stop the "Wonder of the World" publicity machine, which takes an unexpected turn. During Weber's visit to Chichén Itzá, he describes how four years earlier he had received an e-mail from Fernando Barbachano Herrero, owner of the Mayaland Resort, who wrote that he "loved the New7Wonders project and that he would like to help and assist wherever he could and that his family owns Chichén Itzá."

Weber says he was stunned. *Owns Chichén Itzá?* he thought at the time. *In his dreams.* But Weber found out it was true. While the Barbachanos' ownership is well known in Yucatán, not so in the rest of Mexico. Weber inadvertently "unleashed a national polemic," as Jose Alfonso Suárez del Reay puts it. Suárez was a member of the House of Deputies, the Mexican equivalent of the House of the Representatives. "And we are all asking, 'How can a Wonder of the World have owners? A World Heritage site cannot be at the whim of a family.'"

Apparently, at least as the federal government is concerned, it can't. One day after Weber's visit to Chichén, INAH and the Barbachanos are in court, precipitated by one of the first actions taken by Perez de Heredia upon assuming the directorship at Chichén—he shut down the gift shops operated by the Barbachanos inside the archaeological zone.

It is unlikely that Perez de Heredia acted on his own. It is possible he is being set up as a fall-guy ("the Spaniard is temporary," is how one INAH official put it in a private conversation). Months later, Perez de Heredia is demoted and the real story emerges: INAH wants Chichén Itzá—all of it. For months the federal agency had been trying to arrange a purchase of the site. It had appropriated $14 million Mexican to purchase historic sites throughout Mexico. According to one INAH official, the agency offered the property owners of Chichén Itzá $8 million Mexican (approximately $750,000 U.S.). In a move apparently designed to motivate the owners to sell, INAH threatens to expropriate the property, that is, take it by eminent domain rather than a negotiated price. To further motivate them, INAH shuts down the gift shops.

With the death of family patriarch Fernando Barbachano Gomez Rul, it falls to his grandson Hans Thies Barbachano to defend the interests of the family. Thies Barbachano does not retreat or relent, nor does he stand his ground; he instead goes for the jugular. He counters Perez de Heredia's closure order by filing an appeal unique in Latin America, the amparo indirecto. The amparo, similar to habeas corpus in the United States, is the legal mechanism by which a Mexican citizen can fight the federal government on grounds his or her constitutional rights have been violated. The amparo was a creation of a Yucatecan, Manuel Crescencio Garcia Rejón y Alcalá, in the 19th century. At the time the federal government of Mexico was attempting to crush Yucatán under its heel, so the state declared its independence in 1841. To ensure protection of the constitutional rights of citizens of the new republic, Crescenio Rejón fought to have the amparo written into the Yucatán constitution, which eventually was signed into law by vice-governor Miguel Barbachano, Thies Barbachano's great-great-great-great-great uncle. When Yucatán was absorbed back into Mexico, the amparo was added to the federal constitution.

Thies Barbachano's lawyer, Ricardo Rabasa Gamboa, bases the amparo indirecto on several counts, namely that his client is the legal owner of the property of Chichén Itzá and that he has the legal permission from the town of Tinúm (which includes Chichén Itzá) to operate a business. But the most potentially devastating argument in his amparo strikes at the foundation of INAH, that its very existence at Chichén Itzá was unconstitutional.

The legal argument goes something like this: In 1988, the president of Mexico declared Chichén Itzá an "archaeological zone," which gave INAH authority over the site. That decision, according to lawyer Rabasa, stripped his client of some of his rights as a property owner. In Mexico, property rights are almost sacrosanct, but the government can and does take property with great regularity. When it does, there is an appeal process available to the property owner to fight the taking. But when the president of Mexico declared Chichén Itzá an archaeological zone and had INAH take over, there was no legal mechanism for the Barbachanos to fight that decision. As such, it represented an illegal taking by the government, which violated the Mexican constitution.

Rabasa Gamboa is confident his client will prevail because he had an ace up his sleeve—the Mexican Supreme Court in 1984 and 1989 had already ruled in similar cases that the president's action was unconstitutional, although in those instances it was for historic structures, not pre-Columbian ruins.

When he presents his client's case to a federal district judge, the appeal is denied because the judge "said we didn't prove the property was owned by Hans," Rabasa says later. The lawyer suspects the real reason may have been because this case is politically red-hot and the judge does not want to be the one to find INAH's authority unconstitutional.

Rabaso appeals to the *Tribunale Colegiado de Circuito*, a three-member judiciary panel that reviews cases by district courts. The Tribunale Colegiado, however, decides it cannot act upon the appeal until the constitutional issues are resolved, so it passes the legal hot potato up to the Suprema Corte.

During the tug-of-war between INAH and the Barbachanos, Chichén Itzá wins the contest and becomes one of the new Seven Wonders of the World, joining the Taj Mahal in India, the Great Wall of China, Petra in Jordan, Brazil's giant statue of Christ the Redeemer, Peru's Machu Picchu, and the Colosseum in Italy. Yucatán readies for what authorities believe will be a tidal wave of tourists, but it never materializes. A global recession cripples international travel. Then, just as the economy begins to revive, an outbreak of H1N1 "swine flu" erupts in Mexico and the president shuts down the country to stop the spread. That crisis passes relatively quickly, but tourism does not recover, thanks in no small part to another epidemic, this time of narcotics-related homicides in other parts of Mexico. The state of Yucatán has been all but immune to the violence of the drug cartels (the state is far safer than almost anywhere in the United States) but all the rest of the world seems to know is what they read in the newspapers, that thousands are murdered each year in Mexico.

In the midst of these crises, Yucatán selects a new governor, Ivonne Ortega Pacheco, niece of the late Governor Victor Manuel Cervera Pacheco. Even before she takes office, Gov. Ortega Pacheco promises to bring more change to Chichén Itzá than any governor since Felipe Carrillo Puerto. In many respects, she is the modernized embodiment of Carrillo Puerto. Before winning election as governor, she had served as mayor of Dzemul, a small community not far from Carrillo Puerto's hometown of Motul. She later represented Motul in the Mexican Congress.

Like Carrillo Puerto, Ortega possesses a broad vision. A few weeks before taking the oath as governor, she announces a giant public infrastructure project, a "bullet train" between Mérida and Cancun that will include a stop at Chichén Itzá—a project that will cost an estimated $18 billion Mexican. Ironically it was Gov. Carrillo Puerto's road projects, including the road to Chichén, that made the train obsolete in Yucatán.

It becomes evident, though, that her administration is less keeping with Carrillo Puerto than her uncle, Cervera Pacheco, who was among the first to realize that Chichén Itzá was a revenue gold mine. Gov. Cervera Pacheco's first administration created the department *Patronato de las Unidades de Servicios Culturales y Turisticos del Estado de Yucatán*, better known as CULTUR, for the purpose of exploiting tourism in the state. To help finance its activities, the new agency implemented a state ticket fee at Chichén Itzá.

During Gov. Cervera Pacheco's second term, his administration came up with another way to make money off Chichén Itzá—host a concert there. Although rare, Chichén Itzá had been used as a performance space in the past. Archaeologist Sylvanus Morley in the 1920s and 1930s would set up a record player in the Great Ball Court to entertain his guests. In later years, small groups of singers or musicians would perform to limited audiences. But Cervera Pacheco wasn't interested in limited entertainment that would draw 100 people. His administration brought in the great Italian tenor, Luciano Pavarotti, to perform in front of El Castillo. More than 17,000 attended, some paying as much as $14,000 Mexican for a single ticket. The concert was broadcast around the world to more than 200 countries. It also brought scorn and protest by INAH archaeologists and by various Maya groups. It would be the first and, many thought, the last concert ever performed at Chichén Itzá. Others attempted to host events, but found themselves stymied by INAH's archaeologists or by politicians who objected to using sites of public patrimony for private concerts—until the election of Cervera Pacheco's niece, Gov. Ivonne Ortega Pacheco.

A few months into her first term, her administration announces it will bring Spanish tenor Placido Domingo to Chichén Itzá. One state official reports that they have permission from INAH to hold the concert, although the claim is met with some credulity because only five years before INAH had blocked a proposed Placido Domingo concert at Tulum. Later, as more details about the concert negotiations emerged, Gov. Ortega admits that she does not have INAH's permission, but implies that she does not need it, for she has gone over INAH's head to the Secretariat of Education, of which INAH is a department.

Domingo proves to be a canny choice to headline a concert because his professional roots are in Yucatán. His family had moved to Mexico when he was eight and in 1957 the tenor made his stage debut in Mérida performing with his mother. To make the concert critic-proof, the governor announces that Domingo will be joined by Armando Manzanero, Mexico's most famous composer and, more significantly, a Mérida-born mestizo whose ancestors are Maya, the very people who built Chichén Itzá. "When I feel more Maya is when I'm among my people," Manzanero tells reporters during the governor's announcement of the concert.

The concert may be critic-proof, but it is not INAH-proof. INAH's *Consejo de Arqueología* (Council of Archaeology) rejects Yucatán's request to hold the concert at Chichén Itzá. The Council lists several reasons for its denial, declaring that Chichén Itzá too fragile to withstand thousands of attendees as well as the stage and other infrastructure required for the concert. Furthermore the event will complicate the federal government's relationship with the Barbachanos, with whom it was engaged in negotiations.

And what of those negotiations? Two weeks later the Supreme Court of Mexico issues its ruling on the Hans Thies Barbachano appeal. Mexico's highest court, no doubt grasping the ramifications of the precedent this case would establish, decides not to decide. "The Supreme Court of Mexico did not establish the unconstitutionality of the law," says Thies Barbachano's lawyer Rabaso. There is too much at stake. Had they ruled the law unconstitutional, as they had twice in the past in other cases, they would have had to return Chichén Itzá to the Barbachanos—including the monuments, says Rabasa. Furthermore, it would have set a precedent for the thousands of other archaeological sites in Mexico that are private property.

But the case is still a victory, says Rabaso. The court "established a very important matter—that Hans Barbachano, my client, was the owner of the property."

The Supreme Court remands the case back to the Tribunal, which overrules the authority of INAH by granting the amparo. More importantly, the highest court in the land determines that Hans Thies Barbachano is the undisputed owner of the archaeological zone of Chichén Itzá, which opens the door for the biggest transformation of the site since the Spanish Conquest.

INAH's leverage over the Barbachanos evaporates. For the next several months, INAH representatives make noises about expropriating Chichén Itzá or using other legal means, but it has run out of options that would not mean a messy legal battle. Thies Barbachano has demonstrated he is willing to take the fight to the Supreme Court to challenge INAH's very constitutionality.

Gov. Ortega had been a vocal supporter of INAH's attempts to acquire the site. But after the court decisions went against the federal agency, she takes a different tact. Her administration launches an initiative to create a master plan for Chichén Itzá and in a speech on "World Tourism Day" the governor asks the federal government to spend money for Chichén Itzá as it did to create the tourism magnet of Cancun in the 1970s. "Yucatan is in real need of support in terms of tourism, preservation of its resources, and development of its communities," she says. "Truthfully, one cannot even imagine the potential that exists in tourism in this land and we cannot wait another generation for things to get started." She calls for the federal government to take "decisive action" at Chichén Itzá to prevent further deforestation, water table pollution, and rampant, unregulated urban development. "I have not lost my confidence in the federal government where there is such good intention and energy," she concludes.

That confidence melts over the weeks that follow. Perhaps it is because the federal government abandons plans to expropriate Chichén Itzá. Or perhaps it is INAH's resistance to the governor's concerts at Chichén. INAH never officially grants permission for Placido Domingo. Despite the resistance, the concert goes off without any major hitches and the state announces plans to hold more—Sarah Brightman, Elton John, even Paul McCartney.

Gov. Ortega's designs for Chichén Itzá are bigger than just concerts. As she nears the end of the second year of her term, someone leaks her real plans: "Disneyfication" of Chichén Itzá. Some unknown person posts on the internet a promotional video reportedly produced by the state of Yucatán announcing plans for a "macro tourism development." On property near Chichén Itzá the state proposes to encourage development of twelve new hotels, a convention center, artificial lakes with artificial beaches, a large aquarium, water park, golf courses, spas, restaurants, and shopping centers. The proposal is as ambitious, if not more so, than the original plan for Cancun. According to one dubious source, the project already has received a commitment from French, Chinese, and Canadian investors, and the budget for the initial phase will top $2 billion Mexican ($175 million U.S.). A state official later denounces the video, claiming that it had been created by an unnamed foreign partner and without the authorization of the state. The denial comes too late, for the video tipped everyone to the scope of the governor's plans. But she has one big surprise that no one sees coming—she buys Chichén Itzá.

In the spring of 2010 Gov. Ortega announces that the state of Yucatán has come to terms with Thies Barbachano and will purchase the central archaeological zone of Chichén Itzá for $220 million Mexican ($17.6 million U.S.), almost thirty times the amount that had been offered by INAH. Thies Barbachano has little to say about the transaction. "I reiterate my support that every day, including the times ahead, to play a positive and productive role in the future of Chichén," he says at the press conference announcing the sale. "The transfer of property does not conclude my responsibility and affirms my desire of continued support."

Three years later, representatives of Carmen Barbachano y Gomez Rul announce they have come to terms with INAH and have sold ninety-nine hectares, the area of the archaeological zone known as *Chichén Viejo* (Old Chichén), for $232 million pesos. She retains ownership of the buildings that make up the Hacienda Chichén Resort and Spa.

Like Edward Thompson, *la familia Barbachano* over time will fade into the history of Chichén Itzá. They were but caretakers, and the sale of the archaeological zone marks the beginning of the passing of the torch. The future of Chichén Itzá no longer rests with the Barbachanos, but with the government and politicians. Will the vision of Gov. Ortega be realized, the so-called Disneyfication of Chichén? Or will the desires of INAH archaeologists, who rope off monuments to "protect" them from the public, hold sway? Or will the vendors who shout "One dollar! One dollar!" as they have for more than a decade decide the final fate of Chichén Itzá? ¿*Quién sabe?*

EPILOGUE

'WAS EDWARD THOMPSON A GOOD MAN?' Bibiano asks me, a question seemingly out of the blue. From the look on his face, it is one that has been on his mind, probably since our first meeting.

He asks me this during one of my regular visits. I return to Yucatán every year, sometimes twice, and for as long as three weeks. Every trip includes a stop to see Bibiano and his family. Victoria prepares a meal, always some traditional dish. We catch up on the news of our families and people we know. There usually is a quick lesson in Maya and my struggles with the language always bring giggles from Victoria and the rest of the family.

During these visits, I fill everyone in on the progress on the book. On this most recent trip, I announce I have completed my research and that I will finish the book later in the year. Bibiano poses his question as I am about to get into my rental car and return to Mérida. "Was Edward Thompson a good man?"

I smile. "Of course," I say. What I don't tell him is that I have been struggling with that very question.

Most biographers apotheosize their subject, many fall in love with him or her. I have come to like Edward Thompson, even admire him. I can see bits of his personality and character in his descendants, both on the American side and on the Mexican side. There is a romantic spirit among them, an ability to dream beyond their circumstances. They also don't appear to be adept at making money, but at the same time monetary riches don't seem that important.

Was Thompson a "good" man? Not in the minds of many of today's Mexican archaeologists, who have never forgiven the removal of the Cenote Sagrado artifacts even though it occurred long before they were born. That Thompson was acquitted by Mexico's highest court is either unknown or dismissed as corruption. But the truth, like it or not, is that Mexico never had a case. Dredging the Cenote Sagrado was not illegal under Mexican law. Owning artifacts was not against the law. It was illegal to smuggle the artifacts out of Mexico, but the penalty was a mere 500 pesos.

Under Mexican law, the treasures from the Cenote Sagrado belong to Edward Thompson, free and clear.

The case of the Cenote Sagrado artifacts is not unique in archaeological circles. Every nation usually has *something* it wants back, the hometown version of the Elgin Marbles. "Repatriation," where museums return artifacts, is a hot trend these days. In recent years, the Peabody Museum at Yale returned to Peru its collection of objects from Machu Picchu. The museum had agreed to "borrow" the artifacts for eighteen months, which became a century.

But the case of the treasures of the Sacred Well is unique. The ownership of the artifacts has been fully litigated by the highest possible court in the land where the objects were taken. Furthermore, this was not some rubber stamp decision by puppets of the Porfiriato, but one made by judges born from the loins of the Mexican Revolution.

No, the excavations on behalf of the Peabody Museum do not bother me. But I am unsettled by Edward's Thompson's private life. Not that he had a son by a Maya woman, although this shocked some of his contemporaries. June James refused to visit the Hacienda Chichén after learning of Thompson's "left-handed progeny." What gnaws at me is that it appears Thompson abandoned Victoria and Carlos, leaving them behind to fend for themselves.

After reading countless letters written by Thompson, it is evident that family was important, if not his highest priority in life. That is why Thompson abandoning his child seems so out of character. Apparently I don't know him as well as I think.

I am putting the finishing touches on this book when I receive an unsolicited e-mail out of the blue. The subject line immediately grabs my attention. "i am edward herbert thompsons great grandson," it says. It is from John Lord Jr. Inside he writes, "Edward Gilbert Thompson was my grandfather.

"I write you, sir, because I would like the record to be set straight about something that troubled my grandfather until his death in 1977," Lord continues. "As a child I grew up with bedtime stories of the Maya and the jaguar and the Cenote de Sagrado…I don't see much anywhere about my great-grandfather and his works over forty years amongst the Maya. My great-grandfather was not a thief because he was cleared of any wrongdoing by the Mexican court. Please help to clear my great-grandfather's name."

Who the hell is Edward Gilbert Thompson?

Edward H. Thompson had a son named Edward, but his middle name was Josiah, after his father. There was no son named Edward Gilbert. Nor was that the name of any of Victoria's children. My heart sinks. Edward Thompson had children by yet another woman?

I reread Lord's letter and see I missed other details. He claims to be part Maya. His grandfather grew up at the Hacienda Chichén. I look back through my research and find little corroborative clues. One of the American Thompsons had told me that there was a story in the family that one of Edward Thompson's grandchildren had been scandalized when she met someone in Florida who claimed to be related. Also, Sylvanus Morley made a passing mention in his diaries of Thompson's bastard *children*, plural, not just one. I had assumed he had meant Victoria's other children, but now I'm not so sure.

I have to talk to John Lord. I'm thrilled to discover he lives a little more than an hour's drive from me in Massachusetts. We agree to meet.

It's a beautiful late spring day when I pull up in front of John's house. Latin music blares from a nearby car and people of all colors and ethnicities fill the street. It's the melting pot and, while not the bottom, no one who lives here appears to have a lot of money.

John waits for me in front of his house. We shake hands and he introduces me to his son. We make our way into the home where I am introduced to his mother Marilyn, who I am told is Edward Gilbert Thompson's daughter. You can tell she's had a hard life and there is a slight droop on one side of her mouth, which I learn later the family believes was the result of a stroke.

We sit in the parlor. A bird in a cage cheeps to no one in particular. I start up my recorder and away we go.

Marilyn tells me her father was Edward Thompson's son, born and raised in Yucatán, but lived most of his adult life in the United States. I ask if he had any brothers or sisters. He had a brother, she says, "Uncle Al… Alfonso Thompson." And sisters? I ask. "Yes, the only one I remember is Aunt Victoria," Marilyn says. "She was the oldest and I think she lived the longest. I saw her when we went to Yucatán in 1976. She was bedridden, but she still had her mind about her."

Victoria? I show Marilyn a picture of doña Victoria, mother of Carlos Marrufo, taken in the 1950s or so. "That's her," she says, although when they met her hair was white. "She spoke nothing but Spanish," she says, so the two never conversed. "She was living with Alfredo, her son. His name was Marrufo," she says. Carlos Marrufo's younger brother was Alfredo.

So Victoria was his sister? This was drifting into "Chinatown" territory.

Victoria, who reportedly bore Thompson a son, was also his daughter? I know that isn't right. Marilyn thinks her name was Victoria Thompson, but I know from legal documents I have seen that it was Victoria Manjarrez.

Marilyn says that she had been told that Edward Thompson's American wife had been a hypochondriac and she wanted to be back in Massachusetts where her doctors were. After his wife left Mexico, Edward Thompson was at the Hacienda Chichén and "noticed my grandmother, who was a servant girl," says Marilyn. Her name, Marilyn thinks, was "Josefa." Thompson sought a relationship with her, but was blocked by Josefa's mother, who was a shaman or medicine woman and therefore very powerful. There is a story told in the family of a married woman who came to Marilyn's great-grandmother for a potion that would keep her husband from beating her. "She mixed something up and said, 'Give this to him, he'll be fine,'" Marilyn says. "She did and he died."

If Edward Thompson was smart, he was not going to cross a *bruja* (witch), who told Thompson that he had to marry Josefa and agree to raise the children Catholic. "They got married in the church and started a family," she says. Her father, Edward, was born in 1900. Another son, Alfonso, was born five years later.

I told Marilyn that I didn't believe the story and, at least as far as Edward Thompson getting married, it probably wasn't correct. Thompson's wife was in Yucatán when Josefa bore him the two sons. In fact, she was living at the Hacienda Chichén at various times during that period. It also didn't make sense to me that a Maya medicine woman would insist on raising children Catholic, although I had to admit I knew of very devout Catholics in Yucatán who practiced rituals of their Maya ancestors to seek rain and good crops.

How did the family get to the United States? I ask. "T.A. Willard," Marilyn says. He got them jobs in his battery factory in Cleveland.

Of course, Willard, I think. Of all Thompson's friends, he was the one with the resources to be able to hire Thompson's sons. Did Thompson ever have any contact with his sons after they arrived in the United States? Marilyn thinks so.

Marilyn is the daughter of her father and his second wife. According to family lore, Marilyn's father once saved a Maya princess from drowning and, for that, the girl's father told Edward that his first daughter would be a Maya princess. "The kids don't take it seriously about me being a princess," Marilyn says, without a trace of irony. "It was something my father was proud of, it was important."

As I pack up to leave, John says he wants to tell me a story. He lived with his grandfather for five years, beginning when he was five until the elder man's death from cancer. "I was close to him," John says. "He was more of a father than a grandfather. I always felt he was by my side."

One night, long after his grandfather had passed, John had a dream that he and his mother were walking through a cemetery. It was something they liked to do, he says. At one point, Marilyn tells him that she wants to go visit the graves of the children; John says he wants to go visit his grandfather's grave. When he got there, the grave was illuminated in a bright light, "but as bright as it was, it didn't hurt my eyes," John says. The light coalesced into the silhouette of a man. "I turned to my mom, to ask if she saw this, but she was gone." When he turned back, he saw his grandfather standing before him, but with a young, strong body.

"All he said was, 'Johnny, tell your mother I love her and I'm watching her. Take care of my daughter.'" Then he woke up. "It was two-thirty in the morning," he says. The dream was so powerful, so vivid, that he got up, got dressed, and drove over to his mother's house. When he got there, he found the front door ajar, which was something that was simply not done because the home was next to a bar. John says he went inside, found beer cans lying around the living room, but no one around. He went into his mother's room, but she wasn't there. He found her, he says, in the room of one of his brothers. "She was in my brother's bed," John recalls. "I told her about the dream. And what did you tell me after that, ma?" he asks.

"That I was thinking of killing myself," Marilyn says. She had been contemplating taking a baggie of pills that was on the nightstand next to her.

She didn't know why she was in her son's room. She thinks it was because her husband and other sons had been making fun of her being a Maya princess.

When I get back to my office, I scour my research for anything that will corroborate the story of Marilyn and John. It isn't hard to find that they were telling the truth. I can't find a record of Edward Gilbert Thompson but I find his brother Alfonso. According to Ellis Island immigration records, he entered the United States on June 25, 1923 when he was eighteen. The same record states, "Father U.S. Citizen" and that his destination was "Cleveland, Ohio." He was the only passenger who boarded the ship when it docked in Progreso. I have compiled a timeline of Edward Thompson's whereabouts. I knew from memory he had been in Yucatán earlier in the year, for that was the period when the Carnegie Institution representatives first visited and when he revealed to Alma Reed the dredging of the Cenote Sagrado. He had returned to the United States but five days before his son arrived. At the time he was in Swarthmore, Penn. It would have been relatively easy for him to swing by New York, pick up his son and deliver him to Cleveland. I wonder if his American family knew.

Going back over my notes, I find little bits and pieces of additional corroboration. I now remember my conversation with Susan Haskell of the Peabody Museum who showed me the Cenote Sagrado artifacts. She had told me that "representatives" of Thompson's Maya family had been to see the artifacts.

Did this mean Carlos Marrufo was Thompson's grandson and not his son? I think it was far more complicated than that. I believe that Edward

Thompson had a long relationship with Josefa, Victoria's mother. Victoria had been born by another man. And I believe Edward Thompson had a single child with doña Victoria, based on the slightest evidence: Both Victoria and her husband, Carlos Marrufo, were short. Carlos was tall and his sons, even taller. But without DNA testing, it will be impossible to prove. I can find no records, government or church, for Carlos, Victoria, or either of her two brothers, Edward (who was probably "Eduardo") or Alfonso. And I have no last name for Josefa, which was a common name in that part of Mexico in the late 1800s. When the explorer Désiré Charnay explored Chichén Itzá in 1882, he described an incident where he had stayed up late one night writing and was struck by what he thought was a vision. "I suddenly looked up to see standing before me a lovely maiden more like an apparition than a mortal being," he wrote. "Was this the shade of a Maya princess who had returned to the scenes of her former life, conjured up by my imagination? Meanwhile the beauteous figure stood looking and smiling at me. I was amazed, speechless, hardly daring to break the spell, when a third figure stood to from the dark entrance, in whom I recognized the commandant of Pisté."

The post commander said that he had heard Charnay's expedition was without a cook. "I brought you mine," he said.

Charnay's Indian princess turned out to be a fifteen-year-old servant. "I could not believe that so much youth and beauty were put to such a menial occupation," he wrote. The girl brought Charnay a gift, a bottle of liquor, which he said "made me light-headed and, in a fit of somnambulism, I wandered about, spouting poetry at the top of my voice, on the very edge of the pyramid."

The girl's name was "Josepha."

The *commandante* at Pisté later became a good friend of Edward Thompson's after he bought the Hacienda Chichén. It is possible that Josepha sould have moved to the Hacienda Chichén. If she was fifteen as

The Lord family, the 'lost' descendants of Edward Thompson. In front left, Marilyn Lord and back center, her son, John Lord Jr.

Charnay believed in 1882, she would have been thirty-three when Marilyn's father was born and thirty-eight at Alfonso's birth.

After my meeting with John and Marilyn, it isn't too hard to find other descendants. I get in touch with other members of that side of the Thompson family, several of whom are still in Ohio. They tell me they have letters from Edward Thompson to his son, asking for news and telling them to be sure to send money home to their mother, Josefa. Thompson had made certain his Maya sons were provided for. I suspect, but do not know, that he had been the one responsible for getting Carlos a job with the Carnegie Institution's Chichén Itzá Project. Even though the Mexican government had stripped him of his property (unjustly) and left him nearly penniless, Thompson managed to find a way to help provide for the children he had been forced to leave behind. *That* is the Edward Thompson I have come to know.

ACKNOWLEDGEMENTS

THIS BOOK WOULD NEVER HAVE BEEN POSSIBLE without the kindness of strangers, many of whom became close friends along the way.

First and foremost, I am grateful to the late Fernando Barbachano Gomez Rul, who began as an interview subject, became my guide to Yucatán, and later my good friend. His openness and candor form the backbone of this book, and without his unselfish donation of time and resources, this book would never have been possible, not to mention outright dull. I also am grateful to the other members of the Barbachano family and extended family, especially don Fernando's wife, Maruja Herrero Garcia, his sister Carmen Barbachano y Gomez Rul, his daughter Belisa, and especially her husband Bruce Gordon.

Equally important to this project were the descendents of Edward H. Thompson, both in the United States and in Yucatán, especially the late Virginia "Ginny" Kuykendall and her daughters Heleni Thayre and Alex Thayer. I am especially grateful to Bibiano Uh Tun (grandson-in-law of E.H. Thompson), his wife Maria Victoria Marrufo Nah (Thompson's granddaughter), and their children: Maria Indalaecia, Jaime Humberto, Edgar Enrique, Joel Geobani, Josue Natanael, and the late Angelina. I am also indebted to doña Victoria's mother, Maria Luisa Nah Rodriguez, and doña Victoria's brothers (and Thompson grandchildren) Carlos, Ariel, Reynaldo, Javier, Guillermo, and Miguel, for allowing me into their lives. Finally, thanks to Marilyn Lord (granddaughter of Edward Thompson), John Lord Jr. (great-grandson), and family, without whom this book would have ended quite differently.

Others were generous with their time, resources, and suggestions, and without their contributions, sometimes unknowingly, this book would never have come together: Sarah Albright; Stuart Albright; David Bodwell; Lisa Breglia; Keith Brooks; John B. Carlson; Suzanne Carroll; Diane Carter; Quetzil Castañeda; Pedro Castro Martínez; Mindy Todd; Jim Conrad; Chris Craig; Lawrence Desmond; Don Dumond; Don Ediger; Jim and Ellen Fields; Gregory A. Finnegan of the Tozzer Library; Dr. William J. Folan; Stephen Fox; Wilma Jean Garrison; Jocelyn Gibbs at the University of California, Santa Barbara; Curtis Harrison; Curtis Hinsley; George Ann Huck; Jill M. Koelling of the Denver Museum of Nature and Science; Patricia Kervick and Susan Haskell at the Peabody Museum at Harvard; Inga Kimple; Tom and Debi Kuhn; "William Lawson"; Jesse Lerner; Edward F. Maroney; Donald McVicker; Vicki Merrick; the late Ben Muse; Thomas G. Noles; Bob Oakley; Feli Pamploma Marrufo; Dave Pentecost; Eduardo Perez de Heredia; Alan S. Richter; Ryan Sawyer; Adam Sellen; Peter Schmidt; Daniel Schavelzon; Michael Schuessler; CHema Skandl!; Allen Wells; Robert Wintheiser; Manfred Witteman.

Thanks to those who kindly provided art for this book. Special thanks to Peter Pereira, who took many of the contemporary photographs. Don Fernando and Edward Thompson's descendants provided me with access to photos of their respective families. Much of the art and photographs in this book are from public domain sources and have either never been published or not been republished for a century or longer.

Over the course of the decade it took to write this book, I've kept track of the assistance I have received. For anyone I may have omitted, please know I am grateful for your contribution, despite my faulty record keeping.

In the early stages of this book, when I was ignorant of the ways of Mexico, Paul "Pablo" Harding served as my gringo guide. Later, my three amigos, Dr. Steven Fry, Bill Drennon, and Sid Hollander, accompanied me on many an adventure throughout Yucatán in search of information for this book. I am also grateful to Dr. Paul Sullivan, author of the brilliant *Unfinished Conversations*, who always made himself available to answer questions about Maya or translate a phrase or two.

As always, I am especially grateful for the support of my wonderful and patient family, my wife Lori, and my children Sarah and Sam. In all they joined me, in whole and in part, on four excursions to Yucatán. Without their indulgence, none of this would have been possible. Equally important were my parents, Warren and Maxine Albright, whose bequest financed much of the research of this book. If there is one thing I learned in Mexico, it's that family is everything.

Photo by Peter Pereira

AFTERWORD AND BIBLIOGRAPHIC ESSAY

ALTHOUGH THIS IS A WORK OF NONFICTION, certain liberties have been taken. The sections marked "The Past" are straightforward history, and the reader can be assured no literary sleight-of-hand has been employed. In the sections labeled "The Present," some events have been compressed or moved in time to provide an uncluttered, understandable, and more compelling narrative for the reader. Great pains have been taken to be accurate, but there are numerous instances where the reader may infer a conversation or event occurred at a certain time when it may have occurred months or even years earlier or later.

Many of the interviews conducted for this book were with individuals for whom English is a second language (or in the case of many Maya, third language). I have attempted to walk a fine line by correcting grammar and syntax, but leaving enough of the original to give the reader a flavor of what such conversations are like. Often interviews were conducted in Spanish or Maya, and although not indicated, the text has been translated into English. I called upon many friends and colleagues for translation help, but the bulk of the translations in this book are mine, and any errors must be considered my responsibility.

In Latin countries, people tend to have long names. I have tried to put in the full names of individuals on first reference, then truncated their names after that. A standard way of naming individuals became impossible, notably among the Barbachanos who have four Fernandos, four Marujas who aren't named Maruja, three Carmens, and an Isabel who is a Belisa. Once I settled on a naming convention for an individual, I stuck with it. I avoided nicknames—Fernando Barbachano Gomez Rul was known for much of his life "Fernandito," but to me he will always be "Fernando" or "don Fernando."

Throughout this book readers will find derogatory references to peoples, primarily of the Maya, that are contemporary with the historical period in which the chapter is set. Rather than adopt a politically correct stance and sanitize the text or yank the reader out of the narrative to point out racism, I have left it to the reader to apply that sensibility. Sadly, despite the advancements in race relations, I don't believe the Maya, like other indigenous groups in North and South America, are receiving much in the way of respect from those who run government or industry.

Some of the findings and conclusions presented in this book contradict the work of other writers and historians. At times I found myself writing mini-essays explaining the research behind those conclusions, but in the end cut them because it was too "inside baseball." I wish I could have included my footnotes, which number in the thousands, but it became cost prohibitive. Perhaps in a future edition, but for now this brief essay will have to suffice. For any academics or scholars who wish to know where I found a specific piece of information, send me an email c/o the publisher (info@bohlincarr.com).

I am grateful to the following institutions who kindly opened their doors and made their valuable archives of information available:

American Antiquarian Society, Worcester, Mass. (Stephen Salisbury III Papers)
Peabody Museum of Archaeology and Ethnology, Harvard University, Cambridge, Mass. (Frederick Ward Putnam, Peabody Museum Director Papers; Frederick Ward Putnam Papers; Charles P. Bowditch Papers; Alfred M. Tozzer Papers; Edward H. Thompson Papers; L.C. Cole Papers)
Tozzer Library, Harvard University, Cambridge, Mass.
National Archives at College Park, College Park, Md. (Despatches of Consuls, Records of the U.S. State Department records, and Approved Agrarian Claims, the Mexican-American Commission records).
American Philosophical Society, Philadelphia. (Sylvanus Morley Papers)
Archivo de la Biblioteca "Carlos R. Menéndez," Merida, Yucatan, Mexico. (Yucatán and Mexican newspapers collection)
Biblioteca Yucatanense, Merida, Yucatan, Mexico.
Fototeca Pedro Guerra de la Universidad Autónoma de Yucatán, Merida, Yucatan, Mexico.
Architecture & Design Collection, University Art Museum, University of California, Santa Barbara, Calif.
Braun Research Library, Institute for the Study of the American West, Autry National Center for the American West, Los Angeles, Calif.
National Anthropological Archives, Smithsonian Institution, Suitland, Md.
Dumbarton Oaks Research Library, Washington, D.C.
General Manuscripts Collection of the Rare Books and Manuscript Library, Columbia University, New York, N.Y. (Louis Aymé Papers)

Image Archive, Denver Museum of Nature and Science, Denver, Colo. (Walter Austin Papers)

Getty Research Institute, Los Angeles, Calif. (Augustus and Alice Le Plongeon Papers)

Wisconsin Historical Society, Madison, Wisc. (International Harvester Papers)

National Anthropological Archives, Smithsonian Institution, Washington, D.C.

University Archives, George C. Gordon Library, Worcester Polytechnic Institute, Worcester, Mass.

Barnstable County Registry of Deeds, Barnstable, Mass.

Braun Research Library, Autry National Center for the American West, Los Angeles, Calif. (T.A. Willard Papers)

Falmouth Public Library, Falmouth, Mass.

Boston Public Library, Boston, Mass.

Archives, Worcester Polytechnic Institute, Worcester, Mass.

SELECT BIBLIOGRAPHY

American Antiquarian Society. *Proceedings of the American Antiquarian Society*. Worcester, Mass.: Published by the Society, various years.

Breglia, Lisa. *Monumental Ambivalence: The Politics of Heritage*. Austin, Texas: University of Texas Press, 2006.

Brunhouse, Robert L. *Sylvanus G. Morley and the World of the Ancient Mayas*. Norman, Okla.: University of Oklahoma Press, 1971.

Carey, James C. *The Mexican Revolution in Yucatan 1915-1924*. Boulder, Colo.: Westview Press, 1984.

Chamberlain, Robert S. *The Conquest and Colonization of Yucatan 1517-1550*. Washington, D.C.: Carnegie Institution of Washington,, 1948.

Charnay, Claude Joseph Désiré. *The Ancient Cities of the New World.* New York: Harper & Bros., 1887.

Charnay, Claude Joseph Désiré, and Viollet Le Duc. *Cities et Ruinas Americanas: Mitla, Palenque, Izamal, Chichén Itzá, Uxmal.* Paris: A. Morel et Co., 1863.

Coggins, Clemency. "Dredging the Cenote." In Clemency Coggins (ed.), *Artifacts from the Cenote of Sacrifice, Chichén Itzá, Yucatan: Textiles, Basketry, Stone, Bone, Shell, Ceramics, Wood, Copal, Rubber, Other Organic Materials, and Mammalian Remains.* (Cambridge, Mass.: Harvard University Press, 1992).

Desmond, Lawrence, and Phylllis Mauch Messenger. *A Dream of Maya: Augustus and Alice Le Plongeon in nineteenth century Yucatan.* Albuquerque, NM: Univsersity of New Mexico, 1988.

Desmond, Lawrence. *Yucatan Through Her Eyes: Alice Dixon Le Plongeon, Writer & Expeditionary Photographer.* Albuquerque, NM: University of New Mexico, 2009.

Ewing, M. Robert. "A History of the Archaeological Activity at Chichen Itza, Yucatan Mexico," Ph.D. dissertation. August 1972, Kent State University.

Harris, Charles H., and Louis R. Sadler. *The Archaeologist Was a Spy: Sylvanus G. Morley and the Office of Naval Intelligence.* Albuquerque, N.M.: University of New Mexico Press, 2003.

Hinsley, Curtis M. "Wanted: One Good Man to Discover Central American History." *Harvard Magazine*, Nov.-Dec. 1984.

Holmes, William H. *Archaeological Studies Among the Ancient Cities of Mexico*, Field Columbian Museum Publication 8, Anthropological Series Vol. 1 No. 1. Vols. 1, No. 1. Chicago: Field Columbian Museum, 1895.

Maudslay, Alfred P. *Biologia Central-Americana; or Contributions to the knowledge of the Fauna and Flora of Mexico and Central American, Archaeology. Vol. 3.* London: R.H. Porter, 1889-1902.

McVicker, Donald. "A Tale of Two Thompsons: The Contribution of Edward H. Thompson and J. Eric S. Thompson to Anthropology at the Field Museum." *Fieldiana*, New Series, no. 36 (Sept. 2003).

McVicker, Mary. *Adela Breton: A Victorian Artist Amid Mexico's Ruins*. Albuquerque, N.M.: University of New Mexico Press, 2005.

Normal, B.M. (Benjamin). *Rambles in Yucatan: Notes of Travel, Through the Peninsula, Including a Visit to the Remarkable Ruins of Chi-Chen, Kabah, Zayi, and Uxmal*. New York: J. & H.G. Langley, 1843.

O'Neill, John P. "Yucatan Alternative." Institute for the Study of the Americas, University of North Carolina, Chapel Hill, n.d.

Reed, Alma. *Peregrina: Love & Death in Mexico*. Edited by Michael K. Schuessler. Austin, Texas: University of Texas Press, 2006.

Rugeley, Terry. *Yucatan's Maya Peasantry & the Origins of the Caste War*. Austin, Texas: University of Texas, 1996.

Stephens, John Lloyd. *Incidents of Travel in Central America, Chiapas, and Yucatan*. 2 vols. Harper & Bros., 1843.

—. *Incidents of Travel in Yucatan*. 2 vols. New York: Harper & Bros., 1848.

Thompson, Edward H. "Atlantis Not a Myth." *Popular Science Monthly*, October 1879.

—. "Home of a Forgotten Race." *The National Geographic Magazine*, June 1914.

—. *People of the Serpent*. Boston, Mass.: Houghton Mifflin, 1932.

Willard, T.A. *The City of the Sacred Well: Being a Narrative of the Discoveries and Excavations of Edward Herbert Thompson in the Ancient City of Chi-Chen Itzá with some Discourse on the Culture and Development of the Mayan Civilization as Revealed by Their Art and Architecture Here Set Down and Illustrated from Photographs*. New York: The Century Co., 1926.

www.ingramcontent.com/pod-product-compliance
Lightning Source LLC
Chambersburg PA
CBHW050424240426
43661CB00055B/2266